The Demography of Health and Health Care
Second Edition

The Plenum Series on Demographic Methods and Population Analysis

Series Editor: Kenneth C. Land, *Duke University, Durham, North Carolina*

ADVANCED TECHNIQUES OF POPULATION ANALYSIS
Shiva S. Halli and K. Vaninadhu Rao

ANALYTICAL THEORY OF BIOLOGICAL POPULATIONS
Alfred J. Lotka

CONTINUITIES IN SOCIOLOGICAL HUMAN ECOLOGY
Edited by Michael Micklin and Dudley L. Poston, Jr.

CURBING POPULATION GROWTH: An Insider's Perspective
on the Population Movement
Oscar Harkavy

THE DEMOGRAPHY OF HEALTH AND HEALTH CARE
Second Edition
Louis G. Pol and Richard K. Thomas

FORMAL DEMOGRAPHY
David P. Smith

HOUSEHOLD COMPOSITION IN LATIN AMERICA
Susan M. De Vos

HOUSEHOLD DEMOGRAPHY AND HOUSEHOLD MODELING
Edited by Evert van Imhoff, Anton Kuijsten, Pieter Hooimeijer,
and Leo J. G. van Wissen

MODELING MULTIGROUP POPULATIONS
Robert Schoen

POPULATION ISSUES: An Interdisciplinary Focus
Edited by Leo J. G. van Wissen and Pearl L. Dykstra

THE POPULATION OF MODERN CHINA
Edited by Dudley L. Poston, Jr., and David Yaukey

A PRIMER OF POPULATION DYNAMICS
Krishnan Namboodiri

A Continuation Order Plan is available for this series. A continuation order will bring delivery of each new volume immediately upon publication. Volumes are billed only upon actual shipment. For further information please contact the publisher.

The Demography of Health and Health Care
Second Edition

Louis G. Pol
University of Nebraska at Omaha
Omaha, Nebraska

and

Richard K. Thomas
Medical Services Research Group
Memphis, Tennessee

Kluwer Academic/Plenum Publishers
New York   Boston   Dordrecht   London   Moscow

Library of Congress Cataloging-in-Publication Data

Pol, Louis G.
    The demography of health and health care/Louis G. Pol and Richard K. Thomas—2nd ed.
      p. ; cm. — (The Plenum series on demographic methods and population analysis)
    Includes bibliographical references and index.
    ISBN 0-306-46336-9 (hardbound)—ISBN 0-306-46337-7 (pbk.)
     1. Medical statistics. 2. Demography. 3. Social medicine. I. Thomas, Richard K.
1944– II. Title. III. Series.
    [DNLM: 1. Health Planning—methods—United States. 2. Health
Services—economics—United States. 3. Demography—United States. 4. Epidemiologic
Methods—United States. 5. Health Services—supply & distribution—United States. 6.
Health Status Indicators—United States. W 84 AA1 P69d 2000]
RA407 .P65 2000
362.1′042—dc21   00-022102

ISBN 0-306-46336-9 (Hardbound)
ISBN 0-306-46337-7 (Paperback)

©2001 Kluwer Academic / Plenum Publishers
233 Spring Street, New York, N.Y. 10013

http://www.wkap.nl/

10 9 8 7 6 5 4 3 2 1

A C.I.P. record for this book is available from the Library of Congress

Printed in the United States of America

Preface

When *health demography* began to emerge as an applied subdiscipline within demography during the 1980s, few anticipated the developments that would occur in health care to influence its direction. While a distinct body of research categorized under this heading has yet to be formally recognized, the impact of health demography is clearly being felt in the field. The number of health professionals who are using the materials of health demography—perhaps without even realizing it—continues to grow. In fact, most of those involved with health demography are not demographers but sociologists, economists, epidemiologists, and health professionals who are applying the concepts and techniques of health demography to concrete problems in the delivery of health care. The boundaries of this subdiscipline are becoming increasingly visible within demography and the implications of health demography increasingly obvious outside of demography. The US health care system is poised, in fact, to enter the twenty-first century riding on the shoulders of health demography.

Many factors have contributed to the emergence of this new field. The developments affecting the health care industry during the 1980s and 1990s have served to transform a diverse collection of charitable institutions and "mom-and-pop" operations into an industry increasingly dominated by for-profit conglomerates. During the 1980s the industry became market driven and consumer oriented, resulting in an explosion in the demand for both demographic data and health statistics. The need to integrate and interpret data from these two fields has provided a major impetus for the development of health demography. At the same time, the significance of health demography has been confirmed through the reconceptualization of "health" and the growing emphasis on a population-based health care perspective. Now the revolutionary impact of managed care can be added to the list of developments that make the materials and methods of health demography invaluable to the health care industry.

The emergence of health demography as a distinct field has been fostered by several technological advances. These include the development of a microcomputer technology that allows for the processing of large data sets, the development of software that can integrate data from disparate sources, the availability of detailed incidence and utilization rates, and access to heretofore unavailable data on various aspects of health and health care.

The maturing of the field is evidenced by the content of presentations at professional demography meetings and, slowly but surely, by articles in the demographic literature. Not only are demographers demonstrating increasing sophistication with regard to health issues, but they are beginning to approach health-related data as insiders bent on solving concrete problems in health care delivery, not as isolated academicians applying sterile methodologies to distant health issues. The maturing of the field is further evidenced by the increasing variety of constituents for the "products" of health demographers. Once of interest only to selected researchers and funding agencies, the products of health demographers are now demanded by government policymakers, health planners, health care consultants, health care marketers, and other professionals involved in planning, administering, and marketing health services. The "corporatization" of the health care industry has introduced a new magnitude of demand for health data products and the interest in data generated as a by-product of health demography is growing even among parties outside of health care.

This volume has been written for an audience of health care practitioners, academic and private sector demographers, and students in demography and the various health care professions. In fact, the material is of interest to anyone who wants to know more about how and why demographic conditions (and changes in those conditions) affect the supply of and demand for health care and conversely how and why changing health care conditions affect demographic structure. It makes use of data from a variety of sources, using research results, models, theories, and case studies to demonstrate the health care–demography connection from both theoretical and applied perspectives. At the theoretical level, the volume conveys the general principles that serve as the basis for health demography. At the applied level, it demonstrates how the merging of demography and health care has a positive impact on the planning processes of hospitals, physicians' groups, clinics, nursing homes, and other health care organizations.

In producing this work, we have borrowed heavily from disciplines closely related to health care and demography such as social epidemiology, medical sociology, and medical economics. Theories and perspectives from these fields have allowed us to make a more thorough assessment of the origins of the connection between demography and health care. Analytical techniques from these and other fields have contributed to our understanding of current conditions and emerging trends in health care.

Finally, our work in this evolving field has exposed us to the problems and opportunities that require a health demography perspective for their resolution.

It is these real-world applications, which appear as examples in the book, that reflect the dynamic nature of health demography.

ACKNOWLEDGMENTS

Like all authors, we are indebted to several persons who were instrumental in formulating and producing both the first and second editions of this work. First, to Jacqueline Lynch in the College of Business Administration at the University of Nebraska at Omaha whose tireless efforts and seemingly endless patience in the word-processing and rewrite stages of production enabled us to complete our task. We express our deepest appreciation to Virginia McCoy for her valuable suggestions regarding changes in this edition. We also would like to thank our colleagues who revised the first edition for their insights and constructive comments, as well as those who have adopted the work as a text and subsequently "field-tested" it. Their comments have certainly contributed to the improvements in this second edition. As with the first edition, the encouragement received from our fellow members of the Business Demography Interest Group of the Population Association of America, particularly Walt Terrie and Hallie Kintner, helped keep us on course. We also wish to thank our students for the feedback and ideas that they have given us in shaping this work. Any errors of omission or commission, of course, are our own.

Louis G. Pol
Richard K. Thomas

Contents

CHAPTER 1

Health Demography

An Evolving Discipline

INTRODUCTION

Health demography is perhaps best defined as the application of the content and methods of demography to the study of health status and health behavior. *Demography*, of course, is the study of human populations. This includes the study of the size, distribution, and composition of populations, as well as related dynamic processes such as fertility, mortality, and migration. *Health* and *health care* refer, respectively, to the condition of health as experienced by individuals and populations and to the operation of the health care delivery system. (See later chapters for more detailed definitions.) Health demography concerns itself with the manner in which such factors as age, marital status, and income influence both the health status and health behavior of populations and in turn how health-related phenomena affect demographic attributes. Health demography shares an interest in individual-level health issues with clinical medicine and in population-level health issues with social epidemiology.

The scope of health demography is quite broad, and there is little within the discipline of demography that does not have some relevance for the study of health and health care. The scope of the field can be demonstrated by the fact that virtually every aspect of "health" is amenable to study by means of demographic techniques and perspective. Whether the issue is the cause or consequence of disease, variations in health status among populations, utilization levels for various health services, the attitudes of health professionals, the study of medical outcomes, or even the organization of the health care delivery system can be better understood through the use of demographic concepts, methods, and data.

Health demography, as we envision it, is an applied science. Reflecting this applied perspective, the emphasis of this volume is not on the development of basic knowledge, although that is certainly important, but on the application of demographic concepts and methods to the understanding and solution of concrete problems in the delivery of health care. Ultimately, the major contribution of health demography should be to the decision-making process within health care.

THE ORIGINS OF HEALTH DEMOGRAPHY

The subject matter of health demography is not new. Its roots are found in a number of existing disciplines. In fact, this discipline represents to a great extent a synthesis and reformulation of concepts and substantive data previously developed in a variety of other fields. Much of its character reflects the convergence of traditional demography with aspects of biostatistics and epidemiology. In addition to the analytical and methodological contributions of these three disciplines, a number of social sciences have provided important concepts and theoretical frameworks that offer a basis for demographic analysis. These disciplines include medical sociology, medical anthropology, medical geography, and medical economics. Each of these contributing fields is discussed below.

Demographic Roots

Although some aspects of demography are more obviously linked to the study of health and health care than others, there probably is no aspect of the discipline that does not have some relevance. Among the dynamic processes studied by demographers, the analysis of mortality is most directly linked to the health of a population. The study of morbidity is of increasing importance due to the changing nature of illness in contemporary society. Although fertility is not always directly considered a health-related phenomenon, it has numerous indirect implications for health and health behavior. Even the outcomes of migration flows are contributors to the health status and health behavior of the affected populations.

Among the demographic attributes associated with health status and health behavior are basic population characteristics such as size, distribution, and composition. Size and distribution have definite implications for health services demand and utilization, while the compositional factors of the population (e.g., age, sex, and race) are not only linked to health behavior but also are excellent predictors of health status. Other compositional attributes, such as marital status, socioeconomic status, and religion, are correlated with both health status and health behavior. It is perhaps these demographic attributes that most directly relate to health status and health behavior in the contemporary United States.

Historical Demography

Historical demography involves the study of population characteristics during past periods as a basis for gaining an understanding of the social and cultural attributes of earlier societies. This is one of the more challenging aspects of demography, since adequate and systematic records are seldom available for dates before the twentieth century for many areas of the United States. Using sometimes incomplete data from registries of vital events, parish records, listings of inhabitants, and early censuses, demographic "facts" about populations are generated. These facts are used to reconstruct family composition, estimate age structure and life expectancy, and determine the approximate sizes and growth rates of premodern populations. In turn, these data provide the baseline figures that furnish an historical perspective on phenomena such as infant mortality and cause of death. This information allows researchers to put into better perspective the relationships between demographic characteristics, social and environmental factors, and health conditions during periods of time when the demographic landscape was much different.

Applied Demography

Applied demography involves the use of demographic methods, perspectives, and data to understand and address concrete problems in a wide variety of fields. It is oriented toward decision making in both the private and public sectors. As noted earlier, this volume focuses on the application of demography to the field of health care. While the demographic methods and data used are not unique, the applications are.

Early work in applied demography placed the emphasis on the use of demographic methods, many of which focused on estimating and projecting population size and composition, in the public policy arena. More recently a different family of applications has arisen and is being termed *business demography*. Applications to business concerns draw from the common body of demographic data and methods; by merging them with business data and perspectives, a unique way of looking at business problems and opportunities emerges. A growing number of applications in health demography reflect a business demography approach.

Contemporary applied demography is truly an interdisciplinary endeavor. The focus may be on public or private sector issues, and its approach requires the use of demographic tools, techniques, and perspectives to arrive at better decisions. Applied demographers contend that sound demographic data, methods, and perspectives, merged with information related to the "issues at hand," improve the quality of the decisions being made.

Epidemiological Roots

Epidemiology literally means the study of epidemics. Its modern usage, however, refers to the study of the origin and progression of illness within a population. The scope of the field has steadily broadened from a focus on the etiology of acute illnesses to the study of the cause, course, and correlates of a wide variety of health conditions. Many epidemiologists are physicians (epidemiology is one of several medical specialties), while other epidemiologists reflect a broader conceptualization of the field. The notion of "social epidemiology" has become widely accepted by a variety of disciplines and emphasizes the distribution of illness within the population and the health behavior of various social groups.

Epidemiology remains the "detective work" of health care, and its emphasis on populations rather than individuals makes it a kin of demography. Epidemiological investigation has increasingly shifted from the relationship between environmental disease agents and human health conditions toward the link between demographic characteristics and the prevalence and distribution of various health risks. In fact, much of the epidemiological research of the 1980s and 1990s focused on the impact of changing demographic attributes on health status.

Social Science Origins

Medical Sociology. By the 1950s, *medical sociology* had developed as a distinct subspecialty within sociology. Although there always had been an epidemiological influence within the field, medical sociology was historically characterized as a sociology *of* medicine rather than a sociology *in* medicine. Medical sociology's early practitioners were primarily on the outside of medicine looking in; their focus was on the application of concepts from other areas in sociology to the study of the organization of health care.

By the 1960s, however, medical sociology had taken on a strong social epidemiology character. Research findings that established a connection between poverty and poor health, for example, generated interest in the social and demographic correlates of health status and health behavior. As medical sociologists emphasized a sociology in medicine, one directed toward problems in the delivery of care, the significance of differences in health status attributable to demographics became increasingly appreciated.

In addition to contributing some of the key concepts in the field, medical sociologists have led the effort to document the relationship between health characteristics and age, sex, race, marital status, religion, and other demographic variables. They also have demonstrated the extent of interaction among various demographic factors, indicating the complexity of such relationships. The work of medical sociologists has been influential in the redefining of the concepts of health and illness that has occurred in recent years. As the paradigm in the field has shifted from "medical care" to "health care," the discipline has become redefined as the sociology of health and health care.

Medical Anthropology. Although anthropologists were among the first social scientists to become involved in research on the provision of health care, *medical anthropology* as a distinct subdiscipline is of recent origin. Traditionally, anthropologists have emphasized non-Western cultures in their research, and the study of health care generally has not been a distinct component of their ethnographic fieldwork. The limited social differentiation of primitive societies along demographic dimensions has not lent itself to the development of a strong social epidemiological perspective.

In recent years, however, medical anthropologists have turned their attention to the health care systems of contemporary societies. In the United States in particular, applied medical anthropology has gained momentum. From a health demography perspective, the main contributions of medical anthropology lie in four areas. The first relates to an appreciation of the subcultural differences associated with health status and health behavior. As a result of this perspective, an understanding of the cultural context for disease definition and subsequent response is now well established.

The second contribution reflects the emphasis of anthropologists on lifestyles and the impact of lifestyles on health status and health behavior. An understanding of the implications of subcultural variations in lifestyles on health status and behavior has contributed to advances in a number of areas. The third contribution relates to the emphasis in anthropology on alternative health care systems. An appreciation of alternative systems, as often found among ethnic subcultures in the United States, has provided a framework for analysis of health behavior patterns. The fourth contribution relates to the application of a set of qualitative research methodologies to study the internal operations of the health care system.

Medical Geography. *Medical geography* is a newly emerging field that nevertheless has made important contributions to the development of health demography. Geography, of course, is concerned with the spatial distribution of various phenomena and the relationships of different phenomena within space. Medical geography is concerned with the spatial distribution of disease, health conditions, health care providers, and health facilities. As such, the discipline introduces aspects of social epidemiology as it links health phenomena to geographic referents.

Once health phenomena have been plotted spatially, it becomes possible to relate them to demographic variables that then can be used to explain the onset and progression of health conditions. Epidemiological detective work is impossible if the cases under study cannot be linked to geography. An understanding of physician practice patterns and patient behavior, for example, only can be developed within a framework that identifies spatial relationships between the need for health care and the existence of facilities and personnel.

Recent developments in spatial analysis (e.g., gravity models and accessibility analysis), along with the increasing power of geographic information systems (GIS), are now being applied in health care settings. The ability to geocode health-related phenomena, that is, to link them to a specific latitude and longitude or geographic area, has greatly enhanced the ability of health demographers to relate health phenomena to demographic variables. The development of user-friendly GIS software that makes it possible to view health phenomena in a spatial dimension has provided impetus for the development of medical geography.

Medical Economics.   *Medical economics*, a subarea of economics focusing on health care, has been well established since the 1960s. The health care sector is unusual among the various segments of the economy owing to its unique economic characteristics. It does not have the attributes typically associated with other industries and consequently has required separate attention by economists. The concern with spiraling health care costs during the 1980s further contributed to the interest in medical economics both among economists and health professionals. By the 1990s, the economic dimension of health care had come to overshadow many other aspects of health care delivery.

The interface between economics, health care, and demography is evidenced at the system, practitioner, and consumer levels. Health care expenditures at the national or system level are influenced by the demographic makeup of the national population. The fee structures, practice patterns, and locational decisions of physicians, all economic considerations, are functions of the demographic characteristics of both their patients and physicians themselves. The type of care chosen by consumers, indeed, the decision to seek care at all, is a reflection, partly at least, of their economic status. This, in turn, is a reflection of the demographic attributes of the consumers. As the emphasis of the field has shifted to a more contemporary approach, medical economics is increasingly being referred to as health economics.

MAJOR TRENDS AFFECTING THE DEVELOPMENT OF HEALTH DEMOGRAPHY

The US population has undergone a major transformation in this century in terms of both demographic attributes and health care characteristics. This transformation has involved significant changes that have had a major impact on the development of health demography as a discipline. Three of the more important trends are discussed below.

Changing Population Characteristics

Until the early years of the twentieth century, life expectancy at birth in every society was relatively short. Infant mortality claimed many lives, and only a portion of the population survived to adulthood. By the beginning of the twentieth century, however, living conditions in the United States and other industrializing countries had improved to the point that life expectancy was rapidly extended. Increased longevity resulted in a modification of the age structure, and improved survival rates became one of the most important determinants of the health characteristics of today's population. As populations of modern societies have begun to age, the older age cohorts have become disproportionately represented. Indeed, for the first time in history most societies are made up of significantly older populations. This unprecedented situation has resulted in health-related attributes different from those of any populations that have ever existed.

The aging of the US population also has contributed to the growing feminization of American society. Relatively early in the twentieth century, females came to constitute a numerical majority. As the population continues to age, the gap between the number of women and men grows. A disproportionately large female population has important social, economic, and political implications. It also has significant implications for both health status and health behavior.

At the same time that life expectancy was increasing and the age structure was being transformed, other dimensions of the population composition of Americans were undergoing change. Socioeconomic conditions improved dramatically, and major shifts were occurring in the occupational and educational characteristics of the population. In addition, several waves of foreign immigrants not only introduced a variety of national, cultural, and ethnic influences to US society, but also helped contribute to the heterogeneity of lifestyles that has come to characterize American culture.

A demographic trend often overlooked in discussions of health care is the changing structure of American families and households. The past two decades have witnessed significant changes in marital status within the population. There has been a decline in the proportion of the population that is married and a proportionate increase in the size of the single, divorced, and widowed populations. Further, family structure has been significantly modified, to the extent that the "traditional" husband–wife–children family accounted for only one fourth of all households in 1990. Nontraditional family and household structures have become the rule rather than the exception. Average household size has declined and there has been a large increase in the proportion of the population that lives alone.

These changes in age structure and in compositional attributes paralleled the social, political, and economic trends that have reshaped US society. The relatively homogeneous society of the post-World War II era has evolved into one of great diversity. The differentiation that has developed along socioeconomic, racial, and ethnic lines has had a continuing influence on both health status and health behavior. These factors, along with the growing complexity of the economic structure, have led to an increasingly heterogeneous population with complex health characteristics. The significance of these changes are reviewed in the appropriate chapters that follow.

The Changing Nature of Health Problems

The nature of health problems in industrialized societies has changed dramatically during the twentieth century. At the turn of the century, the major health problems were acute conditions. These conditions were usually caused by a disease agent in the environment, had a rapid onset, and either quickly ran their course or resulted in death. Disease agents "attacked" individuals with no respect for age, sex, race, or social status; all segments of the population were essentially at equal risk. These *acute* conditions were epitomized by the "killer" epidemics (such as yellow fever, cholera, influenza, and whooping cough) common in the United States through the early part of the twentieth century. While these conditions have been virtually eliminated in modern industrial societies, they still constitute major health threats in some less developed countries.

As acute illness has declined as the pervasive type of disorder, chronic conditions have emerged as the dominant type of health problem in developed countries. This shift from a preponderance of acute conditions to a preponderance of chronic conditions is referred to as the "epidemiological transition." This shift is usually characteristic of populations that have benefitted from both improving standards of living and public sanitation. The "older" population that results from these developments perpetuates the dominance of chronic conditions.

Chronic conditions tend to be gradual in their onset, of long or infinite duration, and often cumulative in their effect. Chronic conditions are less likely to originate external to the victim (although some are clearly exogenous) and more likely to arise from within an individual. That is, chronic conditions are more frequently linked to lifestyle, heredity, and even psychological state; well-known examples include arthritis, rheumatism, hypertension, and diabetes. Although sometimes resulting in death, chronic conditions generally do not contribute directly to mortality, but often are cited as underlying causes of death. They are more likely to interfere with the quality of life, since they often result in some form of disability.

Once chronic conditions become predominant, the composition of the population becomes a powerful predictor of both health status and health behavior. Since chronic conditions are linked closely to age and lifestyle, the demographic composition of the population becomes a key to understanding the nature of health and illness in a society. One need only examine the demographic characteristics of persons affected by heart disease, diabetes, or AIDS to develop an appreciation for the demographic dimension.

Changing Perceptions of Health and Illness

Since the mid-1960s, health care in the United States has been experiencing a revolution with regard to the conceptualization of health and illness. Since the beginning of this century, the dominant paradigm in medical science has been the medical model of disease. Built on the germ theory formulated late in the nineteenth century, the medical model provided an appropriate framework within which to understand and respond to the acute health conditions prevalent in the United States until the early part of this century. The treatment modalities generated by this conceptualization of the illness process are often, but perhaps without justification, credited with the elimination of the various epidemic diseases responsible for most deaths prior to World War II.

As acute conditions waned in importance and chronic and degenerative conditions came to be predominant, the medical model began to lose some of its relevance. Once the cause of most health conditions ceased to be microorganisms within the environment and became aspects of lifestyle, a new model of health and illness was required. Medical science itself has contributed to the lessened saliency of the medical model, not only by helping eliminate communicable diseases but also by medicalizing many aspects of human existence for which the medical model has limited application. Once such states as pregnancy and aging become defined as "medical" conditions, the traditional medical model begins to be less applicable.

These trends, along with other developments involving health care, have resulted in the reconceptualization of "medical care" as "health care." Medical care reflects the influence of the medical model on our thinking with regard to health and illness. The narrow, biologically based explanation of the operation of disease rooted in germ theory is slowly giving way to a new paradigm. This health care orientation involves a much broader view of health and illness. It depends less on a biological basis for illness definition and is much more appropriate for addressing the chronic conditions affecting contemporary Western society.

The reconceptualization of medical care as health care has been accompanied by the emergence of a biopsychosocial model of health and illness that has more relevance for contemporary health problems. This model emphasizes the interaction of biological factors, psychological states, and social and environmental conditions in the etiology and progression of health conditions within a population. It seeks to replace the simple etiologic framework of the medical model with a much more complex explanation that involves the interplay of biology, social factors, and psychological states.

OVERVIEW OF THE VOLUME

Objectives

The goal of the volume is to delineate the nature and scope of the evolving discipline of health demography. As such, it has multiple objectives. The first objective is to further refine the scope of the field of health demography. Given the far-ranging topics that conceivably could fall under that heading, this in itself is a challenging task. In order to make this task manageable, the authors work systematically through the various concepts in demography and relate each to health and health care.

Even though the term "health demography" is increasingly appearing in the demographic literature, only now is the concept becoming well developed and the content of the field becoming distinct. The approach here is to integrate materials from epidemiology, the social sciences, and the clinical and administrative aspects of health care. The ultimate goal is a book that defines the concepts that have saliency for health demography, identifies the relevant theoretical frameworks, and traces the various disciplinary streams that are contributing to its evolution as a distinct field.

The second objective of the volume is to demonstrate the relevance of demography for the study of health status, health behavior, and health care delivery. To fully appreciate the nature of health conditions in contemporary society, it is essential to understand the demographic context in which these conditions exist. An examination of the distribution of health problems within the US population makes it clear that virtually no health problem is randomly distributed within the population. For virtually every health condition, certain groups are at greater risk than others. All other things being equal, males and African Americans are at greater risk of mortality than females and whites, the elderly are at greater risk of chronic disease than the young, the young are at greater risk of certain acute conditions than the elderly, and the single are at greater risk of mental illness than the married.

The salience of this approach for the study of health and health care has been underscored by the now-massive volume of research linking health status to individual lifestyles. Since lifestyle variations are rooted to a great extent in demographic traits, health demography provides the framework for an examination of the correlates of health status and health behavior.

The third objective of the volume is to illustrate the application of demographic techniques to the study of health and health care. The authors' professional orientations are toward applied demography, and the material herein is designed to demonstrate the variety of ways in which demographic analysis is useful in the study of health status, health behavior, and health care delivery, particularly as it relates to decision making. Demographic techniques such as cohort analysis and survival analysis, along with population estimation and projection methodologies, are increasingly becoming tools for health services research, planning, and marketing.

One final point on demographic applications is appropriate in view of the changes occurring in the health care field. In the mid-1980s, health care administrators came to realize that the delivery of health care in a competitive market place required some business acumen. Increasing competition and reduced profit margins transformed philanthropic operations into business entities, forever changing the characteristics of health care organizations. Not only are business principles being applied in the operation of health care organizations, but new functions, long common to other sectors, are becoming increasingly important in health care. Activities like research and development, planning, marketing, and program evaluation are being incorporated along with this new management paradigm. The one factor that all of these have in common is an underlying foundation in demographic techniques and data.

The questions being asked today in health care—Who are my "customers?" What is the market for this service? What products are the most profitable? What is the least costly way to delivery services?—must be addressed through demographic analysis. The decision-making process, at both the societal and the organizational levels, increasingly is being guided by demographic, not clinical, considerations. What has become the driving force behind national health care policy? The aging of the US population. What has become perhaps the major concern for the health care entities at the operational level? The demographic profile of potential "customers." Today, in fact, virtually no discussion takes place among policymakers or institutional planners that is not prefaced by an exploration of the demographic context of the issues at hand.

This volume, perhaps more than anything else, describes what demography can do for health care. Health care planners and administrators increasingly are in need of the variety of contributions the field can offer. The major contributions of demography to the study of health and health care are in the areas of concepts, techniques, and data.

An understanding of key demographic *concepts* has become increasingly important for health professionals. Health care has already begun incorporating the terminology of business into its vocabulary; it is rapidly expanding its demographic vocabulary as well. Terms like cohorts, population pyramids, survival curves, excess mortality, and standardization are increasingly heard in discussions on health care planning. The new emphasis on patient characteristics, quality assessment, and market analysis all mandate the incorporation of demographic concepts. The "new wave" in health care—managed care—further contributes to the need for an adequate grasp of demographic processes.

The health care field is also manifesting a growing need for *techniques* developed by demographers. As competition has increased and profit margins have dwindled, health care organizations are facing unprecedented challenges to their survival. There is a great need for substantive content from demography and for the incorporation of standard demographic techniques into the health care planning process. In the past, it may have sufficed to purchase demographic or health care data from vendors and to use them unquestioningly. In today's environment, an appreciation of the underlying analytical techniques has become increasingly necessary. The use of "canned" population projections or simple birth trends, for example, opens the door for all types of miscalculations.

These issues must be faced with an in-depth understanding of projection methodology and fertility measurement. Cohort analysis has become essential for studying the aging of populations, since the types of services needed and the types of financial reimbursement may directly or indirectly be a function of the age mix of the provider organization's patients. Migration estimation methodologies have become increasingly important in the determination of future market needs.

The health care field also requires demographic *data*. The 1980s witnessed an explosion in both the demand for and the supply of health care data, much of which are demographic in their orientation. Indeed, a whole new industry has emerged that is dedicated to the provision of data to the health care field. Today, few health care organizations can survive without an in-depth understanding of the demographic dimensions of their markets, and managed care plans and other corporate forms of health care delivery rely heavily on data in their decision-making processes.

Health care planners and administrators need to be able to speak knowledgeably about the demographic profiles of the users of various services, the respective needs of populations with varying demographic characteristics, and the attributes of various categories of patients. A knowledge of such basic information as regional variations in practice patterns or the factors that distinguish a rural service area from an urban one may mean the difference between a program's success and failure. With the newly emerged concern over consumer perspectives and patient satisfaction, the link between the demographic characteristics of the patient population and the patient's knowledge and perceptions of a particular provider of health care becomes crucial information.

Ultimately, health care professionals must develop a demographic *perspective* on the factors that influence health status and health behavior. In today's health care environment, there is a pressing need to understand the motivations behind consumer behavior and the manner in which these behaviors are linked to demographic characteristics. After all the projections are made and all the equations solved, it may be that demography's unique perspective is the primary contribution that health demography can offer to the health care field.

It should be apparent by now that the authors consider health demography a social science. While it is true that some aspects of the population's health status may be linked clearly to biology (e.g., only women have uterine cancer and sickle-cell anemia is limited primarily to African-Americans), the emergence of chronic conditions as the major health problem clearly has introduced a social dimension to any study of epidemiology. Ultimately, knowledge of a population's social behavior patterns is the most direct route to an understanding of its chronic health condition.

More important, however, is the fact so often forgotten by the medical community that health behavior is social behavior. Whether one is considering the behavior of individual physicians or patients, of hospitals administrators, or of national insurance carriers, social factors play a major role in the actions carried out. The patient's decision to visit a particular physician, the psychiatrist's choice of therapy, the hospital board's decision not to allow induced abortions, and the insurer's decision to increase its premiums for male hairstylists and interior decorators all reflect social, political, and economic considerations to a greater extent than clinical considerations. In today's environment, an understanding of the social dimension of health behavior is crucial. In turn, an appreciation of the social factors in health behavior demands an understanding of the demographic attributes of the population.

The Audience

This second edition of *The Demography of Health and Health Care* is designed to appeal to academic and professional audiences alike. Within both groups it is expected to have relevance for a wide variety of disciplinary areas. Within academia, the primary audience is expected to be within demography. Demography instructors should benefit from a presentation of this evolving field, while demography students will be exposed to an area that is of growing relevance. Virtually all substantive areas within demography are included, and illustrations of the applications of many of the methods developed by demographers are presented.

Students in other disciplines will also constitute important audiences. Social science students can benefit from the application of demographic concepts and methods to the solution of problems in health care delivery. This volume should provide a useful framework and some practical examples of applied social science, especially at a time when health care providers are increasingly asked demography-related questions. In addition, students in health care marketing will increasingly require an appreciation of demographic issues. In the 1980s, health care became market driven and demographic analysis, of course, is an important component of the market research process.

Another academic audience includes students in the various health professions. Not only do clinicians find themselves in increasing need of demographic information, but most clinical training programs now include an administrative or management component. Medical sociology and related courses have long been recognized as essential background for clinicians and nonclinicians alike. A well-rounded education for health care professionals will increasingly call for an understanding of health demography, particularly as the emphasis moves away from the treatment aspect of health care and toward education and prevention.

Perhaps an even greater need exists among health care administration students. As health care has become more competitive and health care organizations have begun acting more like other businesses, the need for demographic information on the part of administrators has grown. Health demography provides the basis for performing such tasks as planning, business development, marketing, and program evaluation. Without such capabilities, few health care providers will be able to survive.

The volume also is expected to have wide appeal among a broad range of health care practitioners. Its illustrations of the application of demographic techniques to concrete problems will allow health professionals to improve their clinical and administrative skills. Clinicians should be better able to understand their client populations, while administrators should be able to improve their management effectiveness through the use of these techniques. The volume should serve as a basic reference for planners, researchers, and epidemiologists who are working in varied health care settings. Similarly, health care consultants should find this a useful guidebook for the incorporation of demographic data and methods into their projects.

Independent practitioners such as physicians, dentists, and optometrists require demographic information for practice planning and development. The health care market has become increasingly segmented along demographic dimensions, with medical specialists often focusing on patients segmented along the lines of sex (obstetrics, gynecology) and age (pediatrics, geriatrics). This segmentation has increased as health care programs have come to specialize in women's health, child health, ethnic health, or rural health, among other areas. Now hospitals are developing "product lines" that are geared specifically toward particular demographic categories (e.g., a geriatric product line) or have their foundation in some demographically based variable (e.g., a cardiology product line).

Health care planners at both the system and organizational levels find their analyses increasingly predicated on demographic data. Discussions regarding services to be offered and the placement of facilities and personnel are more and more demographically oriented. Health care planners are being asked to determine the most appropriate sites, health care marketers are being asked to target the market for particular services, and health care consultants are being asked to develop plans for the expansion of clinics or physician practices. The basic knowledge underlying all these activities can be found primarily within the scope of what we have defined as health demography.

It should be noted that there are several things this volume is not. Although it introduces basic demographic concepts and methodologies to readers who may not be familiar with them, it is not a demography textbook. The technical aspects are kept to a minimum and equations are notably absent. On the other hand, working "models" that can be applied to concrete health care problems are common.

While the material is adequately documented, an attempt has been made not to encumber the narrative with too many references. This is not intended to be a standard textbook but a guidebook for practitioners. To this end, more attention has been given to the selected readings offered at the end of each chapter than to references within the text. Traditional demographers may even find that some of the "standard" references are absent. This reflects the objective of providing a working document for practitioners, rather than convincing readers that the authors can cite the conventional sources.

Finally, readers are not expected to read this book cover to cover in order to achieve maximum benefit, although we hope that most readers will do so. The intent has been to structure the material to allow the experienced demographer or health services researcher to skip over familiar material and directly access the appropriate sections. Practitioners can use it as a reference work and quickly locate the one concept or method that is needed. It is hoped that these approaches can be utilized without interrupting the overall flow of the book.

ORGANIZATION OF THE VOLUME

This volume is organized in such a manner as to meet the needs of both those with limited knowledge of demography and/or health care and those with extensive knowledge of one or both of these areas. Two chapters are presented that provide an overview of the US health care system and introduce the basic concepts necessary for an intelligent discussion of its components and operation. Those with extensive health care background may want to forgo this section, although important linkages between health care and demography are discussed. These two chapters further provide a framework within which to examine the demographic dimensions of health and health care.

Chapters 4 through 8 are the most demographic in their orientation because they focus on the basic concepts and processes within the field. Each chapter contains a section that defines the relevant demographic concepts, describes the measures or indexes utilized, presents recent trends, and discusses the various techniques appropriate for analysis in that particular substantive area. Population size, distribution, and composition are discussed, along with the dynamic processes of fertility, mortality, and migration. Trends within the US population are described and the implications of each for health and health care are discussed. Those with extensive demographic backgrounds may wish to skip over some parts of these chapters, although all contain worthwhile examples and illustrations from health demography and useful substantive information relevant to these trends.

Because of the uniqueness of the health care field, Chapter 9 is devoted to data issues. Research in health care settings has its peculiar characteristics and the sources of data are often obscure. While it is possible that more data are generated in health care than in any other sector of society, the availability of these data is probably more restricted in health care than in any other field. Because of the nature of the health care system, there is no central coordinating unit to serve as a clearinghouse for health care data. Consequently, the location, form, and accessibility of health care data are extremely problematic.

Chapters 10 and 11 represent a synthesis of much of the earlier discussion. They are devoted to the demographic correlates of health status and health behavior for both physical and mental illness and perhaps illustrate the essence of health demography. It is here that the issues of who gets sick, why they get sick, and how they respond are addressed. Chapter 12 discusses the future of health demography, offering insights into how demographic trends will be major determinants of the supply and demand of health care and how present health policy decisions can have implications for the size and composition of subsequent populations.

It should be noted that this volume generally is limited to the study of health and health care in the United States. Although occasional references are made to situations in other societies for comparison purposes, no attempt is made to generalize the material here to all societies. It should be made clear, however, that the demographic concepts discussed here have relevance for other social systems as well.

ADDITIONAL READINGS

General

Atchley, R. C. (1994). *Social Forces and Aging: An Introduction to Social Gerontology.* Belmont, CA: Wadsworth.

Bogue, D. J. (1985). *The Population of the United States.* New York: Free Press.

Carlson, R. J. (1975). *The End of Medicine.* New York: Wiley.

Cockerham, W. C. (1998). *Medical Sociology* (7th ed.). Upper Saddle River, NJ: Prentice Hall.

Duncan, G. J., and Brooks-Gunn, J. (eds.) (1997). *Consequences of Growing Up Poor.* New York: Russell Sage.

Engle, G. L. (1977). The need for a new medical model: A challenge for biomedicine. *Science* 196: 129–136.

Farley, R. (ed.) (1995). *State of the Union: America in the 1990s.* (Vol. 1: *Economic Trends*; Vol. 2: *Social Trends*). New York: Russell Sage.

Feldstein, P. J. (1992). *Health Care Economics.* New York: International Thomson.

Hughes, J. W., and Seneca, J. J. (1999). *America's Demographic Tapestry.* Piscataway, NJ: Rutgers University Press.

Johnson, T. M., and Sargent, C. F. (eds.) (1996). *Medical Anthropology.* Westport, CT: Greenwood.

Kertzer, D. I., and Fricke, T. (eds.) (1997). *Anthropological Demography: Toward a New Synthesis.* Chicago: University of Chicago Press.

Lilienfeld, D. E., and Stolley, P. D. (1994). *Foundations of Epidemiology.* New York: Oxford University Press.

Lewith, G. T., Kenyon, J. N., and Lewis, P. J. (1996). *Complementary Medicine: An Integrated Approach*. New York: Oxford University Press.

National Center for Health Statistics (annual). *Health, United States*. Hyattsville, MD: US Public Health Service.

Plane, D. A., and Rogerson, P. A. (1994). *The Geographic Analysis of Population*. New York: Wiley.

Shi, L. (1996). *Health Services Research Methods*. Florence, KY: Delmar.

Starr, P. (1982). *The Social Transformation of American Medicine: The Rise of a Sovereign Profession and the Making of a Vast Industry*. New York: Basic Books.

US Department of Health and Human Services. (1997). *Healthy People 2000 Review, 1997*. Hyattsville, MD: US Public Health Service.

Historical Demography

Farley, R. (1996). *The New American Reality*. New York: Russell Sage.

Robey, B. (1985). *The American People*. New York: Dutton.

US Bureau of the Census (annual). *Statistical Abstract of the United States*. Washington, DC: US Government Printing Office.

Wrigley, E. A. (1974). *Population and History*. New York: World University Library.

Population Characteristics

Jones, L. Y. (1980). *Great Expectations*. New York: Ballantine.

US Bureau of the Census (annual). *Statistical Abstract of the United States*. Washington, DC: US Government Printing Office.

Applied Demography

Murdock, S. H., and Ellis, D. R. (1991). *Applied Demography*. Boulder, CO: Westview Press.

Pol, L., and Thomas, R. K. (1997). *Demography for Business Decision Making*. New York: Quorum.

Swanson, D. A., Burch, T. K., and Tedrow, L. (1996). What is applied demography? *Population Research and Policy Review* 15(December):403–418.

Selected Journals and Magazines

American Demographics
American Journal of Public Health
Demography
Health Affairs
Health Care Financing Review
Health Economics
Health Services Research
Inquiry
Medical Care
Population and Development Review
Population Index
Population Research and Policy Review
Population Studies
Public Health Reports

Websites

US Bureau of the Census (http://www.census.gov)
National Center for Health Statistics (http://www.cdc.gov/nchswww/)
National Institutes of Health (http://www.nih.gov)
University of Michigan (http://psc.isa.umich.edu)

Health and Health Care
An Introduction

INTRODUCTION

Health care is one of the more complex components of US society. Its complexity is such that it is difficult to define and even more complicated to describe in meaningful terms. Is health care an industry? A system? An institution? In actuality, it is all of these and more. However, what health care "is" ultimately depends on one's perspective.

To further complicate the picture, the nature of health care is constantly changing. During the 1980s the health care system underwent a dramatic and rapid transformation. This transformation, perhaps more significant than that ever affecting any other industry, brought about major changes in the views of health and illness, the settings in which health care is provided and the practitioners who provide it, the organizational structure of the industry, and the mechanisms for financing care. These trends continued into the 1990s, with new developments in this decade further contributing to the reformulation of American health care.

An encyclopedia would be required to fully describe the multiple dimensions of American health care and that is certainly not appropriate here. The material that follows is restricted to the information necessary to appreciate the health care system relative to the field of health demography. While some will no doubt be critical of what has been included and excluded, the authors have made their best efforts to restrict this material to that relevant within the context of the remainder of this volume.

At the outset, the concepts of health and health care must be defined, and this is no simple matter. In fact, most books on the topic make no attempt to define either concept. Despite the fact that Americans are obsessed with their "health," there is no consensus on a definition among either professionals or laypersons. In the final analysis, what constitutes health—and its counterparts sickness and disease—depends on one's frame of reference. Medical sociologists and others studying the meanings of these terms have had to settle for several definitions, each linked to a different explanatory model. To the demographer, each conceptualization should be considered important. The various definitions and the perspectives they represent are discussed later in the chapter.

The concept of "health care" also is difficult to define. Although hospital-based medical services involving advanced technology automatically come to mind when the issue is raised, the provision of this intensive level of care is more the exception than the rule. In the United States today, only a fraction of the activities of the health care system is directed toward the management of life-threatening conditions.

Even if health care were to be defined simply in terms of its existing structure, this also represents a challenge. The difficulty of such an approach is exacerbated by the system's size, complexity, and technological emphasis, as well as by its diversity of functioning units, its various levels of "control," its combination of public, quasi-public, and private interests and its mixture of for-profit and not-for-profit entities.

In the final analysis, health care is what society defines as health care. In the contemporary United States, health care has come to include formal, institutionalized care, along with "alternative" therapies, self-care, and any other activities designed to prevent the onset of disease, treat illness, improve the quality of life, and/or preserve health.

For our purposes, "health" hereafter refers to the health status of the population in terms of both its individual and aggregate dimensions. "Health care" refers to society's arrangements for improving the health status of the population, again either individually or collectively. Both concepts are modern in their origin. Health, as an objectified state, was generally not recognized in premodern societies. A rational view of the world (along with a scientific orientation toward disease) was required before society could conceptually distinguish between health and sickness. It is only in this century that the concepts of health and health care have come to be recognized as distinct concepts.

Although this volume is not intended to be a sociological or political work, the issues noted above are central to the demography of health and health care. The social, economic, and political characteristics of a particular society are both a consequent and a determinant of the demographic composition of that society's population. At the same time, the way society views the sick and disabled reflects its demographic attributes quite independently of clinical perceptions. It often has been stated that a society should be judged by how well it treats its sick, and ultimately the way society treats its sick is a reflection of demographic attributes as well as social, economic, and political concerns.

THE RELATIONSHIP AMONG HEALTH, HEALTH CARE, AND DEMOGRAPHY

Before examining the nature of health and health care in depth, it is worthwhile to discuss the relationship among health, health care, and demography. This complex relationship is illustrated by the model depicted in Figure 2.1. As can be seen, each of the three components of the model interfaces with the other two in a reciprocal relationship.

The relationship between demography, health, and health care is rooted in the parallel development of these three concepts. The evolution of health care as a distinct institution within the social system required the modernization of society, with the concomitant *demographic transition.* The demographic transition has accompanied the modernization of societies around the world and initially involves a period of declining death rates as a result of public health measures and rising standards of living. The birth rate, however, remains high initially, causing an unprecedented surge in population growth. This phase is followed by declining birth rates resulting from improved educational and socioeconomic levels and changing conditions within the modernizing society. Ultimately, the birth rate drops to a level only slightly exceeding the death rate, resulting in a relatively stable population, thereby completing the transition.

The evolution of the concepts health and health care has paralleled the trends in demographic processes characterizing the United States in the twentieth century. Initially, the demographic transition that had modified the demographic

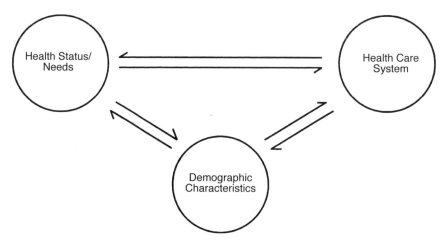

Figure 2.1. The interdependence of health status, health care, and demographic characteristics.

processes during the nineteenth century began to be reflected in the nature of the health care system. Then, in the twentieth century, the *epidemiological transition* that occurred led to a major restructuring of the organization of health care (Omran, 1971). (The epidemiological transition is discussed in more detail below.)

The demographic characteristics of US society serve as both determinants and consequences of the development of the relationship between the US population and its system of health care. Thus, a population with high health status can be expected to have low mortality rates and a relatively old age structure, since attrition due to death is low. At the same time, the demographic characteristics of a population will have an effect on its health status and needs. For example, the age composition of the population will be reflected in the types of health disorders that are common.

A direct relationship obviously exists between a population's health and its health care system. A population's health care needs ideally are reflected in the organization of the health care delivery system. For example, health problems stemming from the effect of communicable diseases demand a system that emphasizes public health measures such as improved sanitation and immunization. Health conditions that are a function of chronic disease and problems of living demand a system that emphasizes medical management and lifestyle-oriented health services.

At the same time, the operation of the health care system affects, to a great extent, the health status of the population. A highly developed health care delivery system should (but does not always) result in higher health status. A system that prolongs life, for example, contributes to the transition from a population characterized by acute conditions to one characterized by chronic conditions. Thus, there is a shift in the nature of the problems as the transition occurs, not an overall decrease in the incidence of health problems.

The operation of the health care system is, to a great extent, a reflection of the demographic traits of the participants in the system. Every aspect of health care, from differential health status to differential utilization patterns, reflects demographic considerations. At the same time, demographic attributes and indicators are a consequence of variations in health status and health services utilization. Mortality rates, for example, reflect both the health status of the population and its use of health services.

The demographic characteristics of the population interface with the health care system to form a complex relationship. The age structure, for example, influences the nature of health care delivery. Thus, a very young population requires quite different services than a very old population.

At the same time, the functioning of the system influences the demographic profile of the population both directly and indirectly through its impact on health status. Therefore, a system that aggressively attempts to reduce mortality contributes to the development of a population that is both older and numerically female dominated. A system that aggressively promotes birth control as a health measure would similarly affect the age and sex structure of the population. Box 2.1 addresses the interface of health, health care, and demography.

TWENTIETH-CENTURY TRENDS

The demographic changes that led to the development of modern American medicine are well documented. The beginning of the twentieth century in effect was the takeoff point for the development of a complex, industrialized, urbanized society. These developments were accompanied by changes in fertility, mortality, and morbidity patterns. Furthermore, dramatic changes also occurred in other demographic indicators. Educational levels improved, as did all other measures of socioeconomic status. The occupational and industrial structures were greatly transformed. Geographic mobility became the norm, quite in contrast to the relative immobility of the traditional, agricultural society of preindustrial America.

The demographic changes of the twentieth century were accompanied by dramatic changes in health status and health behavior. The US population overall became healthier. There was a reduction in mortality, a reduced overall level of morbidity, and a concomitant increase in life expectancy. To a great extent, this health enhancement took place independently of the operation of the health care delivery system. A higher standard of living, better housing, and better nutrition were instrumental in changing the health status of the population. In fact, it has been argued that the elimination of the major "killer" diseases; that is, the communicable diseases, beginning around the turn of the century should really be attributed to these factors and not to medical science. In actuality, the scientific breakthroughs given credit for the elimination of the more deadly communicable diseases typically occurred after the decline of the epidemic in question (McKinlay and McKinlay, 1977). Box 2.2 discusses the fate of the epidemics.

A paradoxical relationship existed in the United States in the twentieth century between health status and health care utilization. At the turn of the century, when infant mortality and maternal mortality were everyday facts of life, few Americans utilized the health care system. As the US population became healthier, however, it began to utilize the system at an increasing rate. The healthier people became, it seems, the more they availed themselves of health services. This situation has become so common in the US health care system that it is now a truism that those who need the most health care get the least, while those who need the least get the most.

The changes in utilization patterns during this century can be attributed in part to changes in the demographic attributes of the US population. These changes include increased incomes, higher educational levels, and the development of an industrial structure that subsidizes health care services. Better education has

Box 2.1

The Interface of Health, Health Care, and Demography:
A Tale of Two Societies

Perhaps the best way in which to illustrate the interrelationships among health, health care, and demography is to present two contrasting examples. This might be done by depicting two quite different societies and the connections among these three factors in each. An appropriate contrast exists between contemporary US society and any number of societies generally referred to as "developing." Examples of the latter might include Mexico, India, and the Philippines.

The developing society is characterized demographically by relatively high levels of fertility and mortality. These dual processes result in a "traditional" age structure. The population is relatively young (with a median age of perhaps 17 or 18) and has approximately equal numbers of males and females. Population growth rates tend to be high, since death rates have fallen below birth rates. The standard of living is generally low and educational attainment is limited.

The developing nation will invariably be characterized by poor health status in terms of both morbidity and mortality. The most common health problems are acute rather than chronic conditions. The health threats of modern societies (such as heart disease and cancer) are rare, since few in the population live long enough to develop these conditions. Instead, the major health problems are communicable diseases, such as yellow fever and tuberculosis, and infectious diseases affecting the digestive system. The rate of infant mortality is relatively high, with infants accounting for a larger share of deaths than the elderly. Wide variations in mortality by age do not exist, since the major killers do not discriminate in terms of age (or gender or any other factor, for that matter). Because of the structure of the society, the health needs of mothers and children tend to be the most pressing.

The health care delivery systems in developing societies generally are poorly developed, at least by modern Western standards. This lack of development reflects to a certain extent an absence of the technology, medical personnel, and financing necessary for the establishment of a modern health care system. It also reflects the absence of certain cultural values that underlie the transition to a modern health care system; for example, an emphasis on science rather than religion as the explanatory framework and an active rather than passive orientation to events in the world are required.

Most important, however, the health needs of the population dictate a health care system quite different from that of the United States. The greatest needs are in the areas of public health, disease prevention, and education. Sophisticated surgical techniques are of limited usefulness; few live to an age where this type of intervention would be appropriate. The elimination of contagious disease has to be the focus of the system, and the community, not the individual, must be considered the "patient." The population's needs mitigate against the development of a Western-style health system that emphasizes longevity and quality of life for all members of society.

Here we see that demographic processes such as fertility and mortality affect the health status and the needs of the population, as well as the form of the health care system. At the same time, the population's health status contributes to its demographic profile, and its health needs are reflected in the form the health care delivery system takes. The health care system can make only limited contributions to individual health status but can have some impact on the overall health of the community by reducing epidemic diseases. Its main impact demographically takes the form of the population growth that results from reductions in mortality.

The relationships that exist among these three factors in the United States reflect the differences between the societies in question. Demographically, the United States is characterized by relatively low rates of fertility and mortality. This has resulted in a bullet-shaped population pyramid; the narrow base reflects decades of low fertility, while the wider top reflects the aging of the population as a result of low mortality. The median age is over 30 years, and the proportion of females is well over 50% due to the fact that in modern societies women outlive men. Income levels and educational levels are relatively high.

The health problems that exist are those of a modern society. The main factors in morbidity are chronic conditions such as arthritis, diabetes, hypertension, and chronic respiratory diseases. Acute conditions are proportionately rare, with the common killers being heart disease, cancer, and stroke. Deaths from communicable diseases are rare as well. The overall health status is considered high. Mortality tends to be highly age specific, since a wider variety of conditions account for death than in developing societies with each age group exhibiting a characteristic mortality profile.

The health care system in the United States is highly developed and complex. Its main focus, however, is on individual (not community) health. The public health component is not emphasized, and the medical management of chronic illness consumes a large portion of the system's resources. Since the need to address life-threatening conditions is not as pressing as it is in developing societies, the system focuses on activities that enhance the quality of life. Thus much of the resources are devoted to mental health services, cosmetic surgery, and elective surgery that contribute to lifestyle more than to longevity. The aging of the population has mandated the development of services geared to the elderly population.

In this case, it is seen that in the United States low fertility and low mortality yield an age–sex configuration with health needs quite different from those of developing countries. High socioeconomic and educational status have contributed to relatively high health status. The demographic trends of the society have in turn transformed the major health threats from acute to chronic conditions. This is reflected in a health care delivery system that increasingly focuses on the quality of life rather than the elimination of life-threatening diseases. The system subsequently contributes to the improved longevity of the population and to the relative importance of chronic conditions for health status.

Box 2.2

What Happened to the Epidemics: Medical Science or Demographics?

During the twentieth century the United States, along with the rest of the world's developed nations, experienced a dramatic decline in mortality. From 1900 to 1973, the mortality rate (adjusted for age and sex) in the United States dropped from nearly 17.5 per 1000 population to barely 5 per 1000. Over this period, a 69.2% decrease in overall mortality was recorded, with most (92.3%) of this occurring during the first 50 years of the twentieth century. It is likely that the decline in mortality, for some causes of death at least, actually commenced during the 1800s. Due to a lack of data, however, the "documented" decline in mortality is usually reported to have occurred during the first half of the twentieth century.

The most direct explanation for the decline in mortality is well documented. This period of history witnessed the virtual eradication of several of the contagious diseases that had been the leading causes of death since the Middle Ages. In the United States in 1900, 40% of the deaths were attributable to 11 major infectious conditions. These included measles, tuberculosis, pneumonia, diphtheria, scarlet fever, typhoid, influenza, whooping cough, poliomyelitis, smallpox, and diseases of the digestive system. By 1973, these conditions combined accounted for only 6% of the nation's deaths. While death rates due to these conditions were dropping precipitously, little decline was seen in the rates for other, noncontagious conditions. In fact, chronic conditions were dramatically increasing their share of the mortality rate.

The ultimate question becomes: What was responsible for the virtual elimination of these killer diseases during the first half of the twentieth century? This question is conventionally answered by pointing to breakthroughs on the part of medical science that led to the eradication of these diseases. Many cite this period as conclusive proof for the efficacy of medical science in dealing with these nearly universal health threats. Medical science has perpetuated the notion that its efforts in the development of cures for these killers were the primary factors in reducing their threat to the population. The general public has accepted this argument and has become a willing supporter for this explanation of the elimination of epidemic diseases.

An increasing number of researchers in both Europe and the United States, however, have argued that medical science has had a limited impact on these killer diseases and therefore has made little contribution to the reduced mortality experienced since 1900.

While conceding that some major breakthroughs occurred during the late 1800s and early 1900s in terms of our understanding of the causes and cures of these epidemic diseases, it is argued that factors other than medical care were responsible for the dramatic drop in mortality. McKinlay and McKinlay (1977) contend, after examining the relationship between mortality trends and developments in medical science, that the timing of the development of "cures" for these conditions virtually eliminates them as an explanation for the recorded reduction in mortality. The McKinlays argue that, for the ten infectious conditions for which there is adequate information available, the therapeutic agents developed to counteract them were introduced long after declines in mortality had begun occurring. For example, by the time a vaccine had been developed in 1943 to combat influenza, this condition had virtually ceased to be a significant cause of death. In fact, 75% of the decline in mortality from influenza between 1900 and 1973 had occurred by the time the cure was introduced in 1943.

Similar scenarios can be constructed for most of the other major infectious diseases. It is further noted that most of the reduction in mortality in the United States overall occurred prior to 1950, that is, before expenditures for health services reached an appreciable level. The McKinlays contend that "3.5 percent probably represents a reasonable upper-limit estimate of the total contribution of medical measures to the decline of mortality in the United States since 1900" (McKinlay and McKinlay 1977, p. 425).

If medical science cannot be credited with the elimination of these epidemic diseases, what can? There is now widespread support for the notion that changes in the demographic characteristics of the population, rather than medical care, accounted for the bulk of the mortality decline documented. Changes in the political, economic, and social environment in the United States had brought about changes in the demographic structure of the population. There had been general improvement in socioeconomic conditions and educational levels, as well as improvements in nutrition. A similar pattern of demographic change characterized industrialized European countries as well.

McKeown et al. (1972) concluded that the decline in mortality in several European countries during the second half of the nineteenth century was attributable to rising standards of living (especially improvements in diet), improvements in hygiene, and a healthier environment. Therapy, it was argued, made virtually no contribution to this improvement. Dubos (1959) argued convincingly for nonmedical— primarily demographic—explanations for the decline in mortality, and Fuchs (1974) clearly implicates rising incomes, not medical technology, in the reduction in mortality beginning in the middle of the nineteenth century.

While conventional beliefs concerning the elimination of the epidemic diseases are still maintained by many within both medical circles and the general public, by the 1970s the research emphasis had substantially shifted from its focus on the medical factors involved in the reduction of morbidity and mortality. The importance of demographic characteristics such as age, income, education, and even marital status as determinants of the nation's mortality levels now has become widely recognized.

increased the population's appreciation of health services and raised its level of expectations. Higher incomes and employer-sponsored insurance have both been enabling factors in the utilization of health care.

THE SOCIETAL CONTEXT OF HEALTH AND HEALTH CARE

The Institutional Framework

The health care system of any society can be understood only within its sociocultural context. No two health care systems are exactly alike, and the differences that are found between health care systems are primarily a function of the contexts in which they exist. The social structure of the society, along with its cultural values, defines the system. The form the system takes and the functions it performs reflect the form and functions of the society in which it resides.

Every social system or society has certain functions whose performance is prerequisite to survival. These include reproduction, socialization, distributing resources, maintaining internal order, providing for defense, providing for the health and welfare of its population, and providing a means for dealing with the supernatural. Each society establishes institutions for meeting these prerequisites. Thus, some form of family evolves to deal with reproduction, some form of educational system to deal with socialization, some form of economic system to deal with the allocation of resources, and so forth. A health care–social services system of some type evolves to deal with the health and welfare of the population.

Obviously, not all societies are populous enough or complex enough to support fully developed institutions of each of these types. In cases where this situation exists, a single institution may perform the functions of two or more institutions. For example, the family within a traditional society may perform the functions of the educational institution, the economic institution, and others as well. Functions usually allotted to the health care system in modern societies are typically performed by the family or the religious institution in premodern societies.

The form that a particular institution takes varies from society to society. The society's cultural history, its environment, its relationship with other societies, and its demographic attributes all contribute to the shaping of its various institutions. There are numerous forms that can be taken by the family, the political institution, and the economic institution, with the particular form being uniquely tailored to the situation of that society. Similarly, the health care institution can be configured in various ways. One might speak in terms of "traditional" health care systems (e.g., shamanism among American Indians), capitalistic systems (e.g., for-profit health care in the United States), socialized systems (e.g., the National Health Service in the United Kingdom), and so forth. No one system is intrinsically better or worse than any other; each has evolved in response to social, cultural, and environmental considerations, and each is uniquely suited to its particular society.

It is only in modern industrial society that health care has developed as a distinct institution. For most of human history, society's provision for the health care needs of the population has occurred within the framework of the family or the religious institution. Traditional societies lack the scientific underpinnings for the development of health care systems. An absence of emphasis on rationality and a dependence on the supernatural as an explanatory factor in the existence of health, illness, and death historically precluded the development of a distinct health care system within premodern societies.

The rise of the health care institution in this century was given impetus by the growing dependence on formal institutions of all types. The political institution began to "legislate" much of society's behavior and the educational system came to be seen as responsible for functions far beyond that envisioned by its creators. Even the arts and leisure activities became commercialized, spawning major industries.

Health care provides possibly the best example of this emergent dependence on formal solutions, since it is an institution whose very development was a result of this transformation. Our great-grandparents would have considered formal health care as the last resort in the face of sickness and disability. Few of them ever entered a hospital, and not many more regularly utilized physicians. Today the health care system is seen as the first resort when health problems arise rather than a necessary evil. In fact, the system's influence is such that Americans turn to it not only for clear-cut health problems, but also for a broad range of psychological, social, interpersonal, and spiritual problems.

The industrialization and urbanization occurring in the United States involved a transformation from a traditional, agrarian society to a complex, modern society in which change, not tradition, is the central theme. This transformation clearly influenced the direction of development for the health care system, as the traditional managers of sickness and death—the family and church—gave way to more complex responses to health problems. The "management" of health became a responsibility partly of the economic, educational, and political systems and eventually of a fully developed and powerful health care system. Traditional, informal responses to health problems gave way to complex, institutionalized responses. "High-touch" home remedies could not compete in an environment that valued high-tech (and subsequently high status) responses to health problems.

These developments firmly established the health care institution in the United States in this century as a major societal force. By the late 1990s, it claimed over 14% of the gross national product, generated over one trillion dollars in annual expenditures, and was one of the leading sources of employment in the economy. It came to be accorded high prestige and exerted a major influence over other institutions. The system has succeeded to the point that there are few

members of society today who are not under some type of "medical management." Some observers have even described America as a "medicalized" society.

The Cultural Framework

The transformation in the US social structure that occurred during this
century was accompanied by a cultural revolution resulting in significant value
reorientation within American society. The values associated with traditional
societies that emphasized kinship, community, authority, and primary relationships became overshadowed by the values of modern, industrialized societies.
Such societies place emphasis on economic success, educational achievement,
and technological advancement. An activist orientation evolved that called for a
proactive approach to all issues, including individual health. Health came to be
recognized as a distinct value in American society, with the quest for health coming to dominate much of the activity of the American population.

The extent to which societal values influence the nature of the health care
system cannot be overemphasized. The emphasis Americans place on economic
success led to the establishment of the world's most profit-oriented health care
system. The emphasis placed on education assured a premium for the long training
period required for medical personnel. The value placed on technology clearly
influenced the direction of the health care system. Most important, perhaps, is the
emphasis on activism noted above in that it called for a health care system that
featured an instrumental orientation that demanded direct, aggressive action in the
face of health problems.

The nature of the society's values are clearly a reflection of that society's
demographic makeup. Traditional societies with high death rates and large numbers of children clearly have a different perspective than populations with an older
age structure, few births, and low death rates. This influence is probably nowhere
more clearly reflected than with the baby boom cohort in contemporary American
society. This large cohort has developed a set of values that set it apart from any
previous generation. By virtue of its demographic legacy, it is introducing a new
value orientation into society.

To a great extent, these shifts in value orientation reflect the demographic
transformation of US society in this century. While it is true that the development
of modern scientific medicine required the formulation of germ theory as its foundation, the evolution of contemporary US health care corresponded substantially
with the demographic changes characterizing the first half of the twentieth century. It is one thing to develop the capacity for inoculating against various disease
organisms—this is readily done in developing countries—but it is quite another to
establish a value system that fosters a mammoth, highly specialized industry that
not only accounts for a disproportionate share of the gross national product but
also exerts a tremendous influence over the everyday lives of society members.

THE STRUCTURE OF HEALTH CARE SYSTEMS

The *health care system* in any society can be separated into two components: the disease theory system and the service delivery system. The disease theory system involves the underlying explanatory framework that provides meaning to the system. This component is unique to each society and reflects the particular society's worldview. The disease theory system addresses such issues as the nature of health and illness, the meaning of life and death, the appropriateness of intervening in the face of sickness, and/or the prolongation of life for the terminally ill. In effect, it encompasses the assumptions that underlie the system and provides the basis for the creation of health care delivery mechanisms. The disease theory system will not be discussed further here, but it should be noted that this underlying paradigm is both a consequence and a determinant of the demographic attributes of the population. Most observers, in fact, argue that the US health care system has experienced a paradigm shift involving the disease theory system during the last years of the twentieth century; this development is discussed below.

The second component, the health care delivery system itself, is our main concern. The delivery system is the mechanism through which society discharges its responsibility for providing for the health and welfare of its members. As such, it involves both structural aspects (such as facilities, organizational arrangements, and role relationships) and functional aspects (such as treatment, research, and education).

In the case of the US system, a discussion of health care delivery is considerably more complex than for any other society. In fact, the US system is unique in a number of ways. Most notable are the lack of any centralized control mechanism and the fractionated state of its structural components. Coupled with the fact that the system is incredibly complex, this means that a useful description of the US system is difficult, if not impossible, to find. The description that follows is geared toward the needs of those interested in the demographic aspects of the system. We hope that it will provide those with limited knowledge of the system adequate background information.

Medical Care and Health Care

At this point it might be worthwhile to distinguish between medical care and health care. *Medical care* is narrowingly defined in terms of the formal services provided by the health care system and refers primarily to those functions of the health care system that are under the influence of medical doctors. This concept focuses on the clinical or treatment aspects of care, and excludes the nonmedical aspects of health care. *Health care* refers to any function that might be directly or indirectly related to preserving, maintaining, and/or enhancing health status. This concept includes not only formal activities (such as visiting a health professional) but also such informal activities as preventive care (e.g., brushing teeth), exercise, proper diet, and so forth.

Since the 1970s, there has been a steady movement of activities and emphasis away from medical care toward health care. Despite the ever-increasing sophistication of medical technology, the importance of the nonmedical aspects of care has become increasingly appreciated. The growing awareness of the connection between health status and lifestyle and the realization that medical care is limited in its ability to control the disorders of modern society have prompted a move away from a strictly medical model of health and illness to one that incorporates more of a social and psychological perspective (Engel, 1977).

A number of factors have contributed directly or indirectly to this shift in orientation. Clearly, the *epidemiological transition*, whereby acute conditions have been displaced by chronic disorders, has played a major role. Quite independently of this trend has been the growing level of patient dissatisfaction with the operation of the health care system. Further, the runaway costs of the system have led observers of all persuasions to question the wisdom of pursuing a one-size-fits-all approach to solving all health problems.

Demographic factors have played no small role in this process. Unquestionably, the influence of the large baby boom cohort has been felt with regard to these issues. The peculiar circumstances surrounding the emergence of this large cohort have set the stage for wholesale reorientation. This population more than any other has led the movement toward a value reorientation as it relates to health care. It has been this cohort that has emphasized convenience, value, responsiveness, patient participation, accountability, and other attributes not traditionally found in the US system of health care delivery. It also has been the cohort that has been instrumental in the emergence of urgent care centers, freestanding surgery facilities, and health maintenance organizations as standard features of the system.

Despite this changing orientation, an imbalance remains in the system with regard to the allocation of resources to its various components. Treatment still commands the lion's share of the health care dollar, and most research is still focused on developing cures rather than preventive measures. The hospital remains the focal point of the system and the physician continues to be its primary gatekeeper. Nevertheless, each of these underpinnings of medical care was substantially weakened during the 1980s, with a definitive shift toward a health care orientation evident during the 1990s. By the 1990s, references to medical care in the press—both public and professional—had become rarer, as references to health care came to dominate. As those financing care become more convinced of the value of "health" measures relative to "medical" measures, this trend can be expected to accelerate.

The Organization of US Health Care

A useful starting point for attempting to examine the organization of US health care would be to inventory its component parts. The US health care system has an incredible number of functioning units, including approximately 6,400 hospitals, over 15,000 nursing homes, and an estimated 300,000 clinics providing physician care (US Department of Health and Human Services, 1997a). These figures do not include nonphysician providers and paramedical personnel such as chiropractors and mental health counselors.

The providers of care typically are autonomous parties operating under a variety of guises and means of control. Health care providers, whether facilities or practitioners, can be organized as private for-profit organizations, private not-for-profit organizations, public organizations, and quasi-public organizations, among others. Similarly, they may be owned by private investors, publicly held, local government owned and operated, or run by a religious denomination, foundation, or some other not-for-profit entity.

The complexity of the US health care system is reflected in the proliferation of occupational roles, the levels and stages of care that are provided (along both vertical and horizontal continua), and the almost unlimited points at which a patient might enter the system. The end result, many observers contend, is a "non-system" that is poorly integrated, lacks centralized control and regulation, and is characterized by fragmentation, discontinuity, and duplication.

The health care delivery system of any society theoretically reflects the health-related needs of its population. The demographic makeup of the society thus has a major influence on the character of the system. In the case of the United States, this means a population that is large and relatively dispersed and one that in recent decades has become increasingly characterized by a relatively mature age structure. The population is characterized by low levels of fertility and mortality and by a modern morbidity profile that features a preponderance of chronic conditions over acute ones. The younger age cohorts have shrunken relative to the older age cohorts, with all that this implies for health services. In addition, as the population has aged, it has become numerically dominated by females; this trend is expected to continue into the future. It also is a well-educated population and one that can generally afford state-of-the-art health care.

While the existing organizational structure appears to meet the majority of the needs for most of the population, there are some mismatches between population characteristics and the attributes of the health care system. As noted above, the United States has a rapidly aging population. However, except for the tertiary care aspects of the system, that is, those involved in extreme, life-threatening situations, the system is not very accommodating of the elderly. The system is structured to meet the needs of a younger population, and of the nation's 625,000 physicians only 1,000 have specialized training in the needs of the growing geriatric population. Similarly, the development of long-term care facilities has lagged behind that of other components of the system in terms of both the establishment of facilities and services and the development of financing mechanisms.

The United States is characterized by a very heterogeneous population in terms of race, ethnicity, religion, social class, lifestyles, and orientation to the health care delivery system. However, the existing system is relatively inflexible in its response to this diversity of needs. One mode of health care is considered to be the standard; members of subcultures or other social categories outside the mainstream are expected to conform to the system. As a result, subsystems develop geared toward the needs of these populations (e.g., *curanderos* for Hispanics; acupuncturists for Asians). The existence of these "alternative" therapies further contributes to the complexity of the system.

A final area of mismatch reflects the fact that the US population has come to be characterized by chronic rather than acute health care conditions. The US system is organized primarily to handle acute conditions and the primary goal of the system remains curing disease. The medical training and the hospital-based, technology-oriented nature of the system are more appropriate for handling acute episodes than for managing chronic conditions. Thus the system's trauma care is widely heralded, but its capacity for the rehabilitation of chronic patients is seldom noted. The situation is exacerbated by the fact that for the most part these chronic conditions are conditions of modern living. Unlike acute conditions that primarily reflect natural biological threats, chronic conditions are a result of nutritional patterns, exercise patterns, work conditions, and exposure to environmental threats. Many chronic conditions arise "naturally" as an outgrowth of aging. This means that not only are many chronic conditions largely preventable, they also are amenable to management by nonmedical means. (It should be noted that contradictions also exist with regard to the financing of acute and chronic care and this will be discussed in a later section.)

The existing system, with its emphasis on treatment and cure, historically has placed much less emphasis on prevention, health education, chronic disease management, and rehabilitation. In the best of all worlds, these factors would be emphasized in order to meet the needs of the US population. Because systems have a way of perpetuating themselves, however, the US system of health care remains geared primarily to the treatment of acute conditions. Training and research are concentrated on the major killers, not on the chronic conditions that afflict a high percentage of the population. This situation, of course, reflects the inability of the system to respond quickly to changes in health status resulting from various demographic trends.

Unlike most other societies, the United States typically provides care at the local level only. There is no national system for the provision of care, nor are there regional or even state structures for the provision of health services. The only national level providers involve the Veterans Administration hospital system and related military facilities. Many states have statewide systems of mental health care, but these are generally considered outside the mainstream of medicine. The local, autonomous provider is the norm in the US system of health care delivery.

Another characteristic of the US system is its historical focus on the individual rather than the community or the population as a whole. Under the medical care model, the goals of the system are thought to be best reached through one-on-one interaction between physician and patient. Except for providing the basics in terms of sanitation, public health is relegated to a minor role. The epidemiologist continues to toil in obscurity, while the heart surgeon is venerated.

This situation has begun to change as the health care model becomes more widely accepted in clinical settings. In fact, we are currently witnessing the emergence of a "new" concept in health care that involves a population-based approach. This approach shifts the focus of health care management from individuals to populations and, as such, is very much a kin to the epidemiological approach discussed earlier in this chapter.

The Vertical Dimension of the Health Care System

A useful approach to understanding the health care system is to conceptualize it in terms of *levels* of care. The framework is illustrated graphically in Figure 2.2. These levels are generally referred to as primary care, secondary care, and tertiary care. Additionally, some observers have identified a fourth category—quaternary care—to be applied to superspecialized services such as organ transplantation. These levels can be viewed as the vertical dimension of the health care delivery system.

Primary care refers to the provision of the most basic services. These generally involve the treatment of minor, routine problems, along with the provision of general examinations and preventive services. For the patient, primary care usually involves some self-care, perhaps followed by the seeking of care from a non-physician health professional such as a pharmacist. For certain ethnic groups, this may involve the use of a folk healer.

Formal primary care services generally are provided by physicians with training in general or family practice, general internal medicine, obstetrics–gynecology, and pediatrics. These practitioners typically are community based (rather than hospital based), rely on direct first contact with patients rather than receiving referrals from other physicians, and provide continuous rather than episodic care. Physician extenders like nurse practitioners and physician assistants are taking on a growing responsibility for care. In the mental health system,

Procedure	Site	Physician
	QUATERNARY CARE	
Organ transplant Complex trauma	Multiinstitution medical centers	Teams of superspecialist physicians
	TERTIARY CARE	
Specialized surgery Complex medical cases	Large-scale comprehensive hospitals with extensive technological support	Physician subspecialists
	SECONDARY CARE	
Moderately complex surgical and medical cases	Moderate-scale hospitals Some freestanding surgery and diagnostic centers	Physician specialists
	PRIMARY CARE	
Routine care Standard tests Simple surgery Prevention	General hospitals Clinics Physician offices "Urgicenters"	Primary care physicians Physician "extenders" (e.g., nurse practitioners, physician assistants, nurses)

Complexity
Severity
Specialization

Figure 2.2. The levels of US health care.

psychologists and other types of counselors constitute the primary level of care. Medical specialists also provide a certain amount of primary care. See Box 2.3 for the separate treatment of mental health.

Primary care generally is delivered at the physician's office or in some type of clinic setting. Hospital outpatient departments, urgent care centers, freestanding surgery centers, and other ambulatory care facilities also provide primary care services. For certain segments of the population, the hospital emergency room serves as a source of primary care. The home has increasingly become the site of choice for the provision of primary care. This trend has been driven by a number

Box 2.3

The Special Case of Mental Health Services

Mental health services are viewed differently enough from other types of health services to require separate discussion. Although services provided for those with mental disorders could be considered under the same umbrella as health care for physical illness, a clear distinction is made between the two in the US system. While some mental health services are provided by general hospitals and many physicians provide some care for conditions that could be considered mental disorders, mental health services are provided for the most part by separate practitioners in separate settings.

In fact, parallel systems have developed in the United States for the management of physical and mental illnesses. This system includes clinics and hospitals designated specifically for the care of mental disorders. Psychiatric clinics may be operated by psychiatrists or nonphysician mental health professionals as private facilities or by governmental agencies. Most of the latter are operated by local (i.e., city or county) governments, although states and the federal government may operate certain types of psychiatric facilities. Many of these clinics are classified as "comprehensive community mental health centers," founded in the 1960s as part of a national initiative to make mental health services accessible to the general public. Care also may be provided by psychiatrists or other mental health professionals operating in office settings.

For institutional care, a parallel system of psychiatric hospitals is in place. Like the clinics, these hospitals may be either private or public. Although private psychiatric facilities may be operated by religious groups or other sponsors on a not-for-profit basis, most private psychiatric hospitals are run as for-profit institutions that cater to select populations. Public psychiatric hospitals have historically been the responsibility of the various states, and until the 1970s most states operated thousands of psychiatric beds. Local governments also operate some psychiatric facilities. Interestingly, this has been the only form of illness treatment that has been considered the direct responsibility of the government.

Public mental hospital patients are frequently committed involuntarily, while private hospital patients are typically admitted on a voluntary basis. While mental hospitals at one time dominated the treatment of mental patients, they have become less significant over the past two decades. During this period the number of inpatient admissions declined dramatically, while the number of outpatient visits multiplied manyfold.

A certain portion of the hospitalized mentally ill are treated in general acute care hospitals, although usually in separate units. The 1980s actually witnessed an in-

Continued

Box 2.3. (Continued)

crease in the number of psychiatric patients treated in general hospitals. This reflects the availability of more efficacious management techniques and the fact that psychiatric care had not yet come under the Medicare prospective payment system. It also reflects the fact that included among the conditions now classified as mental disorders are alcoholism, drug addiction, and eating disorders. Such patients are viewed much differently from patients with extreme psychosis who once were typically associated with a mental institution. An unknown number of patients with psychiatric conditions are "treated" in nursing homes due to a lack of more appropriate facilities or a failure of medical personnel to appreciate the nature of their condition.

Because of changing reimbursement arrangements, the trend has been away from inpatient care for psychiatric patients. Financial pressure is pushing patients from the hospital setting to the clinic setting, the community setting, and the home. At the same time, these pressures are pushing patients away from psychiatrists and toward practitioners with lower skill levels.

While physicians in general practice are likely to encounter and treat many patients with psychiatric symptoms, mental illness is treated for the most part by a separate set of health professionals. The best known of these, of course, are psychiatrists, who (historically at least) have been the pivotal practitioners in the area of mental health. Since the 1970s, however, the importance of psychiatrists relative to other mental health professionals has declined. Today, psychiatrists treat only a fraction of those with mental disorders, frequently treating them in their roles as employees of various institutions rather than as private practitioners. By the 1980s, most individuals with mental disorders were being treated by social workers, clinical psychologists, and the variety of other therapists that had emerged to address the growing numbers of Americans seeking psychiatric services. This pattern of treatment continued in the 1990s.

Mental health services are, for the most part, financed separately from other health services. Historically, mental health services were obtained from private

---

of factors, including financial pressures on inpatient care, changing consumer preferences, and improved home care technology. In addition, there is now a substantial body of research indicating the efficacy of home-based care and the therapeutic effect of being in a familiar environment.

In terms of hospital services, primary care refers to those services that can be provided at a general hospital. These typically involve routine medical and surgical procedures, diagnostic tests, and obstetrical services. Primary care also includes emergency care (although not major trauma) and many outpatient services. Primary hospital care tends to be unspecialized and requires a relatively low

psychiatrists and private mental institutions at great expense to paying patients or were obtained free from government institutions. Thus, in the past, such services were available to only the rich and the poor. The community mental health movement mentioned above represented an attempt to make mental health services accessible to the working and middle classes. By subsidizing mental health services in community settings, the federal government helped to "popularize" such treatment. By the 1980s, community mental health centers had become the major source of such care. In recent years, an increasing portion of Medicare and Medicaid dollars has been devoted to the treatment of mental disorders.

By the 1980s, both federal and state governments had begun reducing their support for mental health services. Although most established clinics continued to operate, other sources of funds were required in the absence of government subsidy. Many of these funds came from increases in fees to patients of community mental health centers. In addition, part of this financial shortfall had begun to be covered by private employer-sponsored insurance. Until the 1980s, few insurers had offered mental health services as part of their coverage, and few employers provided these services as a benefit. However, various factors in the 1970s gave impetus to a trend toward the provision of mental health benefits as a standard part of employee insurance packages. While well received by the insured, these provisions had become a significant burden to employers and insurers by the end of the 1980s, and attempts have been under way since then to modify or limit this sort of benefit for employees. The end result is that today mental health services are financed through a variety of mechanisms, including government subsidy, private insurance, and out-of-pocket payments.

In recent years, mental health care has been redefined as "behavioral health care." The reconceptualization of the field reflects a more contemporary view of mental health problems. This view is much broader in scope than previous iterations and calls for a much different treatment approach than the traditional psychiatric model.

level of technological sophistication. In actuality, there are few hospitals remaining today that could truly be considered to provide primary care. Even the smallest hospital today is likely to have equipment that may not have been available in major hospitals only a few years ago.

Increasing attention is being paid to the role of self-care in the provision of basic medical services. Self-medication has long been an activity carried out by the American population. Now the availability of home diagnostic tests and mail-order remedies has further encouraged the "do-it-yourself approach" to health care. Research has now verified that much of what occurs under the umbrella of "primary care" actually takes place outside the formal medical arena. Self-care and other informal alternatives appear to be firmly entrenched in the American health care ethos.

Secondary care reflects a higher degree of specialization and technological sophistication than primary care. Physician care is provided by more highly trained practitioners such as specialized surgeons (e.g., urologists and ophthalmologists) and specialized internists (e.g., cardiologists and oncologists). Problems requiring more specialized skills and more sophisticated biomedical equipment fall into this category. Although much of the care is still provided in the physician office or clinic, these specialists tend to spend a larger share of their time in the hospital setting. Secondary hospitals are capable of providing more complex technological backup, physician specialist support, and ancillary services than primary care hospitals. These facilities are capable of handling moderately complex surgical and medical cases and serve as referral centers for primary care facilities.

Tertiary care addresses the most complex of surgical and medical conditions. The practitioners tend to be subspecialists and the facilities highly complex and technologically advanced. Complex procedures such as open-heart surgery and reconstructive surgery are performed at these facilities, which provide extensive support services in terms of both personnel and technology. Tertiary care cases are usually handled by a team of medical and/or surgical specialists who are supported by the hospital's radiology, pathology, and anesthesiology physician staff. Tertiary care is generally provided at a few centers that serve large geographical areas. Frequently, a single hospital is not sufficient for the provision of tertiary care; a "medical center" may be required. These centers typically support functions not directly related to patient care, such as teaching and research.

The ability to extend this level of technology to the community is limited by the number of subspecialists and the availability of state-of-the-art technology. However, secondary facilities are increasingly performing what were previously considered tertiary procedures. The routinization of previously uncommon procedures reflects to a great extent improvements in technology and the increased numbers of specialists with advanced surgical training.

Some procedures often performed at tertiary facilities may be considered quaternary care. Organ transplantation, especially involving vital organs like heart, lungs, and pancreas, are included here. Complicated trauma cases are another example. This level of care is restricted to major medical centers often in medical school settings. These procedures require the most sophisticated equipment and are often performed in association with research activities.

This review of the levels of care ignores some other important structural aspects of the system that are not as directly related to patient care. In addition to physicians' offices, clinics, and acute care hospitals, mention also should be made of specialty hospitals and nursing homes. Specialty hospitals include facilities for the treatment of specific categories of conditions such as mental illness, substance abuse, or tuberculosis. They also are established for the treatment of certain categories of patients such as women, children, or the elderly. Federally operated facilities such as those run by the Veterans Administration also should be considered as a special category of facilities. The various specialty facilities are operated under different guises, ranging from poorly funded state-operated facilities to upscale, privately owned, for-profit facilities. The nation's 15,000 nursing homes provide extensive custodial care to nearly 2 million residents each year. Add to these the growing number of newly defined care settings (e.g., assisted living facilities, extended care facilities), and the variety of care settings continues to grow.

The Horizontal Dimension of the Health Care System

The discussion so far has focused on the vertical organization of the health care system. The system also can be viewed as having a horizontal dimension in that health care episodes can be viewed as linear phenomena that proceed through various stages. If the assumption is made that individuals are naturally in a state of "health," a scenario can be developed whereby prevention, screening, and routine self-care are typical of this stage (see Figure 2.3).

With the onset of symptoms, the individual makes a transition to the point of diagnosis and treatment at an outpatient facility. This may result in assignment to the patient category (sickness), whereby the stages of the vertical axis (primary, secondary, tertiary, and quaternary) come into play. Assuming the patient survives the illness episode, he or she may move out of the patient care model back into the community as a "well" person. Alternatively, the patient may require follow-up care or chronic disease management (e.g., by a home care agency), temporary institutionalized care (e.g., a subacute facility), long-term nursing care (e.g., a nursing home), or rehabilitative services of some type (e.g., physical or occupational therapy). These postpatient stages extend the model horizontally.

This patient "career" actually could be thought of as involving three stages: prepatient, patient, and postpatient. Significant aspects of the prepatient and postpatient stages fall outside the vertical dimension of the model. Some of the structural components that are involved in these stages are noted above; others

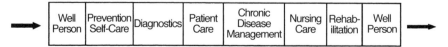

Figure 2.3. The horizontal dimension of health care.

would include public health agencies (for prevention and screening) and hospices (for care of the terminally ill).

Because of the emphasis historically placed on treatment and cure by the health care system, the components in the horizontal integration model not involving direct patient care have not been emphasized until recently. However, research has demonstrated that much of the care received by Americans takes place outside the mainstream of formal care. Importantly, as will be seen in Chapters 10 and 11, certain demographic attributes are correlated with the propensity to utilize different types of care.

Health Care Personnel

An examination of the structure of the health care system requires a discussion of the personnel involved in the provision of health care. The health care system is highly labor-intensive and involves 11 million or more workers, depending on what occupational definitions are utilized. In fact, the health care sector accounts for more employees than almost any other sector of the economy. Increasing from 1 million employees in 1970, its more than 11 million employees accounted for 9% of the US labor force in 1995. The typical hospital has three or more employees per hospital bed, and there are enough physicians in practice to staff several hundred thousand clinics nationwide.

In terms of those who provide patient care, the key player is the physician. There are over 700,000 licensed physicians in active practice in the United States today, most of whom are in direct patient care (American Medical Association, 1997). In 1995, 93% of US physicians were involved in patient care; most of this number (73%) were in office-based practices, with most of the remainder in hospital-based positions. About 16% are residents in training, and small proportions of the physician pool are involved in research, teaching, or administration.

As of the mid-1990s, approximately one fourth of the physicians providing patient care were involved in primary care; this includes general and family practice, general internal medicine, obstetrics–gynecology, and pediatrics. These practitioners are considered primary because they usually serve as family doctors, are the initial point of entry into the system, and generally treat routine, less complex conditions. The remainder of the nation's physician pool is divided among 13 major specialties. Despite greater interest in "family medicine" in the 1980s and 1990s, the trend toward increased specialization is only slowly abating. Changes in reimbursement, more than any other factor, have contributed to the beginning of a shift in training priorities away from the specialties and toward primary care. See Table 2.1 for a breakdown of specialties.

The physician is considered the key player within the system because of the control he or she maintains over the utilization of health services. Only physicians are allowed to diagnose illness, perform most procedures, hospitalize patients, and

Table 2.1. Breakdown of Physician Specialties

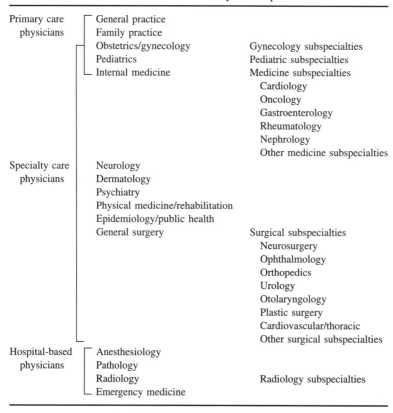

prescribe drugs. It is the physician who determines what type and length of treatment is appropriate, when the patient should enter and leave the hospital, and what other types of specialists or services the patient needs.

This situation allows the physician a great deal of control over utilization by allowing the supplier of services to determine the demand. In fact, it was estimated that during the mid-1980s individual physicians accounted for some 80% of the nation's health care expenditures (although less than 25% goes for physician services) due to their gatekeeper function (Eisenberg, 1986). Because of shifts in the focus of control in the health care system, it is now estimated that less than 65% of the nation's health care expenditures are controlled by individual physicians.

Most office-based physicians are self-employed, even when part of a group practice. Some physicians are hospital based, and these are often employed by the hospital rather than practicing independently. Hospital-based physicians include

---

Box 2.4

The Changing Demographics of American Physicians

The characteristics of the physician personnel pool in the United States have been changing dramatically over the past two decades. Not only has the number of physicians and their distribution among specialties changed, but the demographic composition of this category of professionals has been radically modified. In 1960, there were fewer physicians in the United States per 100,000 population than there were in 1900. However, between 1960 and 1995, the number of physicians per 100,000 population increased from 150 to 236. This represents a rate of growth much greater than that for the population as a whole. This increase in the physician pool was attributable partly to the establishment of new medical schools and increasing the size of medical school classes during the 1960s and 1970s. It also was attributable to a relaxing of immigration and eligibility policies that resulted in the influx of tens of thousands of foreign-trained physicians.

The change in the demographics of the physician pool has been equally dramatic. Once the almost exclusive province of upper-middle-class white Anglo-Saxon males with close relatives who were physicians, the medical community has clearly taken on a different flavor. Between 1980 and 1995, the number of physicians who were women increased by 288%, compared to only 31% for males. In 1995, the proportion of active physicians that were female stood at over 19%, nearly twice the proportion recorded in 1980. By the 1990s, African Americans who at one time were almost totally excluded from all except the few African-American medical schools accounted for around 5% of the physician pool. These new medical students are less

---

specialists like radiologists, anesthesiologists, and pathologists, who generally do not have their own patients but provide related services such as X-ray interpretation or laboratory analysis. Many hospital-based physicians (e.g., radiologists, pathologists) practice under a contract with the hospital. Increasing numbers of patient care physicians are becoming employees of large physician groups, health maintenance organizations, or other corporate entities. In fact, the increasing "corporatization" of the providers of care is one of the major features of US health care today. The changing characteristics of physicians is discussed in Box 2.4.

Physicians are considered independent practitioners because they are licensed to practice without supervision or oversight. Other practitioners who, although less important in the system, are considered independent practitioners include chiropractors, optometrists, podiatrists, dentists, and some "marginal" practitioners such as mental health counselors. All other health workers are

likely to be science majors or to come from affluent backgrounds with physician relatives.

Because of the manner in which the physician pool increased, today's active practitioners are younger and more likely to be foreign born and/or educated. The grandfatherly family doctor is an endangered species, since the largest single age cohort of physicians is those under 36 years of age (31%). The next largest cohort is 35–45, accounting for another 29%.

Until the 1960s, the physician pool included few non-Americans. Foreign physicians who did enter practice in this country came from the traditional bastions of medical education in England, Scotland, and Germany. The 1970s and 1980s witnessed the influx of tens of thousands of foreign physicians. By 1995, foreign medical graduates in the United States totaled about 154,000 out of a total physician pool of 720,000. Now they originate from India, the Philippines, and different European countries; the new immigrant physicians from Iran, Southeast Asia, and Latin America are added to them.

What are the implications of this new physician pool, one that is more female, is younger, is more ethnic, and comes from different socioeconomic backgrounds? These new doctors have different priorities than the "good old boys" of the past. They are more likely to emphasize primary care and have helped resurrect the concept of the family doctor. They are less interested in big incomes and want security, stable working conditions, and time for their families. They are much more likely to become employed as physicians in clinics, health maintenance organizations, or other corporate settings. Finally, they bring a diversity—demographically and otherwise—to medical science that has never been experienced in the United States.

dependent on physicians or these other providers since they must typically practice under the supervision of one of the independent practitioners. In fact, the dependent workers often cannot be paid for their services unless a physician "signs off" on them. The degree of independence of a practitioner is typically a reflection of the licensing practices of the particular state.

The most prominent of the nonphysician providers of care are nurses of various types. This is the largest occupational group within health care. Most nurses are registered nurses, indicating that they have received certain training. These are joined by licensed practical nurses, nursing assistants, and nurse's aides. Nurse practitioners—registered nurses with graduate training—have become more common and often can perform some of the functions usually reserved for physicians. Most nurses and related personnel are employed by hospitals, and some of these positions are found only within hospital settings.

Table 2.2. Active Health Personnel, United States, 1995

Personnel	Number	Rate per 100,000 population[a]
Physicians	672,859	255.9
Federal	21,153	8.0
Nonfederal	651,706	247.9
Doctors of medicine[b,c]	617,362	234.8
Doctors of osteopathy	34,344	13.1
Dentists[a]	146,600	58.8
Optometrists	28,900	10.9
Pharmacists[d]	182,300	68.9
Podiatrists	10,300	3.9
Registered nurses	2,115,800	797.6

[a]Rates for physicians and dentists are based on civilian population; rates for all other
health occupations are based on resident population.
[b]Excludes United States possessions.
[c]Excludes physicians not classified activity status.
[d]Excludes dentists in military service; figure is for 1990.
SOURCE: National Center for Health Statistics (1998).

Physician assistants and other physician extenders (including nurse practitioners) have been introduced into the health care system over the past two decades. The intent has been to "extend" the capabilities of the physician through lesser-trained midrange medical professionals. For a variety of reasons, this level of care has never been well accepted by the medical community. It is likely, however, that the continued pressure from managed care for the provision of care by lower-level professionals will once again boost the interest in physician extenders.

The US health care system is noteworthy for its specialized roles. Beyond the basic physician–nurse tandem, there are a variety of technicians, therapists, and ancillary personnel who perform various tasks. Again, these personnel are found primarily within the hospital setting, although, as more and more procedures are performed on an outpatient basis, these paraprofessionals increasingly are found in clinics and freestanding facilities of various types. It should be noted that the mental health profession has a variety of practitioners and paraprofessionals to further complicate the personnel picture.

The health care system has become increasingly characterized by personnel who are not involved in patient care. Even within the hospital setting, a growing proportion of employees are involved in ancillary activities. Although nurses still are the largest occupational category within hospitals, the greatest growth has occurred in noncare areas such as administration, data processing, medical records management, planning–marketing, and financial management. Some of the components of health care not involved in patient care are discussed below under the functions of the system. The health care field continues to be one of the most fertile sectors of the economy in terms of employment opportunities. In fact, health care occupations figure prominently in the list of projected fast-growing occupations, according to the US Department of Labor.

The demographics of health personnel are worth examining because of their unusual characteristics. In many ways, the demographic makeup of the nation's health personnel replicates the demographic configuration of the US population as a whole; in other ways, it does not. Clearly identifiable patterns of distribution among demographic characteristics are found in health care that represent a microcosm of social stratification in the United States (Conrad and Kern, 1986). Physicians are predominantly male, with nurses and related professionals being almost exclusively female. In fact, as in many other sectors, males tend to occupy positions associated with high status and rewards, and females the converse.

A similar pattern is found with regard to race. High-status positions are occupied primarily by whites and low-status positions by nonwhites. Even among physicians, doctors who are female, nonwhite, or of non-American origin are likely to be allocated to lower-status positions within the profession. This is true not only in the area of patient care but in some medical schools and research facilities as well. A nationwide study (Aguirre et al., 1989) documented the continued differences in health occupation prestige on the basis of race–ethnicity and gender despite the increasingly heterogeneous nature of the health care system.

Control in the System

The complexity of the US health care system makes any discussion of control somewhat problematic. The lack of centralized control or even coordination means that power in the system is fragmented and diffuse. Decision making is shared by administrators and clinicians, as well as by "outside" parties such as insurance plan representatives.

Perhaps the most orderly way to approach this is by dividing the system into public and private sectors. This distinction is not an issue in most industrialized countries, since virtually all health care functions in those systems are "public." In the United States the public sector includes those activities that are operated directly (or indirectly through financial sponsorship) by federal, state, and local governments. Various units of government operate facilities and programs for the direct provision of care, finance others through the subsidization of private organizations, and regulate the activities that come under their purview. Note that the federal government has few constitutionally mandated health care responsibilities, so most of these functions revert to the state level.

Some of these government-sponsored activities have been historically assigned to the public sector. These include provision of care for veterans and the tracking of communicable diseases (the federal government), providing mental health services and training physicians (primarily state governments), and the assurance of a sanitary environment (primarily local governments). Some facilities directly involved in the provision of care are operated by the various levels of government, with certain types of hospitals and clinics operating under government auspices.

Governments at various levels participate in the financing of health services and related activities. The federal government during the mid-1990s accounted for more than two fifths of the nation's expenditures for medical care, primarily through its funding of the Medicare and Medicaid programs (Health Care Financing Administration, 1996). States provide matching funds for the Medicaid program, and the administration of the program is the responsibility of the participating states. Other state-level activities include the licensure of health care professionals, the accreditation of health care facilities, and the regulation of the insurance industry, along with the limited amount of health planning that takes place. Federal regulatory activities generally involve interstate commerce issues and the monitoring of goods and products through such agencies as the Food and Drug Administration.

The private sector is essentially divided into two major components for the provision of care: the for-profit sector and the not-for-profit sector. The overwhelming majority of ambulatory care and a significant proportion of hospital care is provided in for-profit settings. Physician services account for around 25% of health care expenditures and are typically provided on a for-profit basis. The exceptions would be physician services in public clinics or other entities that are operated on a not-for-profit basis. A growing proportion of the nation's hospitals are operated on a for-profit basis, although the majority remain not-for-profit entities. Other parts of the system that are primarily for-profit include the nursing home component, pharmaceutical and medical supplies, and the commercial health insurance industry.

Most hospitals historically have been operated as public entities (under the ownership of state or local governments) or as voluntary not-for-profit hospitals associated with religious organizations. There always have been a few "proprietary" hospitals, often owned by physicians, that have been operated on a for-profit basis. Although the number of such hospitals declined dramatically during the 1970s and 1980s, their disappearance has been offset by the emergence of the multifacility, investor-owned chain. The number of the nation's general hospitals owned by for-profit chains increased from 420 in 1977 to around 1000 by 1997 (*Modern Healthcare*, 1998). The growth has been even more dramatic for chain ownership of mental hospitals.

There was a shift during the 1980s toward more of a profit orientation on the part of traditionally not-for-profit health care organizations. The growing competition for patients, along with the cost-containment measures that reduced revenues for hospitals, resulted in a new for-profit health care component. Many institutions have had to downplay their charitable orientations and develop more aggressive "business" stances. During the 1980s, many not-for-profits began diversifying into related areas, often in the form of for-profit subsidiaries or joint ventures, and the consolidation of hospitals led to the rise of bottom-line-oriented health care conglomerates. These developments have further clouded the picture in terms of the division between the for-profit and not-for-profit components in health care.

Financing Health Care

Health care expenditures accounted for 14.2% of the gross national product in 1995. Despite the introduction of cost-containment efforts in the 1980s, health care expenditures continue to increase and to produce wealth for the more efficient and opportunistic providers of health services. The for-profit components of the system, such as pharmaceuticals and medical supplies, are among the most profitable industries in the US economy. These industries now have been joined by the national conglomerates offering various managed care plans in the health care arena.

One of the more complex aspects of the US health care system and one that sets it apart from virtually all other systems is the manner in which health care is financed. The fragmentation of the system, the variety of entities that can provide services, multiple reimbursement arrangements, and powerful third-party payers create a very complicated picture. (The financing of patient care is the only consideration here; the financing of research, education, and other components are discussed in their respective sections.)

During this century, the financing mechanism has been transformed from one in which each patient was essentially responsible for paying for whatever care he or she received into a system involving multiple payers. Although some charitable hospital care was provided historically, most treatment up until the early part of this century was paid for out-of-pocket. Since the 1920s, however, the financing of health care in the United States has undergone a dramatic transformation. The patient is confronted with a bewildering array of payment and reimbursement arrangements that serve to increase the difficulties in understanding how health care is paid for.

Government statistics indicate that in the mid-1990s about one sixth of health services expenditures was contributed by patients, one third was contributed by private third-party payers such as commercial insurance companies, and over two fifths was contributed by government entities (Health Care Financing Administration, 1996). The bulk of government funds subsidize treatment under the federally supported Medicare and Medicaid programs. Physician services are paid for out of pocket or by insurance plans (commercial or government), while the bulk of hospital services are covered under insurance plans. The situation is made more complex by indirect payments made by patients to insurance programs or government-sponsored health care programs. It is not unusual for patients to have their medical costs covered by all three sources.

It might be argued that the major developments in the transformation of US health care from a cottage industry to a medical–industrial–government complex did not occur in the research laboratories. This transformation has been a function of political and economic decisions related to health services. The transformation reflects, more than anything else, changes that took place in the mechanisms for paying for health care. The documented elasticity in the demand for health services is in fact to a great extent a function of the nature of the financing mechanisms available.

The first major development in the transformation of the system was the introduction of insurance plans to protect individuals from major medical expenses. First proposed in the 1920s, health insurance progressed from a mechanism for the sharing of risk among co-workers to one of the major industries in the US economy. Commercial insurance and its not-for-profit kin, Blue Cross, became widespread after World War II. The industrialization and more importantly the unionization of American society resulted in nearly universal coverage for employed Americans by the 1960s. Its main effect, beyond the obvious one of making health care more accessible and affordable, was to insulate the patient from the cost of care.

Insurance came to be seen as a third-party payer since it existed outside the traditional doctor–patient relationship. Under this arrangement, the patient seldom knew how much health services cost; furthermore, he or she did not care how much they cost or even whether or not he or she needed the services, since someone else was paying for them. By the 1960s, insurance companies were paying for a large share of the treatment historically paid for out-of-pocket. This traditional form of insurance is referred to as indemnity insurance.

The next major development was the introduction of Medicare and Medicaid coverage during the 1960s. The purpose of the former was to provide medical insurance for the elderly and of the latter to insure the poor. Medicare is available to all citizens 65 years and older, to some individuals under age 65 if certain conditions are met, and to the disabled. (Congress has considered raising the age to 67 over a period of years, while the Clinton Administration has proposed expanding coverage to those as young as 55.) Part A of Medicare covers hospitalization and Part B covers physician care. Participation in Part A is mandatory, with a nominal premium being withheld from Social Security payments to individuals. There are no other qualifications to be met for Medicare participation.

Medicaid, although federally sponsored, is administered through the states, which provide matching funds. Beyond certain basic coverage, the degree of participation is left up to the individual state, so that a wide range of benefits is evident among the states. Individuals must qualify on the basis of income level to participate in the Medicaid program.

The next major change in reimbursement arrangements came in the 1970s with the emergence of some alternative financing mechanisms for the coverage of health care costs. The early thrust came in the form of *health maintenance organizations* (HMOs) that theoretically were geared toward health "maintenance" rather than cure. Enrollees paid a monthly premium, and essentially all their health care costs were covered without additional out-of-pocket expenditures. Regular checkups, preventive care, and health education were emphasized on the grounds that more expensive "downstream" care could be avoided by spending funds on upstream prevention. By 1996, there were over 600 HMOs nationwide with a total enrollment of over 51 million individuals (Health Care Financing Administration, 1996).

HMOs were soon joined by a variety of *preferred provider organizations* (PPOs) that attempted to contain costs by controlling the utilization of physicians and hospitals. Unlike traditional insurance, which generally rubber-stamped reimbursement for whatever care was provided by physicians and hospitals, these alternative arrangements demanded justification for hospitalization and the provision of most services before they would authorize the treatment (Sultz and Young, 1999).

The 1980s witnessed another development in the transformation of the health care financing system. This involved the widespread reaction on the part of those ultimately responsible for the financing of care to the continued escalation of health care costs. This in fact became the era of cost containment. The most obvious crusader for cost containment has been the federal government, in particular the administrators of the Medicare program. With spiraling health care costs and an aging population, it was obvious that the Medicare program could not spend health care funds as if its resources were infinite. Further, measures aimed at reducing the federal deficit required reductions in federal spending for health care, a heretofore protected area.

The most significant step in this regard has been the introduction of "prospective payment" as the basis for reimbursement for health care rendered under the Medicare program. Hospitals, physicians, and certain other providers of health care are informed at the beginning of the financial accounting period as to the amount that the federal government will pay for a particular category of patient. This is in stark contrast to the retrospective payment arrangement originally built into the Medicare program, which was essentially a cost-plus approach that contained no incentives for cost containment. The prospective payment system (PPS) limits the amount of reimbursement for services to each category of patient based on rates predetermined by the Health Care Financing Administration, the federal agency that administers the Medicare program.

Cost containment measures on the part of Medicare primarily have affected hospitals whose clientele are mostly Medicare enrollees. Commercial insurers and the various Blue Cross organizations, some of which had started incurring losses by the 1980s, began following the example of the Medicare administration. Their cost containment measures have affected more than the elderly population, as they have placed reimbursement limits and utilization restrictions on all their plan enrollees.

These developments have contributed to the emergence of the "managed care" concept. While traditional indemnity insurance is reactive, managed care programs attempt to be proactive. They are designed to have input on the front end, even prior to the occurrence of an illness episode, to monitor the patient throughout the episode, and to follow the patient through convalescence and rehabilitation. In their most extreme form, managed care programs dictate the conditions under which various types of care can be provided, negotiate with specific providers of care for discount services, and indicate before the services are rendered the amount of reimbursement they are willing to provide for a particular case. With regard to the covered individual, managed care plans frequently place part of the responsibility for justification of care on the insured and frequently offer a variety of copayment arrangements.

By the 1990s, "capitated" reimbursement plans had become common under managed care. This variation on managed care arrangements involves a set payment to providers (e.g., physicians, hospitals) for a defined range of services for a specified population. This is usually stated in terms of a per member/per month payment. If the provider can provide the necessary care under these circumstances in a cost-effective manner, he will be rewarded for his efficiency. If the provider is unable to provide the required services for the money expended, the provider must bear the risk for the shortfall.

One final thrust, and perhaps the most significant, for cost containment was initiated by major purchasers of health care. These were primarily large employers who, through commercial insurers or their own self-insurance programs, had been saddled with ever-increasing costs for an ever-growing active and retired work force and their dependents. The extent of health care benefits offered by employers and the spiraling overall costs led to drastic measures. Employers began offering scaled-down plans, providing options for enrollees (including HMOs), and introducing various copayment schemes. In addition, they began exercising much more oversight regarding the utilization of services. The drive for cost reductions resulted in more careful review of utilization patterns, including preadmission certification, concurrent review (while in treatment), and discharge planning. This intensive monitoring came to be the hallmark of managed care. By the mid-1990s, the growth in self-insurance by large employers and the general trend toward a declining proportion of employees being covered by employer-sponsored insurance resulted in a large and growing uninsured population.

One final development, also initiated by major purchasers of care, was the leveraging of health care buying power. Major employers, HMOs, PPOs, commercial insurers, and government funding agencies began negotiating with various providers of care for the best price in exchange for all of their health care business. As a result, the corporate purchasers of care and the corporate providers of care have become key players; to a great extent, the physician and the patient have become excluded from the decision-making process. While no major advances in controlling costs have been documented due to this development, it clearly has changed the manner in which the business of health care is being conducted.

ADDITIONAL FUNCTIONS OF THE HEALTH CARE SYSTEM

While patient care receives the bulk of attention in the US health care system, there are a number of other components of the system that, while less visible, involve important functions. These components are each important in their own right and some are critical to the health and safety of the population. Each is also particularly "American" in its characteristics.

Public Health

Public health is perhaps the only component of the US system that focuses on the community rather than the individual. In contrast to the situation in most other industrialized nations, the public health component of the US health care system is poorly developed. The establishment of the US Public Health Service was predicated on its not being involved in any way in patient care; that was to be left to the private sector. Thus many functions characterizing the public health components of other industrialized countries are almost nonexistent in the US system.

The public health function is carried out at the national level by the Public Health Service within the Department of Health and Human Services and by such specialized agencies as the Centers for Disease Control and Prevention (CDC). The small portion of federal health care expenditures devoted to public health activities is utilized for contagious disease control, monitoring of health problems, and reporting of health and vital statistics data. Each state also has an agency responsible for health services planning and for monitoring health and environmental conditions. The individual states generally have responsibility for the provision of mental health services. At the local level, county government typically has public health responsibility; a limited amount of patient care is provided at the local level to indigent patients through public health clinics.

From a health demography perspective, the activities of public health entities have two benefits. First, some of the organizations under this heading conduct research that has relevance for health demography. These agencies include the

CDC, the National Center for Health Statistics, and various entities within the National Institutes of Health, described in the next section.

Second, the data collection function of public health agencies at the federal, state, and local levels provides valuable information not available elsewhere. National vital statistics and morbidity data are compiled by federal agencies. Much of the data used by health planners are routinely gathered by the National Center for Health Statistics, while the National Center for Health Services Research and the Agency for Healthcare Research and Quality conduct and support research related to the financing and provision of care. State agencies maintain records on health facilities, health care personnel, and vital statistics. Local health departments are the primary source of information on fertility, morbidity, and mortality. (Chapter 9 on sources of health care data provides detailed descriptions of these resources.)

Health Care Research

Research is a major function performed within the US health care system. This is an area in which the federal government plays a significant role through the establishment of research institutes and the funding of research conducted by universities and research laboratories. In addition, funding for health care research is often provided by foundations. State governments fund some of the research conducted at medical schools. Private corporations, such as pharmaceutical companies and medical suppliers, often conduct internally funded research on products hoped to be commercially viable and subsidize clinical trials at medical schools and research institutes. In fact, by 1989, the amount of funds spent on research by pharmaceutical companies exceeded that spent by government agencies.

In 1995, the federal government invested over $13 billion in health-related research (US Department of Health and Human Services, 1997a). The National Institutes of Health within the Department of Health and Human Services are the primary sites of federally supported health research. They conduct research intramurally and also provide grant support to external research organizations. There are 11 institutes, each with a different focus. Two are particularly important in the generation of data useful to health demographers: the National Institute of Aging and the National Institute of Child Health and Human Development.

The Food and Drug Administration (FDA) is the interface between research units and the public distribution of most such products. The FDA has responsibility for regulating introduction into the US market of all drugs and specified medical devices. While not a research organization per se, the FDA regulates and monitors the product testing that it requires of manufacturers.

In keeping with the emphasis of the US health care system, government-sponsored research has focused on treatment and cure rather than prevention or education. The bulk of research funds is devoted to the major killers (e.g., heart disease, cancer, and stroke), with limited attention paid to the increasingly common chronic conditions. There is growing interest, however, in health services research focusing on the delivery of care and especially on factors involved in the cost of health care.

Education

The education of health professionals is an important function of the US health care system. Large amounts of funds are devoted to the training of physicians, nurses, technicians, hospital administrators, and various other health professionals. The 126 medical schools in the United States are major training organizations, graduating nearly 16,000 medical doctors each year. Schools of osteopathy, podiatry, and optometry, among others, train nonphysician practitioners. Over 1500 nursing schools and various related institutes train registered nurses, licensed practical nurses, and nursing assistants.

Health education frequently is funded at the state level, with federal funds often infused in cases of perceived medical personnel shortages. Most medical schools are state funded, although a few private schools remain in operation. Specialized medical training has been supported to a great extent through the Medicare program since the 1960s. Most major hospitals have educational programs for the training of various levels of professionals, from hospital attendants to residents and fellows in specialty medical training. Because of the demand for health personnel, numerous proprietary health care institutes have been established, mostly to train technicians and lower-level personnel.

Planning and Regulation

Although health care providers often contend that they are overplanned and overregulated, neither one of these functions is highly developed in the US health care system. Except for brief periods during the 1960s and 1970s, virtually no health care planning has taken place at the national level. This function has been left to state and local agencies. Little in the way of formal planning, however, takes place at any of these levels. State and local health planning agencies primarily serve as boards for review of new projects and/or as data compilation agencies. Essentially the only health "planning" activity carried out at the federal level today involves the Healthy People initiatives of the US Public Health Service.

The brief periods during which health planning has flourished represented a boon for demographers with an interest in health care. The legislation mandating the establishment of health planning agencies empowered them to compile and disseminate data on a wide variety of health issues. Most importantly, these agencies were able to obtain information on hospitals and other providers of care that would not have been available otherwise. The deemphasis on health planning that occurred during the 1980s has left health planners with fewer local data resources than were available to them in the 1970s.

The regulation of health care for the most part is not considered an appropriate function of the federal government. The exceptions that exist are those that would relate to any other industry, such as interstate trade activities and postal service violations. Regulation is left primarily to the individual states, who have responsibility for monitoring both facilities and personnel. The states frequently accredit and monitor educational programs as well. There are some national organizations that provide accreditation and exert varying degrees of regulation. Some, such as the Joint Commission on the Accreditation of Healthcare Organizations (JCAHO), have the force of law, with withdrawal of accreditation from a health facility being an effective "death penalty." Others are more voluntary with regard to their members' participation, with limited regulatory powers. Physicians and certain other health professionals are allowed a great deal of self-regulation, although this is usually based on state statutory support.

Medical Supplies–Equipment–Pharmaceuticals

An often overlooked but important component of the health care system involves the various entities providing medical supplies, equipment, and pharmaceuticals. This sector of the health care industry is the most profit oriented of any of the sectors. Americans spend nearly $50 billion per year on prescription drugs alone (Health Care Financing Administration, 1996).

Producers and distributors of supplies, equipment, and pharmaceuticals are typically national and international megacorporations. They often have their own research capabilities and may spend as much as 25% of their revenues on marketing. They tend to be highly profitable industries by any standard and are generally unaffected by the factors that serve to constrain costs in the other parts of the health care system. Although many products in this category are bought directly by the consumer (e.g., over-the-counter drugs), the biggest market for these products are hospitals and other large medical institutions, physicians' clinics, and pharmacies.

REFERENCES

Aguirre, B. E., Wolinsky, F. D., Niederauer, J., Keith, V., and Fann, L. J. (1989). Occupational prestige in the health care delivery system. *Journal of Health and Social Behavior* 30(September): 315–329.

American Medical Association. (1995). Medical education in the United States. *Journal of the American Medical Association* 274(9).

Conrad, P., and Kern, R. (Eds.) (1986). *The Sociology of Health and Illness* (2nd ed.). New York: St. Martin's.

Dubos, R. (1982). *Man Adapting*. New Haven: Yale University Press.

Eisenberg, J. M. (1986). *Doctors' Decisions and the Cost of Medical Care*. Ann Arbor, MI: Health Administration Press.

Engel, G. L. (1977). The need for a new medical model: A challenge for biomedicine. *Science* 196: 129–136.

Fuchs, V. R. (1974). *Who Shall Live?* New York: Basic Books.

Health Care Financing Administration. (1996). *Health Care Financing Review* 18(1).

McKeown, T., Brown, R. G., and Record, R. G. (1972). An interpretation of the modern rise of population in Europe. *Population Studies*, 9:119–141.

McKinlay, J. B., and McKinlay, S. J. (1972). The questionable contribution of medical measures to the decline of mortality in the United States in the twentieth century. *Milbank Memorial Fund Quarterly/Health and Society*, Summer, 405–428.

Modern Healthcare, May 25, 1998, 48–52.

National Center for Health Statistics. (1998). *Health, United States, 1998*. Washington, DC: Department of Health and Human Services.

Omran, A. R. (1971). The epidemiologic transition: A theory of the epidemiology of population change. *Milbank Memorial Fund Quarterly* 49:515ff.

Sultz, H. A., and Young, K. M. (1999). *Health Care USA*. Gaithersburg, MD: Aspen.

US Department of Health and Human Services (1997a). *Health, United States, 1996–97*. Washington, DC: US Government Printing Office.

US Department of Health and Human Services. (1997b). *Healthy People 2000 Review: 1995–97*. Washington, DC: US Government Printing Office.

ADDITIONAL RESOURCES

Coile, R. C., Jr. (1990). *The New Medicine: Reshaping Medical Practice and Health Care Management*. Rockville, MD: Aspen.

Kleinke, J. D. (1998). *Bleeding Edge: The Business of Health Care in the New Century*. Gaithersburg, MD: Aspen Publishers.

Lee, P. R., and Estes, C. L. (Eds.) (1994). *The Nation's Health* (4th ed.). Boston: Jones and Bartlett Publishers.

McKeown, T. (1976). *The Modern Rise of Population*. London: Edward Arnold.

Mechanic, D. (1994). Establishing mental health priorities. *The Milbank Quarterly* 72:501–514.

Osterweis, M. (Ed.) (1996). *The US Health Workforce: Power, Politics and Policy*. Washington, DC: Association of Academic Publishers.

Ratzan, S. C., Filerman, G. L., and Le Sar, J. W. (2000). *Attaining Global Health Challenges and Opportunities*, 55(1). Washington, DC: Population Reference Bureau.

Rockett, I. R. H. (1999). Population and health: An introduction to epidemiology. *Population Bulletin* 54(4). Washington, DC: Population Reference Bureau.

Starr, P. (1982). *The Social Transformation of American Medicine*. New York: Basic Books.

US Bureau of Labor Statistics. (1997). *Employment and Earnings*. Washington, DC: US Government Printing Office.

CHAPTER 3

The Language of Health Care

INTRODUCTION

The concepts used to define and organize any system of health care reflect the social organization and culture of the society in which it exists. These concepts are a function of the unique worldview characterizing that society. Many of the health-related concepts that are so familiar to members of contemporary US society did not exist in premodern societies. Notions of "health," "sickness," and "disease," although taken for granted in contemporary Western societies, are modern social constructs; they have no counterparts in earlier social systems. For premodern societies, these health states were an inherent part of the nature of things and could not be separately objectified.

These concepts related to health and health care are so basic to an understanding of the US health care system that they are discussed in some detail in the sections that follow, along with other terms necessary for an appreciation of the material in subsequent chapters.

HEALTH, SICKNESS, AND DISEASE

Health is perhaps one of the most difficult of health care terms to define. It is a very nebulous concept, one that is even difficult to define by example. A variety of definitions have been offered, all of which have some shortcomings. In the final analysis, the acceptable definition depends on one's perspective. The same is true of health's theoretical opposites: sickness and illness.

There are at least three commonly used paradigms for dealing with the concepts of health and illness (Wolinsky, 1988). The historically dominant model in US society is referred to as the medical model. The medical model had its genesis in the establishment of germ theory as the basis for modern scientific medicine. This perspective emphasizes the existence of clearly identifiable clinical symptoms, reflecting the conviction that illness represents the existence of biological pathology. Thus, illness is a state involving the presence of distinct symptoms; health is the negative residual condition reflecting an absence of symptoms.

In the medical model, health and illness are conceptualized in terms of biological "normality" and "abnormality." While many would argue for a more meaningful definition of these concepts, this view of health and illness continues to be widely accepted, since it is the view supported by medical practitioners. The manner in which most health problems are conceptualized and managed reflects this orientation. Both medical education and the organization of care reinforce this perspective. Health insurance constitutes an excellent example in that no reimbursement for treatment is allowed in the absence of a physician's (i.e., a medical model orientation) diagnosis.

The medical model has been widely accepted because of its scientific basis and its usefulness in addressing certain types of disorders. It has been criticized, however, for its focus on acute rather than chronic conditions, its inability to account for nonphysical and/or asymptomatic conditions, and its reliance on professional "consensus" on what is considered normal and abnormal (Wolinsky, 1988).

On the last point, it should be noted that medical science is not quite the exact science that it is often made out to be. There are numerous problematic aspects with regard to the accuracy of diagnosis, the interpretation of symptoms, and the appropriateness of various treatment modalities. Yet, the reporting of most health problems reflects a "disease" orientation, on the assumption that only a clinically identifiable pathological state can be an illness. This means that a variety of conditions—most mental disorders, for example—become problematic when attempting to determine the level of pathology within a population.

A second context for defining health and illness is referred to as the functional model. This model contends that health and illness reflect the level of *social* normality rather than physical normality characterizing an individual (Parsons, 1951). This approach de-emphasizes the biologically based medical model in favor of a model based on social role performance. This view reasons that an individual with clinically identifiable symptoms, but who is adequately performing his or her social functions, should be considered "well." Conversely, if an individual has no clinically identifiable symptoms but is unable to function, it may be appropriate to classify this individual as "sick."

Examples of this situation would include the alcoholic who for years is able to perform his or her job and maintain an adequate family relationship. This person would be considered sick under the medical model but not under the functional model. Conversely, an individual complaining of chronic back pain would be considered sick under the functional model (assuming that the symptoms interfered with his or her social role performance), even if physicians could not identify any underlying pathological disorder. Another example would involve individuals with disabilities; an amputee may be considered sick from the medical model perspective but actually may be capable of performing all required social roles.

Although the medical and functional models are considered the dominant paradigms, the psychological model also should be introduced (Antonovsky, 1979). Alternately referred to as the "stress model," this is by far the most subjective of the three approaches. This model relies solely on self-evaluation by the individual for the determination of health and illness. If the individual feels well, he or she is well; if the same individual feels sick, he or she is sick. This approach focuses on the importance of stress in the production of sickness and argues that much of physical illness is a reaction to stress on the part of the individual. This perspective has gained some respect with the rediscovery of the mind–body connection and the increasing emphasis being placed on psychosomatic conditions. In fact, the interrelationship between stress and demographic attributes is gaining increasing attention.

One final model that should be noted primarily applies to mental illness. This is the legal model, and it is applied in situations where the legal "health" or competence of the individual is in question. A legal definition comes into play in cases where competence must be determined for involuntary hospital admission, guardianship, or custody decisions and in cases where the individual's ability to manage his or her affairs is in question. Although a physician is generally required to certify the individual's competence, it is ultimately the courts that decide based on criteria established by the legal system. Thus, in the case of involuntary commitment a psychiatrist must determine the extent to which the individual is a threat to himself or herself or others and the extent to which he or she is competent to properly take care of himself or herself. Although a psychiatrist performs the examination, the courts determine competence or incompetence in the final analysis. The situations in which the legal definition might be applied to physical illnesses would be in the case of certain "reportable" diseases and conditions requiring quarantine.

To summarize the definitions of health and illness from these various perspectives, the following might be considered: From the medical model perspective, health is a state characterized by the absence of disease and disability. Under the functional model, it is a condition characterized by the optimum performance of social roles, regardless of the individual's physical state. From the psychological perspective, health is a state of well-being identified by the individual and as such is idiosyncratic to the individual. From the legal perspective, health—or, more appropriately, illness—is a state defined by the legal system that may or may not have any relation to other definitions of health and illness.

One other definition of health that might be noted is the one formulated in the 1960s by the World Health Organization (WHO), the health arm of the United Nations. Health is defined by the WHO as a state of complete physical, psychological, social, and spiritual well-being and not merely the absence of disease and infirmity (World Health Organization, 1999). While this rather idealistic definition generally has been rejected as unworkable in today's health care environment, it is ironic that the US health care system has come to be seen by the public as serving the disparate needs encompassed by this definition. American society today expects the scope of health care to extend far beyond the treatment of physical problems and into the management of psychological, social, and spiritual problems.

Illness and Sickness

In the preceding section, the concept of health from the perspective of various models was addressed. It is the sickness aspect of the health–illness continuum, however, that has been more significant for the US health care system. The system's emphasis continues to be on sickness and not on health, despite all the press coverage the wellness movement has received over the past two decades. It is "sick" people, after all, that the health care delivery system is set up to serve.

In one sense, a state of illness or sickness constitutes "ill health" and is the converse of a state of "health." However, the subjective nature of conditions of health and illness has led medical sociologists to formulate a more complicated depiction of these concepts (Wolinsky, 1988). A major distinction in this regard is made between illness and sickness. *Illness* refers to the individual, private, and usually biological aspect of the state of ill health. The term illness relates to the set of symptoms known only to the individual, and in this sense is private as opposed to public. It is argued that illness (but not sickness) is a state shared by human beings with all other animals; that is, it is a state of biological dysfunction known only to the individual organism. Under this definition, it could be contended that the actual level of illness is similar from society to society, reflecting the primarily biological nature of illness.

Sickness refers to the public or social component of ill health. Illness is transformed into sickness when the condition becomes publicly known through announcement by the affected party, observation by significant others, or professional diagnosis. Thus, while illness is primarily a biological state, sickness is a social state. Sickness is social not only because it is recognized beyond the bounds of the individual per se, but also because it has implications for social role performance and interpersonal interaction.

Some simple examples may help clarify the distinction between illness and sickness. An individual who feels bad (e.g., headache and nausea) is clearly ill. However, if the individual never discloses his or her symptoms to others (or they go unobserved by others) and continues to perform social roles adequately, he or she would not be considered sick. Conversely, if an individual is unable to perform social roles due to some generalized condition, although clinically identifiable symptoms cannot be found, this individual would be considered sick. Unlike illness, the amount of sickness varies widely from society to society and within the same society at different times. Because of the constraints of biology, variation in the amount of illness is limited; since sickness is a social construct, the amount of sickness is highly elastic. Examples of the elasticity of sickness can be found in wartime when military physicians at induction centers adopt a quite different standard of what constitutes disability than in peacetime.

United States society today in fact reflects this notion of elasticity in that a larger proportion of the population is under medical management than at any time in the past. However, it could be argued that the population as a whole is healthier than it has ever been. In this situation, there is a relatively low level of illness but a relatively high level of sickness. In fact, it has even been argued that the truly ill get the least medical care while those who are healthiest receive the most.

Disease

The concept of disease is one of the most problematic within health care. Like all the concepts being discussed here, it is modern in its origin. Originally referring to a state of "dis-ease," the term has come to be used in a variety of ways; the most significant one involves the identification of a medically recognized pathological condition. Technically, this means a syndrome involving clinically identifiable and measurable signs and symptoms reflecting underlying biological pathology. This view of disease clearly reflects an orientation derived from an environment dominated by infectious illnesses. This conceptualization continues to be important, since it underlies the medical model perspective on health and illness and is the definition instilled in health professionals.

In actual practice, the term "disease" is applied rather liberally to a wide variety of conditions that do not precisely fit the definition. One of the more controversial areas relates to mental illness. It could be argued that many, if not most, mental disorders would not be considered diseases under the definition above. The same could be said of other conditions that have been identified as diseases. Examples include alcoholism and drug abuse. These conditions do not have the requisite clear-cut symptomatology and underlying biological pathology. They nevertheless are frequently treated as if they were diseases. One explanation for this is clear: In order for a condition to be treated by the health care system, it must be identified as a disease. Therefore, there is a tendency toward an overly broad conceptualization of disease.

Obviously, the general public is not attuned to the academic definitions of health, sickness, and disease described above. "Folk" conceptualizations of health, sickness, and disease are common, with wide variation in perspectives on these concepts found among various subpopulations. Interestingly, the variations that exist typically reflect differences in the demographic characteristics of sub-segments of the population. Subgroups based on demographic attributes (e.g., ethnic groups) are likely to maintain distinct conceptualizations of health, sickness, and disease, conceptualizations that may vary significantly from the formal definitions of these concepts.

PHYSICAL ILLNESS AND MENTAL ILLNESS

The US health care system clearly distinguishes between physical illness and mental illness. This distinction is well established today, but it has been only in this century that it has been widely applied in health care. Traditional societies viewed all illnesses under the same umbrella. Whatever the form of the malady, it was thought to be a function of disequilibrium on the part of the individual, the intervention of some supernatural force, or some other nonscientific phenomenon. Differential diagnosis (i.e., the precise classification of disease) was not empha-sized, and the etiology (cause) of the problem was the main consideration in evaluating a symptomatic individual.

Modern Western thinking led to a clear distinction between the physical and the mental domains. This perspective was reinforced by the deep entrenchment of germ theory in the medical model paradigm. This model's emphasis on biological causes led to the separation of conditions that demonstrated clear biological pathology (physical illnesses) from those that did not (mental disorders). This distinction is reflected in what is essentially a separate sector within the health care system for the treatment of mental disorders, with distinct facilities and practi-tioners. A clear distinction is maintained today between general hospitals and mental hospitals and, in medical science between psychiatrists (i.e., physicians trained in the treatment of mental disorders) and other physicians. (See Box 2.3 in Chapter 2.)

Mental illness and physical illness do differ from each other in a number of ways. Physical illness is generally characterized by clear-cut, clinically identifi-able symptoms, while mental illness is not. The symptoms of mental illness reflect disorders of mood, behavior, and thought patterns. Clearly, the diagnosis of most mental disorders is more subjective than that of physical disorders because of the lack of clinical diagnostic tests. Although a small portion of mental disorders can be attributed to some underlying biological pathology (e.g., nervous system damage), most mental conditions are thought to reflect either internal psychologi-cal pathology or the influence of external stressors. Neither of these lends itself to traditional medical diagnostic techniques.

Note that the definitions of mental health and illness reflect the same models or perspectives associated with physical health and illness. The medical model remains important, primarily due to the pivotal role of the psychiatrist. However, the functional model is particularly relevant in that mental pathology is more likely to be identified based on some functional impairment rather than a biological impairment. Ironically, the psychological model probably has the least salience in that it assumes the individual making an assessment of healthiness is in his or her "right mind." It also should be remembered that mental health or illness is sometimes defined from a legal perspective.

Mental illness also differs from physical illness in that most mental disorders are considered to be both chronic and incurable. The basic goal of medicine is the treatment and cure of disease, yet most mental disorders are considered to be permanent and cannot be cured, only managed.* This makes the medical model of limited usefulness as a framework for viewing mental illness. Mental illness also is perceived much differently by the general public than is physical illness. Mental illness carries more of a stigma than do most physical illnesses: one can recover from the latter, but not the former. At the same time, the unpredictability of the behavior of the mentally ill tends to make the "normal" person uncomfortable in the face of psychiatric symptoms.

One final distinction relates to the treatment of physical and mental illnesses by medical science. In general, mental disorders do not lend themselves to treatment by the modalities derived from the medical model. In some cases, drug therapy is utilized for mental disorders; in rare cases, surgery is as well. However, most mental disorders are treated by counseling and psychotherapy. "Talk" therapies rather than the standard armamentarium of the medical scientist are commonly used, further reinforcing the conceptual gap between physical and mental illness.

THE CLASSIFICATION OF PHYSICAL ILLNESSES

As has been often noted, one of the major concepts underlying science is the notion of categories. The classification of objects, whether natural or manmade, is a prerequisite for the rational development of any conceptual categories and ultimately the development of science. Medical science, especially the contemporary Western version, is highly dependent on classification systems or disease nosology. The emphasis placed on the diagnostic process and the obsession with causation mandate a concise and accurate classification system.

Despite the presumed objectivity of medical science, the development of a workable disease classification system has been difficult. The use of modern diagnostic techniques and sophisticated biomedical testing equipment notwithstand-

*The distinction between physical and mental disorders in many instances is becoming less clear. Chronic fatigue syndrome, for example, long thought to be a form of mental illness, recently has been linked to chemical imbalances in the brain.

ing, no real consensus exists with regard to the classification of disease. Part of the problem stems from controversy over exactly how to define disease. Even if this were not an issue, the reality is that disease syndromes are not necessarily clear-cut and mutually exclusive, diagnostic tests are far from precise, and conventional standards for defining diseases tend to shift in accordance with new research findings, new treatment modalities, and even nonclinical developments. These problems—and the concomitant criticisms—are exacerbated when attempts are made at classifying mental disorders. Therefore, the systems that have been developed, although used widely, are not without their critics. While less than perfect, these existing classification systems provide the framework within which medical science operates. Although the explication of these classification systems that follows may be tedious, it is impossible to understand the functioning of the US health care system without a working knowledge of the manner in which conditions and procedures are classified.

International Classification of Diseases

The most widely recognized and utilized disease classification system is the International Classification of Diseases, now in its tenth version (abbreviated ICD-10). The ICD system, whose major disease categories are shown in Table 3.1, is the official classificatory scheme developed by the WHO within the United Nations. In the United States a version of the ICD system is utilized that reflects

Table 3.1. Major Categories of Diseases and Injuries ICD, Version 9

1	Infectious and parasitic diseases
2	Neoplasms
3	Endocrine, nutritional, and metabolic diseases and immunity disorders
4	Diseases of the blood and blood-forming organs
5	Mental diseases
6	Diseases of the nervous system and sense organs
7	Diseases of the circulatory system
8	Diseases of the respiratory system
9	Diseases of the digestive system
10	Diseases of the genitourinary system
11	Complications of pregnancy, childbirth, and the puerperium
12	Diseases of the skin and subcutaneous tissue
13	Diseases of the musculoskeletal system and connective tissues
14	Congenital anomalies
15	Certain conditions originating in the perinatal period
16	Symptoms, signs, and ill-defined conditions
17	Injury and poisoning
V	Classification of factors influencing health status and contact with health service
E	Classification of external causes of injury and poisoning

modifications necessary in keeping with current medical practice in American hospitals (US Department of Health and Human Services, 1999). For the present, the ICD-9 system continues to be utilized in the United States, although it is currently undergoing revision.

The ICD system is designed for the classification of morbidity and mortality information and for the indexing of diseases and procedures that occur within the hospital setting. (A different system is used for conditions seen in physicians' offices.) The present classification system includes two components: diagnoses and procedures. Two different sets of codes are assigned to the respective components; the codes are detailed enough that very fine distinctions can be made among specific diagnoses and procedures.

Originally, the ICD system was designed to facilitate communication concerning diseases worldwide, to provide a basis for statistical record keeping and epidemiological studies, and to facilitate research into the quality of health care. Today, the system is also used as a coding scheme for facilitating payment for health services, evaluating utilization patterns, and studying the appropriateness of health care costs. While the epidemiologist may find this classification system invaluable for studying the distribution and spread of disease, its primary use within the US health care delivery system has come to be related to financial management (i.e., as a coding system for patient billing).

The disease classification component utilizes 17 disease and injury categories, along with two "supplementary" classifications. Within each major category, specific conditions are listed in detail. A three-digit number is assigned to the various major subdivisions within each of the 17 categories. These three-digit numbers are extended another digit to indicate a subcategory within the larger category (in order to add clinical detail or isolate terms for clinical accuracy). A fifth digit is sometimes added to further specify any factors associated with that particular diagnosis. For example, Hodgkin's disease, a form of malignant neoplasm or cancer, is coded as 201. A particular type of Hodgkin's disease, Hodgkin's sarcoma, is coded 201.2. If the Hodgkin's sarcoma affects the lymph nodes of the neck, it is coded 201.21.

The supplementary classifications are a concession to the fact that many nonmedical factors are involved in the onset of disease, responses to disease, and the utilization of services. These additional categories attempt to identify causes of disease or injury states that are external to the biophysical system.

In ICD-9, procedures are divided into 16 categories. Of these, 15 are keyed to specific body systems (e.g., nervous system, digestive system) and one involves diagnostic procedures and residual therapeutic procedures. A two-digit scheme is utilized, with a code being carried out to two decimal places when necessary to provide more detail. The system was designed to accommodate usage in both hospital and ambulatory care settings. Table 3.2 illustrates ICD-9 as applied to the condition of ischemic heart disease.

Table 3.2. Sample of Disease Classification Using ICD-9-CM

Condition	Coding		
Ischemic heart disease	410–414		
Other forms (i.e., not coded elsewhere)		414	
Coronary atherosclerosis		414.0	
Aneurysm of heart		414.1	
Aneurysm of heart wall			414.10
Aneurysm of coronary vessels			414.11
Other aneurysm			414.12
Other specified forms of chronic ischemic heart disease		414.8	
Chronic ischemic heart disease, not elsewhere specified		414.9	

Much like the disease-coding scheme, the procedure classificatory system has come to be heavily used for financial management and the determination of patterns of utilization, although it retains its uses for epidemiological studies. The categories for classification are listed in Table 3.3.

Current Procedural Terminology

While the ICD classification system focuses on procedures performed under the auspices of a hospital or clinic, the Current Procedural Terminology (CPT)

Table 3.3. Major Categories
of Medical Procedures ICD, Version 9

1	Operations on the nervous system
2	Operations on the endocrine system
3	Operations on the eye
4	Operations on the ear
5	Operations on the nose, mouth, and pharynx
6	Operations on the respiratory system
7	Operations on the cardiovascular system
8	Operations on the hemic and lymphatic system
9	Operations on the digestive system
10	Operations on the urinary system
11	Operations on the male genital organs
12	Operations on the female genital organs
13	Obstetrical procedures
14	Operations on the musculoskeletal system
15	Operations on the integumentary system
16	Miscellaneous diagnostic and therapeutic procedures

system relates exclusively to procedures and services performed by physicians. Physician-provided procedures and services are divided into five categories: medicine, anesthesiology, surgery, radiology, and pathology and laboratory services. In its fourth version (CPT-4), this system identifies each procedure and service with a five-digit code number. This method attempts to facilitate accurate, specific, and uniform coding (American Medical Association, 1994).

Examples of coded procedures include surgical operations, office visits, and X-ray readings. The most accurate descriptor is determined from the CPT guidebook by the provider and that code is assigned. In addition to the identifying code, the five-digit number allows for modifiers to be appended. Modifiers may indicate situations in which an adjunctive service was performed, where another physician participated, or where only part of a service was performed. The manual also contains some useful information on accepted definitions for levels of care and extensiveness of consultation. Some 7000 variations of procedures and services are cataloged. Table 3.4 presents a section from the CPT code book.

Another set of codes have been developed to supplement the CPT codes. The Health Care Financing Administration's Common Procedure Coding System (HCPCS) involves a listing of services provided by physicians and other providers that are not covered under the CPT coding scheme. These include certain physician services along with nonphysician services such as ambulance, physical therapy, and durable medical equipment (Health Care Financing Administration, 1999).

Diagnostic Related Groups

Spiraling health care costs during the 1980s launched an era of cost containment. Efforts aimed at slowing health care expenditures have been initiated primarily by the federal government in response to the financial demands placed

Table 3.4. Sample Codes of the Current
Procedural Terminology Coding System

Procedure	Coding	
Surgery	10000–69999	
Bladder incision	510–	
Aspiration of bladder by needle		51000
Aspiration of bladder by trocar or intracatheter		51005
Cystotomy or cystostomy		51020
Cystolithotomy		51050
Transvesical ureterolithotomy		51060
Drainage of perivesical space space abscess		51080

on the Medicare program, the Medicaid program, and other federally supported health care initiatives. The most significant step in this regard has been the introduction of prospective payment as the basis for reimbursement for health services rendered under the Medicare program.* Under the prospective payment system (PPS) hospitals, physicians, and certain other providers of health care are informed at the beginning of the financial accounting period the amount that the federal government will pay for a particular category of patient.

This approach is in stark contrast to the retrospective payment arrangement originally built into the Medicare program, which was essentially a cost-plus arrangement with no incentives for cost containment. The prospective payment system limits the amount of reimbursement for services provided to each category of patient based on rates predetermined by the Health Care Financing Administration (HCFA), the federal agency that administers the Medicare program.

The basis for prospective payment is the diagnostic related group (DRG). Using the patient's primary diagnosis as the starting point, HCFA has developed a procedure for grouping all hospital patients into 470 DRGs. The idea is to link payment to the consumption of resources, with the assumption that a patient's diagnosis should be the best predictor of resource utilization. The primary diagnosis is modified by such factors as other coexisting diagnoses, the presence of complications, the patient's age, and the usual length of hospital stay in order to create the 470 diagnostic categories.

The significance of the introduction of the PPS cannot be overemphasized, as it has had implications for the entire health care system. The PPS probably has done more to modify practice patterns than anything since the introduction of the Medicare program in the 1960s.

Before presenting representative examples of DRGs, it should be noted that for many purposes—general reporting, statistical analysis, planning—the 470 DRGs represent too fine a distinction among conditions. For these purposes, DRGs have been grouped into 23 major diagnostic categories (MDCs). These MDCs are based primarily on the different body systems. Table 3.5 lists the MDCs currently in use.

Each MDC contains anywhere from a handful to as many as two dozen DRGs. The DRGs listed under each MDC are subsequently divided into medical DRGs and surgical DRGs. In the calculation of reimbursement for these services, each of these DRGs is given a weight. This weight is the major factor in a complicated formula for determining the rate of reimbursement for each hospital participating in the Medicare program. Note that physicians are reimbursed for their services under a separate payment system involving payment levels established by the Health Care Financing Administration that are considered reasonable for the

---

*Refer to Chapter 2 for discussions of the financing of health services in the US health care system.

Table 3.5. Major Diagnostic Categories Used in the Prospective Payment System

Major diagnostic category	Code
Diseases and disorders of the nervous system	1
Diseases and disorders of the eye	2
Diseases and disorders of the ear, nose, and throat	3
Diseases and disorders of the respiratory system	4
Diseases and disorders of the circulatory system	5
Diseases and disorders of the digestive system	6
Diseases and disorders of the hepatobiliary system and pancreas	7
Diseases and disorders of the musculoskeletal system and connective tissues	8
Diseases and disorders of the skin, subcutaneous tissue, and breast	9
Endocrine, nutritional, and metabolic diseases and disorders	10
Diseases and disorders of the kidney and urinary tract	11
Diseases and disorders of the male reproductive tract	12
Diseases and disorders of the female reproductive system	13
Pregnancy, childbirth, and the puerperium	14
Newborns and other neonates with conditions originating in the perinatal period	15
Diseases and disorders of the blood, blood-forming organs, and immunity	16
Myeloproliferative diseases and poorly differentiated neoplasms	17
Infectious and parasitic diseases	18
Mental diseases and disorders	19
Substance use and substance-induced organic mental disorders	20
Injury, poisoning, and toxic effects of drugs	21
Burns	22
Factors influencing health status and other contacts with health services	23

particular geographic area in question. Table 3.6 presents a partial list of DRGs grouped under a particular MDC.

One other development worth noting with regard to classification systems relates to the current discussion of the use of a relative-value scale as a basis for setting physician fees (Hsaio et al., 1988). Presently there is no standard mechanism for determining the charge for a specific procedure performed by a physician. Subsequently, subjective bases are often utilized to set fees. This has resulted in a great deal of variability in the fees that are charged by different physicians for the same service. Furthermore, the independent evolution of fee schedules for various procedures has resulted in some notable imbalances in fees. This means that, when objective criteria are applied, some procedures are identified as overpriced and others as underpriced. This has led to the development of a scale that would determine the relative value of a procedure or service based on such factors as the skill level required and the amount of training needed in order to perform that procedure. When a relative-value scale becomes the basis for reimbursing physicians, the fee structure is greatly modified.

Table 3.6. Representative Listing of DRGs Used
in the Prospective Payment System

DRGs under MDC 3: Diseases/disorders of ear, nose, throat	Code
Surgical	
Major head and neck procedures	49
Sialoadenectomy	50
Salivary gland procedures	51
Cleft lip and palate repair	52
Sinus and mastoid procedures (Age > 17)	53
Sinus and mastoid procedures (Age 0–17)	54
Miscellaneous ear, nose, and throat procedures	55
Medical	
Ear, nose, and throat malignancy	64
Dysequilibrium	65
Epistaxis	66
Epiglottitis	67
Otitis media and upper respiratory infection (Age > 69)	68
Otitis media and upper respiratory infection (Age 18–69)	69
Otitis media and upper respiratory infection (Age 0–17)	70

Ambulatory Patient Groups

As the prospective payment system based on DRGs was being implemented to control the cost of inpatient care for Medicare, much of the treatment was being shifted to an outpatient or ambulatory setting. Any cost savings realized by the Medicare program on the inpatient side were now being eroded by growing expenditures for ambulatory services. This situation prompted the development of a system similar to DRGs for the outpatient environment referred to as Ambulatory Patient Groups (APGs).

As with the DRGs, APGs focus on the facility component of health care costs and not on physician charges. The intent by HCFA is to contain outpatient facilities costs, introduce some controls on outpatient services utilization, and create a prospective system similar to the DRG situation. The basis for the fee is the *patient visit* rather than the entire episode as in the case of DRGs. An APG-specific diagnosis code has been developed and current procedural terminology codes are used to classify procedures and ancillary services.

The APG classification system had not been adopted for use by HCFA at the time of this writing. However, some states are already beginning to adopt it, and it is clear that some form of ambulatory care classification system will become standard in the future.

THE CLASSIFICATION OF MENTAL ILLNESS

Since mental illness is conceptualized differently from physical illness, a separate classification system has been established for mental disorders. Mental illness involves disorders of mood, behavior, or thought processes. This sets mental health problems apart from physical disorders; differences in etiology, symptomatology, disease progression, diagnostic procedures, and treatment modalities are clearly distinguished when it comes to physical and mental illness. The fact that mental disorders generally are not amenable to clinical diagnostic procedures also has important implications for the classification system that has evolved (Spitzer and Endicott, 1978).

The definitive reference on the classification of mental disorders is the *Diagnostic and Statistical Manual of Mental Disorders*, Fourth Edition (1994), commonly referred to as DSM-IV, which is published by the American Psychiatric Association and, despite long-standing criticism, remains the last word in mental disease classification. Since it is published by the professional association representing psychiatry, it reflects a medical model bias. Its 17 major categories of mental illness and over 450 identified mental conditions are considered exhaustive.

The DSM classification system is derived in part from the ICD system discussed earlier. It is essentially structured in the same manner, with a five-digit code being utilized. The fourth digit indicates the variety of the particular disorder under discussion, and the fifth digit refers to any special considerations related to the case. The nature of the fifth-digit modifier varies depending on the disorder under consideration. Unlike the other classification systems discussed, the DSM system contains rather detailed descriptions of the disorders categorized therein and serves as a useful reference in this regard. Tables 3.7 and 3.8 indicate the major classifications within DSM-IV and present a representative sampling of the coding of mental disorders.

Alternative Mental Disorder Classification

Although the DSM system is widely used by mental health professionals in clinical settings, it has been criticized on a number of grounds. Conceptual and technical considerations aside, the system probably is overly complex for health care professionals who are not involved in mental health care but nevertheless must interface with mental health services. Further, this classification system has not been utilized extensively by those who set policy and distribute resources for the treatment of mental disorders (Cockerham, 1998).

It may be worthwhile, therefore, to present another conceptualization of the categories of mental disorder that is more straightforward (oversimplified, some might say), but is both more useful for general discussions of mental health care and more in keeping with popular conceptualizations of mental disorders. This

Table 3.7. Diagnostic Categories Used in the DSM-IV

Disorders usually first diagnosed in infancy, childhood, or adolescence
Delirium, dementia, and amnestic and other cognitive disorders
Mental disorders due to a general medical condition
Substance-related disorders
Schizophrenia and other psychotic disorders
Mood disorders
Anxiety disorders
Somatoform disorders
Factitious disorders
Dissociative disorders
Sexual and gender identity disorders
Eating disorders
Sleep disorders
Impulse-control disorders not elsewhere classified
Adjustment disorders
Personality disorders
Other conditions that may be a focus of clinical attention

system begins by distinguishing between organic and nonorganic mental disorders. Only a small fraction (approximately 5%) of mental disorders fall into the organic category, and many would classify these as physical illnesses because of the presence of brain damage or dysfunction, neurological dysfunction, or chemical imbalance. This small proportion of cases is noteworthy, however, since they

Table 3.8. Representative Sampling
of DSM-IV Codes for Mental Disorders

Mental disorder	Code
Anxiety disorders	
Anxiety disorder due to a general medical condition	293.89
Generalized anxiety disorder	300.02
Panic disorder with agoraphobia	300.21
Agoraphobia without history of panic disorder	300.22
Social phobia	300.23
Specific phobia	300.29
Obsessive–compulsive disorder	300.3
Acute stress disorder	308.3
Posttraumatic stress disorder	309.81

often require total care and account for a large share of mental health expenditures. Further, the significance of this category is expected to increase as victims of Alzheimer's disease become more numerous. Brain-damaged patients generally do not benefit from active medical intervention and are typically cared for in custodial-type institutions (Lipowski, 1978).

The remainder of disorders are classified as nonorganic, or functional. They are termed functional disorders because their common characteristic is interference with social role performance and interpersonal relationships. Unlike the organic disorders, functional disorders typically do not have an identifiable underlying biological basis, and in fact their etiology is generally not known. These conditions are manifested primarily by disorders of mood, thought processes, and behavior.

Functional disorders are commonly divided into three major categories: anxiety disorders, psychoses, and personality disorders. Anxiety disorders (historically referred to as neuroses) include the relatively mild disorders that are generally associated with low intensity care (e.g., psychological counseling) and include such conditions as anxiety, compulsiveness, and various "nervous" conditions. These are conditions that typically affect only one dimension of a person's being; the remaining aspects of personality are essentially normal. These disorders are virtually always cared for on an outpatient basis and have limited significance for the formal health care system.

Psychoses are sometimes thought of as more serious forms of anxiety disorders, although many contend that there is a qualitative difference between the two. Psychotic conditions are often extreme in their manifestations and tend to completely disorder the lives of the individuals so affected. This category includes schizophrenia, depression, and extreme paranoia, conditions that often require institutionalization in mental hospitals since they are usually too severe and disruptive to be treated in a general hospital setting. These are the conditions that often entail psychotropic drug therapy, electroconvulsive shock treatment, and in some cases psychosurgery.

The final category, personality disorders, represents something of a residual category. It includes a variety of conditions that do not fit neatly into the other categories. Disorders such as antisocial behavior, sexual deviance, and alcohol and drug abuse are included. The contents of this category seem to be the most variable, since this is the "bucket" in which newly diagnosed or redefined conditions often end up. Although these disparate conditions are difficult to categorize, they could be said to share the characteristics of unpredictability, unclear etiology, and unresponsiveness to any type of therapy other than behavior modification techniques. Personality disorders are of growing significance for the health care delivery system in that some like substance abuse and eating disorders are receiving inordinate attention at this time.

Even this approach to the classification of mental disorders is too complex for some uses and an even more basic classification system has been adopted de facto for many uses. The concept of "severe mental illness" has evolved and this category includes a group of discrete mental disorders that differ in cause, course, and treatment. Severe mental illness includes schizophrenia, schizoaffective disorders, autism, affective disorders (e.g., bipolar depression), and other psychotic disorders, as well as certain anxiety disorders. Patients with these conditions often carry a "dual diagnosis" (i.e., psychiatric and substance abuse) and/or have serious physical problems. Although accounting for only 3% of the population, these patients account for a major proportion of mental health expenditures.

It should be noted that mental health practitioners are rapidly moving away from terms like "mental illness" and "mental health." The field, in fact, is becomhing reconceptualized as "behavioral health." To an extent, this is a concession to both the realization that external factors play a major role in such disorders and the fact that symptoms can be addressed more readily than causes. The term "behavioral health" also carries less of a negative connotation. In any case, the emphasis on behavioral health calls for a broader approach to mental disorders and allows for a wider range of treatment modalities.

KEY CONCEPTS FROM EPIDEMIOLOGY AND HEALTH CARE

Like all sciences, demography and the other disciplines converging to form health demography have their own languages. A technical vocabulary is essential in order to communicate in an accurate and precise manner. This need is particularly great in the health care field. Its vocabulary reflects a combination of technical scientific terms, terms peculiar to health care administration, and lay terms. Thus, the terminology in use in health care does not always have the specificity or consensus generally found in more "scientific" fields.

The paragraphs that follow discuss some of the basic concepts that have not been presented in earlier sections. Box 3.1 features a more extensive listing of terms and definitions from epidemiology, medical sociology, and health care administration.

Acute and Chronic Conditions

Health problems are generally grouped into two broad categories that primarily reflect the course of the condition. *Acute* health conditions involve problems that might be considered "episodic" (i.e., they are characterized by a one-time occurrence). Acute conditions also are characterized by fairly direct causation (e.g., exposure to a disease organism or an accident), relatively rapid onset, rapid progression and short duration, and a disposition involving either recovery or death. These types of problems are often self-limiting, in that the organism either responds and overcomes the pathological assault or its immune system fails and

---

Box 3.1

Key Concepts in Health Care from Medical Sociology,
Epidemiology, and Health Care Administration

Acute condition   Health condition characterized by episodic occurrence, relatively
direct causation, relatively rapid onset, rapid progression and short duration,
and a disposition involving either recovery or death.

Age adjustment   Procedure whereby incidence and prevalence rates are adjusted to
consider the age structure of the population being studied. This is one of the
more common techniques used to "standardize" rates.

Average daily census   The average number of inpatients (excluding newborns)
receiving care in a hospital each day during a particular reporting period.

Average length of stay (ALOS)   The average number of inpatient days recorded by
hospitalized patients during a particular time period. ALOS is calculated by
dividing the total number of patient days recorded during the time period by the
number of patients discharged from the hospital.

Case finding   The various procedures used to determine the numerator to be utilized
in calculating incidence and prevalence rates. Case finding involves both determining what constitutes a "case" and procedures for calculating the number of
cases within the population at risk.

Chronic condition   Health condition characterized by a relatively complex etiology, slow onset and progression, extended (even lifelong) duration, and no
clear-cut disposition. Chronic conditions typically cannot be cured, only managed.

Cohort   Refers in its broadest usage to any segment of the population that has some
characteristic in common. In epidemiology, cohorts refer most often to segments of the population that have been exposed to a certain health risk. In
demography, cohorts refer most often to age groups within a particular population. In either case, cohorts can be traced over time to determine changes in the
composition of the group and the disposition of its members.

Disease   Technically, a scientific construct referring to a medical syndrome involving clinically identifiable and measurable signs and symptoms reflecting underlying biological pathology. The term "disease" actually is utilized in a much
broader sense than this clinical conceptualization, often referring to any condition treatable by the health care system.

Endemic   Situation in which a pathological condition is common to a large portion
of a population, to the extent that its presence might be considered "normal."
The prevalence of endemic conditions does not fluctuate much over time.

Epidemic   Refers to a health condition not normally present within a population but
whose appearance represents an "outbreak" of the particular condition. Gener-

Continued

Box 3.1. (Continued)

ally refers to a condition that is contagious or communicable (which contributes to its abnormally high but usually short-lived occurrence).

Epidemiology   Literally, the study of epidemics, but has come to mean the study of the etiology, distribution, and course of disease within a population.

Etiology   The cause of a health condition. The etiology may be relatively simple and direct as in the case of most acute conditions, or it may be complex and indirect as in the case of most chronic conditions.

Health status   Indicator of the overall state of health of an individual or, more often in health demography, a population. There is no one measure of health status, with existing health status indicators utilizing outcome measures (e.g., morbidity and mortality) and utilization measures (e.g., physician office visits or hospital admissions).

Incidence   The rate at which the onset of new cases of a particular health condition occurs. Incidence is calculated based on the number of new cases diagnosed during a particular time period (usually 1 year), divided by the population at risk.

Illness   The existence of a clinically identifiable medical syndrome in an individual or a population. Social scientists often distinguish between illness and sickness, with the former referring to the presence of some biological pathology and the latter referring to the presence of some condition recognized by society as a state of ill health.

Morbidity   The level of sickness and disability existing within a population. There is no overall indicator of morbidity, so it usually is looked at in terms of the incidence or prevalence of specific conditions.

Mortality   Refers to the rate at which deaths occur within a population. Mortality rates are calculated by dividing the number of deaths occurring within a particular time period (usually 1 year) by the total population alive during that time period.

death results. From an epidemiological perspective, the entire population is generally at risk from acute conditions, since they are no respecters of age, sex, race, or social class. Examples of acute conditions include infectious diseases, colds, and injuries.

Until this century, acute conditions were the most frequent causes of morbidity and mortality. The epidemic diseases characterizing nineteenth-century America and prevalent even today in less-developed countries represent the "classic" acute conditions. The prevalence of these conditions during the formative years of modern medicine has biased medical science and the health care delivery

Occupancy rate   The proportion of a hospital's beds (or those of some other health care facility) that are occupied on the average during a particular time period. The occupancy rate is calculated by dividing the average daily census for a particular time period by the number of hospital beds available during that time period.

Population at risk   The portion of a population that has been exposed to a particular health threat or is susceptible to a particular health threat. The population at risk is used as the denominator in calculating incidence and prevalence rates when the condition in question does not affect the total population.

Prevalence   The total number of cases of a particular health condition within a population at a particular point in time. Prevalence is calculated by dividing the number of known cases at a particular point in time by the population at risk at that point in time.

Relative risk   The probability of the occurrence of a particular health condition within a population relative to the risk for some other population. Relative risk is calculated by determining how much more likely a condition is to occur among one population (e.g., smokers) compared to another (e.g., nonsmokers). The relative risk is often contrasted to the absolute risk of the occurrence of a condition.

Sickness   The presence of ill health in individuals or populations based on whatever definition the particular population uses for ill health. Social scientists distinguish between sickness and illness, with the former referring to the social construct of "sickness" and the latter referring to the presence of measurable biological pathology.

Sign   A manifestation of a health condition or disease syndrome that can be identified through clinical tests or through the observation of a health care professional.

Symptom   A manifestation of a health condition that is experienced by the affected individual. Symptoms are often "internal" (e.g., pain) in the sense that they can only be identified by the individual.

system toward the treatment of such conditions. Indeed, the development of germ theory and the medical model of health and illness evolved within a framework dominated by infectious disease. Even today an acute care orientation, with its emphasis on treatment and cure, dominates the provision of health care.

Chronic conditions are those characterized by a relatively complex etiology, slow onset and progression, and no clear-cut disposition. Unlike many acute conditions, most chronic conditions are not self-limiting nor do they result in death. Today, chronic conditions are also referred to as diseases of civilization, since in most cases they reflect the impact of lifestyles on health status. Chronic conditions typically cannot be cured, only managed. Examples include hypertension (high blood pressure), diabetes, arthritis and rheumatism, and chronic obstructive respiratory disease. Most forms of mental disorder would fall into this category.

Twentieth-century America has come to be dominated increasingly by chronic conditions as they have replaced acute conditions as the major causes of morbidity, disability, and mortality. At the same time, they do not fit well within the medical model conceptualization of disease. Their complex etiology and absence of curative treatment options are problematic for medical science. Since treatment and cure, not management, are the focus of the US health care delivery system, chronic conditions historically have received limited attention in terms of medical education, biomedical research, health care administration, and financial subsidization.

The chronicity inherent in chronic diseases also has implications for society. At the macrolevel, chronic conditions are a major drain on health care resources and account for much of the losses in productivity reflected in work-loss days and school-loss days. Chronic conditions also account for an increasing share of health insurance costs. At the individual level, chronic disease often portends a lifetime of medical management; in the most extreme cases, chronically disabled patients may require perpetual care.

Unlike acute conditions, chronic conditions are selective in their distribution. Epidemiologists have linked a variety of demographic, sociocultural, and economic factors with the distribution of chronic disorders. Consequently, the epidemiological picture is much more complex, with certain chronic conditions prevalent among some segments within the population and other conditions among other segments. (Chapter 10 addresses the demographic correlates of acute and chronic conditions.)

Some conditions cannot be categorized easily as acute or chronic. Many of the more common chronic conditions may have one or more acute episodes associated with them. In some cases, acute conditions may result in secondary chronic conditions. Many health problems associated with heart disease, for example, are likely to have both acute and chronic components.

Incidence and Prevalence

One of the most important aspects of the study of health problems and their management involves a consideration of the amount of ill health (in its various manifestations) found within the population. The level of illness, morbidity, disability, and disease is generally referred to in terms of incidence and prevalence. Virtually every measure of ill health is a rate or ratio that reflects one or the other of these concepts. Although often used interchangeably, the two terms are quite distinct in their meanings and implications.

Incidence refers to the rate at which the onset of new conditions occurs. The incidence rate, expressed in terms of number per 1000 population or some similar basis, indicates the number of new cases of a condition that have been diagnosed or reported for a given time period (usually one year). Thus, the 1996 incidence rate for lung cancer of 71.5 indicates that about 72 out of every 100,000 residents in the United States in 1996 developed or were diagnosed as having lung cancer (Centers for Disease Control and Prevention, 1999). Incidence is an extremely useful indicator for epidemiological purposes such as monitoring the course of an epidemic condition, determining demographic correlates of a condition, or examining the etiology or cause of a particular condition (Haberman, 1978).

Prevalence refers to the total number of cases of a particular condition or disease at a specified point in time. Prevalence includes all previously existing cases along with any newly identified cases of the disease in question. Thus the number of cases utilized to determine the prevalence rate also includes those utilized to determine the incidence rate. Prevalence is less useful than incidence with regard to epidemiological investigations; its usefulness is derived from its ability to assist in the planning of facilities and services and the allocation of funds for health care programs.

Incidence rates are more meaningful for the reporting of acute conditions than chronic conditions due to the volatility in the amount of acute conditions. Prevalence rates, on the other hand, are more meaningful in the examination of chronic conditions, for which the rate of onset is not as important as the total volume of such cases within the population. The prevalence rate is invariably higher than the incidence rate, since prevalence includes incidence. The gap between incidence rates and prevalence rates is the least when acute diseases of epidemic proportions are under study. The gap is greatest for chronic conditions where a small number of new cases each year are added to an already large population of affected individuals.

Case Finding

The basis for all epidemiological analysis is the determination of the types and levels of morbidity, disability, and mortality characterizing a particular population. The denominator in this equation—the population at risk—is usually readily available. The problematic aspect of the equation is the numerator, that is, the existing number of cases of the condition within the denominator. As a consequence, much of the research that takes place with regard to disease incidence–prevalence focuses on identifying the number and characteristics of these cases.

Case finding involves a variety of activities, and some of these are discussed in more detail in Chapter 9 on data sources. Essentially, there are two major sources from which to determine the number of cases of a particular condition:

Box 3.2

How Crazy Are We? Case Finding in Mental Illness

Conventional wisdom suggests that as America became more industrialized and urbanized, the population also became crazier. Three or four generations ago, most citizens could live their entire lives without knowing anyone who was considered insane. There was the occasional "retard," "eccentric," or "truly certifiable" lunatic, of course, but for all practical purposes the American population was relatively free of the mentally ill. Today, in stark contrast, it seems that mental illness is rampant. Startling figures are quoted for the number of individuals with various mental conditions, and millions of Americans are reported to be seeking treatment for one psychiatric condition or another. In fact, a large proportion of the patients who present themselves to physicians offices with "physical" symptoms actually are suffering from emotional disorders.

If "new" mental disorders (such as drug abuse and eating disorders) are included, the size of the affected population is truly staggering. Unlike our forefathers, virtually everyone today knows someone with some type of psychiatric problem. In fact, there is a good chance that each of us has at some time or another experienced a condition diagnosable as a mental disorder.

What is the explanation for this apparent dramatic increase in the official prevalence of mental disorders? Are we truly crazier as a people or is there some other explanation? The answer to these questions depends on an understanding of case finding or the manner in which individuals are identified as having a disorder (or being a "case"). Historically, a major problem has been a lack of data on the existence of mental illness within the population. No comprehensive system for tracking mental disorders, or any condition for that matter, had ever been available. The fact that most mentally disturbed individuals in the past were handled informally, that is, by the family, meant that most never came to be officially recognized.

Until well into this century, the only source of information on the extent of mental disorders in the population was the official records of institutions charged with treating these cases. The main sources of such data were the asylums and mental institutions, along with other agencies of social control such as jails, who maintained records on their inmates for administrative purposes. These records were subsequently utilized to develop estimates of the amount of mental disorder in the population.

Not surprisingly, such records indicated a strikingly low level of disorders within the US population, although those who were insane were seriously impaired. It was further determined from these records that most mentally ill individuals were nonwhite, poor, poorly educated, and/or of foreign descent.

Many of the deficiencies of this method of case finding were addressed with the introduction of the community survey method for identifying the prevalence of mental disorders. The nation's first known attempt at a community mental health study was conducted in 1917, and since then scores of community surveys have attempted to determine the extent of mental illness within the US population. While there is little agreement as to which of the various studies most accurately reflects the true prevalence of mental disorder, all community surveys have had one thing in common: They have demonstrated that the prevalence of mental disorders identified using the reported cases approach represents only the tip of the iceberg. Every community study has found a level of mental disorder many times higher than that previously assumed.

Then how crazy are we really? After the administration of scores of community surveys, there is still little consensus on the answer to this question. A review of 60 community studies conducted in the United States over several decades found estimates of prevalence ranging from less than 1% to well over 50% (Dohrenwend and Dohrenwend, 1974). These studies included one rural area where the prevalence rate of functional psychiatric disorders was placed at 69%! More recent studies employing more sophisticated research methodologies have demonstrated less variation in the levels of disorder identified. A 1980 review of prevalence studies (Dohrenwend 1980) found for all types of psychopathology that an average of 21% of the population were affected. Applying statistically acceptable standards of preciseness, the review concluded that between 16 and 25% of the US population have a clinically significant disorder at any one time. The most extensive study to date, the federally funded Epidemiological Catchment Area Program, reported that in the course of a year as many as 22% of the US population meets the criteria for one or more mental disorders. However, only 9% report significant disability associated with a mental disorder (Regier et al., 1995).

How is it possible to explain the apparent increase in mental disorders during this century or the discrepancy between various studies conducted in presumably the same manner? These questions get at the heart of case finding. It is always the situation and it is particularly true for mental illness that what constitutes a "case" is what the researcher calls a case. As the mental health field has evolved in US society, it has developed a much more precise classification system for mental disorders. One implication of this is a greater sensitivity to many conditions that in the past may have been passed off as eccentricities. Over time mental health officials have expanded their notion as to what constitutes a mental disorder. Many conditions that would have been considered historically as weirdness, immorality, or crime are now classified as psychiatric disorders. In the final analysis, there is probably no "true" prevalence of mental illness. Our level of sanity or insanity will always be a function of the case finding techniques in use at the time.

reported cases and community surveys. The reported cases approach involves some type of mechanism for tracking or reporting cases of a particular disorder. The reporting of certain conditions is required by law, and these data are entered into a national data bank; the monitoring of sexually transmitted diseases would be an example. Also, local health departments or individual health care institutions might maintain registries for such purposes. Hospital-based registries of cancer or heart patients are examples of this.

In other instances, the number of reported cases may be compiled through periodic surveys of the organizations that deal with a particular condition. For example, the National Center for Health Statistics might assemble data on all hospital discharges for a particular time period to determine the number of cases of a given condition treated within the nation's hospitals. Similarly, the Health Care Financing Administration within the Medicare program might collect data from all providers of services to Medicare patients in order to determine the magnitude of a specific health problem.

The reported cases method of case finding has both advantages and disadvantages. With the computerization of many health care databases, the compilation of comprehensive data on a wide range of health problems is easier today than at any time in the past. A large volume of data is readily available and an extensive amount of information useful for epidemiological studies is often accessible for reported cases. On the other hand, this method suffers to the extent that not all sources of care are included in reporting and data collection, and the criteria for reporting and even defining conditions vary from area to area. Multiple reporting of the same case is always a possibility.

The major drawback to using reported cases as the basis for the numerator, however, is inherent in the process itself. Reported cases are just that: cases that have been both diagnosed and entered into an appropriate data bank. Many cases are never diagnosed, especially for such conditions as mental disorders. (Box 3.2 discusses case finding for mental disorders.) In fact, the "known" cases of many diseases may represent only the tip of the iceberg. More cases may go undetected than are detected. Further, reporting is less than complete and is often selective. Therefore, uncritical utilization of reported data can result in misleading conclusions (Kituse and Cicourel, 1963).

The other source of data for case finding is community surveys. The community survey typically involves the interviewing and/or clinical examination of a sample of the population under study. Information might be collected from the study population on existing symptoms, conditions previously diagnosed, any treatment received, and any other factor appropriate for determining the extent of morbidity and disability within the population. Clinicians may be involved in the survey process in order to perform examinations or diagnostic procedures.

The objective is to identify all cases of the condition under study within the population, not just those that have come to the attention of the various reporting mechanisms. Invariably, the incidence and/or prevalence of a particular condition is found to be much higher using the community survey approach than when relying on the reported cases approach.

Today, both official records and community surveys are relied on for case finding for both physical and mental disorders. Many of these research approaches have become quite sophisticated, and some are discussed in Chapter 9 on data sources. Enough accurate information has now been developed to allow for relatively precise estimates and projections of incidence and/or prevalence ⌐ı particular conditions within a given population.

REFERENCES

American Medical Association. (1994). *Physician's Current Procedural Terminology* (4th ed.). Chicago: American Medical Association.

American Psychiatric Association. (1994). *Diagnostic and Statistical Manual of Mental Disorders* (4th ed.). Washington, DC: American Psychiatric Association.

Antonovsky, A. (1979). *Health, Stress and Coping.* San Francisco: Jossey-Bass.

Centers for Disease Control and Prevention (1999). Website, URL: www.cdc.gov/nchswww/astats/ pdf/ has98+58.pdf

Cockerham, W. C. (1998). *Medical Sociology* (7th ed.). Upper Saddle River, NJ: Prentice Hall.

Dohrenwend, B. P., and Dowhrenwend, B. S. (1974). Social and cultural influences on psychopathology. *Annual Review of Psychology* 25:417–447.

Dohrenwend, B. P., et al. (1980). *Mental Illness in the United States: Epidemiological Estimates.* New York: Praeger.

Gallagher, B. J. (1980). *Sociology of Mental Illness.* Englewood Cliffs, NJ: Prentice-Hall.

Haberman, S. (1978). Mathematical treatment of the incidence and prevalence of disease. *Social Science and Medicine* 12:147–152.

Health Care Financing Administration. (1999). Website, URL: www.hcfa.gov/stats/anhcpcdl.htm.

Hsiao, W., Braun, P., Becker, E. R., et al. (1988). *A National Study of Resource-Based Relative Value Scale for Physician Services: Final Report to the Health Care Financing Administration.* Boston, MA: Harvard School of Public Health.

Iglehart, J. K. (1982). The new era of prospective payment for hospitals. *New England Journal of Medicine* 307(11 November):1288–1292.

Kituse, J., and Cicourel, A. (1963). A note on the use of official statistics. *Social Problems* 11:131–139.

Lipowski, Z. J. (1978). Organic brain syndromes: A reformulation. *American Journal of Psychiatry* 135:345–349.

Parsons, T. (1951). *The Social System.* New York: Free Press.

Regier, D. A., Bruke, J. D., Manderscheid, R. W., et al. (1995). The chronically mentally ill in primary care. *Psychology Medicine* 15:265–273.

Schwartz, R. A., and Schwartz, I. K. (1976). Are personality disorders diseases? *Diseases of the Nervous System* 37:613–617.

Spitzer, R. L., Andreasen, N., and Endicott, J. (1978). Schizophrenia and other psychotic disorders in DSM-III. *Schizophrenia Bulletin* 4:489–509.

Spitzer, R. L., and Endicott, J. (1978). Medical and mental disorder: Proposed definition and criteria. In R. L. Spitzer and D. F. Klein (Eds.), *Critical Issues in Psychiatric Diagnosis* (pp. 15–40). New York: Raven.

Strauss, A., and Corbin, J. M. (1988). *Shaping a New Health Care System.* San Francisco: Jossey-Bass.

US Department of Health and Human Services. (1999). *International Classification of Diseases* (10th rev.). Washington, DC: US Government Printing Office.

Wolinsky, F. D. (1988). *The Sociology of Health*. Belmont, CA: Wadsworth.

World Health Organization. (1999). Website, URL: www.who.int/aboutwho/en/definition.html.

ADDITIONAL RESOURCES

Brown, F. (Ed.) (1999). *ICD-9-CM: Coding Handbook, with Answers*. Chicago: American Hospital Association.

Freudenheim, E. (1996). *Healthspeak: A Complete Dictionary of America's Health Care System*. New York: Facts on File.

Medicode, Inc. (1999). *2000 DRG Guide*. Salt Lake City, UT: Medicode.

Segen, J. C. (1998). *Dictionary of Alternative Medicine*. Chicago: McGraw-Hill.

Timmreck, T. C. (1997). *Health Services Cyclopedic Dictionary*. Sudbury, MA: Jones & Bartlett.

Toth, A. (1998). *Decoding the Codes: A Comprehensive Guide to ICD, CPT & HCPCS Coding Systems*. Chicago: McGraw-Hill.

Population Size, Concentration, and Distribution

INTRODUCTION

The number of people (i.e., the size of the population) found within a geographic area is typically the simplest and most straightforward of demographic attributes. At the same time, it is often the most important. While population composition, health status, and other factors are significant in determining the health care needs and in estimating the health services demand for a specific place, the size of that population is arguably the most important factor in making these assessments. After size, the pattern of concentration and distribution of persons within and across geographic areas probably are next in importance for health researchers and planners.

Demographers generally begin telling a "demographic story" about a location by presenting information on population size in very basic terms. Statistics that describe the size and location of various populations are common in the popular press. For example, much has been written about the lack of population growth that characterized several midwestern states during the 1990s. The concomitant population increases in California, Florida, and Texas have been duly noted in the context of a rise in demand for health services. When the Census of Population and Housing is conducted, population losses and gains are reflected in lost and gained seats in the US House of Representatives. Between the 100th Congress (1987) and the 103rd Congress (1994), for example, California gained seven House seats (from 45 to 52) and New York lost three (from 34 to 31). These gains and losses reflect the population growth differentials experienced by California and New York during the 1980s. In 1996, nearly one-fifth of all of the electoral votes needed to secure the presidency for William Jefferson Clinton were garnered when he won the popular vote in California.

Data on the size and location of the population also provide the basis for descriptive statistics such as rates and ratios. Population counts, whether for the total population or for subsegments, serve as the denominators for rates like the incidence of heart disease per 10,000 population and the number of hospital beds per 100,000 population. The calculation of rates facilitates comparisons between areas of different size. The observation that deaths in California substantially outnumber those in Montana is not an indicator that health conditions are necessarily worse in California. A comparison of death rates—deaths per 1,000 population, for example—would provide the basis for a meaningful comparison. For planning purposes, in health care as well as other fields, rate calculation is one of the first steps in determining the need for services, facilities, and personnel.

CONCEPTUAL AND MEASUREMENT ISSUES

Population Size

The first demographic "fact" usually desired about a population is its *size*. Size involves a simple count or enumeration of the number of residents and/or households for "a specified area at a specified date" (Bogue, 1985, p. 13). The enumeration of persons in the United States vis-à-vis the census is accomplished using a person's residence (i.e., where she normally sleeps and eats) as the geographic point of reference. Almost all persons have a residence as a frame of reference. A count implies that some organized and systematic effort is made to identify and record individuals and households. These data are then aggregated at one or more levels of geography (e.g., a county). In addition, every population count must be specific with respect to a date.

The most complete count of a population takes the form of a census. Decennial census counts in the United States refer to April 1 of years that end in zero, since that is the day the population is officially enumerated. In years when full counts are not made, population estimates are generated and these figures serve as substitutes for direct enumeration. Population estimates usually refer to July 1 (midyear) of the year in question or in some instances December 31 (end of year). Such a distinction, of course, may be crucial in the examination of an area undergoing rapid population change. Box 4.1 describes how the size of the population is used to approximate the distribution of patients.

In the process of gathering data on the number of persons in households and other living units, information on the unit's specific location (e.g., a street address) is collected. Aggregating the individual living unit data from the census to any geographic area desired (e.g., a zip code) generates size data for that area. As

Box 4.1

Where Are Our Customers?
Geographic Identifiers for Health Care Providers

Only a few years ago, hospitals, physicians, and other health care providers had limited interest in the characteristics and location of their patients. The health care market was considered to be unitary, and there was little need to distinguish one kind of patient from another. Most health care providers maintained quasi-monopolies, and as long as the patients and revenue flowed there was no pressure to understand the market.

This "golden age" of market hegemony ended abruptly in the 1980s, when almost overnight cutthroat competition was injected into the health care arena. An oversupply of hospital beds, facilities, and some types of personnel, coupled with declining utilization for some services, meant that there was now a smaller pie that had to be sliced into more and more pieces. The providers of health services had to adapt the ways of the business world quickly if they were to survive. A new way of looking at the market was necessary, and this involved transforming health services into "products" and patients into "customers."

This new health care environment demands that health care providers know who their customers are and what they are like. It also demands that providers know where they are. A competitive environment requires constant monitoring of the sources of customers. The ability to plan systematically for product introduction, expansion, or withdrawal depends on current data on patient origin.

In response, hospitals and other providers have turned to their data-processing centers and research departments in an attempt to get a handle on the geographic distribution of their patients. All record-keeping systems maintain street address and zip code identifiers for patients, for billing purposes if for nothing else. The obvious first step is to determine the origin of patients or users of other services by zip code (or some smaller unit of geography, if possible). In rural areas, of course, zip codes may be meaningless, so it may be necessary to aggregate zip codes into county combinations if patients have not been assigned already to a county.

These zip code-based data present an overview of the distribution of users or the provider's customers. While a tabular presentation may be useful, it is much more descriptive to present these data on a map. Nothing seems to say it better than a map, particularly one that pinpoints the exact location of customers. Clusters are identified and areas of weak or strong market penetration are easily located. In the past, it was common to obtain a street map and create a dot map manually using colored dots or pushpins. For health care providers, however, this is not very practical, since even the smallest hospital or physician practice will generate thousands of customer

Continued

Box 4.1. (Continued)

encounters annually. Fortunately, computerized mapping packages are available that can quickly generate maps that graphically depict the distribution of whatever phenomenon is being examined.

Regional hospitals and other providers that serve multicounty or multistate markets may find the zip code or even the county level of geography to be adequate. Most health care providers, particularly those in urban areas, are more local in their orientation. Smaller urban hospitals as well as clinics often cater to a certain segment of the community that demonstrates a particular geographic distribution. The practices of primary care physicians may be restricted to a limited geographic area. See Box 4.4 on the use of zip code geography.

All providers certainly need to know the economic characteristics of their patients in a cost-conscious environment, and while zip code-level data give an indication of the socioeconomic status of the patient this information is generally not specific enough. For many purposes, then, a lower level of geography is required for health care providers. The next lowest level after the zip code is the census tract, with a zip code being roughly composed of several tracts. Unfortunately, since zip codes and census tracts have been developed independently, there is little correspondence between the boundaries of the two types of units. (Many computer mapping packages do have the capability of depicting zip codes and census tracts on the same map.) Plotting one's customers on a map by census tract presents much more detail than could ever be achieved using zip codes.

Even this level may not be precise enough for some purposes. For example, there may be some extremely localized services (such as a minor medical center) or certain products that are to be offered to a very restricted population. As health care providers have turned more to direct mail for promotional purposes, even greater degrees of specificity have become necessary. For these reasons, the provider may want to use the block group as the basis for analysis. This approach brings the analysis essentially to the neighborhood level. Although most providers are not likely to need block-level information, it is available. In fact, it is now possible to obtain certain information all the way down to the household level.

Once, the hospital or physician's practice has zip code-level data, how does it

---

noted above, postcensal population estimates and projections, which are discussed later in this chapter and in Chapter 9, provide information beyond the time for which an actual count was conducted. These data are particularly valuable for planning purposes.

Several issues must be addressed in the counting of the population. The first concerns who is to be counted. By definition, censuses try to enumerate every

get down to the census tract, block group, block, or household? The assignment of lower-level geographies to a particular customer may be done through the process of geocoding. Although geocoding involves some technical stumbling blocks, the geocoding process itself is quite simple. With access to appropriate computer capabilities and software, any address can be identified as to its tract or block group; all that is required is the assigning of a latitude and longitude to the address in question. Once a geocode is assigned, any other geographic identifier can be determined.

This can be done because the US Bureau of the Census and data vendors have undertaken the herculean task of geocoding every address in the United States. A list of addresses can be quickly scanned and geocodes assigned to most of them. Of course, the list must be "clean" in order to reduce the number of nonmatches. These systems do have the ability to eventually convert the most imprecise address into at least a zip code. Health care providers can submit their patient lists, for example, to a data vendor who has geocoding capabilities and a geocoded list can be developed. At present, this is a relatively expensive process, although, as with all such technology, the costs seem to be dropping rather quickly. Software packages are now available that allow the health care analyst to geocode addresses on his or her own computer.

Once geocoding has been accomplished, patient information can be depicted on a census tract map or even a block group map if the provider has the technical capabilities. In addition, this linkage to lower level geography means that a wide range of data now can be obtained on customers because you now "know where they live." For example, a hospital is not likely to have income or educational data on its patients, but these characteristics can be inferred from the census tract- or block group-level data available as a result of the decennial census. Furthermore, it is now possible to initiate a precisely targeted direct mail campaign. For example, the block groups with the characteristics that you want to target can be identified and their identities provided to a mailing list vendor. These block group identifiers can be used by the vendor to generate a mailing list that is tailored to the specified target markets and only those markets.

These developments indicate the extent to which health care has taken on the characteristics of other industries. It seems clear that, as of the late 1990s, health care providers who expect to be successful must place as much emphasis on tracking their markets as they do on providing quality health care.

individual. Every 10 years from 1790 through 2000, the US Bureau of the Census has attempted to count everyone who resides in the United States, regardless of their legal status. This enumeration also includes certain US citizens residing abroad (such as US military personnel and members of diplomatic missions).

The assigned location of individuals in terms of geography is also of concern, and people are generally counted at their usual place of residence. Since the place of residence is defined as the location where the individual usually sleeps and eats, the usual place of residence is easy to establish for the vast majority of the population. Definitional complications may arise, however, for subpopulations such as college students, migrant workers, persons with two or more residences, and the homeless. While college students are assigned to the location of their educational institution, the determination of a usual residence for the remaining groups involves the application of specific rules, enumerator judgment, and special counting attempts (e.g., visiting rooming houses to count the homeless). Greater detail regarding these issues can be found in Robey (1989).

A further distinction between an individual's usual place of residence (nighttime) and his workplace location (daytime) is important. The downtown areas of many US cities teem with people during working hours only to become virtual ghost towns in the evening. The opposite is often true for residential areas. In many situations, information on the location of the daytime population may be more useful than information on place of residence. Locational decisions relating to medical emergency facilities, vehicles, and staffing, for example, require a sensitivity to differentials in daytime and nighttime populations. The ability to provide at least minimal services to all parts of the community requires either a count or an estimate of these distinct populations. Daytime populations can be estimated using Census Bureau information on daily commuting patterns, although postcensal estimates are required in order to keep these data as current as possible.

Another issue relates to the coverage of the enumeration. An enumeration implies that everyone has been counted. While censuses conducted in the United States come very close to full coverage, a portion of the population is inevitably missed. An evaluation of the 1980 census indicated that, while about 99% of the white population was accounted for, only 94% of the black population was enumerated. Furthermore, the undercount for African-American males between the ages of 25 and 54 was estimated to be about 15% (Fay et al., 1988). Estimates of undercount for the 1990 census indicated that for the first time in the history of the census the count was less accurate than its predecessor. Specifically, the undercount was 33% higher than that for 1980, with a similar pattern of racial and ethnic disparities seen as in the 1980 census. However, it should be emphasized that the overall undercount was 1.6%, a figure clearly acceptable in virtually every other data collection activity. Plans to officially adjust the data for the 1990 census based on undercount information were rejected. While the Census Bureau has developed methodologies for adjusting counts and other data for the 2000 census, the issue of adjustment has become politicized. In 1998, the US Supreme Court ruled against adjustment for purposes of reapportionment, but did not preclude the Census Bureau from producing adjusted figures. Analysts working with data from the 2000 census are likely to be faced with the decision of which numbers to use (adjusted versus unadjusted).

Although an actual census only takes place only once every ten years in the United States (special censuses are an exception), data on population size are available during intercensal periods for many geographic units and at regular intervals by virtue of *population estimates and projections.** Population estimates and projections are produced by combining data from the most recent counts available (or most recent estimate), with measures of population change (i.e., births, deaths, and migrants), symptomatic data (e.g., housing starts and utility connections), and assumptions about likely demographic change. Using this approach, data on population size and in some instances population characteristics are produced for past, present, or future time periods. Population estimates and projections sometimes are viewed as surrogates for enumeration data. In many instances, however, they contain a relatively large degree of error. Worse yet, the amount of error is likely to be unknown. In any case, population estimates and projections should be used with caution. More information regarding the calculation and use of population estimates and projections can be found in Haub (1987) and Tayman and Swanson (1996). Box 4.2 discusses the accuracy of estimates and projections.

Data on population size are meaningful only if linked to a geographic unit. Units of geography usually refer to political and/or census bureau boundary delineations such as *census blocks* and *block groups, census tracts, metropolitan areas*, cities, and counties. Census blocks, which average about 30 persons, represent the smallest unit of census geography; they are generally well-defined rectangular pieces of land whose boundaries are delineated by streets and roads, though irregular boundaries such as those created by streams and railroad tracks are sometimes seen. Block data were first available for all areas in the United States in 1990. Before 1990, block data were produced only for metropolitan areas. Relatively homogeneous blocks are aggregated to form block groups. Block groups have vast potential for application in health planning, since they can be thought to represent a "community." More extensive data are available from the census for block group levels than for blocks.

Blocks and block groups are combined to form census tracts. On average a tract contains about 4000 persons, and this census unit historically has been the most widely used for small-area analysis. In nonmetropolitan areas the census tract equivalent is the *block numbering area* (BNA). BNAs average the same population size as tracts, although the land area is somewhat larger. BNAs also are divided into blocks. BNA blocks are larger in average population size—about 35 persons—and in land area than their metropolitan counterparts. Additional subcounty data can be found for census designated places, incorporated places, minor

---

*In 2003, the Census Bureau will fully implement the American Community Survey. The survey is designed to provide intercensal demographic, housing, social and economic data estimates for all counties in the United States.

Box 4.2

Which Numbers Can You Trust?
Evaluating Population Estimates and Projections

The US census of population is only conducted every 10 years. During the intercensal period, official population counts are not available, so estimates are required to provide information on the number of residents. Moreover, population size data for future dates—population projections—are often required in the planning process.

Population estimates and projections data come from a variety of public and private sources. For example, the US Bureau of the Census, in cooperation with state data centers, produces annual population estimates for states and counties. Numerous state data centers and other government agencies generate population estimates for smaller units of geography such as cities and census tracts. Many vendors generate annual estimates for each zip code and smaller units of geography. The US Bureau of the Census also makes available annual population projections for the country up to 100 years into the future.

Most of the estimates available for larger geographic units (e.g., states) are relatively reliable. Estimates for smaller geographic units (e.g., counties) are less reliable. Projections are inherently more problematic, especially those for small geographic units. Since the producers of estimates and projections utilize different methodologies, the figures generated for smaller geographic units may vary substantially. When making or purchasing population estimates, consider the following:

1. Estimates are only as good as the population baseline data from which the figures are derived. If the base figure is another estimate (with the strong possibility that it contains error), further estimates may compound the original error. In general, the further from a sound baseline figure (e.g., census data), the greater the amount of error.

2. Estimates are only as good as the assumptions underlying them. All estimation procedures require several underlying assumptions concerning fertility, mortality, migration, land use (zoning), and/or the growth in housing units. To the extent that assumptions are unsound, the estimates will be in error. Therefore, assumptions underlying population estimates must be carefully examined. For example, the population estimates for many geo-

civil divisions, census county divisions, and zip codes. Extended discussions of geographic concerns can be found in Shryock et al. (1973). More detail concerning the use of tract and block data can be found in Pol and Thomas (1997, pp. 147–188). Box 4.3 focuses on identifying boundaries for market areas.

The collection of population data for blocks, block groups, tracts, and BNAs,

graphic areas are too high because the organization making the estimate did not account for the area's *carrying capacity*, that is, its physical limit to growth. In the instance where a geographic area cannot "hold" any more housing units, an assumption of continued growth probably cannot be justified.

3. Estimates are only as good as the data on the components of change needed to make those estimates. Aside from the quality of population base data discussed above, without reasonably good nonpopulation data, estimates may contain substantial error. For example, if a given method requires accurate information on housing starts and utility connections, the resulting estimate may well contain a large amount of error if only general estimates of these two components exist or there are errors in the data.

4. Estimates for small and rapidly changing areas are subject to more error than those for large and stable areas. If a geographic area contains few people or it is changing rapidly (growing or declining), estimating population size becomes more problematic. It takes little absolute error to translate into large percentage error for small populations.

The same basic concerns drive the evaluation of population projections though more attention must be paid to the recency of base period data. Projections are usually trickier than estimates, since assumptions are being made about future trends in the various components of population change. Assumptions about births, deaths, and migration each carry the potential for error. The most important assumption is that future developments are a function of past trends. Error also tends to be compounded as the age of the baseline data increases. In fact, many demographers argue that national projections extending more than 20 years into the future are of little value. For smaller and/or rapidly changing areas, the useful projection period is almost certain to be much shorter, and in some instances no more than two or three years.

Though many users of population estimates and projections purchase data from someone else, the concern for data quality should not be treated lightly. It is important that users compare and contrast baseline data, underlying assumptions, and overall methodology among vendors before purchase and use of the data takes place. The more the provider already knows about his or her own market area, the better the ability to evaluate the work of data vendors.

the geographic areas that experience the greatest amount of change over time, occurs only every 10 years. Between censuses, the population must be estimated for these geographic units. Before any estimates are used, however, it is important to ascertain on which data they are based and how they were derived.

Metropolitan statistical areas (MSAs) were created by the US Bureau of the

---

Box 4.3

Identifying a Health Care Market Area

Increased competition among health care providers has made the accurate delineation of market areas crucial to the success of health care organizations. Market boundary information is used in conjunction with population data, competitor information, and patient records to better understand the distribution of patients, justify adding new services and/or facilities, and determine shifts in the locations of competitors.

Correctly identifying a health care market area involves the use of carefully chosen geographic units. Market areas are sometimes approximated in order to adhere to existing standard geographic boundaries such as those for census tracts, zip codes, and counties. While the use of standard boundaries is particularly attractive, since data sets are often available for these units, underbounding or overbounding may occur. It is incumbent upon the analyst to ascertain whether data for exact boundaries (street-specific in some markets) can be found and to identify the advantages and disadvantages of boundary approximation if no such data exist.

A number of methods are useful in establishing market area boundaries, and it is good practice to compare boundaries using more than one measure. One method is to establish the maximum distance or driving time that people are willing to travel for a given service, using the locations of the service as the center of a circle or other shape that encompasses the market. Computer software is available to perform this task, though in rapidly changing areas driving times can be significantly altered over a relatively short period of time. In general, this method simply involves identifying the location of the service/facility and allowing the software to establish boundaries, given that travel time data have been provided.

Census to standardize statistical comparisons among highly urbanized areas. MSA designation requires a central city of at least 50,000 persons or Census Bureau-defined urbanized areas of at least 50,000 inhabitants and a total MSA population of at least 100,000 (75,000 in New England). Counties or county equivalents (cities and towns in New England and parishes in Louisiana) are the building blocks of MSAs, and a central city may spread over more than one county. Counties adjacent to the central county (or counties) are designated as part of the MSA if they meet certain commuting and residential density criteria. More detail regarding the MSA designation may be found in US Bureau of the Census (1996) publications.

Sometimes it is useful to think of MSAs as being made up of a hierarchy of components. MSAs are composed of counties or county equivalents. Counties are

A second method is to plot on a map the residences of a sample of recent patients or health care enrollees specific to the service in mind. The distribution of residences can be assumed to replicate the market area. The market area for general hospital services may be different and much smaller than that for more specialized offerings. Therefore, multiple market areas will exist for almost all larger health providers. The delineation of market areas also should account for patients who do not come from traditional residences but from other facilities such as nursing homes, offices, or industrial sites.

A third method focuses on establishing market area boundaries for a service or services not yet offered. Establishing these boundaries is much more difficult and usually requires multiple techniques. Initially, the residential and/or workplace distribution of patients using similar services should be plotted. If another organization is offering the same or similar services, then its market area boundaries also should be estimated. Distance/driving time data must be evaluated as well. However, a more subjective approach may be required because the service in question is new to the area. Data on the same service offered in a different market area may be available through professional networks. These data could help establish time–distance parameters. Surveys of potential consumers of these services (e.g., physicians and patients) also may provide valuable time–distance sensitivity information.

A final issue is worthy of consideration. Market area boundaries must be continuously monitored for change. Traffic patterns and driving times change and, along with the entrance or exit of competition, market area boundaries may be significantly altered over a short period of time. Changes in tastes and preferences for services either on the part of physicians (e.g., increased preference for home infusion therapy) and/or patients (e.g., increased demand for outpatient services) as well as changing patterns of managed care enrollment also must be monitored in regard to how they may affect market area boundaries.

subdivided into census tracts. Census tracts are subdivided into block groups, and block groups into blocks. For nonmetropolitan areas, counties are divided into BNAs, which are further divided into blocks.

Zip code geography is independent of these geographic units. Box 4.4 addresses the use of zip code geography in health care applications. Zip codes were developed by the US postal service for mail delivery administration, but have become a commonly used unit for the planning of health services.

Concentration and Distribution

When population concentration and distribution are considered, two types of measurement are of interest. The *concentration* of the population is usually

Box 4.4

To Zip or Not to Zip: What Unit of Geography Is Best?

The most commonly used geographic patient identifier, especially in urban areas, is the zip code. The wide use of zip codes by health care managers and planners reflects the facts that (1) market area delineation and information are crucial in a more competitive marketplace, and (2) the easiest-to-obtain geographic identifier is the zip code because it is a part of the patient record. Because many marketing efforts contain a direct mail component, targeting by zip code and postal carrier route has become a standard mode of operation for many institutions.

There are both advantages and disadvantages in the use of population and household counts by zip code. On the advantage side, intercensal data often are readily available for zip codes. For example, a number of data vendors sell demographic data by zip code, and this represents a relatively inexpensive source of easy-to-use information for all zip codes comprising a market area. Some vendors offer more than 100 variables for each zip code. Moreover, current and potential customer data, some of which are available through mailing lists, often contain a zip code identifier allowing for the easy match of demographic and industry data. Direct mail is organized on the basis of zip codes and postal carrier routes. The desire to have population and household estimate data for both of these levels of geography makes their use attractive. More recently, psychographic (lifestyle) data have been made available for zip codes and other units of geography, allowing for a greater knowledge of the geographic areas from which customers are drawn.

On the downside, zip codes are large in terms of both population and area and are relatively unwieldy units of geography. They seldom correspond to the actual boundaries of a market area. Moreover, zip code and carrier route boundaries change frequently, and new zip codes are regularly carved out of old ones. It is exceedingly difficult if not impossible to reconstruct boundaries used in the past, thereby making comparisons over time difficult. In addition, population counts for zip codes and carrier routes are estimates and are subject to the errors addressed in Box 4.2.

Presently, the technology exists for and use is being made of geographic-based information generated for market areas defined by street addresses from patient records. These addresses can be matched against a list of addresses that contain geographic identifiers (e.g., census blocks and latitude and longitude), making it possible to fine-tune market area boundaries. Many vendors are providing demographic data for these smaller, more customized areas. Though caution is advised in the use of these data (see Box 4.2), the precise identification of boundaries is superior to the use of zip code boundaries in many instances.

measured in terms of density. *Distribution*, on the other hand, is measured by the proportion of the total population living in specified geographic areas and sub-areas. Each measure yields different but related pieces of information. Concentration stated in terms of density and usually measured as persons-per-square-mile provides information regarding a population's concentration within a given geographic area. On the other hand, proportional measures of distribution relate a population count or estimate for a certain area to a larger total, such as that of the United States (e.g., the percentage of the US population that lives in California or the proportion of Nebraska's population that lives in the Omaha MSA). Both measures assume that there are reasonably accurate population count or estimate data available and that the size of the land area is known. Both concentration and distribution measures also depend on precise boundary delineations. Both measures are crucial in the study of the location of health services personnel and facilities.

When changes in population concentration or distribution are analyzed, any boundary changes must be taken into consideration. For example, MSA boundaries expand through the addition of counties, making it misleading to determine decade-to-decade change unless the boundaries are standardized. The geographic units utilized in the next several pages are found in Figure 4.1. The regional, divisional, and state boundaries seen in this figure are useful because they remain constant over time. This stability in boundaries facilitates many types of comparisons.

Rates of Change

Population count and estimate data are frequently used in the calculation of ratios, indices, and/or rates of change. Demographers and other users of demographic data often wish to describe or analyze changes in population size, concentration, or distribution for two or more time periods and/or across different geographic units. Several options are available and the method employed depends on the needs of the analyst. Initially, absolute differences—simply taking one number and subtracting the other—may be used to indicate the change in size. If more than two time intervals are being studied, then multiple differences may be generated, including measures for the entire time span as well as for each of the segments comprising that span. The advantage of decomposing longer time intervals into shorter components is that the figure for the entire interval may mask differences between and among component parts. For example, a population may have increased by 5 million persons over the three decades being studied, though almost all the growth actually took place over the most recent decade. The smaller the geographic unit analyzed, the greater the chance of uneven growth over a long time interval.

Proportional and percentage measures of population change are useful as well. A choice of the base population must be made, and this affects the interpre-

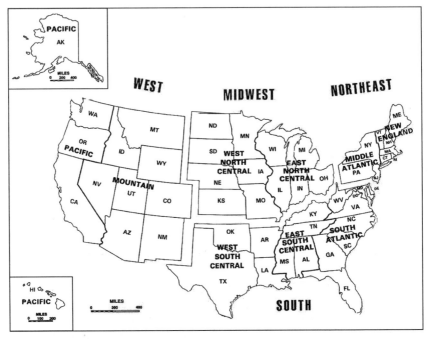

Figure 4.1. Census regions and divisions of the United States. (SOURCE: US Census Bureau. On-line at www.census.gov/geo/www/gaim.html)

tation of figures derived. If there are two time periods and the difference in the two figures (e.g., 1999 total minus 1990 total) is the numerator, then choosing the 1990 figure as the base for rate calculation results in a figure for percentage change, either positive or negative, since 1990. However, if the 1999 figure is chosen as the base, then the interpretation shifts to indicate the percentage of the 1999 population that was added (or subtracted) during the decade of the 1990s. In rapidly changing areas, the two rates may be quite different, perhaps resulting in two sets of conflicting conclusions.

It is important to use both absolute and relative measures in focusing on health-related phenomena. Looking at state comparisons, suppose the question concerns which state grew the fastest during the 1980s. Change in size is being measured in this case. Two answers are correct: California with an increase of 6 million persons and Nevada with an increase in population of 50.1% (US Bureau of the Census, 1996: Table 27). Even though the absolute population increase was only 402,000 persons during the 1980s in Nevada, its base population in 1980 was so small (800,000) that it yielded the nation's largest percentage growth. It is only when the changes in population size and percentage are compared that meaningful information can be produced. These two measures provide two very different pieces of information. The selection of a measure is predicated on and limited by the specific use intended by the analyst.

TRENDS IN POPULATION SIZE, CONCENTRATION, AND DISTRIBUTION

The continuous increase in the size of the population has been a major force historically in the political and economic development of the United States. From a nation of roughly 4 million persons in 1790, the population of the United States has increased to the present estimate of approximately 274 million (US Bureau of the Census, 2000). At the same time that the population was growing, political and economic institutions were evolving that helped make the United States a world power. While political and economic strength do not have their most important base in the size of a nation's population, the skills and creativity of a diverse population that has at least some minimal size can contribute significantly to overall vitality.

Table 4.1 presents data on population size and density for the United States from 1950 to 2010. When compared to other nations, the United States is the third most populous country, trailing the People's Republic of China and India. As can be seen in the table, the population is large, has grown by 116 million persons since 1950, and is projected to be 275 million persons in 2000. The population was projected to grow by over 81% between 1950 and 2000. During the decade of the 1990s, the increase was projected to be about 10%.

Population growth in the United States has varied in both absolute and

Table 4.1. US Population Growth and Density, 1950–2010

Year	Population	Population per square mile	Increase over previous decade	Percent change
1950	151,325,798	42.6	19,161,229	14.5
1960	179,323,175	50.6	27,997,377	18.5
1970	203,302,031	57.4	23,978,856	13.4
1980	226,545,805	64.0	23,243,774	11.4
1990	248,718,301	70.3	22,176,102	9.8
2000[a]	274,634,000	77.7	25,915,699	10.4
2010[a]	297,716,000	84.2	23,082,000	8.4

[a]Population projection.

sources: US Bureau of the Census (1996), Tables 1 and 17; Campbell (1997), Table 1.

percentage terms in recent decades. While the percentage increase has declined in each decade since the 1960s, absolute increases in excess of 22 million persons have been recorded for each decade since 1960. The 10.4% increase for the 1990s translates into the addition of nearly 26 million Americans during that decade.

Population density in the United States was approximately 72 persons per square mile in 1992. When compared to that of some other nations, however, this figure is relatively low. In the mid-1990s, the density figures per square mile for five other countries were: China, 336; Germany, 618; India, 829; Japan, 823; and Belgium, 871 (US Bureau of the Census, 1996: Table 1325). Population density at the national level for the United States is of limited concern because there is insignificant year-to-year change. However, when subnational geopolitical units such as regions, states, counties, and cities are studied, the dissimilarities in the change in concentration of persons across geographic areas becomes very important in assessing health care needs and evaluating the supply of health services.

Overall, the US data demonstrate that, while the rate of population growth is slowing, substantial numbers continue to be added to the US population each decade. These increased numbers will continue to drive population-sensitive aspects of health care demand for the foreseeable future. However, as will become evident in Chapters 5 through 8, the characteristics of those needing care are changing rapidly, thereby altering the nature of the health care demanded beyond that implied by size data alone.

Census Divisions

Although growth is slowing and density is increasing for the US population as a whole, wide geographic variation exists with regard to both size, growth, and density. Table 4.2 provides population data for the census divisions identified in Figure 4.1 at 10-year intervals from 1970 to 2010. Examining data for 1990, wide variations among the divisions can be seen. The range in count and percentage concentration is from 13.2 million, or about 5%, in the New England division to 43.7 million, or 17.6%, in the South Atlantic division. Differentials in growth among the divisions are evident as well. While the first four divisions in the table exhibit relatively modest increases in population between 1970 and 2010, the increase for the South Atlantic division is 24.7 million (80%) and for the Pacific division the increase is 23.8 million (90%) over the 40-year period! Conversely, each of the first four listed divisions as well as the East South Central division shows a decline in its percentage share of the total US population.

An examination of decade-by-decade growth trends yields additional information. While all divisions were expected to experience slowing growth during the last decade of this century, increases will still be at or above 10% in the South Atlantic, West South Central, Mountain, and Pacific divisions. On the other hand, virtually no population growth is anticipated for the East North Central, Mid-

Table 4.2. US Population Distribution by Census Division, 1970–2010

Division	1970		1980		1990[a]		2000[b]		2010[c]	
New England	11.8[c]	(5.8)[d]	12.3	(5.5)	13.2	(5.3)	13.6	(4.9)	14.2	(4.8)
Mid-Atlantic	37.2	(18.3)	36.8	(16.2)	37.6	(15.1)	38.5	(14.0)	39.5	(13.3)
East North Central	40.3	(19.8)	41.7	(18.4)	42.0	(16.9)	44.4	(16.2)	45.8	(15.4)
West North Central	16.3	(8.0)	17.2	(7.6)	17.8	(7.2)	19.1	(6.9)	20.1	(6.8)
South Atlantic	30.7	(15.1)	37.0	(16.3)	43.7	(17.6)	50.1	(18.3)	55.4	(18.6)
East South Central	12.8	(6.3)	14.7	(6.5)	15.2	(6.1)	16.9	(6.2)	18.1	(6.1)
West South Central	19.3	(9.5)	23.7	(10.5)	26.7	(10.7)	30.5	(11.1)	34.0	(11.4)
Mountain	8.3	(4.1)	11.4	(5.0)	13.7	(5.5)	17.7	(6.5)	20.2	(6.8)
Pacific	26.5	(13.1)	31.8	(14.0)	39.2	(15.8)	43.7	(15.9)	50.3	(16.9)

[a]1990 data are from the 1990 Census of Population and Housing.
[b]Data are population projections.
[c]The left column under each year presents population data in millions. The right column under each year presents the population data as a percent of the total US population.
[d]Column percent distribution in parentheses.
SOURCES: US Bureau of the Census (1988), Table 28; Campbell (1997), Table 1.

Atlantic, and West North Central divisions. Slow growth in these divisions has initiated a cycle whereby the population composition changes in such a way as to hamper future growth. This phenomenon is discussed in more detail in Chapter 5. Box 4.5 illustrates the ways in which patterns of population change affect the distribution of health care resources.

States

Table 4.3 provides percentage growth figures for the states with the highest and lowest growth rates for the decades 1980–1990 and 1990–2000. The upper panel contains the ten states with the highest growth rates, and as can be seen the figures for percentage increase are substantial. The high growth rates for Arizona, Florida, California, Texas, and Georgia are especially evident. These rates are particularly noteworthy in view of these states' large base populations in 1980. The second portion of the panel shows projected growth from 1990 to 2000 and indicates a significant decline in growth rates when compared to the previous data. Furthermore, the change in the rank order of states and the substitution of Idaho, Colorado, New Mexico, and Oregon for Alaska, Florida, New Hampshire, and California illustrate the tendency of these rates toward instability.

The second panel lists states with the lowest growth rates. During the 1980s, four states and the District of Columbia lost population. The lowest growth states were located in all regions of the country. For the 1990s, three states are projected to lose population, and all of the low-growth states are found in the Northeast and Midwest regions, with the exception of the District of Columbia. Table 4.4

Box 4.5

The Maldistribution of Health Services

Differential regional, divisional, state, and substate population growth patterns have led to what many health care experts see as a maldistribution of both health personnel and facilities. Areas undergoing rapid population growth are frequently underserved (e.g., not enough hospitals or physicians), while those areas experiencing slow growth or even population loss often have a relative excess of services. Nebraska, for example, is a typical midwestern state that has experienced little population growth in the last two decades. On the surface, this implies a fairly stable ratio of health services to population. However, the situation at the substate level is much different, in that many rural counties are losing population while the state's urban areas continue to grow. This means that at the local level imbalances between supply and demand develop or are exacerbated over time.

As is often the case, population redistribution does not bring with it a concomitant redistribution of resources. Health care facilities represent major investments and are not opened or closed in the same way one would open or close a small retail business. For example, while some rural hospitals may experience occupancy rates lower than 20% (compared to the national average of about 65%), there is resistance to closing those hospitals. Community hospitals are sources of local pride and generate jobs and income. They are seen as a part of the infrastructure that must be maintained. There is concern that once a hospital closes, related jobs and other parts of the community's infrastructure will be adversely affected. Major efforts at preventing closure are often initiated, including increasing the local tax burden. However, based on most objective criteria (e.g., population served, occupancy level, and profitability), a strong argument for closure often can be made.

The imbalance between distribution of health facilities and physicians and population distribution has been evident for some time in the United States. Maldistribution is a function not only of population redistribution patterns but also of demographically based locational preferences of physicians. Simply put, to the extent that physicians make rational decisions with regard to choice of practice location, they base these decisions in part on the demographic characteristics of the populations in various sites. Thus, physicians' offices tend to be overrepresented in communities of high socioeconomic status.

The maldistribution issue does not lend itself to easy remedy. Without clear and properly directed health care policy that present viable and acceptable alternatives, small communities will continue to engage in heroic efforts to keep their hospitals open. States and localities will continue to offer enticements to get physicians to staff these hospitals and practice in rural areas. Without a mechanism for providing adequate health services should a hospital be closed, it can be argued that these communities have no choice in their actions. Many observers argue that hospital closure will leave a substantial number of persons without a reasonable level of care. Given that a large number of rural hospitals have closed during the 1990s despite attempts to save them, it is important that health care decisionmakers develop mechanisms to assure that the affected populations are provided at least a minimal level of care.

Table 4.3. Population for the 10 States
with Highest and Lowest Growth Rates, 1980–1990 and 1990–2000

	1980–1990			1990–2000	
Rank	State	Percentage change	Rank	State	Percentage change
1	Nevada	50.1	1	Nevada	27.3
2	Alaska	36.9	2	Idaho	15.5
3	Arizona	34.9	3	Arizona	15.1
4	Florida	32.7	4	Colorado	13.7
5	California	25.7	5	Utah	13.3
6	New Hampshire	20.5	6	Washington	11.6
7	Texas	19.4	7	New Mexico	11.2
8	Georgia	18.6	7	Georgia	11.2
9	Utah	17.9	9	Oregon	10.5
10	Washington	17.8	10	Texas	10.2
51	West Virginia	−8.0	51	District of Columbia	−8.7
50	District of Columbia	−4.9	50	Rhode Island	−1.4
49	Iowa	−4.7	49	Connecticut	−0.4
48	Wyoming	−3.4	48	North Dakota	0.4
47	North Dakota	−2.1	47	New York	0.8
46	Pennsylvania	0.2	46	Massachusetts	0.9
45	Louisiana	0.3	45	Maine	1.1
44	Michigan	0.4	44	Pennsylvania	1.6
43	Ohio	0.5	43	West Virginia	1.9
42	Nebraska	0.5	42	Iowa	2.3

SOURCE: US Bureau of the Census (1996), Table 28.

Table 4.4. Population Gains in Absolute Numbers
for the Top 10 and Bottom 10 States, 1995–2000 (Projection)

	Largest gains			Smallest gains	
Rank	State	Population gain	Rank	State	Population gain
1	Texas	1,395,000	51	District of Columbia	−31,000
2	Florida	1,068,000	50	Rhode Island	8,000
3	California	932,000	49	Connecticut	10,000
4	Georgia	674,000	48	New York	10,000
5	North Carolina	582,000	47	West Virginia	13,000
6	Arizona	580,000	46	Maine	18,000
7	Washington	427,000	45	North Dakota	20,000
8	Colorado	422,000	44	Vermont	32,000
9	Tennessee	401,000	43	Wyoming	44,000
10	Virginia	379,000	42	South Dakota	48,000

SOURCE: Campbell (1997).

provides absolute change figures by state for the 1995–2000 time period. Three states—Texas, Florida, and California—account for a combined increase of 3.3 million persons. Only the District of Columbia is projected to lose population during the interval.

There is substantial state-to-state variation in population per square mile. Excluding the District of Columbia, which had 9531 persons per square mile in 1992, New Jersey had the highest population density at nearly 1054. Three other states, Rhode Island (958), Massachusetts (765), and Connecticut (677), recorded densities exceeding 500 per square mile. On the low side, Alaska had a density of 1 person per square mile, followed by Wyoming, 5; Montana, 6; South Dakota, 9; and North Dakota, 9 (US Bureau of the Census, 1994: Table A).

Counties

An analysis of population trends at the county level indicates even more variation than in any of the previous discussions. Table 4.5 provides population size data for the 10 most populous and the 10 least populous counties in the United States. As can be seen, the range in size is substantial (from 141 people to over 9 million). The counties display a tendency toward some geographic concentration with five of the most populous counties in either California or New York. Six of the 10 least populous counties are found in the adjacent states of Colorado and Nebraska. Another three are located in Texas.

Table 4.6 presents population change data for the 10 US counties experiencing the greatest absolute increases and for the 10 counties showing the greatest absolute declines in population from 1980 to 1992. As can be seen, the size for both the increases and decreases are substantial. Of the 10 counties with population in-

Table 4.5. Ten Largest and 10 Smallest Counties
Based on Population, 1992

Largest		Smallest	
Los Angeles, CA	9,053,645	Loving, TX	141
Cook, IL	5,139,341	King, TX	339
Harris, TX	2,971,755	Kenedy, TX	439
San Diego, CA	2,601,055	Arthur, NE	457
Orange, CA	2,484,789	Hindsdale, CO	499
Kings, NY	2,286,167	Petroleum, MT	511
Maricopa, AZ	2,209,567	McPherson, NE	528
Wayne, MI	2,096,179	Mineral, CO	571
Dade, FL	2,007,972	San Juan, CO	585
Queens, NY	1,951,034	Blaine, NE	667

SOURCE: US Bureau of the Census (1994), Table 1.

Table 4.6. The 10 Counties with the Largest Population
Gain and Loss, 1980–1992

Gain counties	Number	Loss counties	Number
Los Angeles, CA	1,576,407	Wayne, MI	−241,664
San Diego, CA	739,209	Philadelphia, PA	−135,638
Maricopa, AZ	700,392	Allegheny, PA	−115,799
San Bernardino, CA	639,327	Cook, IL	−114,287
Riverside, CA	625,236	Cuyahoga, OH	−87,191
Harris, TX	562,208	Essex, NJ	−77,884
Orange, CA	551,868	St. Louis, MO	−69,068
Clark, NV	382,546	Orleans, LA	−68,332
Dade, FL	382,463	Baltimore City, MD	−60,645
Tarrant, TX	359,239	Erie, NY	−43,183

SOURCE: US Bureau of the Census (1994), Table 1.

creases, 7 grew by more than 500,000 persons during the 12-year interval. Conversely, each of the counties losing population experienced a decline of at least 20,000 persons during the period. Once again some geographic concentration is evident. Seven of the 10 largest gainers are in California or Texas.

As can be seen in Table 4.7, county-level density comparisons show even greater variation. Although the density for the United States was 72 persons per square mile in 1992, the densities for individual counties ranged from 0.1 persons per square mile in 4 counties in Alaska to 52,432 persons per square mile in New York, New York. Of the 10 counties with the highest population densities, 6 are located in the Northeast region, and 8 of the 10 least densely populated are located in Alaska.

Table 4.7. The 10 Counties with the Most
and Fewest Persons per Square Mile, 1992

Most		Fewest	
New York, NY	52,432	Lake, AK	0.1
Kings, NY	32,428	Peninsula, AK	0.1
Bronx, NY	28,443	North Slope, AK	0.1
Queens, NY	17,834	Yukon-Koyukuk, AK	0.1
San Francisco, CA	15,609	Dillingham, AK	0.2
Hudson, NJ	11,883	Northwest Arctic, AK	0.2
Philadelphia, PA	11,492	Southeast Fairbanks, AK	0.2
Suffolk, MA	10,926	Loving, TX	0.2
District of Columbia	9,531	Bethel, TX	0.3
Baltimore, MD	8,986	Skasway-Yakutat-Angoon, AK	0.3

SOURCE: US Bureau of the Census (1994), Table 1.

Several conclusions can be drawn from the data presented thus far. While the population of the United States is large, its rate of growth is slowing. Divisional, statewide, and county-level growth differentials reflect a continual redistribution of the population away from the Northeast and Midwest toward the South and West. In addition, concentrations of persons as measured by population per square mile show wide variation, with the highest densities being in the Northeast. All these factors and trends impact both the demand for and the supply of health care facilities and personnel.

MEASURING THE SUPPLY OF HEALTH SERVICES

While it is traditional for demographers to discuss size and distribution with respect to population counts, estimates, and projections, a somewhat broader health care perspective takes into account the number and distribution of demographic events (e.g., births) as well as facilities and personnel. In Chapters 6, 7, and 8, data on the number and geographic distribution of births, deaths, and migrants are presented. The number and distribution of health care personnel and facilities are presented in the sections that follow.

National Patterns

While a host of indicators of the availability of health personnel and facilities can be found, the number and distribution of physicians and hospital beds have been selected for presentation here. At the national level, several trends are evident concerning these measures of health care resources. The number of physicians in the United States has increased dramatically since 1960. Expressed as a rate per 100,000 population, this figure increased from 126 in 1960 to 245 in 1997 (US Bureau of the Census, 1999: Table 197). The number of hospital beds per 100,000 persons, on the other hand, declined from 930 to 450 over the same time period. Furthermore, from 1960 to 1997, the average number of beds per hospital was reduced from 241 to 170, and the average length of a hospital stay dropped from 8.0 days to 6.1 days. Between 1960 and 1994, the number of hospital personnel per 100 patients increased from 114 to 573, and the average cost of a stay in the hospital rose from $1851 to $6230 (US Bureau of the Census, 1996: Tables 187, 189, and 190). These figures indicate that health care resource measures can be more volatile than the population figures seen earlier.

State Patterns

The distribution of health care resources varies widely from state to state. Table 4.8 presents rates per 100,000 population for physicians and hospital beds

Table 4.8. Physician and Hospital Bed Rates
(per 100,000 Population) for the 10 States
with the Highest and Lowest Rates, 1990

Physicians		Hospital beds	
Highest rates			
District of Columbia	659	District of Columbia	1,289
New York	335	North Dakota	807
Maryland	333	South Dakota	755
Connecticut	320	Nebraska	640
Massachusetts	300	Mississippi	630
Rhode Island	270	Wyoming	623
New Jersey	263	Kansas	621
Vermont	263	Iowa	598
Pennsylvania	255	Tennessee	573
California	238	Montana	569
Hawaii	215	New York	566
Lowest rates			
Mississippi	129	Washington	307
Isaho	130	Utah	307
Wyoming	136	Nevada	315
Alaska	137	Oregon	332
Nevada	148	California	333
Oklahoma	151	Arizona	339
South Dakota	155	Alaska	340
Iowa	158	Hawaii	355
Arkansas	161	Vermont	378
Montana	167	Idaho	380
US	214	US	366

SOURCE:US Bureau of the Census (1994), Table A, Items 32–47.

for selected states. The 10 states with the highest rates are listed, followed by the ten states with the lowest rates. The rates are somewhat crude in that no compositional factors are considered that might influence the demand for health care (e.g., differences in age structure). This issue is explored in Chapter 5. Looking first at physician rates, the highest concentration of active doctors is in the relatively high-income states along the East Coast. California and Hawaii are the only states on the list not located in that part of the country. On the other hand, low physician concentrations are found across a range of geographically dispersed states.

Interestingly, high bed rates are found to be concentrated in low growth states. Five of the 10 states exhibiting low growth during the 1980–1990 period (Table 4.3) also are states that exhibit high hospital bed concentrations. The list of states with low bed rates is very different from that containing low hospital rates. Nine of the 10 states having low bed rates are located in the West region. Six are found in the Pacific division. For the most part, these are states experiencing more rapid population growth.

County Patterns

At the county level, even wider rate differences in the supply of health services can be found. A large number of US counties have no primary care physicians, as well as no hospital beds. For example, in the early 1990s, of the 93 counties in Nebraska, 19 had no physician and 25 had no hospital (US Bureau of the Census, 1994: Table B). At the same time there were 1603 physicians and 9 hospitals in Douglas (Omaha) County. The bed rate (beds per 100,000 residential population) varied from 0 in 25 counties to 2367 in Garfield County. The physician rate (physicians per 100,000 resident population) ranged from 0 in 19 counties to 385 in Douglas County. The degree of variation in Nebraska can be found in virtually every other state in the nation.

IMPLICATIONS FOR HEALTH CARE DELIVERY

General Issues

The data presented in this chapter point to a number of challenges faced by the health care industry today. Many of these challenges exist because of a maldistribution of resources vis-à-vis population distribution at the regional, state, and substate levels. Some areas can be described as having a critical shortage of health care resources while others report a surplus. At the same time, policymakers propose laws to ameliorate conditions in areas that have limited resources. Of course, the reorganization of the health care system and in particular the consolidation of health service providers further complicate these considerations.

In areas experiencing population growth, the task is to project the relevant dimensions of that growth and to prepare adequately for it. In areas experiencing slow population growth or decline, the challenge of providing adequate health services is greater. For such areas, adjustments must be made when the health care supply exceeds the demand for services. For example, many rural counties that have experienced several decades of population decline can no longer "support" their community hospitals. These communities, along with the hospital owners, must decide whether or not to close or scale back such hospitals. Furthermore, if the hospitals are to be closed, the affected patients must find alternative sources of care. Hospital closings may be in order, but in most communities this type of action meets with resistance. In some urban areas, on the other hand, "competition" has led to an oversupply of hospital beds.

The discrepancy between the rapid growth in health care supply (e.g., physician and hospitals) and the slowing of population growth raises several additional issues. Whether or not there is truly a need for the existing supply is one issue, though the argument that the existing level of service is necessary for quality care may be made. At the local level, the supply–demand issue becomes even more important due to the possibility that rapid population change will occur. In areas showing population growth, service provision may lag and patients may find that supply has not kept up with demand. On the other hand, it may be difficult to convince corporate executives, planning boards, and/or taxpayers to commit the necessary funds to plan for the growth that is projected. Since projections can be wrong, corporations and communities run the risk of overcommitting resources and perhaps paying for unneeded facilities for many years to come.

Population Thresholds for Health Services

Perhaps the most direct link between population size, concentration, and distribution and health care resources relates to the population threshold levels that have been identified for various services. Prior to the introduction of federally supported health planning in the 1960s, little concern was given to the critical mass required to support a facility or service. There was adequate unmet need to absorb any health care resources that might be developed.

By the 1960s, however, concerns were beginning to be voiced with regard to health care oversupplies, shortages, and maldistribution. These concerns prompted efforts to specify the size of population necessary to support health care facilities, specific health programs, and health professionals. These thresholds, it was hoped, would provide guidelines for the establishment of new programs and the expansion of existing ones. Although often established as rough guidelines, these thresholds were in some cases written into law. To the extent that health planning agencies could control the development of resources, these thresholds often became the basis for decision making.

These thresholds were typically presented in one of two ways. In the first case, some minimum number of residents would be identified before a particular project was deemed feasible. For example, a new hospital might require a minimum of 50,000 residents within some geographic area that did not have ready access to a hospital. In another example, a catchment area of 250,000 residents might be considered necessary to support a cardiac catherization laboratory. Note that these figures are typically linked to some geographic area, defined either administratively (e.g., a county or a health planning district) or in terms of distance (e.g., within 50 miles or within 20-minutes driving time). More refined threshold measures have attempted to focus on the affected populations rather than the total population. For example, guidelines for an obstetrical unit or geriatric program may specify a certain number of childbearing-age women or residents over 65 years of age, respectively.

The other approach has been to specify some ratio of resources to population,

Box 4.6

Determining Practice Opportunities for a New Internist

The Stork-Netzel Consulting Agency in Omaha, Nebraska, was approached by a female physician who recently had completed residency training in internal medicine. She was interested in practice opportunities in the Minneapolis-St. Paul metropolitan area. The issues addressed by the consultants concerned the supply of internists in the market vis-à-vis the population (including population characteristics), the relative merits of different sites within the market, options for group practice and hospital affiliation, and the influence of HMOs and PPOs in the Twin Cities area.

Several organizations (e.g., the Minnesota Medical Association) were contacted regarding information about internal medicine physicians practicing in the state of Minnesota. It was found that there were 217 internists in Minneapolis and 105 internists in St. Paul in 1990. These physicians were distributed over 93 practices (61 in Minneapolis and 32 in St. Paul). Population estimates for both cities were available through a data vendor, and internist-to-population ratios were calculated for each market. The ratio for Minneapolis was one intern for every 4201 persons and for St. Paul one intern for every 6209 persons. Using Graduate Medical Education Advisory Committee (GMENAC) guidelines regarding the recommended internist-to-population ratio (1 for every 3500 persons), the initial judgment was that the Minneapolis-St. Paul market had a "shortage" of internists.

The locational aspect of the analysis required the consideration of many factors, including a determination of the sites of existing internal medicine practices as well as the location of acute care hospitals. At this point in the analysis another factor—the sex of the internist—was introduced. This became a consideration because recent studies had shown that women have a strong preference for female medical specialists. Out of the 93 practices identified, 29 included female internists as group members.

Taking into account the number of existing practices (female members considered), the presence or absence of an acute care hospital (presence was seen as a plus), population size data (smaller internist-to-population ratios were seen as a plus), along with other demographic data, five zip codes in Minneapolis and three in St. Paul were targeted for further evaluation. That is, the practice environment and demographic profile of these zip codes were judged to be consistent with the client's practice goals. The final step was to provide the client with a list of practices within those zip code areas to approach regarding possible affiliation. Armed with appropriate demographically based market data, the internist was now much better informed for the purpose of practice decision-making.

for example, the number of hospital beds per 1000 population, the number of alcohol and drug treatment "slots" per 100,000 population, or the number of physicians per 1000 population. This approach is more useful as a guide for planning, although data from the first approach can be converted into such ratios.

These thresholds can be utilized as both guidelines and standards. In the latter case, they might be used to assess the adequacy of existing facilities. The extent to which an area is underserved or overserved can be determined by applying these standards, assuming that an acceptable standard is available. If the guideline for hospital beds is 4 beds per 1000 population, this figure can be used to determine adequacy. If there are more than 4 beds per 1000 population, the area might be judged to be overbedded. Conversely, if the ratio is less than four, the area might be regarded as underbedded.

Similarly, such standards are utilized to determine the adequacy of physician supply. In this case, different specialties have different thresholds. A population of 4000 residents may be required to support a family practitioner, but perhaps 20,000 residents are needed to support an ophthalmologist. Box 4.6 addresses the issue of thresholds from a private sector perspective.

It should be noted that there are no widely accepted criteria for what is considered "adequate" for health care resources. The determination of guidelines often turns out to be a political rather than a scientific issue. Since no agencies exist in most communities to enforce such guidelines, they generally serve as a rule of thumb and not a hard standard. However, the US Public Health Service uses such standards as a basis for officially designating "health professions shortage areas."

REFERENCES

Barton, L. J. (1997). A shoulder to live on: Assisted living in the US. *American Demographics* (July):45–51.

Bogue, D. J. (1985). *The Population of the United States*. New York: Free Press.

Fay, R., Passel, J., and Robinson, J. G. (1988). *The Coverage of Population in the 1980 Census*. US Census Publication PHC80-E4. Washington, DC: US Government Printing Office.

Haub, C. (1987). Understanding population projections. *Population Bulletin*, Vol. 42, No. 4. Washington, DC: Population Reference Bureau.

Pol, L., and Thomas, R. (1997). *Demography for Business Decision Making*. Westport, CT: Greenwood Press.

Robey, B. (1989). Two hundreds years and counting: The 1990 census. *Population Bulletin*, Vol. 44, No. 1. Washington, DC: Population Reference Bureau.

Shryock, H. S., Siegel, J., and Associates (1973). *The Methods and Materials of Demography*. Washington, DC: US Government Printing Office.

Tayman, J., and Swanson, D. A. (1996). On the utility of population forecasts. *Demography* 33(November):523–528.

US Bureau of the Census. (1988). *Statistical Abstract of the United States, 1988*. Washington, DC: US Government Printing Office.

US Bureau of the Census (1994). *County and City Data Book 1994*. Washington, DC: US Government Printing Office.

US Bureau of the Census. (1996). *Statistical Abstract of the United States, 1996*. Washington, DC: US Government Printing Office.

US Bureau of the Census. (1999). *Statistical Abstract of the United States*. Washington, DC: US Government Printing Office.

US Bureau of the Census. (2000). Website (www.census.gov/population/estimates/nation/intfile/ _/.text)

ADDITIONAL RESOURCES

Anderson, M., and Fienberg, S. E. (1999). *Who Counts?* New York: Russell Sage Foundation.

Fosler, R. S., Alonso, W., Meyer, J. E., and Kern, R. (1990). *Demographic Change and the American Future*. Pittsburgh, PA: University of Pittsburgh Press.

Robey, B. (1985). *The American People*. New York: Dutton.

US Bureau of the Census. (2000). *Geographic Areas Reference Manual*. www.census.gov/geo/www/ gaim.html

CHAPTER 5

Population Composition

INTRODUCTION

While population size, concentration, and distribution provide a general picture of a market area, additional information on the composition of a population is necessary to fully appreciate the characteristics of a population. Since not all individuals or groups are at equal risk of becoming ill or consuming health services. Demographic factors such as age, income level, and sex provide valuable information for identifying individuals and groups with greater or lesser than average risk. Together, these variables are labeled compositional measures.

Population composition refers to the demographic makeup of persons within a geographic area. The composition of an area's population is useful in projecting the incidence of disease and death, and thus health care needs and demand. Two communities of equal size do not have the same health care needs if one has a younger, more affluent and racially homogeneous population than the other. Health-related behavior, such as the percentage of persons who smoke cigarettes, may vary as well.

Knowledge regarding changing demographic composition over time is also important. Though the present demographic composition of a given area may indicate a relatively low level of demand for a specific health service, the impact of fertility, mortality, and migration processes (Chapters 6, 7, and 8, respectively) or its present composition may result in a much different level of demand in the future.

Variables related to population composition are usually thought of as descriptive. Initially, their usefulness is derived from their ability to profile a population in terms of its traits. An area's age distribution, racial makeup, income level, and dominant religion are the types of characteristics that give a population its "personality." When these variables are related to health status and health behavior, however, they go beyond description and become powerful predictors of the health status of a population and its patterns of health services utilization. The use of composition-based models to predict and understand health phenomena are an important component of demographic research.

When compositional characteristics are merged with health care indicators, a great deal of insight can be gained into the utilization and delivery of services. For example, research has shown that higher-income patients undergoing dialysis treatment are substantially more likely to receive kidney transplants than lower-income patients. In a study of Medicare beneficiaries, whites had more physician office visits, more ambulatory surgeries, more cancer treatments, and more laboratory tests than African Americans after controlling for the social and economic differences in the two populations (Lee et al., 1997). Both lower income and more hazardous occupations have been linked to higher levels of mortality (Duleep, 1989; Moore and Hayward, 1990). Affluent women are more likely to give birth by cesarean section than poor women. In one study the cesarean section rate for women in families with incomes of $11,000 or less was 13.2% versus 22.9% for women with family incomes over $30,000 (Winslow, 1989). Hypertension, often called the "silent killer," is a disorder heavily concentrated within the low-income population, and poor people are less likely than the affluent to be on a treatment regime designed to counteract the disease.

It may be of passing interest to note that a population is 15% elderly (age 65 and over), 40% African American, mostly at a working-class income level, has an average educational level of the tenth grade, and has an average family size of 3.5. This information becomes more than interesting when it is linked to health status and health behavior. These facts can be converted to information on the death rate, the level of sickness and disability affecting the population, the type of health problems that can be anticipated, the number of hospital admissions, the number of surgeries to be performed, and the demand for various medical specialists, among many other factors.

Information of this type has become crucial in the planning and management of health services. The list of attributes and compositional factors can be expanded beyond traditional demographic measures to include factors such as health insurance status. Uninsured persons report more difficulties in accessing needed care, are less likely to have a regular health care provider, and rate the care that they receive as lower in quality compared to persons who have health insurance coverage (Schoen et al., 1997). They also suffer from a higher mortality rate (Rogers et al., 1999). The level and type of services needed can be accurately predicted only if these compositional variables are available to supplement data on population distribution size.

COMPOSITIONAL MEASURES

For purposes of this volume, compositional factors are divided into two categories: biosocial and sociocultural. *Biosocial characteristics* are those that have an underlying biological or physical component. As such, they tend to be "ascribed" characteristics present at birth and not amenable to change. The biosocial factors include age, sex, race, and ethnicity. With the exception of ethnicity, all are rooted squarely in biology, although for those of mixed race parentage, issues regarding race are blurred. Ethnicity has its basis in a common cultural heritage, but endogenous marriage within ethnic groups often results in the development of a gene pool that fosters common physical characteristics. Biosocial characteristics have significant social connotations in that there are behaviors associated with persons who have various combinations of ascribed characteristics.

Sociocultural factors are those associated with the operation of the social system. Sociocultural factors, in US society at least, are primarily "achieved" rather than ascribed. These are not traits one is born with but ones that are acquired (voluntarily and involuntarily) and reflect one's position in the social system. Unlike biosocial factors, sociocultural factors are amenable to change. The most frequently utilized sociocultural factors are marital status–living arrangements–family structure, income, education, occupation–industry, and religion. Each variable is discussed in turn in the sections that follow.

Biosocial Factors

The biosocial characteristics of a population are identified by researchers through questions asked in censuses and surveys and/or through government or administrative records such as birth or death certificates, tax filings, Medicare and Medicaid records, and Social Security reports. In each instance, the person providing the information is asked to disclose his or her own age, sex, and racial–ethnic identity. However, in cases where data for an entire family or household are being requested, the person completing the form may provide data for other individuals. In most such situations, a reference person provides data for all members of a household.

Age.   *Age* is measured in chronological terms beginning at a person's date-of-birth. Age questions take two forms. Individuals may be asked to disclose their age at last birthday or simply to provide their date of birth. In the latter case, exact age is derived by subtracting the birth date from the current or reference date. For example, a person born on October 31, 1970, is considered to be 29 years old at the time of the 2000 census (i.e., April 1, 2000). In general, it is thought that age data in the United States are of good quality, though some age "heaping" is seen for milestone years such as 21, 62, 65, 100, and for years that end in zero. A larger than expected number of persons reported at certain ages is evidence that some respondents are not accurate in reporting their age.

Age data are usually grouped in intervals (e.g., the number of persons aged 20 to 24) to simplify data presentation. Standard intervals are 5 years in length, with the exception of the youngest intervals (under 1, 1 to 4), and the oldest (age 85 and above). However, users of these data should keep in mind that there is no substantive reason for utilizing these particular intervals. Others that are more relevant to the health care issue at hand may be more appropriate, such as the identification of a 12-to-17 age group for purposes of studying adolescent health. In addition, means, medians, and measures of statistical dispersion also are calculated and used as indicators of the overall age distribution. Age data are generally aggregated for a specific geographic unit (e.g., census block, zip code, or market area).

Sex. The *sex* or *gender* of an individual is perhaps the most straightforward attribute to determine, given that there are only two possible responses, male and female. Sex composition has important implications in all societies and has a major impact on health status and health behavior. In the study of health-related factors, the relative number of males and females within a service area is of paramount importance. The sex distribution is typically presented in terms of percentage breakdown (e.g., 52% female and 48% male) or converted into a "sex ratio" (i.e., the number of males per 100 females). Because of the simplicity of measurement and its importance in the study of health care issues, analyses of sex differentials for a variety of health-related concerns are frequently conducted.

Race and Ethnicity. Race and ethnicity are at the same time biologically determined and socially constructed. Racial identity is based on physical characteristics such as skin color. Ethnic identification, on the other hand, is based on a common cultural heritage. *Racial* groups include whites, African Americans, Asians (several subgroups), and Native Americans (including Alaska Natives). Since race is a societally determined concept, racial categories vary from society to society. *Ethnic* identification requires a person to specify ancestry or national origin, such as Hispanic–Latino (several subgroups), Italian, German, or Thai. Subgroup totals are often summed and presented as an aggregate such as are figures for the Hispanic–Latino population.

Racial–ethnic identification is less clear than that for age or sex because the guidelines for placement in a category are not well defined. With regard to race, the lack of clarity is the result of the fact that millions of Americans are of mixed parentage. Many individuals may not even know their racial background; when they identify themselves as African American or Asian American, for example, placement in that group may be as much a product of historical association (e.g., I was raised by African Americans, I live with African Americans, therefore I am African American) as one of biological distinction. The same can be said for ethnic identification, where historical association plays a bigger role than for race, given the lack of distinctive physiological features.

The racial and ethnic characteristics of a population are determined by asking respondents in censuses and surveys to identify the appropriate racial and/or ethnic group(s) to which they belong. The option for respondents to choose more than one racial category is being offered for the first time for the census scheduled for 2000 (US Bureau of the Census, 1997b; O'Hare, 1998). In some instances, persons may claim membership in both a racial group and an ethnic group, for example, an African American of Hispanic heritage.

Sociocultural Factors

Marital Status–Living Arrangements–Family Structure. Marital status, living arrangements, and family structure are all ways of looking at household characteristics. Historically, marital status was the primary measure used for this phenomenon. However, as the traditional family gave way to new household organizational structures, other measures of household characteristics became necessary. Individuals are grouped into four or five marital status categories: married, separated, widowed, divorced, or never married.

Several pieces of information are required to specify living arrangements.* First, the identification of households must take place. A *household* is made up of one or more persons living in a housing unit. A *housing unit* is defined as one or more rooms that comprise separate living quarters. To meet the separate living quarters standard, residents must have access to the unit from the outside or through a common hall and have a kitchen or cooking equipment for exclusive use. Therefore, individual apartments and duplex halves are separate housing units, while dormitories and military barracks are not; the latter are referred to as *group quarters*.

Establishing whether or not persons in a housing unit or elsewhere constitute a family is also important. A *family* is defined as two or more persons related by blood, marriage, or adoption who live together. As part of census and survey inquiries, questions are asked about the relationship among persons living in households and other domiciles. If the relationship described meets the family definition requirement, those persons are considered a family. Two unrelated persons living in the same housing unit are designated as a household; if they are related, they are classified as both a household and family. When data for households and families are published, the first distinction made is between persons who live in households and those who live in group quarters. Households are then subdivided between family and nonfamily categories. Family households are distinguished from nonfamily households based on the marital status of their members and whether or not spouses are present.

This distinction between households is important for several reasons. Family households have legal standing, while nonfamily households most often have

---

*See US Bureau of the Census (1998) for a more detailed discussion of the definition of households, housing units, and families.

none. Family households are typically larger than nonfamily households. Family household income is typically greater. The health service needs of family and nonfamily households differ as well, not to mention the differences found in health insurance coverage. In the final analysis, whether members of a housing unit are "related" by marriage, blood, friendship, convenience, or some other basis has important implications for health care.

Income.   *Income* statistics generally refer to income received in a particular year and are collected in one of two ways. Income data are collected in terms of absolute dollars (e.g., $25,500 per year) or for a predetermined interval (e.g., $20,000 to $24,999, $25,000 to $29,999). In most instances, respondents are asked to disclose the amount of money income they earned from all sources during the previous year. Income data may be collected on an individual or for all members of the household or family collectively. Additional detail may be obtained on the source of income (e.g., wages and salaries, interest, or income from estates and trusts) for the individual and/or the family–household. Income data are typically presented in intervals, and summary measures like median household income are often used.

Education.   *Education* is typically stated in terms of years of school completed and/or degrees attained. Persons may be asked to report the number of years of schooling they have completed (e.g., completion of high school equals 12 and college graduate equals 16). Alternatively, respondents may be asked about the degrees they have completed (e.g., associates degree or masters degree). Educational attainment is frequently expressed in mean or median years, though an analysis of the distribution of years of education completed by individuals in a population is often important.

Work Status–Occupation–Industry.   *Work status*, *occupation*, and *industry* data all relate to one's position in the labor force. These data are collected through a variety of sources. Work status is a more general heading and includes information on labor force participation, employment history, and episodes of unemployment. For individuals who are employed, additional information on the number of hours worked may be collected. Part-time and full-time classifications may be used based on the number of hours per week and weeks per year worked. Occupation refers to the kind of work a person normally does. Examples of specific occupations include registered nurse, gasoline engine assembler, and teacher's aide. The very large number of occupations is often aggregated into nine or ten major groupings (e.g., professional and technical, sales, and management). Industry refers to the business or industry within which the occupation is performed, for example, health services, publishing, or retail sales.

Occupation and industry data from individuals and businesses are assigned code numbers developed for the standard industrial code (SIC) listing and the dictionary of occupational titles (DOC). SIC and DOC data for market or service areas are particularly valuable in that they provide information regarding where people work and the type of work they perform. This information provides clues to the level of insurance coverage and the extent and type of occupational injuries that can be anticipated. Recently, the North American Industry Classification System (NAICS) replaced the old SIC system. NAICS is an improvement over SIC because it identifies more industries, particularly in the service sector (US Bureau of the Census, 2000). In addition, the North American Product Classification System has been introduced.

Religion. Questions regarding *religious affiliation* or level of religiosity are typically not included in censuses, government-sponsored surveys (one exception is the National Health Interview Survey), or through any government registration system. However, data collected through other surveys (e.g., the Louis Harris Poll), health care administrative records (e.g., hospital admission forms), and church registries can provide partial information on religious affiliation. The types of questions usually asked concern religious affiliation (e.g., Roman Catholic), level of participation (e.g., number of times attending church per month), and degree of religiosity (e.g., depth of beliefs). Because health care-related questions infrequently are asked at the same time religious inquiries are made, the relationship between the two factors is not well understood.* The smaller the geographic unit, the less likely that data on religion will be available. Box 5.1 presents methods for accessing compositional data via the world wide web.

MEASURES OF COMPOSITIONAL VARIATION

Compositional traits are often expressed in proportion terms (e.g., 25% of the population in Orange County, Florida, has a college education or above), along with summary measures such as means and medians. These summary measures often can provide useful insights into the nature of a population. When using percentage distribution information, it is generally better to include data for several categories for comparison purposes (perhaps the entire distribution), even though the focus may be on only one level of aggregation. This will give the reader a more complete picture of the conditions being addressed.

The mean refers to the arithmetic average and the median to the midpoint of a distribution, and these two measures of central tendency are likely to be used for

---

*Recent research by Hummer et al. (1999) shows that the difference in life expectancy is over 7 years more for persons who attend church more than once per week compared with those who do not attend at all.

Box 5.1

Accessing Census Data On-Line
http://www.census.gov/

New technology has made demographic data easier to access and use than ever before. Data from the 1990 Census, Census Bureau surveys, and other census-related activities (e.g., population projections) are readily accessed via CD-ROMs at little or no cost. Data required for specific market areas can be downloaded from compact disks (CDs) to diskette and analyzed using one of many available spreadsheet software applications. Now, even easier access is possible via the Internet.

The Census Bureau's website contains a wealth of demographic data. The information is organized by category, with the main menu containing eight major categories including *News*, *Access Tools*, *Subjects A–Z*, *Search*, and *Related Sites*. Under subjects A–Z, for example, there is an alphabetized list of subjects that can be accessed. Key word searches also can be performed. The ability to manipulate a mouse, that is, simply pointing and clicking, is the main skill needed to view, print, purchase, and/or electronically transfer information. Each of the main menu categories is organized into submenu items. Submenus allow the user to identify the states and counties for which the data are needed. Additional menu-driven commands allow for the data to be printed and/or electronically transferred to a hard drive or diskette. The website is entered using this Internet address: http://www.census.gov/.

The Census Bureau website is much more than a data archive. National, state, and substate maps are available and these can be printed directly or electronically transferred. Information about the organization and history of the Bureau of the Census is also available. Press releases, organized by topic, can be viewed. For example, the authors of this volume have a research interest in health insurance coverage. Examining press releases under the topic *Health* on the menu bar yields several useful press releases on recent publications based on Current Population Survey data. Specific reports are referenced in the press releases and, if more information is needed, these can be purchased or in some instances accessed electronically.

CD-ROMs, computer tapes, publications, and map products also can be ordered through the Census Bureau's website. Clicking on *Catalog* calls up descriptions of data available on CD-ROM. Purchases are made by telephone, mail, or fax.

Finally, Census Online provides a "bridge" to other websites that offer demographic data. Websites at the Universities of Michigan, Missouri, and California–Berkeley, for example, provide information on and access to maps and data on CDs that can be printed or electronically transferred.

different purposes. It is generally better to rely on the median, though the use of both these statistics, along with an examination of the entire distribution, is the best approach. A given mean or median may be the result of an infinite number of combinations of distributional data. Therefore, utilizing the mean or median without analyzing the distribution from which those figures are derived may result in an incomplete understanding of the data. This is particularly important when examining income and age distributions.

Many discussions of composition are descriptive and focus on simple percentage comparisons. However, there are a number of demographic measures that facilitate compositional analysis. Many of these methods are relatively simple to use, and those that are more complex are available through appropriate computer software.

Most of these methods require that the population be expressed in a distributional format. That is, the population is divided into different categories based on the compositional factors being considered. For example, the population of the United States is frequently subdivided by age, race, and sex categories. The number of age groupings is generally large—nine or more if 10-year intervals are used. The number of racial categories is usually small (e.g., white, African American, and other). Given two classifications for sex, three for race, and 18 for age, there would be 108 pieces of sex–race–age data in a typical distribution format. The advantage of having data at this level of precision is that a multitude of arithmetic and statistical operations on the data are possible, all of which result in increased insight into the characteristics of an area.

Population Pyramids

Population distributions are sometimes presented visually in the form of *population pyramids*. The age–sex distribution of a population is typically presented in a series of stacked bars (Newell, 1987, pp. 25–26; Pressat, 1972, pp. 263–276). Each bar represents the percentage of the total population at that age, though absolute numbers may be used as well. The bar also has two sides; on the left the percentage for males is displayed, and on the right is the same information for females. Pyramids that are "bottom heavy" have younger age structures, while old age structures demonstrate consistent age-to-age percentages and appear bullet-shaped.

Figures 5.1 and 5.2 present the population pyramids for Garfield and Sarpy Counties in Nebraska for 1990, created by a readily available computer software package. Garfield County is a rural county located in the north central part of the state. Sarpy County is part of the Omaha Metropolitan Statistical Area and is the fastest growing county in the state. As can be seen, the age structure of Sarpy county is much younger and has a lower "center of gravity." Garfield County has a top-heavy distribution. About 25% of the population of Garfield County is age

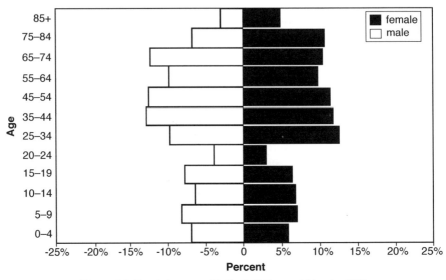

Figure 5.1. Population pyramid, Garfield County, Nebraska, 1990.

65 and over while the corresponding proportion for Sarpy County is approximately 6%. The median age differences are large, with median ages of approximately 40 years for Garfield County and 29 years for Sarpy County.

Dependency Ratios

A dependency ratio is the quotient of an area's dependent population divided by its theoretically "supporting" population. Dependent and supporting populations are defined in terms of economic dependence and support (Bogue, 1969, pp. 154–156). The supporting population in the United States usually is considered those individuals between the ages of 18 (or 20) and 64, while dependent populations are those under age 18 (or 20) and over age 64. Dependency and support are general notions regarding economic activity, and the population aged 18 (or 20) to 64 is seen as economically active (income earning).

The *youth dependency ratio* for the United States in 1950 can be calculated as follows:

$$\frac{\text{number of persons under age 20}}{\text{number of persons 20–64}} = \frac{51,100,000}{87,327,000} = 0.58$$

This ratio of 0.58 converts to 1.72 persons of approximate working age for every person under age 20. By the year 2000, the ratio will shrink to 0.49 or 2.04 persons of approximate working age for each person under age 20.

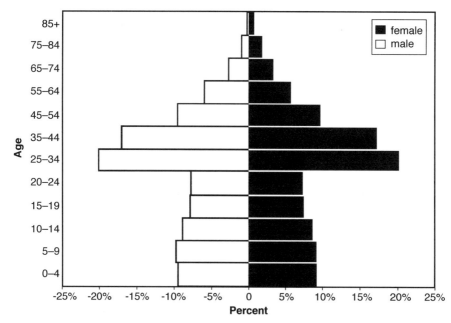

Figure 5.2. Population pyramid, Sarpy County, Nebraska, 1990.

The *age dependency ratio* for 1950 can be calculated as follows:

$$\frac{\text{number of persons aged 65 and over}}{\text{number of persons 20–64}} = \frac{12,270,000}{87,327,000} = 0.14$$

This ratio of 0.14 converts to 7.14 persons of approximate working age for each person age 65 and over. In the year 2000 the ratio will increase to 0.21, or 4.76 persons of approximate working age for each person age 65 and over. The age dependency ratio is frequently used to illustrate the growing burden of persons aged 65 and over on the Social Security or Medicare systems.

The *total dependency ratio* takes the sum of both dependent populations (under age 20 and over age 65) and divides by the number of persons aged 20 to 64. In 1950, the total dependency ratio was 0.72, or 1.39 persons of approximate working age for every person under age 20 or over age 64. In 2000, the total dependency ratio will be 0.70, or 1.43 when inverted. As can be seen, the total dependency ratio is virtually the same for both years, despite the substantial rise in the age dependency ratio. The increase in the older population has been offset by a decrease in the younger population.

These ratios exhibit a great deal of variability across geographic areas. For example, in 1990 the youth dependency ratios for Tallahassee and St. Petersburg,

Florida, were 0.41 and 0.49, respectively. In contrast, the age dependency ratios were 0.14 and 0.48, respectively (US Bureau of the Census, 1992: Table 61). In other words, St. Petersburg had approximately two workers for every person age 65 and over, while Tallahassee had seven!

Sex Ratios

The sex ratio is calculated by dividing the total number of males by the total number of females. This ratio can be calculated for all ages combined or for specific age groupings. For 1996, the sex ratio calculation for all ages in the United States was:

$$\frac{131,883,000}{138,119,000} = 0.95 \text{ (or 95 men for every 100 women)}$$

Since the age distribution for males and females is usually different, an overall sex ratio may mask some information. For example, for the category persons under 5 years of age, the sex ratio is 1.05 (or 105 males for every 100 females). At ages 25 to 29, the ratio declines to 1.0. At ages 65 to 74 and 75 and over, the sex ratio is 0.81 and 0.58, respectively; thus, at ages 65 to 74 and 75 and over there are 123 and 172 women for every 100 men, respectively.

Sex ratios can show even more variability for smaller units of geography. For example, in Florida the ratio of males to females for all ages was 0.94 in 1980 but was 0.89 in 1990 (US Bureau of the Census 1992; table 18). However, in St. Petersburg, Florida, the sex ratios were 0.87 in 1980 and 1.01 in 1990, respectively (US Bureau of the Census, 1992: Table 61).

Cohort Analysis

Another way to examine compositional data is through *cohort analysis*. A cohort is a group of persons with a common characteristic. Cohort analysis typically involves following a cohort over time to measure such facts as the outcome of exposure to toxic material, the impact of health care intervention, or the increase or decrease in the prevalence of a disease. This characteristic is one that the data user finds valuable for understanding the issue at hand. For example, military personnel who were exposed to Agent Orange during the Vietnam war or persons born during a particular time interval might be the cohort of interest.

Age is the most frequent basis for cohort identification used by demographers. Age cohorts are identified by grouping together persons of similar age. The US cohort aged 50 to 54, which currently contains the oldest of the baby boomers, is made up of persons who were born between 1946 and 1950. The "notch" cohort, which has received a great deal of attention because of its unique status with respect to Social Security benefits, was born between 1917 and 1920. It is assumed, though not always correctly, that persons within a cohort share experiences and behavior because of their common characteristic.

Cohort analysis is sometimes used as a basis for ascribing experiences and behavior patterns to a cohort when individual data are not available. Cohort analysis can range from measuring the change in the number and proportion of persons in various age groupings over time to ascertaining how cohort experiences affect different types of behavior (Glenn, 1977). Cohort-to-cohort comparisons allow an assessment of change in cohort behavior over time.

Cohort analysis can be particularly useful in a health care setting. For example, persons born during a particular time interval might be the population of interest. Since health problems are frequently age specific, cohort analysis can determine future patterns of morbidity and mortality. Age cohorts also may exhibit varying types of health-related behavior or levels of exposure to a particular type of carcinogen that is unique to the age group in question. The cohort in question could be tracked over time to provide insights, for example, into disease prevalence.

In a comparison of age cohorts, one task is to examine the relative size of specific cohorts over a set period of time. The population of persons age 60 to 64 (the cohort born approximately between 1906 and 1910) numbered 8.6 million in 1970. By 1975, that cohort was replaced by a larger one (born between 1911 and 1915); the total number of persons in this group was 9.1 million. The size of the 60-to-64 age cohort was 10.1, 10.6, and 10.2 million in 1980, 1990, and 1998, respectively, and is projected to increase to over 16 million in 2010 (Campbell, 1997). To the extent that persons aged 60 to 64 are unique in their needs and demands, the information on fluctuating cohort sizes is quite useful.

Studying the transition or aging of a cohort from one period to the next involves the use of mortality data and a technique called survival analysis, both of which are discussed in Chapter 7. For example, the cohort aged 65 to 69 in 1995 was made up of those persons aged 60 to 64 in 1990 minus those who died during the interval (not accounting for immigration). Tracking change in cohort size tells the analyst a great deal about the health service demands that are likely to characterize this cohort in the future.

Cohort analysts need to take into consideration that population change in the United States is affected by factors other than mortality. Persons are added at the youngest ages via births and this establishes the initial size of a cohort. Once a cohort is born, its size change can only be altered through death, in-migration, and out-migration. By factoring emigration and immigration into the analysis, however, the analyst may be violating some of the "spirit" of cohort analysis. Considering additions or subtractions due to any other factor beside births or deaths complicates the comparison over time. For example, if the health status and health behavior of a cohort of persons aged 65 to 69 in Orlando, Florida, in 1997 is being tracked for 5 years, the fact that the population aged 70 to 74 has increased 5 years later (in 2002) by virtue of in-migration confounds the analysis. The analyst is no longer measuring the mortality–behavior experiences of only the initial cohort and must isolate the recent in-migrants for a separate analysis. In-migrant contribution to growth by age interval is examined more closely in Chapter 8.

In the military example introduced earlier, the cohort of personnel exposed to Agent Orange in Vietnam was analyzed to determine whether they had higher rates for selected conditions thought to be related to their exposure. This cohort can be compared to other military cohorts who were not exposed, and statistical tests can be used to determine whether any identified morbidity or mortality rate differences are likely to have occurred by chance. Veterans of the Gulf War may be studied in the same way, but the analysis is more complicated, because Gulf War syndrome may well be the product of several different types of exposures (e.g., inoculations and burning oil).

As stated earlier, one health care application of cohort analysis involves the tracking of a cohort's morbidity–mortality experiences over time. The cohort under age 5 in the United States in 1950 (approximately 16.1 million persons) will be aged 50 to 54 in the year 2000 (a projection of 17.2 million persons). Mortality has reduced this cohort somewhat, but immigration has more than offset the number of deaths. Assuming that immigrants can be identified and separated, the goal is to follow only the cohort that was under 5 and living in the United States in 1950. Health experiences, sickness, death, medical treatment, and preventive activities could be documented over a specified time period. The resulting profile would be very valuable in studying actual health-related events and in planning for the health care needs for this cohort in the future. Additional value is gained, moreover, if health experiences of several cohorts are compared, for example, the under 5 cohorts in 1950, 1960, 1970, 1980, and 1990. This would allow the analyst to study the relationship among improved medical technology, changes in health care strategies, exposure to environmental hazards, and health care experience.

Standardization

Population sizes between different areas vary, and without holding size differences constant, comparisons between two or more populations can be misleading. Rates can be used to control for differences in size, allowing for the comparison of data for two or more regions, states, metropolitan areas, or market areas with respect to mortality, morbidity, level of health care resources, or health practices. However, even a simple comparison of rates can lead to misleading conclusions.

For example, if two communities of 10,000 people were being compared and analysts found that one had twice the incidence of breast cancer as the other, would it be correct to assume that environmental, behavioral, and/or health care factors were responsible for the rate differences? While such factors may be able to provide some explanation for the observed differential, demographic explanations must be considered as well. The simplest demographic analysis would determine whether there were marked differences in the proportion of males and females between the two communities. In other words, a heavily female community (with a sex ratio of 0.90 or less) would clearly be expected to have more cases of breast cancer, *ceteris paribus*. Or suppose that one community has a much older age structure than the other. Since breast cancer is more common among older women, the older community would be expected to report more cases of breast cancer.

Up until this point, it has been argued that the age–sex structure differences in the two communities must be studied before cancer incidence is evaluated. Are there any other demographic variables that might help explain a difference in breast cancer rates between the two communities? The researcher may want to consider racial–ethnic compositional differences and/or any other demographic factors known to be associated with breast cancer (e.g., occupation). The ultimate goal is to account for as many of these factors as possible in order to eliminate any nonenvironmental or nonbehavioral explanations.

Standardization is used to control for competing demographic explanations (Barclay, 1958; Bogue, 1969, pp. 121–125; Pressat, 1972, pp. 101–106). As an example, a standard population is chosen and breast cancer rates for the two populations being compared are applied to the standard population's age and sex composition. A standard population (e.g., one of the communities involved) is used to hold age, sex, and other differences constant. Application of the other community's rates to the first community's population structure yields the number of cases that would occur *if* the community in question had the same age–sex composition as the first. An adjusted rate for the second community can then be calculated.

The simple example shown in Table 5.1 illustrates the advantages of adjusting for age and sex differences. Both communities are equal in size and have the same incidence of breast cancer. However, as seen in the table, community A has 50,000 females, while community B has 60,000 females. Because breast cancer is very rare in males, it makes better sense simply to calculate a female-specific rate. The new rate per 1000 females for communities A and B are 10.00 and 8.33, respectively.

However, suppose that community A had the same sex structure as that for community B. How many breast cancer cases would there be? The rate, 10 per 1000, would have to be multiplied by the size of the female population in community B, or 60,000. The result of 600 cases is 20% greater than the 500 cases observed. The same adjustment can be made in the other direction; that is, the number of expected breast cancer cases in community A (assuming it has the same rate as that of community B) can be calculated. Multiplying 8.33 per 1000 by 50,000 yields 416 cases, a 17% reduction from the 500 cases observed.

Table 5.1. Age–Sex Composition and Incidence of Breast Cancer
for Two Fictitious Communities

Age	Community A				Community B			
	Males	Females	Cases[a]	Rate[b]	Males	Females	Cases[a]	Rate[b]
60–64	13,000	13,000	100	7.69	10,000	12,000	100	8.33
65–69	12,000	12,000	75	6.25	10,000	12,000	100	8.33
70–74	10,000	10,000	75	7.50	12,000	14,000	100	7.14
75–79	8,000	8,000	125	15.42	10,000	12,000	100	8.33
80 and over	7,000	7,000	125	17.86	8,000	10,000	100	10.00
Total	50,000	50,000	500	10.00	40,000	60,000	500	8.33

[a]Cases of breast cancer.
[b]Rate per 1000 females.

The difference in age structure also may be addressed during standardization. First, a standard population (either community A or B) is chosen. The analyst might be interested in the rate that community A might have if it had community B's age structure. In this example, only the female population is utilized. The calculations are straightforward:

Age	Rate per 1000	Female population		Cases
0–67	7.69	12,000	=	92
65–69	6.25	12,000	=	75
70–74	7.50	14,000	=	105
75–79	15.62	12,000	=	187
80 and over	17.86	10,000	=	179
Total		60,000		638

The results show that, if community A had the same age structure as community B, there would have been 638 breast cancer cases, or an increase of about 6.3% over the observed figure. The new "adjusted" rate is 638/60,000, or 10.63 per 1000.

From an applied standpoint, the analyst may have hypothesized that health care conditions were the same in each community, given that each had the same initial "rate" of breast cancer. However, after adjusting for age and sex, that analyst might conclude that health conditions with respect to breast cancer in community A are more favorable than in community B. Of course, other factors would have to be considered before the analysis was complete.

This technique has been advanced through the application of log linear models to the same sets of data (Clogg and Eliason, 1988; Yu, 1989). The use of a log linear model addresses some of the shortcomings in traditional standardization techniques and allows for the isolation and identification of the effect of age structure as well as other variables on the rates being studied.

COMPOSITIONAL CHARACTERISTICS AND TRENDS FOR THE US POPULATION

Age

Age is the single most important compositional factor for many health care analyses. Table 5.2 provides a historical perspective on age structure in the United States. The data for 1900, 1950, and 1990 are from the decennial census of population and the data for 2000 are population projections.* The figure presented here is the Census Bureau's middle series projection (series 14) and assumes constant fertility and immigration rates from 1990 (the base year) to 2000, along with a slight increase in life expectancy (Campbell, 1997). Aside from the substantial increase in population size (+361%), the most marked shift over the 100-year period can be seen in the age structure. For example, while 4% of the population was 65 years old and over in 1900, the projected proportion of older persons for 2000 is nearly 13%. Looking at broader age categories, the comparative age distribution for 1900 and 2000 is as follows:

	1900	2000
Under age 20	43.3%	28.7%
20–49	43.8%	43.5%
50 and over	12.9%	26.6%

While the percentages for the middle age cohorts (ages 20 to 49) are virtually identical, the projected population for 2000 is clearly older.

The comparison between figures for 1950 and 2000 shows a considerable difference as well. Using the same age categories, the results are as follows:

	1950	2000
Under age 20	33.9%	28.7%
20–49	43.7%	43.5%
50 and over	22.4%	27.6%

Once again, the middle ages have virtually the same proportional representation. The 1900–1950 comparison shows a decrease of about 10% under age 20 and an

*Population estimates and projections are discussed in more detail in Chapter 9.

Table 5.2. Age Structure of the US Population, 1900–2000

Age	1900[a,b] Number	Percent	1950 Number	Percent	1990 Number	Percent	2000[c] Number	Percent
Under 5	9,171	11.8	16,164	10.7	18,846	7.5	18,987	6.9
5–9	8,874	11.4	13,200	8.8	18,055	7.2	19,920	7.3
10–14	8,080	10.4	11,119	7.4	17,187	6.9	20,057	7.3
15–19	7,556	9.7	10,617	7.0	17,759	7.1	19,820	7.2
20–24	7,335	9.4	11,482	7.6	19,133	7.7	18,257	6.6
25–29	6,529	8.4	12,242	8.1	21,229	8.5	17,722	6.3
30–34	5,556	7.1	11,517	7.6	21,908	8.8	19,511	7.1
35–39	4,965	6.4	11,246	7.5	19,977	8.0	22,180	8.1
40–44	4,247	5.4	10,204	6.8	17,790	7.1	22,479	8.2
45–49	3,455	4.4	9,070	6.0	13,821	5.5	19,806	7.2
50–54	2,943	3.8	8,272	5.5	11,368	4.6	17,224	6.3
55–59	2,211	2.8	7,235	4.8	10,473	4.7	13,307	4.8
60–64	1,791	2.3	6,059	4.0	10,618	4.2	10,654	3.9
65 and over	3,080	4.0	12,270	8.1	31,235	12.5	34,709	12.6
75 and over	—	—	—	—	13,137	5.3	16,575	6.0
Total	74,994		150,697		249,398		274,634	
Median age	22.9		30.2		32.8		35.7	

[a]Numbers for left most column under each year are expressed in thousands.
[b]Figures in right most column under each year reflect the percentage age distribution.
[c]Population projection (middle series from US Census Bureau).
SOURCE:US Bureau of the Census (1975), Table A 119–134; Campbell (1997); US Bureau of the Census (1998).

increase of 10% at 50 and over. Overall, the median age of the US population increases from less than 23 years in 1900 to almost 36 years in 2000.

While the data in Table 5.2 illustrate the substantial shifts in US age structure since 1900, they do not provide information regarding the internal variations that are reflected in their need for very different arrays of health services. Table 5.3 presents age structure data for the cities of Tallahassee and St. Petersburg, Florida, for 1990. Tallahassee is a fast-growing city housing two universities and is the capital of Florida. St. Petersburg to a great extent is a retirement community and currently is losing population. While St. Petersburg was more than three times the size of Tallahassee in 1980, the size difference is rapidly narrowing. In 1990, St. Petersburg was less than twice the size of Tallahassee.

Looking at the percentage distribution figures (in parentheses), substantial differences in age composition can be seen. Over 41% of the population of St. Petersburg is over age 44, and 32% is over age 54; the comparable percentages for Tallahassee are 22% and 14%. On the other hand, 44% of the Tallahassee population is aged 15 to 34; in St. Petersburg, 28% of the population falls in this age category. As noted earlier, the age dependency ratios for Tallahassee and St. Petersburg are 0.14 and 0.48, respectively.

Table 5.3. Age Structure Differences Between
Tallahassee and St. Petersburg, Florida, 1990

Age	Tallahassee		St. Petersburg	
	Number	Percent	Number	Percent
Under 5	6,868	5.5	14,281	6.0
5–9	6,778	5.4	13,154	5.5
10–14	6,358	5.1	12,133	5.1
15–19	13,276	10.6	13,419	5.6
20–24	23,946	15.2	14,585	6.1
25–34	22,269	17.9	38,708	16.2
35–44	17,136	13.7	33,597	14.1
45–54	9,744	7.8	22,754	9.5
55–64	7,352	5.9	23,053	9.7
65–74	6,453	5.2	?5,916	10.9
75 and over	4,493	3.6	27,029	11.3
Total	124,773		238,629	

SOURCE: US Bureau of the Census (1992), Table 61.

Overall, this comparison illustrates the radically different health care demand structures that can exist in different communities. Superficial observation indicates that obstetrical services are in greater demand in Tallahassee, while the number of geriatric specialists needed in St. Petersburg is large. Though national trends are instructive for comparison purposes, data for the market or service area under consideration are considerably more useful, especially when patterns such as those seen in Table 5.3 exist.

Sex

Additional insight into the nature of the population can result from adding sex as a variable to the examination of the age distribution. Age and sex data for the US population in 1998 are presented in Table 5.4. Of the 1998 estimated population 51% was female and 49% was male. There were more males than females at all age intervals under age 30, as a result of the ratio of male to female births of 105 to 100. Selective immigration by sex (i.e., more males) also contributes to the larger number of males at the younger ages. These two issues are addressed in greater detail in the chapters on fertility and migration.

At all ages above 30, females outnumber men. In fact, with each successively older cohort, the numerical difference increases. For example, at age 75 and over the sex ratio is 0.58 or 58 males for every 100 females. Stated conversely, 63% of this population is female and 37% male. As expected, the age structures of the male and female subpopulations are different. The male age structure is more than

Table 5.4. US Population by Age and Sex, 1998

Age	Total		Female		Male	
	Number	Percent	Number	Percent	Number	Percent
Under 5	19,117	7.1	9,336	6.8	9,780	7.4
5–9	20,024	7.4	9,773	7.1	10,252	7.8
10–14	19,371	7.1	9,451	6.8	9,920	7.5
15–19	19,426	7.2	9,470	6.9	9,955	7.5
20–24	17,451	6.5	8,598	6.2	8,853	6.7
25–29	18,568	6.9	9,289	6.7	9,279	7.0
30–34	20,189	7.5	10,143	7.3	10,046	7.6
35–39	22,579	8.4	11,333	8.2	11,246	8.5
40–44	21,811	8.1	11,013	8.0	10,798	8.2
45–49	18,813	7.0	9,588	6.9	9,225	7.0
50–54	15,707	5.8	8,071	5.8	7,635	5.8
55–59	12,401	4.6	6,443	4.7	5,957	4.5
60–64	10,261	3.8	5,413	3.9	4,847	3.7
65–74	18,365	6.8	10,141	7.3	8,224	6.2
75 and over	15,919	5.9	10,055	7.3	5,865	4.4
Total	270,002		138,119		131,883	
Median age	35.2		36.3		34.0	

SOURCE: Campbell (1997).

2 years "younger"; the median age for males is 34.0 and for females 36.3. The percentage distribution by age (in parentheses) within each category indicates the relative youth of the male population.

Race–Ethnicity

Data on the racial–ethnic composition of a population are also very useful. In 1990, whites, African Americans, and Hispanic–Latino persons comprised 77.1%, 12.8%, and 7.3% of the total US population, respectively. No other single racial or ethnic group approached even 1%. However, these data mask substantial regional and local variations in racial–ethnic composition (an issue addressed in Chapter 10). Furthermore, these summary data do not reflect the rapid increase in numbers experienced by some of these subgroups during the 1980s and 1990s. Immigrants from Mexico, Vietnam, and China, for example, not only have contributed to the growth of these ethnic groups in the United States, they also have contributed to changes in the demand for health care in many areas.

Table 5.5 presents historical data as well as projections for the three predominant racial–ethnic groups. Two observations based on these data are worthy of note. The first is the fact that the African-American and Hispanic–Latino popula-

Table 5.5. Population of the United States
by Race and Hispanic Origin, 1950–2000

Year	Total[a]	African American		Hispanic–Latino[b]	
		Number	Percent	Number	Percent
2000[c]	276,242	35,475	12.8	31,164	11.3
1990	249,395	30,598	12.3	22,558	9.0
1980	226,546	26,683	11.8	14,609	6.4
1970	203,235	22,581	11.1	10,500	5.2
1960	179,323	18,872	10.5	6,927	3.9
1950	151,325	15,045	9.9	4,012	2.7

[a]Numbers in thousands.
[b]Hispanic–Latino may be of any race.
[c]Projected.
SOURCES: US Bureau of the Census (1996), Tables 36 and 38; Development Associates (1982), Table 1–2; Bouvier et al. (1983), Table A-1.

tions are increasing much faster than the white population. In 1950, African-American and Hispanic–Latino persons combined made up 12.6% of the US population. By the year 2000 this figure is expected to increase to 24.1%. Differential growth is attributed to the somewhat higher fertility levels of these two populations—a factor discussed in the next chapter—as well as to younger age structures. The second observation is that the Hispanic–Latino population is increasing faster than the African-American population. Some projections even show the Hispanic–Latino population exceeding the African-American population in numbers early in the twenty-first century. These trends have marked implications for the provision of health services.

The Hispanic–Latino population was the youngest of the racial–ethnic groups in 1990, with nearly 49% of its members under age 25. Comparable percentages for the cohorts 25 or younger for whites and African Americans were 33% and 45%, respectively. As expected, at the older ages the percentages are reversed. For example, 26% of the white population was 50 years old or older; comparable percentages for the African-American and Hispanic–Latino populations were 17% and 14%, respectively. The age dependency ratios for the white, African-American, and Hispanic–Latino populations were 0.24, 0.15, and 0.09, respectively. The youth dependency ratios were 0.44, 0.65, and 0.70, respectively.

These data illustrate the importance of the joint effects of race–ethnicity and age on an area's population composition. In general, areas with a higher percentage of African-American and/or Hispanic–Latino persons will contain younger populations. However, areas with a higher proportion of Cuban Americans are exceptions, because this Hispanic–Latino subgroup has an older age structure. It also should be noted that younger populations such as those seen for African-

Americans and Hispanic–Latinos have greater potential for growth because a higher proportion of the female population is or will soon be in the childbearing years. Given the significant difference in age structure, the African-American and Hispanic–Latino populations will continue to grow more rapidly than the white.

Marital Status, Living Arrangements, and Family Structure

As noted earlier, a household is made up of one or more persons living in a housing unit, with a housing unit being defined as one or more rooms that comprise separate living quarters. A family is two or more persons related by blood, marriage, or adoption who live together. Table 5.6 provides historical data on household and family size in the United States. As can be seen, average household size declined by one person between 1940 and 1996, and at the later date the average was about two and two-thirds persons. A drop in family size also is evident, though the decline is not as large as that seen for households.

There are several explanations for these declines. Delayed age at marriage and the increase in the incidence of divorce have resulted in more single-person and smaller multiple-person households and families. At the older ages, longer life expectancies for women (discussed in Chapter 7) have resulted in more widows, and thus smaller households. The decline in fertility in the United States, which is addressed in Chapter 6, is reflected in a larger proportion of couples that are childless (by choice). Fewer children are born in those families who do have children.

Trends in the number of households and families by type (e.g., husband–wife, male head, female head) are changing the US social structure. Between 1940 and 1996, the number of all households increased by 285%, while family households rose by only 220%. As a result, the proportion of all households that were

Table 5.6. Median Household and Family Size
in the United States, 1940–1996.

Year	Median household size	Median family size
1996	2.65	3.20
1990	2.63	3.17
1980	2.76	3.29
1970	3.14	3.58
1960	3.33	3.67
1950	3.37	3.54
1940	3.67	3.76

SOURCE: US Bureau of the Census (1998), website http://www. census.gov/population/www/socdemo/hhfam.html.

classified as families declined from 92% to 70% over the 56-year period (US Bureau of the Census, 1998). In addition, female-headed families/households increased by 367% over the 56-year interval, and in 1996 comprised 12.6% of all households. Thus, of the more than 99 million households in existence in 1996, over 12 million were female-headed.

These same trends have affected parent–child relationships. In 1996, about 74% of all family households with children age 18 or younger had both parents present. If these same data are cross-tabulated by race and ethnicity, a more startling finding is made. While nearly 77% of white families with children have both parents present, the corresponding percentages for Hispanic–Latino and African-American families are 57 and 41, respectively. Nearly 53% of all children-present African-American families are mother-only families (US Bureau of the Census, 1997a: Table 76). Some observers contend that the nation's changing household structure will have more implications for health care than any other trend besides the aging of the population.

An additional household composition variable of particular significance for the delivery of health services is the percentage of persons who live alone. Successful convalescence and the delivery of care at home are often dependent on the presence of another member of the household. Table 5.7 presents the percentages of persons living alone categorized by age and sex. As can be seen, the percentage of persons living alone increases substantially with age. And it is at the oldest ages that persons are most likely to "need" someone else in their household to assist in home health care delivery. There is also a wide difference in these percentages by sex. At the ages 75 and over, over one fourth of all males and one half of all females live alone (Saluter, 1997).

Given the relatively large number of compositional factors and the vast array

Table 5.7. Percent of
Population Living Alone
by Age and Sex, 1995

Age group	Males	Females
18 and over	11.4	14.7
18–24	5.0	4.7
25–34	10.8	7.0
35–44	10.8	6.6
45–64	11.2	13.5
65–74	14.0	32.1
75 and over	22.8	53.5

SOURCE: US Bureau of the Census (1998), website http://www.census.gov/population/www/socdemo/hh-fam.html.

Table 5.8. Selected Compositional Characteristics
for the United States, 1970–1995

Characteristic	1970	1980	1990	1995
Percent with at least high school[a]	52.3	66.5	77.6	81.7
Percent with 4 years of college or more[a]	10.7	16.2	21.3	23.6
Median household income[b]	$32,229	$32,795	$34,914	$34,076
Median family income[b]	$36,410	$38,930	$41,223	$40,611
Percentage labor force in manufacturing	26.4	22.1	18.0	16.4
Percentage labor force in services	25.9	29.0	33.0	35.2
Percentage of females in labor force[c]	42.6	51.1	54.7	59.0

[a]Population 25 years and older.
[b]In 1995 dollars.
[c]Females 16 years and older.
SOURCE: US Bureau of the Census (1997a), Tables 243, 649, 718, 724.

of ways that these variables can be expressed, choices must be made regarding the manner in which population structure is presented. In some instances the choice of measure significantly will alter interpretation, a point worthy of attention in all analyses. Table 5.8 presents data for additional compositional variables (education, income, occupation, and labor force status), with multiple measures of each except for the last. The justification for choosing these indicators is that they serve as evidence of significant change in US population structure over the last three decades. The data are for four time periods: 1970, 1980, 1990, and 1995.

Education, Income, and the Labor Force

As can be seen in Table 5.8, the educational level of the US population increased substantially over the 25-year time interval. The percentage of population aged 25 and over with at least high-school education rose even more markedly, from 52% to nearly 82%, and the proportion with 4 or more years of college rose from 11 to 24%.

Conclusions concerning recent trends in income depend on the measure chosen for analysis. Median household and median family income rose over the interval, though the proportional increase for household income (5.7%) was smaller than that for family income (11.5%). In terms of real dollars, both figures have lost ground to inflation since 1970.

The last three rows in the table present selected data on occupation and labor force characteristics. Since 1970, the percentage of employed persons aged 16 and over working in manufacturing occupations has declined approximately 10 percentage points to 16.4% of all persons employed. The trend toward a services-dominated occupational structure is clearly seen, with the table indicating a rise of nearly 10 percentage points over the 25-year period. Finally, the percentage of all women aged 16 and over who are in the labor force (working or actively seeking work) has increased by more than 16 percentage points.

Statistics for education, employment, income, and poverty vary greatly by race and ethnicity. For example, only 53% of the Hispanic–Latino population aged 25 or over has completed at least 4 years of high school, while the figures for African Americans and whites are 74.3% and 82.8%, respectively. Median income for white households was nearly $13,000 more than that for Hispanic–Latino and African-American households. More than 30% of all Hispanic–Latinos and 29% of all African-American persons live below the poverty level, while the figure for whites is 11%. Unemployment, which generally runs at less than 5% for the white population, was 10.2% and 10.0%, respectively, for the Hispanic–Latino and African-American populations in 1996 (US Bureau of the Census, 1997: Tables 243, 637, 723, 741). Box 5.2 illustrates how the composition of two comparable communities can vary dramatically along demographic lines.

CHANGING POPULATION CHARACTERISTICS: IMPLICATIONS FOR HEALTH CARE

Compositional Shifts

The data presented in this chapter are indicative of the major compositional changes under way in the United States. Each change, whether viewed at the national level or specified for a particular market or service area, has at least one significant implication for health care provision in the future. Together, all the changes outlined demonstrate that significant alterations in the structure of health care provision are required if every citizen is to continue to receive the level of health care we have come to expect.

The most significant shifts are those that are changing the age–race–income composition. A rising median age, a higher number and proportion of persons aged 55 and over, and the rapid rise of the population aged 75 and over translate into the need for disproportionately more health care. Longer life expectancy in many ways brings about changes in health care needs and results in more years of life during which some daily activities are restricted (Crimmins et al., 1989). The prevalence of chronic conditions is rising as a result of these trends. Because the older cohorts are becoming "healthier" and changes in tastes and preferences for care are occurring (e.g., toward more home care), the nature of health services is changing as well.

The increase in the proportion of the US population that is classified as a racial or ethnic minority has significant health care implications as well. For example, African Americans have higher levels of mortality and lower health

Box 5.2

A Tale of Two Counties

While population size and recent growth patterns tell us a great deal about a population, the inclusion of compositional factors for descriptive and analytical purposes is necessary for an understanding of service area characteristics. Two counties in Florida—Alachua and Manatee—are compared below vis-à-vis their compositional characteristics. The data presented in the table are readily available and were extracted from the 1994 *City and County Data Book* published by the Census Bureau.

	Alachua County	Manatee County
Population (1992)	189,409	216,674
Net change (1980–1992)	+38,040	+68,229
1980–1992 growth	+25.1%	+46%
Percentage African American	18%	8%
Percent Hispanic	4%	4%
Percentage age 65 and over	9%	28%
Sex ratio	96	90
Median household income	$22,084	$25,951
Physicians	1180	322
Hospitals	4	2
Hospital beds	1,096	855
Births	2,612	2,695
Deaths	1,210	2,745

As can be seen, the 1992 population size differential is about 27,000 persons, although in 1986 these counties were nearly identical in size. Manatee County grew nearly twice as fast during the 1980–1992 time interval. Large compositional differences also are evident. While nearly 20% of the Alachua County population is African American, the figure for Manatee County is less than 10%. Manatee County is much older as indicated by the proportion of the population age 65 or over. Only 9% of the Alachua County population is 65 and over, while more than one fourth of the Manatee County population is in that age cohort. Finally, there is a $3800 advantage in median household income in Manatee County.

Regarding health-related characteristics, equally significant differences can be seen. The number of physicians in Alachua County is more than three times the number found in Manatee. The Alachua–Manatee ratio for hospital beds is much closer to one. On the other hand, there are nearly an equal number of births in each county but 1500 more deaths in Manatee County. If not for in-migration, Manatee County would be losing population. These figures reflect the composition of the population and can serve as indicators of demand for health services as well as the adequacy of the current health care system.

status than whites (e.g., Berkman et al., 1989). Many African Americans traditionally have been outside of the mainstream of health care provision. Coupled with increases in the number and proportion of persons near, at, or below the poverty level, the need for assistance in paying for services is likely to rise.

It must be remembered that compositional change occurring at the national level is not necessarily reflected in data for regions, counties, and smaller units of geography. Some areas (e.g., some metropolitan counties in Florida) are maintaining a younger age structure because of migration, while others (e.g., some rural counties in Nebraska) are much older than the US average. Some areas exhibit a high proportion of racial and ethnic minorities (e.g., many cities in the South), while others have virtually no minority population at all (e.g., Utah and Montana). Each market or service area is different and must be evaluated on its own merits.

Health Care Needs

When combined with data on size, concentration, and distribution, compositional information is extremely valuable in assessing the level of health services required in a market or service area. Moreover, these data provide direction in identifying business opportunities. By inventorying services presently offered by existing providers, a service area can be categorized as overserved, adequately served, or underserved for a variety of health care services. Many rural areas, for example, are judged to be critically underserved because the supply of health care services (e.g., physicians and hospitals) does not meet the level of need as indicated by the size and composition of the service area. Patients must travel relatively long distances to obtain treatment, and many physicians are overburdened by the sheer volume of patients seeking care. On the other hand, a reduction in population size and changes in composition have caused occupancy rates in some rural hospitals to fall precipitously. The supply–demand imbalance in many areas is an issue that politicians and health care providers will have to address for many years to come.

Projections of compositional change tell planners and health services providers a great deal about the future need for health care. For example, the changing age structure of the United States (seen in Table 5.2) indicates that a growing need for geriatric specialists exists. While it can be argued that this growing need is common knowledge, the data provide specific information on which to base need projections. The data in Table 5.6, which show population projections by race and ethnicity (Hispanic–Latino), serve as indicators of other shifts in structure of needs, given that the disproportionate growth in the African-American and Hispanic origin populations is likely to result in disproportionate increases in the number of persons needing assistance in paying for health services. Furthermore, these are populations that traditionally have been underserved and are among the least likely groups to have health insurance.

Finally, health-related behavior that reflects population characteristics can be used to project future service needs. For example, while the overall incidence of cigarette smoking is falling, specific demographic segments (e.g., black males) continue to exhibit a much higher level of smoking incidence. To the extent that these segments are growing or shrinking disproportionately when compared to the population as a whole, the volume of health service needs specific to the smoking population will change.

Many of these same issues are addressed in more detail in Chapters 10 and 11. In the next three chapters, the demographic processes that drive growth and composition are explored.

REFERENCES

Barclay, G. W. (1958). *Techniques of Population Analysis*. New York: Wiley.

Berkman, L., Singer, B., and Manton, K. (1989). Black/white differences in health status and mortality among the elderly. *Demography* 26(November):661–678.

Bogue, D. J. (1969). *Principles of Demography*. New York: Wiley.

Bouvier, L., Davis, C., and Haupt, A. (1983). *Projections of the Hispanic Population in the United States, 1990–2000*. Arlington, CA: Development Associates.

Campbell, P. (1997). Population projections: States, 1995–2025. *Current Population Reports*, Series P-25, No. 1131. Washington, DC: US Government Printing Office.

Clogg, C. C., and Eliason, S. R. (1988). A flexible procedure for adjusting rates and properties, including statistical methods for group comparisons. *American Sociological Review* 53:267–283.

Crimmins, E. M., Yasuhiko, S., and Ingegneri, D. (1989). Changes in life expectancy and disability-free life expectancy in the United States. *Population and Development Review* 15(June):235–267.

Development Associates. (1982). *The Demographic and Socioeconomic Characteristics of the Hispanic Population of the United States, 1950–1980*. Arlington, VA: Development Associates.

Duleep, H. O. (1989). Measuring socioeconomic mortality differentials over time. *Demography* 26(May):345–351.

Glenn, N. D. (1977). *Cohort Analysis*. Beverly Hills, CA: Sage.

Hobcraft, J., Menken, J., and Preston, S. (1982). Age, period and cohort effects in demography: A review. *Population Index* 48 (Spring):4–43.

Hummer, R., Rogers, R., Nam, C., and Ellison, C. (1999). Religious involvement and US adult mortality. *Demography* 36 (May):273–285.

Lee, A. J., Gehlbach, S., Hosmer, D., Reti, M., and Baker, C. (1997). Medicare treatment differences for blacks and whites. *Medical Care* 35(12):1173–1189.

Moore, D. E., and Hayward, M. D. (1990). Occupational careers and mortality of elderly men. *Demography* 27(February):31–53.

Newell, C. (1987). *Methods and Models in Demography*. New York: Guilford Press.

O'Hare, W. (1998). Managing multiple-race data. *American Demographics* (April):42–44.

Orlando Sentinel. (1989). Lack of insurance raises babies' risks. October 24, p. A3.

Otten, A. L. (1989). Higher-income patients are more likely to get a kidney transplant, study says. *Wall Street Journal* (January 16): p. B4.

Pressat, R. (1972). *Demographic Analysis*. New York: Aldine.

Robey, B. (1989). Two hundred years and counting: The 1990 census. *Population Bulletin* 44(1). Washington, DC: Population Reference Bureau.

Saluter, A. (1997). Household and family characteristics: March 1996 (update). *Current Population Reports*, Series P-20, No. 495. Washington, DC: US Government Printing Office.

Santi, L. L. (1988). The demographic context of recent change in the structure of American households. *Demography* 25(November):509–519.

Schoen, C., Lyons, B., Rowland, D., Davis, K., and Puleo, E. (1997). Insurance matters for low-income adults: Results from a five state survey. *Health Affairs* 16 (September/October):163–171.

Shryock, H. S., and Seigel, J. S. (with E. Stockwell). (1976). *The Methods and Materials of Demography*. New York: Academic Press.

Sweet, J. A., and Bumpass, L. L. (1987). *American Families and Households*. 1980 Census Monograph Series. New York: Russell Sage.

US Bureau of the Census. (1975). *Historical Statistics of the United States, Colonial Time to 1970*. Washington, DC: US Government Printing Office.

US Bureau of the Census. (1992). 1990 Census of Population. Volume 1, Characteristics of the Population. Chapter B, *General Population Characteristics*, Part II, Florida. Washington, DC: US Government Printing Office.

US Bureau of the Census. (1994). *County and City Data Book, 1994*. Washington, DC: US Government Printing Office.

US Bureau of the Census. (1996). *Statistical Abstract of the United States, 1996*. Washington, DC: US Government Printing Office.

US Bureau of the Census. (1997a). *Statistical Abstract of the United States, 1997*. Washington, DC: US Government Printing Office.

US Bureau of the Census. (1997b). Census 2000 Questionnaire to allow multiple race responses: No multiracial category. *Census and You*, 32(11).

US Bureau of the Census. (1998). Website (http://www.census.gov).

US Bureau of the Census. (2000). Website: www.census.gov/eped/www/naics.html

US Department of Health and Human Services. (1989). *Report of the Expert Panel on Detection, Evaluation, and Treatment of High Blood Cholesterol in Adults*. Washington, DC: US Government Printing Office.

Winslow, R. (1989). Affluent women are more likely to have caesareans than poor are, study finds. *Wall Street Journal* (July 27): p. B4.

Yu, K. (1989). An alternative purging method: Controlling the composition-dependent interaction in an analysis of rates. *Demography* 26(November):711–716.

ADDITIONAL RESOURCES

Ambry, M. (1990). *The Almanac of Consumer Markets*. Chicago: Probus.

del Pinal, J. , and Singer, A. (1997). Generations of diversity: Latinos in the United States. *Population Bulletin* 52(3). Washington, DC: Population Reference Bureau.

Exter, T. (1996). *The Official Guide to American Incomes* (2nd ed.). Ithaca, NY: American Demographics.

Griffith, J. E., Frase, M. J., and Ralph, J. H. (1989). American education: The challenge of change. *Population Bulletin* 44(4) (December). Washington, DC: Population Reference Bureau.

Manton, K., Singer, B., and Suzman, R. (Eds). (1993). *Forecasting the Health of Elderly Populations*. New York: Springer-Verlag.

O'Hare, W. P. (1996). A new look at poverty in America. *Population Bulletin* 51(2). Washington, DC: Population Reference Bureau.

Pollard, K. M., and O'Hare, W. P. (1999). America's racial and ethnic minorities. *Population Bulletin*, 54(3). Washington, DC: Population Reference Bureau.

Russell, C. (1993). *Master Trend: How the Baby Boom Generation is Remaking America*. New York: Plenum Press.

Russell, C. (1996). *The Mid-Youth Market: Baby Boomers in Their Peak Earning and Spending Years*. Ithaca, NY: American Demographics.

CHAPTER 6

Fertility

INTRODUCTION

Fertility refers to the reproductive experience of a population. The reproductive experience involves all factors related to sexual behavior, pregnancy, and birth outcome. The number of births, the characteristics of those births, and factors describing the mothers and fathers of the children form the basis for fertility analysis. The primary focus of this chapter is on the population's reproduction patterns and the implications of these patterns for health status and behavior.

Fertility is a social process requiring the biological interaction of two persons in a specific economic, social, and/or political context. Fertility behavior is viewed broadly here and includes prepregnancy behavior, prenatal care, health-related activities during pregnancy (e.g., cigarette smoking), pregnancy outcome (e.g., birth, miscarriage, induced abortion), and short-term postnatal care. From a health care perspective, fertility can be viewed as a process whereby behavior (e.g., contraceptive use and coital frequency) leads to an outcome (e.g., pregnancy). This perspective involves the relationship of culture, technology, and economic conditions with fertility behavior. The analysis of fertility is becoming more complex due in part to changes in technology that make it possible for infecund and subfecund women to become mothers (Kalmuss, 1987; Newman, 1997).

Fertility plays an important role in shaping the demographic makeup of a population. It is one of the three demographic processes. The level of fertility, along with an area's migration and mortality characteristics, determines the size and composition of any market or service area. Knowledge of the size and make-up of a market is crucial for health planning. The ability to project changes in these characteristics of markets provides a health care provider with a strategic advantage.

Fertility patterns and related behavior have numerous implications for health and health care. The obvious linkage involves the health care needs of mothers and children prior to, during, and after birth. Unique service and facility needs related to childbearing are evident. Other requirements emerge when all stages of the reproductive process are considered. For example, health care providers and facilities are major sources of contraception-related services. Disorders related to the male and female reproductive systems place additional demands on health care providers, and infertility treatment is a growing component of the health care system. Together, these activities can be viewed as direct effects of fertility-related behavior on the health care system.

Historically, factors such as the quality of care given during the prenatal, birthing, and postnatal periods have been shown to be related to birth outcomes (Harvey and Satre, 1997), although some recent evidence indicates that prenatal care has a limited effect on factors such as birth weight (e.g., Huntington and Connell, 1997; Rogers et al., 1996). A number of studies indicate that lesser amounts and lower quality of care in the postnatal period substantially increase the likelihood that a young child will be less healthy and require more postnatal services (Clarke et al., 1993).

The demographic characteristics of women who bear children, such as age, race, marital status, income, and education, are good predictors of fertility levels and birth outcomes. Women and children from lower-income groups, for example, do not receive the quality of postnatal care that their middle- and upper-income counterparts receive. More postnatal complications and less healthy children and mothers are the result.

Variations in fertility levels among geographic areas provide valuable information about service needs. Differences in the number of births and the birth rates among regions or local service areas result in variation in the demand for obstetrical and related services. In turn, changing demand affects staffing needs, staff training requirements, facility planning and construction, and overall business planning for existing and new service providers. The extent of the maldistribution of obstetrical services, as demonstrated by the growing number of communities identified as underserved in terms of obstetrical care, points to the need for some level of health planning.

An important fertility-related concern for health care planners and providers, particularly at the local level, is the wide year-to-year variation in the number of births. Because of the influence of social factors on biological reproduction, the level of fertility can fluctuate dramatically. Various nonmedical factors determine at what ages women bear children and indeed whether they have any children at all. This "elasticity" in fertility makes the projection of future births difficult, especially for subnational areas. Over a three-decade span, the United States has experienced a peak of 4.3 million annual births (in the early 1960s), a valley of 3.1 million births (in the mid-1970s), a rise to about 4.0 million births (during the early 1990s), and a recent decline to 3.9 million (in the late 1990s). These short-term fluctuations place heavy demands on a system that cannot easily modify its capacity for providing obstetrical services.

The drop in the number of births of about 1 million per year from the peak of the baby boom from the late 1950s and early 1960s to the mid-1970s meant, at the very least, the elimination of nearly 2 million consumers (mothers and babies) of prenatal, obstetrical, and pediatric services per annum. Currently, the birth deficit (relative to the peak of the boom) is about 400,000 births per year. The average number of children women bear over a lifetime is now about 60% that of the early 1960s; in 2000 the average woman is likely to bear fewer than two children over her lifetime. This decline in births per woman has implications for both total births and the mix of services required for mothers who are now having fewer children.

Longer-term fluctuations in the number of births translates into changes in the size of age cohorts over time. Fewer births result in the shrinking of the overall health care consumer market at the younger ages (i.e., 20 and under). In fact, the under-20 age group will be smaller in the year 2000 than it was in 1970. Projections beyond 2000 indicate reductions in the size of other age groups (e.g., 35 to 50). The continued trend toward smaller households and families as well as the reduction in the proportion of persons living in families means that there will be other as yet indiscernible changes in health care demand, practices, and concerns in the future.

The remainder of this chapter focuses on five specific areas. First, fertility concepts useful to both demographers and health care planners are introduced. Second, a number of fertility measures are presented, and they in turn are used to describe trends in US fertility. Third, the importance of compositional characteristics as factors in understanding and predicting fertility-related behavior is explored. Fourth, sources of data regarding fertility and birth-related concerns are discussed. Finally, the health care implications of fertility trends and differentials are examined. These implications are subsequently related to some contemporary issues in health care.

CONCEPTS, MEASURES, AND TRENDS

Concepts

Fertility involves social interaction that results in a live birth. Fertility most often is measured in terms of the number of births that occur within a population. The conditions of the newborns (e.g., birth weight and Apgar scores) can be determined along with compositional traits (e.g., marital status and age) of the mothers. This information is typically gathered from birth certificates.

Other concepts used by demographers that are of value to health care professionals include *fecundity* (the physiological ability to reproduce), *age at menarche* (the onset of menstruation), *menopause* (the end of menstruation), and *parity* (the number of children women have already had). Since physiological factors can change in response to the physical and social environments (e.g., the historical reduction in age at menarche in the United States), they are likely to affect fertility levels and the demand for health services.

Additional important concepts useful to the health demographer include *pregnancy wantedness* (whether the pregnancy was wanted before, at that time, later, or not at all with respect to when it occurred) and *marital timing* (whether the pregnancy occurred before or after being married). The marital status of the mother also is an important concern from a health care perspective. Pregnancy wantedness and marital timing have been linked to a host of health-related concerns, including behavior before, during, and after pregnancy. For example, women who have unwanted pregnancies are less likely to change behavior that is potentially deleterious to their unborn babies than women who want to be pregnant (Weller et al., 1987). Women who conceive and bear their first child before marriage average more births than those who conceive and bear their first child after marriage (US Department of Health and Human Services, 1997).

Measures and Trends

For statistical purposes births are usually assigned to the mother's *place of residence*, although births reported by *place of occurrence* can provide valuable information to service providers. The distinction between place of residence and place of occurrence is an important one. When the obstetrical facilities and the residence of mother are in the same general geographic area, there are minimal occurrence–residence disparities. However, in situations where women must travel some distance to a hospital (e.g., in some rural areas), the number of births by place of occurrence and place of residence will vary considerably. Even in urban areas where specialty hospitals attract women from a wide geographic area, the occurrence–residence figures can be very different. Health services analysts should understand this distinction and its implications for health services planning. Obstetrics services providers should know the geographic areas from which their patients originate.

Table 6.1 presents the annual number of births in the United States from 1945 to 1996. Figure 6.1 presents the same data in graphic form. As can be seen, the number of births increased from 2.9 million in 1945 to 4.3 million annually from 1957 through 1961. The period from 1946 to 1964 is considered as the era of the *post-World War II baby boom*; after 1964, the number of births did not reach 4 million again until 1989. The interval 1965 to 1972 is seen as the transition to the *baby bust* that lasted from 1972 to 1978. The increase in fertility after 1978 could

Table 6.1. Annual Births, United States, 1945–1998

Year	Births (in millions)	Year	Births (in millions)
1945	2.9	1972	3.3
1946	3.4	1973	3.1
1947	3.8	1974	3.2
1948	3.6	1975	3.1
1949	3.6	1976	3.2
1950	3.6	1977	3.3
1951	3.8	1978	3.3
1952	3.9	1979	3.5
1953	4.0	1980	3.6
1954	4.1	1981	3.6
1955	4.1	1982	3.7
1956	4.2	1983	3.6
1957	4.3	1984	3.7
1958	4.3	1985	3.7
1959	4.2	1986	3.8
1960	4.3	1987	3.8
1961	4.3	1988	3.9
1962	4.2	1989	4.0
1963	4.1	1990	4.1
1964	4.0	1991	4.1
1965	3.8	1992	4.1
1966	3.6	1993	4.0
1967	3.5	1994	3.9
1968	3.5	1995	3.9
1969	3.6	1996	3.9
1970	3.7	1997	3.9
1971	3.6	1998	3.9

SOURCES: US Bureau of the Census (1975); US Bureau of the Census (1990), Table 80; Ventura et al (1999a), Table B.

be considered an *echo baby boom*. In other words, there was an increase in births due to the rapid rise in the number of potential mothers as the early baby boomers reached their childbearing years (Mitchell, 1995). After 1987, there was an increase in the number of births that cannot be explained by the echo effect, although the annual number of births had declined to 3.9 million by 1997 (Ventura et al., 1999: Table 9).

At the state and local levels, fertility trends may vary significantly from those at the national level. For example, the number of births in Florida and California increased from approximately 115,000 and 363,000 in 1970 to 189,000 and 552,000, respectively, in 1995. Thus, the annual number of births in these states increased by 64% and 52%. Births in Ohio and New York, on the other hand, declined from 200,000 and 318,000 to 154,000 and 272,000, respectively, during

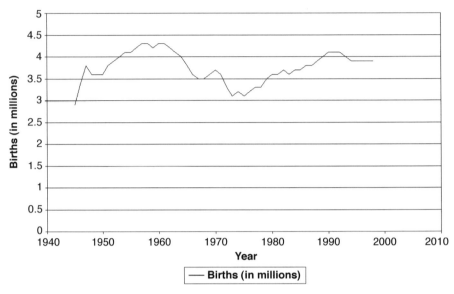

Figure 6.1. Annual birth rates for US women, 1945–1998.

the same interval. These figures represent decreases of 23% and 14% (Ventura et al., 1996). Such subnational differences must be taken into consideration in the development of fertility-related services.

Fertility Rates

The level of fertility is often expressed in terms of rates. The calculation of rates facilitates the comparison of fertility levels across areas that differ in size and/or other characteristics. Comparing the number of births for two cities with populations of 100,000 and 1,000,000, respectively, makes little sense given that the base population producing births is 10 times larger in the latter city. Rates therefore are used to make such comparisons more meaningful. Before any rates are utilized, however, the analyst should fully understand the advantages and potential limitations of those measures.

The *crude birth rate* (CBR) is the most basic measure of fertility. It is calculated by dividing the total number of births for a given year (or the average over 3 years) by the midyear total population for that year (the midyear in the range if a 3-year average of births is taken). This quotient is then expressed as the number of births per 1000 population. The CBR for the United States was 23.7 births per 1000 persons in 1960 and fell to 14.8 by 1995 (Ventura et al., 1996: Table 1).

While the CBR is adequate for making very general comparisons and has the advantage of requiring only two pieces of information, it has two major shortcomings. First, the denominator includes people who are not *at risk* of having a birth. Males, very young females, and females beyond menopause are not at risk of giving birth, yet they appear in the denominator of the rate. Second, the CBR masks differences between the age composition of populations. Fertility rates are greatly affected by age composition, particularly for women, and the CBR cannot account for this. Two populations of the same size could easily have dissimilar CBRs simply because females in the childbearing ages accounted for 20% of one population but 35% of the other. As a result of these shortcomings, more refined measures of fertility have been developed.

The *general fertility rate* (GFR), sometimes referred to simply as the *fertility rate*, represents a refinement of the CBR. Only the *population at risk* is used in the denominator. It is expressed in terms of births per 1000 females aged 15 to 44 (or 15 to 49). In 1960, the GFR was 118 births per 1000 women aged 15 to 44, and by 1995 it had declined to 66 (US Bureau of the Census, 1996: Table 92; Ventura et al., 1999: Table 1).

The GFR also can be decomposed into its birth order components. That is, the existence of first, second, third, and so forth births can be analyzed to determine patterns of fertility. GFR data that have been cross-classified by birth order for three time periods appear in Table 6.2. The drop in GFR from 87.9 in 1970 to 65.6 in 1995 can be seen here. Moreover, a redistribution of births in terms of order also is evident. In 1970, 66.4% of births were either first or second births to women. By 1995, this figure had increased to 74.8%, reflecting the fact that women were bearing a smaller number of children on average. While 15.0% of births were fourth or higher order in 1970, in 1995 only 10.1% of all births were classified the same way.

Table 6.2. General Fertility Rate by Birth Order,
United States, 1970, 1980, 1997

All births	1970[a]		1980		1997	
General fertility rate	87.9	(100.0)	68.4	(100.0)	65.0	(100.0)
First birth	34.1	(38.9)	29.5	(43.1)	26.5	(40.7)
Second birth	24.2	(27.5)	21.8	(31.9)	21.1	(32.5)
Third birth	13.6	(15.5)	10.3	(15.1)	10.6	(16.3)
Fourth birth	7.2	(8.2)	3.9	(5.7)	4.1	(6.3)
Fifth birth	3.8	(4.3)	1.5	(2.2)	1.4	(2.3)
Sixth and over	4.0	(4.6)	1.4	(2.0)	1.3	(1.9)

[a]Percentage distribution in parentheses.
SOURCE: US Bureau of the Census (1990), Table 96; Ventura et al. (1999b).

While the GFR expresses fertility in terms of births per 1,000 women in the at-risk age group, it provides no information on fertility for specific age intervals (e.g., women aged 15 to 19). Additional information can be provided by calculating *age-specific birth rates*. Age-specific birth rates provide the analyst with much needed information regarding trends in service demand. For example, the recent increases in birth rates for females under age 15 and over age 30 point to the rising need for specialized services. On the one hand, children born to younger mothers have a substantially greater probability of being underweight, and on the other hand, older mothers are somewhat more likely to experience childbearing complications. For example, in 1995, 13.5% of all births to females under age 15 were low birth weight, compared to less than 7.3% for women aged 20 to 34 (Ventura et al., 1999: Table 94).

Demographers typically calculate age-specific fertility rates using 5-year age intervals. Five-year intervals are used for convenience, and in cases like adolescent fertility measurement, narrower age intervals may be used. The age-specific fertility rate (ASFR) for women 20 to 24 years of age is derived by dividing the number of births to women in that age group by the number of women in the group (midyear population). The rate is usually calculated for 1 year (or an average is taken for 3 consecutive years), and fertility is expressed in terms of births per 1000 women in the given age range. Table 6.3 presents ASFRs for the United States in 1960, 1980, 1990, and 1995.

ASFRs sometimes reveal considerable short-term fertility variation. For example, in 1960 (during the peak of the baby boom) the ASFR for 20- to 24-year-olds was 258 (258 births per 1000 women in this age cohort). By 1995, this rate had declined to about 110. Overall, ASFRs have declined markedly since 1960. Since 1980, however, a somewhat different trend has become apparent, including an increase in ASFRs at the age intervals 30 to 34 and 35 to 39. Moreover, while the

Table 6.3. Age-Specific Fertility Rates, United States, 1960, 1980, 1990, and 1997

Age interval	1960	1980	1990	1997
10–14	0.8	1.1	1.4	1.1
15–19	89.1	53.0	59.9	52.3
20–24	258.1	115.1	116.5	110.4
25–29	197.4	112.9	120.2	113.8
30–34	112.7	61.9	80.8	85.3
35–39	56.2	19.8	31.7	36.1
40–44	15.5	3.9	5.5	7.1
45–49	0.9	0.2	0.2	0.4

SOURCE: US Bureau of the Census (1996), Table 92; Ventura et al. (1999b), Table 3.

rate for women aged 19 and younger has dropped, the ASFR for females aged 10 to 14 has increased (Ventura et al., 1996).

The *total fertility rate* (TFR) is sometimes utilized as a summary measure of age-specific fertility rates. The TFR reflects hypothetical completed fertility for a population. Technically, the only way to accurately determine how many children a cohort of young women (e.g., those currently under age 15) will bear over their lifetimes is to wait 30 or more years until they have completed their childbearing. Therefore, hypothetical measures that allow an analyst to project the completed fertility of a specified cohort without the long wait have been developed. The calculation of the TFR assumes that a group of 15-year-old females will experience the same age-specific fertility rates presented in Table 6.3 throughout their lifetimes; for example, at ages 15 to 19 the cohort will experience a birth rate of 56.8 births per 1000 women per year. Since the age interval 15 to 19 covers 5 years, the rate is multiplied by five. Adding up all the ASFRs (multiplied by 5) produces a hypothetical total number of births per 1000 women. The TFR calculation yields an average of 1.8 births per woman for 1987 and 2.0 for 1995.

While this hypothetical rate may not precisely reflect actual fertility experience, the TFR represents a good estimation of completed cohort fertility as long as ASFRs remain fairly stable. Recent data, reflected in Table 6.3, suggest that ASFRs, in fact, are becoming more stable. As a result, TFRs are themselves becoming more stable. While the TFR for the interval from 1960 to 1964 was 3.4, it has stayed between 1.8 and 2.1 since 1974 (Ventura et al., 1999: Table 4).

The TFR has been further modified and refined by demographers. One modification, the *gross reproduction rate* (GRR), adjusts the TFR to include only female births. This adjustment makes intuitive sense since it is only females who can bear children. *Replacement-level fertility*, the number of births required for females to exactly replace themselves, is about one birth per woman over a lifetime, or a GRR of approximately 1. While it appears logical to multiply TFR by 0.5, to do so would result in an overestimation of the GRR. Instead, the TFR must be multiplied by the inverse of the sex ratio at birth, which is about 105 male births for every 100 female births. In other words, the TFR should be multiplied by 0.488 in order to arrive at the GRR. More detailed calculations can be performed depending on the need for precision in the GRR.

While the GRR meets the demand for a measure of replacement, it fails to account for the mortality experience of both children and mothers. Therefore, an additional refinement, the *net reproduction rate* (NRR), has been created in order to adjust the measure of replacement by accounting for the deaths to women and female children that are known to occur. Adjusting for mortality results in NRRs that are smaller than GRRs. However, replacement fertility remains at 1; that is, the NRR must be 1 to have a replacement-level fertility. The factors used to adjust the GRR are derived from observed mortality data and the life tables that are based on these data (Palmore and Gardner, 1983, pp. 88–94).

Cohort Measures

The rates discussed thus far are referred to as *period measures*, because the data used in their calculation are specific to a given year or a 3-year interval. Recall that *cohorts* are persons who share a common experience, and that most often demographers use age as a cohort identifier. Cohort measures of fertility also are utilized, although collecting data on cohort fertility in censuses and surveys requires a unique set of inquiries that focus on fertility outcomes. Specifically, women are asked how many children they have ever given birth to and/or how many children they expect to eventually have. These data are then cross-classified by age (the cohort identifier) and the measure *children ever born* (CEB) product. CEB data are expressed in births per 1000 women in a specific age cohort. For example, in 1994, the CEB for women aged 40 to 44 was 2094, or 2094 children ever born for every 1000 women aged 40 to 44 (US Bureau of the Census, 1996: Table 106).

In regard to lifetime *birth expectations*, women are asked on surveys how many children they eventually expect to have (including those already born). This information is then linked to age data to produce the cohort measure. For example, in 1992, the lifetime-births-expected figure was 2092 births for 1000 women aged 18 to 34. Though somewhat like the TFR in that it is a hypothetical measure of completed fertility, the lifetime-expected measure has a birth-to-date (actual experience) component. That is, some expected births have already occurred. Box 6.1 summarizes the calculations of all of the rates discussed thus far.

Another measure, *parity*, refers to the number of children already born to a woman. This includes women who already have completed their childbearing. The data required to calculate measures of parity include the number of women by age cohort cross-classified by the number of live births they already have had. So, if the focus is on women aged 40 to 44, whose fertility is complete, parity data may be examined. Births by parity for women aged 40 to 44 are shown for three time periods in Figure 6.2. As Table 6.2, data from this show that over time there has been a greater concentration of births in the early parity numbers (0–2).

At this stage, several manipulations of the data are possible, including determining the percentage distribution by parity discussed earlier. Data for 1994 show that the cohort aged 40 to 44 had experienced the following parity distribution: zero, 17.5%; one, 17.1%; two, 35.3%; three, 18.9%; four, 7.0%; five, 2.0%; and six or more, 2.1% (US Bureau of the Census, 1995: Table 1). Moreover, the probability of progressing from one parity to the next—the parity progression ratio—can be derived as seen in Box 6.2 (Pressat, 1972, pp. 219–242). For example, the probability of a woman with three children having a fourth is 0.37. The method for calculating progression probabilities is shown in the second panel of the box. Moreover, the cohort fertility rate, which is a measure of average completed fertility, can be derived. The cohort fertility rate seen in the box is 1.93,

---

Box 6.1

The Calculation of Birth Rates

Birth rates are relatively easy to calculate, and in most instances the data required are readily available. Birth data are found in vital statistics sources, and population figures (rate denominators) can be drawn from Census Bureau counts or estimates. The net reproduction rate requires additional data on mortality. Cohort birth measure data are gathered via vital statistics and surveys. The rates expressed below are for the total population, although these rates for various units of geography can be calculated. These rates may be adjusted for factors such as marital status, age structure, and parity.

$$\text{Crude birth rate (CBR)} = \frac{\text{Number of births in year } X}{\text{Population at midpoint (July 1) in year } X} \times 1000$$

$$\text{General fertility rate (GFR)} = \frac{\text{Number of births in year } X}{\begin{array}{c}\text{Population of women age 15 to 44}\\ \text{(or 49) at midpoint in year } X\end{array}} \times 1000$$

$$\text{Age-specific fertility rate (ASFR)} = \frac{\begin{array}{c}\text{Number of births in year } X\\ \text{to women age } y \text{ to } y + n\end{array}}{\begin{array}{c}\text{Number of women age } y \text{ to } y + n\\ \text{at midpoint in year } X\end{array}} \times 1000$$

$$\text{Total fertility rate (TFR)} = \frac{\text{Sum of ASFRs} \times 5}{1000}$$

$$\text{Net reproduction rate (NRR)} = \sum_{i=1}^{n} \frac{B_x}{P_x} - \frac{L_x}{l_0}$$

where B_x/P_x is the female birth age specific fertility rate for age x to $x + n$; L_x/l_0 is the life table survival rate (see Chapter 7) appropriate for that age interval, and $\sum_{i=1}^{n}$ indicates that all the products for each ASFR rate combination are summed. Given that there are eight categories of ASFRs in Table 6.2, n would be equal to 8.

$$\text{Children ever born (CEB)} = \frac{\begin{array}{c}\text{Number of children ever born}\\ \text{to women aged } X \text{ in year } Y\end{array}}{\text{Population of women age } X \text{ in year } Y} \times 1000$$

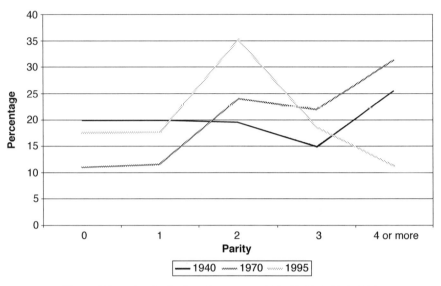

Figure 6.2. Parity distribution of women aged 40–44; 1940, 1970, 1995.

or below replacement level. These probabilities can be used as the basis for assumptions about future fertility by parity. To the extent that the use of obstetric services is tied to parity (e.g., complications are more likely in a first birth), these calculations become very useful.

The major advantage of using cohort measures is that they provide an indicator of completed fertility when the oldest age cohorts are examined. In addition, CEB figures serve as a measure of childbearing status for women who have not completed their childbearing. The latter advantage is particularly marked when data for several time periods are studied. To the extent that parity progression ratios are consistent across several cohorts, the probabilities from older cohorts can be applied to younger ones in order to generate birth forecasts by parity. These comparisons offer considerable insight into the trends in overall fertility as well as those regarding the timing of births (earlier or later in women's lives).

Although the fertility rates discussed above do not include all of the measures developed by demographers, they are representative of those in general use. As noted earlier, when using rates, the analyst must keep in mind both the advantages and shortcomings of each measure as well as the uses being considered for the rates.

The use of rates in health planning is very important. In order to make birth projections for a market area, for example, birth rates and population projections by age and sex are needed. Multiplying fertility rates, adjusted for anticipated

Box 6.2

Computation of Parity Progression Ratio and Cohort Fertility Rate for Population of US Women Aged 40 to 44 (1994)

Children ever born (CEB)	Women 40–44[a]		Women 40–44 with at least this CEB		Parity progression ratio	
0	1,745	(b_0)	9,962	(c_0)	.825	(a_0)
1	1,705	(b_1)	8,217	(c_1)	.793	(a_1)
2	3,520	(b_2)	6,512	(c_2)	.459	(a_2)
3	1,885	(b_3)	2,992	(c_3)	.370	(a_3)
4	698	(b_4)	1,107	(c_4)	.369	(a_4)
5+	409	(b_5)	409	(c_5)		(a_5)

[a]expressed in 1,000s.

Example of ratio calculation:

$$(1)\ c_5 = b_5$$
$$c_4 = b_5 + b_4$$
$$c_3 = b_5 + b_4 + b_3$$
$$\vdots$$
$$c_0 = b_5 + b_4 + \cdots + b_0$$
$$(2)\ a_0 = c_1/c_0$$
$$a_1 = c_2/c_1$$
$$\vdots$$
$$a_4 = c_3/c_4$$

Cohort fertility rate (CFR) $= a_0 + a_0a_1 + a_0a_1a_2 + \cdots a_0a_1a_2a_3a_4a_5$
$$= 1.93$$

SOURCE: US Bureau of the Census, 1995: Table 1.

change, by the number of women in specific age groups yields the projected number of births. Additional assumptions are required in order to forecast the health services needs of the mothers and children.

COMPOSITIONAL FACTORS

Interaction of Factors

Although the analysis of fertility rates provides useful information for health planners, additional information concerning births is required for many purposes. Information on conditions influencing the birth process, as well as the demographic characteristics of both babies and mothers, makes it possible to determine the level and type of health care needs. Composition and fertility-related factors also can provide information about trends in both births and birth rates.

A model for understanding these factors was developed during the 1950s by Davis and Blake (1956) and is still quite useful today. The model is presented in Figure 6.3 and focuses on the factors influencing fertility outcomes. These factors do not act independently of each other, although each category represents a separate stage in the fertility process. That is, intercourse must occur first, followed by conception, and last, by successful gestation. The intercourse variable is operationalized in terms of age at first intercourse, frequency of intercourse, time spent in and out of marriage, and age at first marriage. The second set of factors, "exposure to conception," reflects the levels of contraceptive use, sterilization, and infertility. The last group of factors focuses on pregnancy outcomes measured in terms of frequency of miscarriages, stillbirths, and induced abortions. Together with social factors such as the age, socioeconomic status, race–ethnicity, and marital status of mothers, these intercourse, conception, and outcome factors

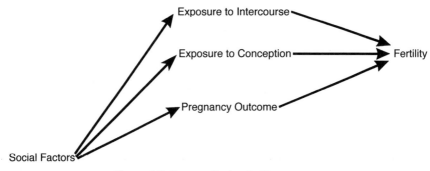

Figure 6.3. Factors affecting fertility outcomes.

produce varied levels of fertility for demographically defined subpopulations. Note that the focus of the Davis–Blake model, as well as that for most fertility analysis, is on the study of women. Few data are available on men in this regard, and interest in fertility analysis from a male perspective is a relatively recent phenomenon (e.g., Kaufman, 1997).

A change in the average age at first intercourse can have important implications for the health of a population. For example, premarital intercourse on the part of teenagers has increased markedly since the 1970s. Earlier age of first intercourse results in an increased risk of pregnancy and increases exposure to sexually transmitted diseases (STDs).

With regard to the likelihood of conception, several trends are worthy of note. Not only has contraceptive use increased since the 1960s, but the pattern of use has changed over time. Currently, about 32% of women of childbearing age are sterile and another 34% use some type of nonsurgical contraceptive (e.g., oral contraception, intrauterine device [IUD], or diaphragm) (Peterson, 1995: Table 1). However, reliance on the pill, IUD, and diaphragm has declined since the 1970s, while sterilization as a means of contraception has become increasingly common. These changes reflect in part the relationship between age and preferences for contraceptive method. Use of the pill declines with age, from nearly 24% for women aged 15 to 24 to less than 5% for women aged 35 to 44. On the other hand, nearly 65% of females aged 35 to 44 are sterile (Peterson, 1995: Table 2). These factors affect the nature of health care needs directly through the demand for contraceptive services and indirectly through their effect on pregnancy outcomes.

Today, induced abortions have a greater impact on fertility outcome than either miscarriages or stillbirths. In 1997, there were nearly 1.4 million induced abortions, a decline of about 200,000 from the early 1980s. The number of abortions per 1000 live births stabilized at about 380 in the 1990s (US Bureau of the Census, 1996: Table 115). Services related to the performance of induced abortion involve a variety of health care components, including medical, counseling, and contraceptive services.

Social Factors

A number of social factors affect fertility levels, and these factors must be examined with regard to health care concerns. The objective is to understand how these characteristics are related to fertility differentials and the health status of newborns. These two concerns viewed jointly yield even more useful information. For example, the distribution of births by birth weight is an important determinant of health care, given that low-birth-weight babies are much more likely to need additional care for a period beyond birth. Currently, about 7% of the births each year exhibit low birth weight (i.e., less than 2500 grams) (Ventura, 1996: Table 44). The age of the mother (a social factor) is linked to the likelihood of having a low-birth-weight baby. Over 13% of all births to the very youngest mothers are low birth weight, while only 6% of the children of mothers aged 25 to 29 fall into this category. To the extent that proportionately more younger women (less than age 17) are having children, more supplemental services are required.

Births by age of mother for three time periods are shown in Figure 6.4, and two phenomena are worthy of note here. First, most births are to women aged 20 to 24 or 25 to 29, regardless of the time period being studied. Second, over time the age at which most mothers give birth has increased, reflecting the higher number of woman 30–39 who are bearing children.

In regard to race and ethnicity, several differences in fertility patterns are apparent. In 1995, the white general fertility rate was 64 births per 1000 women aged 15 to 44, compared to 72 for African-American and 105 for Hispanic mothers (Ventura et al., 1996: Tables 1 and 11). However, variation in the GRF is found for Hispanic subpopulations. The rate ranges from 53 for Cubans to 117 for Mexican Americans. If other fertility measures are examined, a somewhat smaller differential appears. Utilizing the children-ever-born measures (per 1000 women aged 40 to 44), the white, African-American, and Hispanic figures are 1927, 2195, and 2510, respectively (US Bureau of the Census, 1995: Table 2).

Fertility differences by the educational attainment of the mother are even greater than those for race and ethnicity. When all marital statuses are combined,

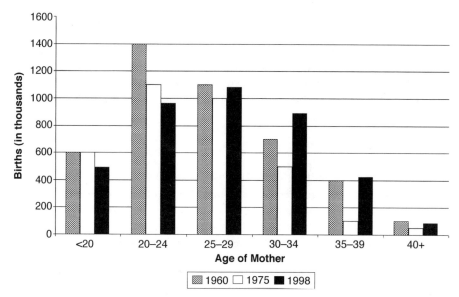

Figure 6.4. Births by age of mother: 1960, 1975, 1998.

women with less than a high school education have a children-ever-born (CEB) figure of 2678 per 1000 women aged 35 to 44. High school graduates have a CEB of 2020; followed by college graduates, 1576; and college graduates who have an advanced degree, 1342 (US Bureau of the Census, 1995: Table 2). College-educated women in particular have shown dramatic shifts to later age of childbearing over the last 35 years.

Marital status differences in fertility levels show the greatest variation of any of those reviewed. Women who have ever been married (not necessarily married now but have been married at least once) who are 40 to 44 years of age have a CEB of 2094 compared to 758 for women who have never been married. While 12.1% of those women ever married are childless, 68% of the never-married women fall into the same category. To the extent that there are higher concentrations of women in the higher fertility rate category (i.e., married) in a given geographic area, a higher than average number of births can be expected. The total fertility rate or CEB measures specific to a market or service area always should be adjusted to reflect these compositional differences.

The marital status of mothers also is of concern given that unmarried mothers typically have limited access to health services. In general, the proportion of all births born to unmarried women is increasing. In 1960, 5% of births occurred to unmarried women compared to 32% in 1995 (Ventura et al., 1996: Table 16). The likelihood of being an unmarried mother decreases markedly as the age of the mother increases. For example, nearly 75% of births to 15-year-old females are to those classified as unmarried, but only 15% of the births to 30- to 34-year-old females. The level of nonmarital fertility reflects the level of nonmarital sex, which has risen in recent years (Nathanson and Young, 1989).

Large racial differences in the marital status of mothers exist as well. In 1995, nearly 70% of African-American births but only 25% of white births were to unmarried women. Both racial groups experienced an increase in this percentage over the previous decade (Smith et al., 1996). The racial difference in premarital birth rates is explained largely by differences in socioeconomic status. African-American women with low socioeconomic status are three times more likely to have a premarital birth than African-American women with high socioeconomic status (Bumpass and McLanahan, 1989). When age of mother is accounted for, the differential narrows. At age 15, 84% and 99% of white and African-American births, respectively, are delivered by mothers who are unmarried (Ventura et al., 1996: Tables 40 and 82).

Other trends in fertility patterns should be considered. For example, there has been a marked increase in out-of-wedlock childbearing over the last four decades, with 42% of US births delivered by unmarried women. However, the percentage of males and females who have never been married has risen sharply since 1970. As can be seen from the data in Table 6.4, the percentage of males and females aged 25 to 29 and 30 to 34 who are not married has more than doubled since 1970.

Table 6.4. Single (Never-Married) Persons
Aged 20 to 39 as a Percentage of the Total Population
in That Age Group, United States, 1970, 1987, and 1998

Age interval	Males			Females		
	1970	1987	1998	1970	1987	1998
20–24	54.7	77.7	76.4	35.8	60.8	60.7
25–29	19.1	42.2	49.4	10.5	28.8	32.9
30–34	9.4	23.1	27.4	6.2	14.6	19.5
35–39	7.2	12.4	26.8	5.4	8.4	13.2

SOURCE: US Bureau of the Census (1989), Table 52; US Bureau of the Census (1996), www.census.gov/prod/99pubs/p20-514u.pdf.

Not only do these data imply changes in health care needs and demands overall due to differences in health status and human behavior of persons married later in life, but they also provide some explanation for the decline in fertility since the 1960s.

As noted earlier, several demographic factors are reflected in the conditions surrounding birth. While 5.8% of white newborns are classified as low birth weight, 13.3% and 6.1%, respectively, of African-American and Hispanic newborns are classified the same way (US Department of Health and Human Services, 1992: Tables 39 and 49). The percentage of all births classified as low birth weight declines from 9.6% for women with 9 to 11 years of education to about 5.0% for those with a college education or more. Moreover, the percent of babies who are of low birth weight is about twice as high for unmarried women as for married women (10.4% vs. 5.7%). When examined jointly, these factors help identify even greater differentials. Nearly 14% of the births to African-American females under age 15 are classified as low birth weight, as are 22.4% of the births to African-American females aged 35 to 39 with 9 to 11 years of education (US Department of Health and Human Services, 1997: Tables 1-108 and 1-110).

These same characteristics can be used in the analysis of differentials in fertility-related behaviors. For example, while 84.9% of white women receive prenatal care in their first trimester, only 64.2% of Hispanic women and 64.0% of African-American women receive such care (US Department of Health and Human Services, 1992: Table 1-47). There also are substantial and complex racial differences in contraceptive use (US Department of Health and Human Services 1997).

The greatest value in this information lies in its usefulness to examining the impact of joint relationships (e.g., age and race), while accounting for compositional changes over time. For example, given racial–ethnic differences in fertility and the younger age structures of the African-American and Hispanic populations, the proportion of all births that are African-American or Hispanic is projected to increase sharply in this decade. Moreover, given that the rates for early prenatal care are lower and the incidence of low birth weight is higher for these populations, the subsequent demand for related health services can be expected to rise markedly.

The above discussion does not present an exhaustive list of the factors having potential impact on fertility, nor of the variations that exist among service areas. For example, data on other racial and ethnic groups would be of interest in the Southwest or on the West Coast. Compositional change (e.g., changing age or racial–ethnic composition) over time is equally important given the population redistribution patterns underway in the United States. Substantial increases in the number of births are possible over relatively short periods of time (3 to 5 years) in rapidly growing areas. The importance of the above information lies in its salience for the level of need for birth-related services. Two service or market areas with same population size may have very different levels of demand given differentials in age, income, race–ethnicity structure, contraceptive use, and marital status of mothers. By anticipating change in these and other factors, service providers can gain a significant competitive edge over those institutions that know little about the reproductive future.

Data Sources

While a more thorough treatment of demographic data sources appears in Chapter 9, several specific comments regarding fertility-related data are appropriate at this juncture. Fertility data are drawn from a variety of sources. Relatively high-quality birth registration systems have functioned in each state since at least 1933, and the standard birth certificate includes a variety of data on the characteristics of the child, father, and mother. Together, these state systems make up the national system. The national system makes aggregated data from birth certificates available to users for a particular study area. Table 6.5 provides a list of items on the standard birth certificate.

By aggregating data from birth certificates, it is possible to determine not only the total number of births but the characteristics of children and their mothers. For example, a health care marketer could determine the number of low-birth-weight babies born to white mothers aged 15 to 19 years within a geographic area for a specified year if such information were desired. These data could be used to forecast the number of low-birth-weight children over the next 5 years by estimating the present and future age and sex structure of the population and making assumptions about future fertility behavior. Combining registration data on the number of births with population data allows for the calculation of birth rates. The resulting rates can provide information on market-to-market variations in fertility.

Table 6.5. Items Included on US Standard Certificate of Live Birth

Child	Mother	Father	Pregnancy
Name	Name	Name	Pregnancy history (live
Sex	Age	Age	births, other
Date of birth	State of birth	State of birth	terminations)
Hospital or facility	Residence (state, county,	Race	Date of last normal menses
name	city, town, or	Hispanic origin	Month prenatal care began
County of birth	location)	(yes, no)	Prenatal visits
Birth weight	Residence (address,	Education	Complications of
Apgar score	inside or outside city	Relation to child	pregnancy
	limits)		Concurrent illnesses
	Race		Congenital malformations
	Hispanic origin		or anomalies of child
	(yes, no)		Birth weight
	Marital status		Method of delivery
	Education		Medical risk factors
	Pregnancy history		Obstetric procedures

SOURCE: National Center for Health Statistics (1995).

In addition to the birth registration system, fertility surveys are a source of data on fertility-related behavior. Surveys provide information on such issues as contraceptive use, infertility levels, and breast-feeding patterns. Table 6.6 provides a list of the types of concerns addressed in the most recent administration of the National Survey of Family Growth. It can be seen, for example, that the change in the contraceptive patterns by age, which can be determined by examining successive fertility surveys, provides valuable market information about the demand for contraceptive products and services.

The US Bureau of the Census makes inquiries about a limited number of fertility issues in both the decennial census of population and the Current Population Survey (CPS). In the decennial census, women are asked how many children (not counting stillbirths) they have had during their lifetimes. These data are then cross-tabulated by a variety of demographic variables such as age, marital status, income, and education. They are made available in published form for the nation as well as regions, states, metropolitan statistical areas (MSAs), and local areas in the form of CEB figures. *Microdata*, that is, data obtained from survey participants, are available on computer tape, computer disk, and on-line, making more customized analyses possible. The names, addresses, and most geographic identifiers are removed from the records to ensure that survey participants remain anonymous.

The CPS has a somewhat more extensive list of fertility inquiries, but the sample size renders most local area data too unreliable to use. Questions with

Table 6.6. Selected Factors Addressed in the 1995 National Survey of Family Growth

Children	Contraceptive use	Intercourse	Other/demographic—mother
Children born	Type of contraceptive—	Frequency	Age
Births expected	current	Age at first	Pregnancy wantedness
Were children	Use prior to pregnancy—	intercourse	Education
wanted	effectiveness		Marital status
Infertility	Contraceptive use at first		Employment status
	intercourse		Race
	Sterilization		Ethnicity
			Income
			Marital timing, as related to
			childbearing
			Use of family planning
			services—frequency
			Breast feeding
			Health insurance coverage
			Cigarette smoking
			Pelvic inflammatory disease
			Sex education
			HIV risk behavior

SOURCE: US Department of Health and Human Services (1997).

regard to actual and expected fertility are asked and cross-tabulated by other demographic factors. The June CPS report of each year focuses on fertility, and in fact is titled, "The Fertility of American Women."

CONTEMPORARY ISSUES

Fluctuations in Births

While there are a number of contemporary health care issues related to births and birth rates, some are particularly relevant for health services planning, marketing, and business development. The first concerns the changing demand for services resulting from fluctuations in the number of births in a given market area. While the number of births in the United States has stabilized at about 3.8 to 4.0 million per year, large area-to-area differentials exist. Some locales have a demographic environment conducive to producing a large number of new "customers" (e.g., a young age structure and little significant out-migration), while others have demographic conditions likely to result in low birth production. If planners merely look at overall population change as an indicator of service demand, errors in judgment will be significant. Changes in population size reflect the specific combination of births, deaths, and migrants in an area. For example, some cities in Florida are experiencing high population growth rates due to in-migration yet record relatively few births. Other cities, particularly those in the Northeast and Midwest regions, exhibit negative growth (population loss), even though a substantial number of births are recorded.

Obstetrical services planners must know their market areas and the relative contribution of births, deaths, and migration to population change. Projecting births for local areas is more difficult and more subject to error than are national or state projections, but such numbers can be produced. It is possible to project some birth- and mother-related compositional characteristics in order to refine the projections and therefore know more about future service needs. Furthermore, birth projections must be seen in the context of normal service delivery (e.g., managed-care limitations on hospital stays following a delivery) if health services needs are to be accurately measured (Kun and Muir, 1997).

Variations in Fertility Rates

Variations in fertility rates over time can be attributed to a number of factors. These include social, economic, and political factors, not to mention more practical matters such as access to contraceptives. In the United States and other postindustrial countries, increases in educational levels and standards of living have contributed to declining fertility since the beginning of the twentieth century. This trend also was influenced by a major shift in the economic structure during this time period. Agrarian economies place a premium on large families; in industrial economies, large families become a liability. In addition, growing numbers of women have entered the labor force, particularly since World War II, further discouraging and/or preventing the establishment of large families.

Within this general trend, fluctuations can be identified that reflect social, economic, and political conditions. Birth rates have historically declined during periods of economic uncertainty (e.g., the Great Depression) and increase during periods of prosperity (e.g., the post-World War II boom). Similarly, birth rates are typically lower during wartime than during peacetime. Although government policy in the United States typically has not been utilized as a mechanism for controlling fertility, it has been argued that the federal tax structure historically has favored families with children. In some other societies (e.g., Prussian Germany and the People's Republic of China), fertility levels have been directly controlled by the ruling government.

Another consideration in the United States is the impact of social psychological factors on fertility. This is another way of saying that reproduction is "trendier" at some points in history than at others. The predisposition of parents to have children is influenced by societal expectations, current fashion, and competing values. Children in the United States were viewed as having a different function at the beginning of the twentieth century than they have now. Function influences the value placed on progeny, which in turn influences the propensity to reproduce. In some societies, such a high value is placed on children (or on the connotations of reproduction for masculinity and femininity) that other factors such as changing socioeconomic status may be overridden (Friedman et al., 1994; Lehrer et al., 1996).

In the final analysis, the elasticity in the fertility rate is a function more of culture than biology. The cultural values surrounding reproduction and family formation seem to override more practical considerations. (Box 6.3 addresses the health care implication of adolescent fertility.)

Provision of Services

Another issue that has emerged recently concerns the providers of obstetric services. Recent data show a marked increase in the number of obstetricians who have given up that specialty at a time when demand for their services remains high. The reasons for dropping out of the pool of service providers (e.g., a substantial increase in malpractice insurance premiums) are important, but from a more general perspective other problems may be created if physician shortages occur. Aside from the question of an adequate supply of service providers overall is the concern that in some areas, due to less desirable living conditions or more litigious populations, the decline in providers could be relatively large. While such a decline creates opportunities for new doctors and other medical personnel, they face the same obstacles as the providers who abandoned their practices in these areas. Many hospitals and clinics have faced difficulties in attracting the requisite obstetrical staff for a number of years.

Providers of obstetrical services also must accommodate the changing tastes and preferences of consumers seeking birth-related services. From an increase in husband participation to having births under water, the market for various birthing techniques has broadened considerably over the last 20 years. In fact, the establishment of "birthing centers" sounded the death knoll for many traditional labor and delivery practices. The increased demand for these techniques is directly related to a host of demographic factors such as marital status, income, and the age of mothers.

Moreover, there is increasing competition for health care consumers, particularly for those who are healthy. The introduction of standard business practices by health care providers has put some competitors at a distinct advantage over others, and some of the advantage is not always direct. For example, some hospitals and clinics have developed ways of attracting quality staff by establishing successful marketing strategies. Maternity units targeting families who wish to have a "total" birthing experience can be found all over the United States. A package price for prenatal, birth, and postnatal services is being offered along with

Box 6.3

Health Implications of Adolescent Pregnancy

One of the most unsettling trends in the United States today is the increasing proportion of births that occur outside of marriage. While only 30 years ago, 95% of all births were to married women, that figure was around 68% in the mid-1990s. The situation is further aggravated by the fact that a large proportion of these births are to adolescents. In 1994, of the roughly 1.3 million children born to unmarried women, nearly one third were born to women under age 20. By comparison, in 1960 there were only 90,000 births to unmarried women under age 20. The fertility rate for unmarried women aged 15 to 19 tripled during this period, from 15.3 births per 1000 women in 1960 to 46.4 in 1995 (US Bureau of the Census, 1996: Table 97).

As with other fertility related phenomena, adolescent pregnancies are not randomly distributed throughout the population. For example, about 55% of all births to white adolescents were born to unmarried women. The comparable figure for black women was over 90%. These births also are likely to be characterized by attributes that mitigate against a satisfactory outcome or a long-term healthy existence. Young mothers are much less likely to receive early prenatal care. While less than one half of young pregnant women between ages 15 and 17 receive prenatal care during the first trimester, nearly 90% of pregnant women aged 25 through 29 receive such care. Furthermore, young mothers are significantly more likely to give birth prematurely.

Being born to a young mother has numerous disadvantages. While nearly 14 of 1000 babies born to females under age 15 are classified as low birth weight, the comparable figure for women aged 25 to 29 is only 6. Though 15% of these youngest mothers produce babies with low one-minute Apgar scores, only 9% of older women do. The combination of low birth weight, prematurity, and the young age of the mother contributes to an increased incidence of birth defects, a higher level of mental retardation, and greater levels of infant mortality. About 80% of all fetuses that die are classified as low birth weight.

In addition, early childbearing has deleterious effects on the mothers. Initially, a greater number of birthing complications occur due to the lack of physical maturity and the lack of prenatal care. Beyond the immediate physiological dangers, there are related consequences such as lower educational attainment, more lifetime births, and overall lessened earning power. The overall economic impact of having a child at an early age can be quite high given the opportunity costs involved.

Finally, the indirect effects of early childbearing must be considered. The higher incidence of birth defects and mental retardation carries an economic and psychic cost for both the mother and society. Many of these children face the long-term prospect of diminished health status and the resulting need for continuous health services. There also is some evidence indicating that where early childbearing is combined with poverty and despair, children are more likely to suffer abuse and neglect. This too carries economic and psychic costs.

marketing efforts to attract young mothers and their families to additional services (e.g., smoking-cessation clinics and exercise programs). Since obstetrical costs constitute the major category of expense for most health plans, those involved in the provision of care must understand these processes. Health care organizations that want to remain competitive must also develop an understanding of demographic information. Box 6.4 focuses on planning issues related to opening a new obstetrics unit.

Implications for Health Care Delivery

Fertility as a demographic process is not inherently linked to the health care delivery system. In many societies, in fact, no linkage is perceived between pregnancy and childbirth and the provision of health care. In the United States and other industrial societies, however, the reproductive process has become redefined as a medical process. It is believed that pregnancy, gestation, and childbirth can take place only under the management of the health care system. For this reason, fertility levels have numerous implications for health and health care.

The level of fertility in US society dictates the level of need for a variety of health-related services. The fertility rate determines the number of deliveries that will take place. This in turn influences the number of hospitals that will be required in general and the number of hospital obstetrical units in particular. In either case, the demand for both obstetrical beds and newborn nursery space is a function of the level of reproductive activity within the area in question. Higher levels of fertility also result in a greater need for neonatal care units.

At the same time, the number of females in the population who are pregnant at any one point in time is a major determinant of the need for ambulatory obstetric services. Pregnancy and associated factors have come to take up an increasing amount of outpatient clinic time since the 1960s. Prenatal and postnatal checkups have become commonplace for most segments of the population. The use of pregnancy-related diagnostic tests has increased dramatically. Ultrasound and amniocentesis testing techniques have become readily available since the 1970s and are increasingly being used to monitor pregnancy progress. Fertility-related problems have engendered industrial segments devoted to the treatment of infertility and impotence.

The demand for obstetrical medical personnel also is a function of the level of fertility. As the level of fertility rises, so does the need for obstetricians and neonatologists. This is true also of other personnel (e.g., neonatal nurses) for whom demand is a function of the level of fertility. Secondary demand is generated for pediatricians and pediatric services for the medical management of the consequences of the fertility rate.

The link between fertility levels and the demand for obstetrical services is complicated by the fact that fertility rates vary widely among various groups of society. The groups in US society today with the highest fertility rates tend to be low users of health services such as prenatal care. High-risk groups are among

Box 6.4

A Case Study in Fertility Services: Planning an Obstetrical Unit

The establishment of an obstetrical (OB) facility may seem straightforward enough. One need only estimate the likely number of births in the area, arrange for appropriate medical staff and physical facilities, and offer the service. This process, however, masks a great deal of the complexity that surrounds the provision of services for OB needs. In fact, there is virtually no aspect of demography that can be ignored in planning for an OB unit.

From the first step on, the process requires considerable research and the application of a number of demographic concepts. The first problem involves the delineation of the service area for an OB unit. How far is it reasonable to expect pregnant women to travel to deliver a baby (or for prenatal and postnatal services if the obstetrician's office is located near the facility)? The administrators already may have some idea of the facility's service area for general care, but are OB patients different? In fact they are, and a hospital is likely to attract OB patients from a broader area than patients for many other diagnoses. The delineation of the OB service area will depend therefore on the availability of competing services, the location of obstetricians' offices, and transportation access.

Having delineated the appropriate service area, it is then necessary to calculate the demand for obstetrical services.* How many deliveries can be expected annually from the population being served? This, of course, can be calculated in a number of ways. The simplest and probably most misleading of these would be to focus on the crude birth rate of the target population. This would be misleading in that it does not take such factors as age, race, and marital status into consideration. Applying the countrywide crude birth rate, for example, to the target population at the zip code level may mean that an average is being used that is skewed due to high birth rates for African Americans, while in actuality the service area population is predominantly white.

It would be more appropriate to use an indicator (e.g., general fertility rate) that takes the age and sex distribution of the area into consideration. It would be best if the actual fertility experience of the target population were known. If it is not, one could apply some standard rate that accounts for age, sex, race, and even income distribution. Any ethnic concentrations within the service area also should be noted, as many such groups (e.g., Hispanics) are likely to display different fertility patterns than the general population.

Incidentally, detailed current population estimates that include age, sex, and racial–ethnic composition may not be readily available. The smaller and more

---

*Obstetrical care is probably the only health service for which the "need" and the "demand" are almost synonymous. Once the process (pregnancy) is set into play, it is irreversible. Many heart patients may back out of bypass surgery, but pregnant women—after a point at least—cannot opt out of the process.

irregularly shaped the service area, the more likely this is to be a problem. The profiling of the service area population may be done by purchasing data from private vendors (usually at the zip code level) or seeking assistance from local planning agencies who often make such estimates. It may be necessary to call on the services of an area demographer if possible, since every service area is likely to have its own peculiar characteristics.

Once the current population has been profiled, it should be possible to apply the appropriate rate and estimate the yield of births from the service area. However, it will be a year or two before the facility is operational, and perhaps 5 years before it attains financial viability. The projected volume of births thus becomes more crucial than the current level. How does one determine the number of potential births for the future? Here the various projection techniques of the demographer come into play. One might first want to examine overall population trends; that is, is the service area population increasing, decreasing, or stable? A projected decline in the population base does not bode well for a new facility. More importantly, however, how is the composition of the population changing? A growing population will not be beneficial if it is rapidly aging. The planner must project the population in terms of the variables discussed above—age, sex, race, and ethnicity. In addition, some projection of socioeconomic status must be made, unless the patient's ability to pay is not a factor.

Projections can be made using straight-line techniques, cohort analysis, or more reality-based approaches that take factors such as housing stock into consideration. In the short run, the rate of natural increase or decrease (difference between births and deaths) is not likely to be significant, but the migration rate certainly is. The identification of in-migrants and out-migrants becomes essential. What type of people, for example, are moving into the community—retirees, young marrieds, middle-aged empty nesters? Can the identified trends be expected to continue into the future? In addition, will known fertility rates be maintained indefinitely?

Obviously a number of assumptions have to be made to develop a profile of the service area population 5 or 10 years into the future, and many of the demographer's tools are necessary for this task. Once a future population has been established, the potential number of births can be projected. The planning does not end here, however, since a number of other factors need to be taken into consideration. The economic status of the target population needs to be evaluated (unless OB services are considered a "loss leader"). Further, the availability of medical manpower needs to be considered, since a new facility with no physician support or an inadequate number of neonatal nurses will not be viable. The risk level of the population also must be considered. Is this a population characterized by high rates of premature and low-birth-weight babies or a population that utilizes little prenatal care? If so, special facilities and services may be necessary.

Two other related factors also must be considered. First, what are the psycho-

Continued

Box 6.4.   (Continued)

graphic characteristics of the service area population? Is this a "yuppie" population interested in innovative birthing arrangements, rather than the traditional delivery format this facility is offering? Or is it a traditional population with no interest in the progressive alternative birthing facility being planned? These questions lead directly to the issue of competition. The perception of the organization offering the OB facility will influence utilization levels, so image becomes a key factor. An understanding of how consumers see this facility relative to its competitors is essential.

The subject of competition raises one final point. The projected birth figure for the service area population is only meaningful if there is no competition. In most areas, there will be more than one facility competing for obstetrical cases. The new facility cannot expect to obtain all potential births, but only its "share." The current distribution of births among existing facilities must be determined in order to estimate the share that the new facility will capture. Information on deliveries often can be obtained from state health agencies or purchased from data vendors who calculate market shares. Some realistic estimate of the capturable market share must subsequently be made in order to determine the true potential utilization for the planned facility.

As can be seen, virtually all aspects of demography are utilized in the planning of this type of facility, and the process can be even more complicated than outlined above. This helps explain the booming business in the sale of demographic data and the growing number of individuals with demographic training being utilized by health care organizations.

---

those least likely to obtain the training and information that would minimize fertility-related health problems. Extensive research continues on the relationship between fertility related behaviors, lifestyles, and the use of obstetrical services.

Implications for Health Status

A statistical correlation can be demonstrated between fertility levels and health status that resembles a J-shaped curve. It appears that the healthiest segments of the population (the most fecund) are not the most prolific (the most fertile). In fact, subpopulations that demonstrate moderate levels of health status tend to have the highest birth rates. However, once health status drops below a certain level, biological factors come into play to reduce the level of fecundity or the physical ability to reproduce. This mechanism operates with regard to the individual's ability to conceive, the ability to carry the fetus to term, the potential for a positive pregnancy outcome, and the potential for a healthy child.

This relationship, more than anything else, reflects the nonbiological aspects of reproduction. Those who are in the best health also are likely to be those who are best educated, most affluent, and most knowledgeable about contraception. Those with less favorable characteristics—the poorly educated, the working poor, the least knowledgeable about contraception—are characterized by high fertility levels. The end result is a link between fertility and health status that is complex and a relationship that is very indirect.

The most important implication of the above is for health consequences for those groups characterized by high fertility rates. The highest fertility rates in the United States today are found among certain racial and ethnic minorities. Members of these groups generally suffer disadvantages that have either a direct or indirect impact on the health of mother and child. Since the mothers are likely to be in relatively poor health themselves, this has implications for the children during gestation. In general, these high-fertility populations suffer from high rates of infant mortality, maternal mortality, birth complications, low-birth-weight babies, birth defects, and mental retardation. Further, these children are likely to be born into environments that are relatively unsafe and/or unsanitary, to be exposed to poor nutritional levels, and generally to suffer from a lack of the resources necessary to maintain a healthy lifestyle. These conditions often dictate that the individual ends up as a multiproblem person. This results in the creation of large numbers of individuals whose health is impaired from before birth and many of whom are never given the opportunity to improve.

REFERENCES

Bumpass, L., and McLanahan, S. (1989). Unmarried motherhood: Recent trends, composition, and black–white differences. *Demography* 26(2):279–299.

Clarke, L., Miller, M., Vogel, B., Davis, K., and Mahan, C. (1993). The effectiveness of Florida's improved pregnancy outcome program. *Journal of Health Care for the Poor and Underserved* 4(2):117–132.

Davis, K., and Blake, J. (1956). Social structure and fertility: An analytical framework. *Economic Development and Cultural Change* 5:211–235.

Francese, P., and Edmondson, B. (1986). *Health Care Consumers*. Ithaca, NY: American Demographics Institute.

Friedman, D., Hechter, M., and Kanazawa, S. (1994). A theory of the value of children. *Demography* 31:375–401.

Harvey, M., and Satre, S. (1997). Impact of a hospital funded prenatal clinic on infant outcomes and hospital costs. *Children and Youth Services Review* 19(3):163–177.

Huntington, J., and Connell, F. A. (1997). For every dollar spent—The cost savings argument for prenatal care. *New England Journal of Medicine* 35(19):1303–1307.

Kalmuss, D. S. (1987). The use of infertility services among fertility-impaired couples. *Demography* 24:575–585.

Kaufman, G. (1997). Men's attitudes toward parenthood. *Population Research and Policy Review* 16:435–446.

Kun, K., and Muir, E. (1997). Influences on state legislators. *Public Health Reports* 112:277–283.

Lehrer, E., Grossbard-Shechtman, S., and Leasure, W. (1996). Comment on a theory of the value of children. *Demography* 33:133–136.

Mitchell, S. (1995). The next baby boom. *American Demographics*:22–31.

Nathanson, C. A., and Young, K. J. (1989). Components of change in adolescent fertility, 1971–1979. *Demography* 26(1):85–98.

National Center for Health Statistics. (1995). *Vital Statistics of the United States, 1992*, Vol. 1, *Natality*. Washington, DC: US Public Health Service.

Newman, A. (1997). The risk of racing the reproductive clock. *Newsweek*, May 5, pp. 96–98.

Palmore, J. A., and Gardner, R. W. (1983). *Measuring Mortality, Fertility, and Natural Increase*. Honolulu: East-West Population Institute.

Peterson, L. S. (1995). Contraceptive use in the United States: 1982–90. *Advance Data*, No. 260. Hyattsville, MD: National Center for Health Statistics.

Pressat, R. (1972). *Demographic Analysis*. New York: Aldine.

Rogers, M., Sheps-Peoples, M., and Suchindran, C. (1996). Impact of a social support program on teenage prenatal use and pregnancy outcomes. *Journal of Adolescent Health* 19:132–140.

Smith, H., Morgan, P., and Koropeckyj-Cox, T. (1996). A decomposition of trends in the nonmarital fertility ratios of blacks and whites in the United States: 1960–1992. *Demography* 33:141–151.

Stephen, E. H., Rindfuss, R. R., and Bean, F. D. (1988). Racial differences in contraceptive choice: Complexity and implications. *Demography* 25(1):53–70.

US Bureau of the Census. (1975). *Historical Statistics of the US, Colonial Times to 1970*, Part 1, Series B1-4. Washington, DC: US Government Printing Office.

US Bureau of the Census. (1989). *Statistical Abstract of the United States, 1989*. Washington, DC: US Government Printing Office.

US Bureau of the Census. (1990). *Statistical Abstract of the United States, 1990*. Washington, DC: US Government Printing Office.

US Bureau of the Census. (1995). *Fertility of American Women: June 1994*. Current Population Reports Series P-20, No. 482. Washington, DC: U.S. Government Printing Office.

US Bureau of the Census. (1996). *Statistical Abstract of the United States, 1996*. Washington, DC: US Government Printing Office.

US Department of Health and Human Services. (1997). Fertility, family planning and women's health: New data from the 1995 National Survey of Family Growth. *Vital and Health Statistics*, Series 23, 19. Hyattsville, MD: Centers for Disease Control and Prevention.

Ventura, S., Clarke, S., and Mathews, J. J. (1996). Recent decline in teenage birth rates in the United States: Variations by state, 1990–94. *Monthly Vital Statistics Report*, Vol. 45, No. 5. Hyattsville, MD: National Center for Health Statistics.

Ventura, S. J., Martin, J. A., Curtin, S. C., and Mathews, T. J. (1999a). Report of natality statistics, 1995. *Monthly Vital Statistics Report*, Vol. 45, No. 11(s). Hyattsville, MD: National Center for Health Statistics.

Ventura, S. J., Martin, J. A., Curtin, S. C., and Mathews, T. J. (1999b). *Births: Final Data for 1997*, National Vital Statistics Report, Vol. 47, No. 18. Washington, DC: US Government Printing Office.

Weller, R. H., Eberstein, I. W., and Bailey, M. (1987). Pregnancy wantedness and maternal behavior during pregnancy. *Demography* 24(3):407–412.

ADDITIONAL RESOURCES

Bianci, S. M., and Spain, D. (1996). Women, work and family in America. *Population Bulletin* 51(3). Washington, DC: Population Reference Bureau.

Easterlin, R. A., and Crimmins, E. M. (1985). *The Fertility Revolution*. Chicago: University of Chicago Press.

Potts, M. (1997). Sex and the birth rate: Human biology, demographic change, and access to fertility-regulation methods. *Population and Development Review* 23(1):1–39.

Riley, N. E. (1997). Gender, power and population change. *Population Bulletin* 52(1). Washington, DC: Population Reference Bureau.

Rindfuss, R. S., Morgan, P., and Swicegood, G. (1988). *First Births in America: Changes in the Timing of Parenthood*. Berkeley: University of California Press.

US Department of Health and Human Services. (1997). Fertility, family planning and women's health: New data from the 1995 National Survey of Family Growth. *Vital and Health Statistics*, Series 23, No. 19. Hyattsville, MD: US Government Printing Office.

CHAPTER 7

Morbidity and Mortality

INTRODUCTION

Of all demographic factors, morbidity and mortality represent the clearest linkage between demography and health care. The morbidity and mortality characteristics of a population reflect both the level of health services needed and the effects of the functioning of the health care system. *Morbidity*, or the level of sickness and disability within a population, historically has been an area of study for both clinicians and population-oriented scientists such as epidemiologists. In recent years, increased activity on the part of demographers has been observed as population researchers apply their methodologies and perspectives to the study of sickness and death. *Mortality* refers to the level of death characterizing a population, and its study includes the characteristics of those who die as well as the causes of death. Mortality is a more traditional focus of demographers, in part because of its direct effect (along with fertility and migration) on population change.

Morbidity has become a growing focus of demographers as the connection between demographic variables and morbidity differentials has become clearer. In fact, many advances in the understanding and management of the health problems of contemporary populations have a demographic component. With acquired immune deficiency syndrome (AIDS), for example, the link between disease and demographic characteristics of those who have AIDS in the United States is direct. Demographically, AIDS victims are young (under age 50), predominantly male, disproportionately from racial and ethnic minorities, and highly concentrated in a limited number of metropolitan areas. Combining this knowledge with lifestyle data, health planners are able to develop strategies for both controlling the spread of the virus and providing for the care of the individuals affected. The population of Uganda, on the other hand, has a different set of demographic correlates. The disease is spread through heterosexual contact, it is concentrated along main transportation routes, and the incidence in both sexes is about the same. These different demographic linkages call for very different prevention and treatment strategies.

Mortality, one of the three components of population change, has always been in the forefront of demographic research. Some of the earliest demographic studies focused solely on the study of the causes of death, the characteristics of those who had died, and life expectancy. In recent years the disciplinary lines between demographically oriented mortality studies and epidemiology have blurred as demographers and medical researchers have combined their efforts to understand differentials in mortality experience within the population.

The relatively large infant mortality disparity between African Americans and whites, for example, illustrates a link between a demographic characteristic and mortality levels. In 1997, the African-American infant mortality rate was 14.2 deaths per 1000 live births, while the white rate was 6.0 per 1000 births (Hoyert et al., 1999: Table c). The racial difference in infant mortality can be attributed to dissimilarities in the causes of death. African-American infants experience a higher rate of infant mortality as a result of their greater likelihood of dying from complications associated with low birth weight and pregnancy, pneumonia, and respiratory distress syndrome.

The purpose of this chapter is to introduce the concepts and indicators of morbidity and mortality, along with the techniques utilized to measure and compare levels of each. The morbidity and mortality trends of particular interest to demographers and health officials are emphasized.

MORBIDITY

Introduction

Morbidity refers to the level and type of sickness and disability within a population. For the demographer, this involves identifying both the static and dynamic aspects of sickness, as well as the ways in which those patterns affect mortality. Static dimensions include not only a profile of diseases within a population, but information on the distribution of these conditions. The dynamic dimension focuses on the connection between population change (in terms of size, composition, and distribution) and the morbidity profile. As national and subnational population change has occurred, the morbidity profile of the affected populations has been altered. Today, for example, the aging of the American population along with advances in medical practice have transformed the morbidity profile for the United States from one dominated by acute conditions such as measles and mumps to one characterized by such chronic disorders as cancer and heart disease. (An additional discussion of morbidity and mortality is found in Chapter 10 on the demographic correlates of health status.)

Morbidity Measures

Several measures are commonly used in morbidity analysis. The first involves the simple counting of officially recognizable conditions for the nation or subnational units of geography. Although little success has been made in establishing a summary measure of morbidity for individuals or populations, indicators for specific conditions are frequently used. Some of the indicators that are used include incidence statistics for specific conditions, symptom checklists, and various measures of disability.*

Reportable (or notifiable conditions) are those diseases that must be reported by law to health authorities. The National Notifiable Diseases Surveillance System (NNDSS) is the mechanism by which notifiable disease data, such as those on gonorrhea, hepatitis, Lyme disease, and pertussis (whooping cough), are gathered. It should be recalled that these particular diseases have been singled out primarily because of their communicable nature. A *notifiable disease* is one for which regular, frequent, and timely information on individual cases is considered necessary for the prevention and control of that disease. Public health officials are particularly interested in these conditions, since they have the potential to spread to epidemic proportions. Note that they are virtually all acute conditions, at a time when the major health problems are attributable to chronic conditions. For this reason, reportable morbid conditions have become less useful as indicators of health status. Box 7.1 provides more information on the NNDSS and its data resources.

Many other health conditions that are monitored through reports from health facilities, sample surveys, and ongoing panel studies. Federal health agencies conduct periodic surveys of hospital inpatients and ambulatory patients utilizing clinics and other outpatient services.† In addition, databases have been established for the systematic compilation of information on inpatient and to a lesser extent outpatient utilization. These data collection efforts allow for the identification of cases for a wide variety of conditions and the monitoring of the level of these conditions over time. While this information is invaluable, coverage is far from complete at this point. It also should be remembered that these compilations include only reported cases. If individuals afflicted by various disorders are not diagnosed and treated, they will not show up in these studies.

---

*In addition, multiple comorbidities have been combined into indices that can be used, for example, to estimate survival rates from breast cancer (Fleming et al., 1999).
†The National Ambulatory Medical Survey and other similar data collection efforts are discussed in some detail in Chapter 9.

Box 7.1

The Collection of Notifiable Disease Data
through the National Notifiable Diseases Surveillance System

In 1878, Congress authorized the US Marine Hospital Service (i.e., the forerunner of the Public Health Service [PHS]) to collect morbidity reports regarding cholera, smallpox, plague, and yellow fever from US consuls overseas. This information was to be used for instituting quarantine measures to prevent the introduction and spread of these diseases into the United States. In 1879, a specific Congressional appropriation was made for the collection and publication of reports of "notifiable diseases." The authority for weekly reporting and publication of these reports was expanded by Congress in 1893 to include data from states and municipal authorities. To increase the uniformity of the data, Congress enacted a law in 1902 directing the Surgeon General to provide forms for the collection and compilation of data and for the publication of reports at the national level. In 1912, state and territorial health authorities, in conjunction with the PHS, recommended immediate telegraphic reporting of five infectious diseases and the monthly reporting of 10 additional diseases.

The first annual summary of the notifiable diseases in 1912 included reports of 10 diseases from 19 states, the District of Columbia, and Hawaii. By 1928, all states, the District of Columbia, Hawaii, and Puerto Rico were participating in national reporting of 29 specified diseases. At their annual meeting in 1950, the state and territorial health officers authorized a conference of state and territorial epidemiologists whose purpose was to determine which diseases should be reported to PHS. In 1961, the Centers for Disease Control (CDC), now known as the Centers for Disease Control and Prevention, assumed responsibility for the collection and publication of data concerning nationally notifiable diseases.

The list of nationally notifiable diseases is revised periodically. A disease may

---

The use of symptom checklists in sample surveys is another approach to the development of morbidity indicators. A list of symptoms that has been statistically validated is utilized to collect data for the calculation of a morbidity index. These are utilized to derive health status measures for both physical and mental illness (Warnecke, 1995). Usually there are 15 or 20 symptoms, since it is difficult to retain respondents' attention much longer. While the symptoms are sometimes examined individually, the main use is in the calculation of an index. Typically, the number of symptoms is simply summed and this becomes the index score for that individual. In some cases, the symptoms may be weighted on the grounds that some symptoms may be more important in the determination of morbidity levels

be added to the list as a new pathogen emerges, or a disease may be deleted as its incidence declines. Public health officials at state health departments and the CDC continue to collaborate in determining which diseases should be nationally notifiable. The Council of State and Territorial Epidemiologists (CSTE), with input from CDC, makes recommendations annually for additions and deletions to the list of nationally notifiable diseases. However, reporting of nationally notifiable diseases to the CDC by the states is voluntary. Reporting is currently mandated (i.e., by state legislation or regulation) only at the state level. The list of diseases that are considered notifiable therefore varies slightly by state. All states generally report the internationally quarantinable diseases (i.e., cholera, plague, and yellow fever) in compliance with the World Health Organization's international health regulations.

Currently, there are 52 infectious diseases designated as notifiable at the national level. Infectious disease data also are available for all 50 states, the District of Columbia, and 122 selected cities. The data are available on a monthly basis in *Morbidity and Mortality Weekly Report*, a CDC publication, and on the worldwide web at http://www2.cdc.gov:81/mmwr/mmwr.htm. Additional information on notifiable diseases can be found at http://www. cdc.gov.

Before the 1990s, data in the National Notifiable Diseases Surveillance System consisted primarily of summary statistics that lacked demographic information for persons with reported diseases. By 1990, all 50 states were using the CDC's National Electronic Telecommunications System for Surveillance to report individual case data that included demographic information (without personal identifiers) about most nationally notifiable diseases. These data are important for evaluating sex-specific differences in the occurrence of infectious diseases; monitoring infectious disease morbidity trends; determining the relative disease burdens among demographically diverse subpopulations in the United States; targeting prevention; and identifying priorities for research and control.

SOURCE: Downloaded reports from the CDC website (1997) URL http://www2.cdc.gov.

than others. For example, occasional chest pains may be given more weight than an occasional cough.

A primary rationale for the utilization of symptom checklists is the fact that much of the population is free of clinically identifiable disorders but is likely to have some, albeit minor, manifestations of ill health. Virtually everyone has vaguely defined symptoms of some type at various times or clearly identifiable ones that cannot be linked to a particular clinical condition. It is further argued, with regard to both physical and mental conditions, that these "everyday" symptoms are more significant measures of health status than are the comparatively rare clinical conditions. Symptom checklists also are attractive because of their objective nature and generally agreed-upon definitions. Virtually everyone is going to agree on what constitutes an "occasional cough" or "occasional dizzy spells," but clinical diagnoses are often misunderstood by patients or obscured by the terminological complexity of the health care setting.

Symptom checklists usually are based on answers directly obtained from survey respondents. Respondents either complete a questionnaire that contains the checklist or provide responses to an interviewer who records them. In some rare cases, the checklist will include signs as well as symptoms, and clinical personnel will be involved in the data collection process to obtain test results. This approach is occasionally utilized, for example, in studies of psychiatric morbidity, in which case the clinician will typically administer various psychiatric tests. The index calculated in this manner generally reflects a combination of symptoms reported by the respondent and signs observed by the clinician.

Another group of health status measures might be generally referred to as disability measures. Like other aspects of morbidity, disability is extremely difficult to operationalize. While it would appear simple to enumerate the blind, deaf, or otherwise handicapped, the situation is actually quite complex. A wide variety of other conditions that are not so clear-cut cloud the picture. Does lower back pain that interferes with work constitute a disability? When does an arthritic condition become disabling? How is mental retardation classified and at what point? Even those disabilities that appear obvious defy easy categorization due to the subjective dimension of disability. There are many hearing-impaired individuals and amputees, for example, who would take exception to being classified as disabled.*

This definitional problem is partly resolved by the utilization of more objective and easily measured indicators as proxies for disability. These might be referred to as "restriction" indicators, since they reflect the extent to which affected individuals are restricted in terms of work or school activities. Measures in this category include: work-loss days, school-loss days, bed-restricted days, and limitation of activity indicators. The number of days missed from work or school, the number of days individuals are restricted to bed, and the extent to which individuals cannot carry out routine daily activities can all be calculated and used as proxy measures of morbidity. While such measures are being used increasingly, it should be remembered that much of this information is available only from sample surveys. It is possible that many "cases" go undiscovered and uncounted. Nevertheless, significant variations have been identified in terms of the demographic correlates of disability as measured in this manner.

Finally, there are health status measures related to ascertaining medical

---

*The extent of this definitional problem has been recognized by the US Census Bureau, which (after an unsuccessful data collection attempt in 1970) decided to discontinue a question on disability. No one could agree on what constituted a disability. Another attempt at calculating the level of functional disability and activity limitations within the population was made with the 1990 census.

outcomes. Medical outcomes measurement is a growing area of interest for both researchers and decision makers, with outcomes seen as indicators of service delivery efficiency and medical success. The short-form health survey (SF-36) is one device used to measure outcomes (Ware and Sherbowrne, 1992). It includes one multi-item scale that assesses eight health concepts: (1) limitations in physical activities, (2) limitations in social activities, (3) limitations in usual role activities related to physical health problems, (4) pain, (5) general mental health, (6) limitations in usual role activities related to emotional problems, (7) vitality, and (8) general health perceptions. The SF-36 is suitable for self-administration, computerized administration, or administration by a trained interviewer in person or over the telephone. Box 7.2 explores the relationship between age, gender, and reasons for visiting a physician.

Assuming that high quality morbidity data are available, several other measures can be utilized. Two of the most useful measures are incidence and prevalence rates. An *incidence rate* refers to the number of new cases of a disease or condition over a certain time period expressed as a number per 1,000, 10,000, or 100,000 population at risk. A *prevalence rate* divides the total number of persons with the disease or condition in question by the population at risk with respect to a specific point in time. Again, the population at risk is the number of persons who have some nonzero probability of contracting the condition in question. For example, the incidence rate for persons diagnosed as having AIDS in 1995 in the United States was:

$$\frac{\text{Number of persons diagnosed as having AIDS in 19995 (71,547)}}{\text{Population at risk in 1995 (262,755,000)}}$$

or 27.2 cases per 100,000 persons in 1995. The prevalence rate, on the other hand, includes the total number of persons with AIDS in 1995 divided by the population at risk. In this instance the population at risk is the total population, minus those who already had AIDS in 1995, since this is a prevalence rate and the entire population has been theoretically at risk. In 1995, the AIDS prevalence rate was about 72.7 persons per 100,000 population (US Bureau of the Census 1996: Tables 14, 134, and 217). The prevalence rate always exceeds the incidence rate, since the former is but a fraction of the latter. The only time the two rates are nearly comparable is when the condition is acute and of very short duration. For example, the incidence rate would almost equal the prevalence rate at the height of a 24-hour virus epidemic since victims recover almost as quickly as they are affected.

Incidence and prevalence rates can both serve a useful planning purpose. If the analyst knows, for example, that the incidence rate for a certain medical procedure is 17 per 1000 population aged 65 years and over and has reason to believe that the incidence rate for that procedure will remain nearly constant for the next 5 years, then the demand for that procedure 5 years in the future can be

Box 7.2

Demographic Characteristics and Reasons for Visiting a Physician

Most individuals with health problems eventually end up at a physician's office. Data on office visits to a physician can be examined in terms of the characteristics of these patients. By examining the presenting symptoms of those representing different demographic profiles, the extent to which health conditions are unevenly distributed within the population can be demonstrated.

The table below presents the most frequent reasons for visiting a physician for three groups of patients based on distinct age and sex characteristics. This comparison is based on rates developed through the National Ambulatory Care Survey, which uses data from the general population and physicians' practices to calculate the rate of physician utilization by health problem and demographic characteristics. This simple example illustrates the differences in morbidity experience for males and females and for individuals of different age groups. The relative occurrence of acute and chronic conditions is apparent in this example. An even more detailed picture of morbidity distribution could be presented if such variables as race, income, and lifestyle were factored in.

Females 15–24	Males 25–44	Females 65 and older
Throat symptoms	Back symptoms	Vision problems
Acne and related	Throat symptoms	Hypertension
Abdominal pain	Skin rash	Cataracts
Headache	Low back pain	Dizziness
Cough	Knee symptoms	Diabetes
Earache/Ear infection	Cough	Back symptoms
Skin rash	Chest pain	Chest pain
Back symptoms	Headache	Leg symptoms
Knee symptoms	Depression	Knee symptoms
Vaginal symptoms	Anxiety/nervousness	Cough
Neck symptoms	Hypertension	Abdominal pain
Colds	Neck symptoms	Skin lesions
Allergies	Shoulder symptoms	Shortness of breath
Urinary tract infections	Anal/rectum symptoms	Arthritis

SOURCE: National Center for Health Statistics. (1998). *National Ambulatory Medical Care Survey, 1993.* Hyattsville, MD: National Center for Health Statistics; unpublished NCHS data.

determined by multiplying the incidence rate by the projected population of persons age 65 and above. The prevalence rate can be used in much the same way when the condition is a chronic one. This is precisely the way in which many hospitals and other health care providers forecast demand for their services. More refined figures can be generated by creating a set of projections (or likely scenarios) based on different assumptions, given that incidence and prevalence rates may change over time and that population projections may vary. Methods of estimating and projecting health care needs are discussed in Box 7.3.

The incidence rate also is a valuable measure in epidemiological investigations. If a new or mysterious condition afflicts a population, epidemiologists can trace the spread of the condition through the population by backtracking using incidence data. The cause or population of origin of a new disease often can be determined only by identifying the characteristics of the victims and the conditions under which the disease was contracted. The exact date of occurrence becomes crucial if the epidemiological detective is to link the onset to a particular set of circumstances. Quite often the key is the demographic characteristics of the victims. AIDS is a case in point wherein the means of transmission is identified based on the characteristics of the victims.

Two additional rates utilized by demographers and useful to health planners are case rates and case fatality rates. A *case rate* is merely an expression of the reported incidence of a disease per 1000, 10,000, or 100,000 persons and is not as finely tuned as a rate that is adjusted for the population at risk. The *case fatality rate* is generated by dividing the number of persons who die from a certain disease by the number of persons who contracted that disease. The quotient is expressed as a percentage. For example, through 1996, 7629 children had contracted AIDS and 4406, about 58%, had died (Centers for Disease Control and Prevention, 1997: website). Most often, cohorts of persons first diagnosed with a disease are followed through time to measure levels of sickness, response to various treatment modalities, and the ultimate cause of death. In a recent study successive cohorts of pediatric AIDS patients who contracted the disease between 1979 and 1991 were followed over time. Although the case fatality rate was high for all cohorts, median survival time increased over the interval. The increase in survival is linked in part to improvements in pediatric AIDS treatment (Barhart et al., 1996). It is possible to refine the above rates to include more narrowly defined populations at risk. However, measurement techniques are in need of further development, especially now that there is access to the detailed data required for such expansion and improvement.

Morbidity Trends

The presentation of morbidity trends that follows should indicate to the reader why morbidity is such an important issue for demographers, health care

Box 7.3

Estimates and Projections of Health Care Needs in a Market Area

From a strategic planning perspective, there is a great deal of need for health services demand estimates and projections. Data requirements for strategic planning vary from certificate-of-need applications to long-range capital improvement projects that involve significant financial investment. Overall, the question most often asked is, "After the building is built and/or the service is offered, will there be enough patients to generate an adequate return on investment?" Part of this question must be addressed from a nondemographic perspective; for example, what is the competitive environment like, and is it likely that technological breakthroughs will significantly alter the nature of the service?

On the demographic side, the number of persons (along with their characteristics) in an area sets the general parameters of the market. As discussed in Chapters 5 and 6, determining boundaries can be accomplished by plotting a sample of patient addresses on a good quality map or utilizing geographic information systems software to plot the data. Demographic data (e.g., size and age distribution) for the area can be obtained through traditional demographic sources (e.g., population estimates by state or local agencies) or from data vendors. In order to produce estimates and projections of the number of persons needing a specific service, an incidence or prevalence rate may be multiplied by a population estimate or projection. Assuming that we already have the requisite population data, then all we need are incidence rates. These can be produced by using national incidence rates (available through the CDC or National Center for Health Statistics) or by calculating market area incidence rates by combining local area population data and morbidity counts or estimates.

The procedure for estimating needs is simple. Multiply the incidence rate by the population estimate or projection to arrive at the size of the population in need for the entire market area. The market area total then can be adjusted for the market share held by the organization in question. Moreover, in making projections it is possible to adjust these projected figures for (1) expected change in regard to market share, (2) projected alterations in market area, and (3) upward or downward movements in incidence and prevalence rates.

If, for example, a certain disease has an incidence rate of 1,650 per 100,000 males aged 55 to 64 and a market area contains 200,000 males in this age range, then the estimated or projected incidence of the disease is 3,300 cases. Given that the provider in question has 20% of the market, 660 patients can be expected. Of course, these are estimates based on other estimates, so the researcher should place confidence intervals (or at least examine several alternative scenarios) around the point estimates in order to set a realistic level of expectation.

planners, and policy strategists. As was discussed in Chapters 2 and 3, there has been a major shift away from acute conditions to chronic conditions in the United States. This is an important shift, because it is responsible for significant changes in the health status of the population and in the type of health services required. The trend away from acute conditions is reflected in the reduction in incidence rates for many infectious and parasitic diseases.

Data for selected notifiable diseases for three time periods are shown in Table 7.1. As can be seen, there has been considerable fluctuation in the number of cases of these diseases over the 26-year period. While there were approximately 47,000 reported cases of measles in 1970, for example, there were only around 300 in 1996. This same downward trend can be seen in the data for mumps (105,000 to 700 cases); malaria (3,100 to 1,500 cases); and syphilis (91,000 to 11,000 cases). At the same time, increased incidence is seen for AIDS, animal rabies, and pertussis.

On the other hand, cardiovascular diseases and cancer, the two leading causes of death in the United States today, typically do not immediately result in death and therefore require a different health care delivery system from one dominated by acute conditions. In fact, an estimated 80% of contemporary health conditions are neither immediately fatal nor curable. Thus, a large proportion of the US population is under lifelong management for hypertension, arthritis, diabetes, or some other chronic condition. For example, in 1995, 22 million, 28 million, and 33 million Americans had heart disease, high blood pressure, and/or an arthritic condition, respectively (US Bureau of the Census, 1996: Table 219).

Table 7.1. Cases of Selected Notifiable Diseases in the United States, 1970–1996

Disease	1970	1985	1996
AIDS	NA[a]	8,249	65,475
Hepatitis A	56,800	23,200	29,024
Hepatitis B	8,300	26,600	9,994
Animal rabies	3,224	5,565	6,676
Malaria	3,051	1,049	1,542
Syphilis	91,000	68,000	11,110
Gonorrhea	600,000	911,000	308,737
Tuberculosis	37,100	22,200	19,096
Measles	47,400	2,800	295
Mumps	105,000	3,000	658
Pertussis[b]	4,200	3,600	6,467

[a]NA, not available.
[b]Whooping cough.
SOURCES: US Bureau of the Census (1996); downloaded data tables from Centers for Disease Control and Prevention website, *Morbidity and Mortality Weekly Report.*

While treatment and cure are still emphasized, long-term disease management and the development of methods for coping with chronic illnesses are the challenges facing the health care system today. The system has attempted to adapt as chronic conditions have become more a part of everyday life. Case management becomes important, since care is continuous and different forms of therapy may be utilized at different stages. Chronic conditions can be expensive to treat, raising both ethical and financial issues that must be addressed.

Diseases and conditions have been linked to the demographic characteristics of those more likely and less likely to be afflicted. Even among the elderly who have higher rates of morbidity, wide differences exist in chronic disease prevalence. While about 45% of the population aged 65 and over has high blood pressure (a chronic condition), about 15% of this population has cancer, diabetes, and/or has had a heart attack. Women are more likely than men to report high blood pressure, cancer, hip fractures, and diabetes (Brown, 1989). Similar sex differences in chronic conditions have been reported for all ages (Verbrugge, 1988). Women are more likely to report having anemia, nervous disorders, and respiratory conditions. The number of hours spent viewing television and fast food meal intake are more highly associated with obesity in women than in men (Jeffrey and French, 1998).

The infectious and chronic disease receiving the greatest amount of current attention is AIDS. The incidence of AIDS increased from 199 new cases in 1981 to about 65,000 in 1996 (Centers for Disease Control and Prevention, 1997). The spread of this disease has become a major concern, since it is fatal in virtually every case and is spread by means of social interaction. By 1995, nearly 497,000 persons in the United States had been diagnosed (prevalence) as having AIDS and almost 306,000 had died from the disease. Over 31,000 persons died from AIDS in 1995 alone (US Bureau of the Census, 1996: Tables 134 and 217). Moreover, there is some evidence that AIDS deaths are underreported by 5 to 8%. Using the 5% undercount figure, over 321,000 persons had died of AIDS in the United States through 1995. In addition, it should be noted that the incidence of AIDS has declined since 1993. From 1993 to 1995, the number of AIDS cases reported declined from 103,533 to 71,547 (US Bureau of the Census, 1996: Table 213).

Issues concerning behavioral, genetic, and environmental factors that are related to morbidity also are of interest. Heart disease, for example, has been linked to health-related behavior in the early years of life. Research shows a strong association between high cholesterol levels in the blood of teenagers and the early stages of atherosclerosis. A combination of smoking and high levels of low-density lipoprotein (LDL) has a deleterious effect on artery walls (Winslow, 1990). In addition, tobacco and alcohol consumption have been directly linked to a host of diseases and ultimately to increased levels of mortality. Public pressure from sources ranging from the Surgeon General's statements with regard to the relationship between smoking and lung cancer to congressional action limiting the advertising of tobacco products have been indirectly linked to a reduction in cigarette consumption.

More recently, *homocysteine*, an amino acid in the blood that damages artery walls and causes heart attacks, has become a focus of medical research. Levels of homocysteine are genetically influenced, although there are ways to artificially decrease the levels. Testing for the level of homocysteine is now urged by some members of the medical community in part because it is relatively easy to lower the level via commonly taken vitamins.

Population researchers have been able to establish a relationship between demographic characteristics and tobacco consumption. For example, while 37% of the 45- to 64-year-olds in the United States have never smoked a cigarette, 55% of the 19- to 29-year-olds have never smoked. About one-third of all adult males in the United States are former smokers (US Department of Health and Human Services, 1989). The relationship between age and smoking status illustrates what demographers call a "period effect." In the case of smoking, members of older cohorts were exposed to a great deal of social pressure to smoke, and many ended up doing so. Today, there are counterpressures with regard to smoking, and lower levels of consumption have resulted. Thus, lower levels of smoking-linked morbidity and mortality can be expected in the future as a result of the reduction in current levels of smoking. Recent reductions in cardiovascular disease rates already have been linked to a reduction in tobacco consumption. Recent anti-alcohol and antidrug campaigns could have a long-lasting impact on alcohol- and drug-related morbidity (and mortality) if behavior patterns are permanently altered.

Changes in the size and composition of the US population must be considered when evaluating trends in morbidity. The aging of the population portends a corresponding increase in chronic conditions. Current estimates place the number of Alzheimer's disease victims at approximately 4 million; projections indicate that this number could rise to 14 million over the next 50 years. A proportionately larger African-American population is likely to generate more cases of sickle-cell anemia.

Figure 7.1 presents data on the age structure of two notifiable diseases: AIDS and tuberculosis. As can be seen, the age compositions of these two populations are markedly different. About 79% of all AIDS cases were ascribed to persons aged 20 through 44 (Centers for Disease Control and Prevention, 1997). On the other hand, nearly 44% of the tuberculosis cases were ascribed to persons aged 50 and over. The age restructuring of the US population is certain to impact the prevalence of these two diseases.

Morbidity analysis and reduction are on the cutting edge of what many describe as the most exciting aspects of medical science. However, some of the excitement has been tempered by the more sobering moral and ethical issues faced as a result of attempting to reduce levels of sickness. For example, several recent

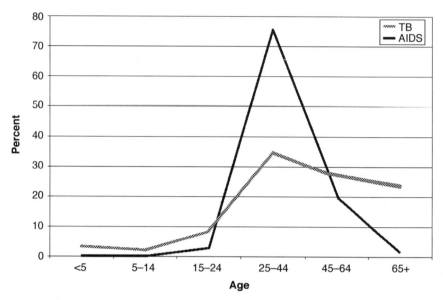

Figure 7.1. Age distribution of persons diagnosed with tuberculosis or AIDS.

breakthroughs in the potential treatment of Parkinson's syndrome and Alz-heimer's disease rely on fetal implants as a method of treatment. Critics of this line of research evoke an image of fetal tissue being extracted before death has occurred, as well as the more general concern that many fetuses will be unethically used in some way should this research continue. Such issues no doubt will surround many future attempts at disease control and elimination.

MORTALITY

Introduction

Mortality refers to the level of death characterizing a population. The study of mortality examines the relationship between death and the size, composition, and distribution of the population. Furthermore, mortality studies investigate the who, how, why, and when issues related to dying. Demographers have contributed greatly to the understanding of mortality and health care issues both in terms of the development of mortality measures and the identification of patterns of mortality within the population. This section begins by discussing concepts and measures utilized in the study of mortality. Following that, trends in mortality are described with respect to the measures previously introduced. The implications of mortality trends for the demand and provision of health care services are then addressed.

Mortality Measures

Death is defined as the complete cessation of life after a live birth has taken place (Shryock et al., 1973). Deaths that occur prior to a live birth—fetal deaths—are allocated to a separate category. Though the words cessation of life may seem to comprise a simple, straightforward definition, medical advances are making the interpretation of death more complex. As the ability to prolong life artificially has improved, the distinction between life and death has blurred. The definition of death is constantly being reconsidered in the light of medical and technological advances.

The primary source of mortality data in the United States is the governmental registry based on certificates filed at the time of death. By law, death certificates must be filed whenever a death occurs, typically with the county health department. In turn, these certificates are aggregated at the local, state, and national levels. The data collected on the certificate include primary cause of death, contributing causes, and individual social and economic characteristics such as sex, age, race–ethnicity, last occupation, place of residence, and place of death. Using these data, demographers can begin to study the relationship between the cause of death and a variety of demographic variables.

The most basic way to measure mortality is simply to count the number of deaths. These counts are usually based on a one-year period and may be reported for the nation as a whole, states, metropolitan areas, or smaller geographic areas. Compiling death counts over a period of years has helped identify trends with regard to increases or decreases in mortality. Deaths also are cross-classified by the medical, social, and economic characteristics of the deceased. Two of the most useful of these characteristics to demographers are the cause of death and the age at which death occurred.

Using a simple count of deaths in the analysis of mortality has several shortcomings. As in the case of fertility analysis, the comparison of deaths among geographic areas or over time generally is not very useful, given the various population sizes generating these deaths. Sometimes it is of little value to compare the number of deaths in community X (population 10,000) with the number of deaths in community Y (population 100,000). Therefore, demographers have created a number of measures of mortality that allow for both area-to-area and longitudinal comparisons (Pressat, 1972, pp. 71–106).

The simplest measure used is the *crude death rate* (CDR). Like the crude birth rate described in Chapter 6, this rate expresses mortality as the number of deaths per 1000 population. The CDR is calculated as follows:

$$CDR = \frac{\text{Number of deaths in year } X}{\text{Midyear population in year } X} \times 1000$$

To avoid single-year anomalies in the number of deaths, especially in small geographic areas, researchers frequently take a 3-year average of deaths, with the population for the middle year used as the denominator. The CDR for the United States in 1997 was:

$$\frac{2,314,245}{267,656,000} \times 1000 = 8.6, \text{ or } 8.6 \text{ deaths per 1000 population}$$

By comparison, the CDR was 8.6 in 1990, 8.8 in 1980, 9.5 in 1970, 9.6 in 1950, and 10.8 in 1940.

Just as everyone in a population is not at risk of pregnancy, not all of the population has the same risk of death. Lumping all deaths into one crude rate, as is done with the CDR, limits this measure's usefulness. Therefore, *age-specific death rates* (ASDRs) are often generated. ASDRs are usually calculated for 5-year age intervals, though for more detailed analyses 3- or even 1-year intervals may be used. ASDRs for 5-year age intervals are calculated using this formula:

$$\text{ASDR} = \frac{\text{Deaths to persons age } X \text{ to age } X + 5 \text{ in year } Y}{\text{Number of persons age } X \text{ to age } X + 5 \text{ in year } Y} \times 1000$$

with X to $X + 5$ signifying the 5-year age interval. As noted above, three-year death averages may be used as numerators if there is substantial year-to-year variation in the number of deaths. In 1997, the ASDR for persons aged 80 to 84 in the United States was:

$$\frac{344,731}{4,642,000} \times 1000 = 75.3 \text{ deaths per 1000 persons aged 80 to 84.}$$

By comparison, age-specific death rates are lowest at the ages 5 to 9 (0.2), stay relatively low through ages 45 to 49 (3.8), and rise again at the ages 65 to 69 (20.6).

Another measure, the *infant mortality rate* (IMR), is used to determine the death rate during the first year of life. The IMR is always expressed as a 1-year rate and is examined separately because of the greatly increased probability of dying during the first year of life as compared with subsequent ages. Persons under age 1, for example, are 20 times more likely to die in a given year than someone in the 1- to 4-year-old category. The IMR is calculated as follows:

$$\text{IMR} = \frac{\text{Deaths to persons under one year of age in year } X}{\text{Live births in year } X} \times 1000$$

Notice that the denominator of the rate is births and not population. In 1997, the IMR in the United States was:

$$\frac{28,045}{3,800,000} \times 1000$$

or 7.4 deaths per 1000 live births. Some confusion arises for persons who are born in one year and die in another. Demographers have formulated "adjustment" factors that reflect the carryover from one year to the next, though the rates change very little when these alterations are made.

Other rates have been designed to specify further the timing of early death. The IMR may be divided into *neonatal* and *postneonatal* components, with the former referring to deaths during the first 28 days of life and the latter reflecting deaths occurring from 29 days to one year. Research on infant mortality has identified causes of death during the first month of life as congenital abnormalities, low birth weight and birth complications, respiratory distress symptoms, and maternal complications of pregnancy. Recent research has revealed the increasingly important impact that prematurity and the associated low birth weight have on infant mortality (Sowards, 1997; Frisbie et al., 1996). Deaths during the remainder of the first year are most often related to environmental factors. The four causes listed above account for nearly 59% of all neonatal mortality. Sudden infant death syndrome (SIDS) accounted for more than 30% of the post neonatal deaths in 1995 (National Center for Health Statistics, 1997: Table 27).

There are several other measures of early life mortality demographers use. The *perinatal mortality rate* combines late fetal and early infant mortality into one rate. This measure is used to assess the quality of antenatal and perinatal medical care (Richarddus et al., 1988). It is calculated by adding the later fetal deaths (usually after 28 weeks of gestation) to early infant deaths (usually those during the first 7 days after birth, but sometimes the first 28 days) for a given year and dividing that sum by the number of live births in that year. The *fetal death ratio* takes the number of late fetal deaths and divides that number by the total number of live births. A related measure, the *maternal mortality rate*, divides the number of female deaths due to childbearing-related causes by the number of births.

As stated earlier, death certificates contain information regarding the primary and contributing causes of death. There are several potential problems with these data. The first is one of correct specification of the primary cause of death. While identifying the cause of death may seem relatively easy to the layperson, in practice it is often difficult and may result in the incorrect recording of the cause. Some deaths are complicated in that more than one condition is present (e.g., cancer and pneumonia) with several bodily systems affected (e.g., lungs and heart). The second problem is closely related to the first in that it is often difficult to distinguish between and among the primary and contributing causes.

Cognizant of these potential problems, demographers calculate *cause-specific death rates*. The method is similar to that of the CDR, with the number of deaths from a specific cause comprising the numerator and the total population as the denominator of the rate. Cause-specific rates can be calculated for specific age intervals as well. It is sometimes useful to decompose the CDR into cause-specific components and to calculate the percentage of total deaths attributable to one cause. These figures, which are derived by dividing the number of deaths from one cause by the total number of deaths represent the proportion of population dying of a specific cause. Box 7.4 discusses standardization techniques (Chapter 5) for adjusting mortality rates for two or more areas for which compositional differences exist.

Life Tables

Although inappropriately named, life tables provide health care planners and demographers with a great deal of useful information (Namboodiri and Suchindran, 1987, pp. 11–50; Schoen, 1988, pp. 3–21). Life tables are a mechanism for combining death data and rates into a summary measure of mortality that is somewhat analogous to the total fertility rate, gross reproduction rate, and net reproduction rate discussed in Chapter 6. That is, age-specific mortality rates are transformed and combined in such a way as to generate a measure of life expectancy. *Life expectancy* is the average number of years a hypothetical group or cohort of persons born today or alive at a particular point in time could be expected to live if current ASDRs remain constant throughout their lifetimes. In other words, as the cohort ages, it is subject to probabilities of dying specific to that age interval, which in turn are based on current ASDRs. Life expectancy projections are made by adjusting ASDRs to match the assumed levels for some time in the future. Table 7.2 presents an abridged life table for the United States in 1995. It has been "abridged" by combining single-age intervals into 5-year intervals. Life table functions are summarized in Box 7.5.

Life tables provide a host of information about mortality conditions, and it is possible to trace trends in mortality by assembling life table data for more than one time period. Comparative life table analysis can yield information on life expectancy differentials by sex and race for any age. For example, while life expectancy at birth is over 6 years greater for females than it is for males, the difference narrows to 5 years at age 40, 3 years at age 65, and less than 2 years at age 80. When one looks jointly at race and sex, larger differentials emerge. African-American females outlive African-American males by nearly 9 years. White females outlive African-American males by over 12 years (Hoyer et al., 1999: Table 6).

Not only do these data have serious social, economic, and political implications, but the differentials indicate that two very different populations exist vis-à-vis the health care system. Health care providers and policy makers alike must take differential life expectancies into consideration in performing their respective tasks. Comparing African-American male and white females, for example, it found that, out of 100,000 white females born (L_0), over 85,000 are still alive at age 65 (L_{65-70}). For African-American males, the number remaining alive at age 65 (L_{65-70}) is about 57,000 or only about two thirds that of the white female population. This differential has serious implications for planning for the elderly

---

Box 7.4

Standardization of Health Data

Standardization is a way to adjust mortality rates or other rates for compositional factors that have an effect on those rates. The rate adjustments can be used to facilitate both longitudinal and comparative mortality analysis. For example, the number of deaths occurring in any year is a function of three components: health status, population size, and age composition. Since mortality rates are frequently used as indicators of health conditions, it is important to hold size and age structure constant when mortality indices are being constructed.

The calculation of rates addresses the concerns over the difference in population size and allows the analyst to compare the health status of two populations that are quite different demographically. The crude death rate (CDR), for example, may be used for this purpose. However, a problem emerges in using the CDR for comparison purposes because it is influenced by differences in age structure. That is, populations with younger age structures and low probabilities of dying for most of the population tend to report low rates. For example, while age-specific death rates (ASDRs) at all ages are higher in Mexico than in the United States, the CDR is lower in Mexico due to its very young age structure. In addition, relatively large state-to-state differences in the CDR exist due to age structure differences. "Old" states such as Florida (10.7 deaths for 1000 population) and Pennsylvania (10.4 per 1000) have higher rates than "young" states such as Alaska (4.0) and Utah (5.5). These differences emerge not because the environment in Alaska is more than twice as healthy as that in Florida, but because the population of Alaska is much younger. Therefore, the unadjusted CDR is not a good comparative measure. Direct comparison of ASDRs is more useful and quite instructive but cumbersome at the same time.

It is possible to adjust or standardize rates in order to control for age structure differences. One way to accomplish this task would be to select a given age structure, apply the ASDRs from two different populations, and then compare both the number of deaths and death rates (CDR) that resulted. This standardization is based on the number of deaths hypothetically generated if the age structures were the same. The analyst would simply multiply two or more sets of ASDRs (one set for each county, city, or time period being considered) by the standard age structure and generate a total number of expected deaths given the set of mortality rates. The number of expected deaths is divided by the size of the base population to yield an age adjusted CDR. The adjusted rate combining the ASDRs then can be compared and the differences assumed to represent true differences in health conditions. Demographers distinguish between "direct" and "indirect" standardization to refer to the use of different age structures for base population. The same basic principles of standardization can be used to adjust rates for other factors, such as education, race, and ethnicity. Similarly, they can be used to adjust fertility rates to hold constant certain factors.

Table 7.2. Abridged Life Table for the United States, 1995

Age interval: Period of life between two exact stages stated in years (x to $x + n$)	Proportion dying: Proportion of persons alive at beginning of age interval dying during interval ($_nq_x$)	Of 100,000 born alive		Stationary: In the age interval ($_nL_x$)	Stationary population: In this and all subsequent age intervals (T_x)	Remaining lifetime: Average number of years of life remaining at beginning of age interval (e_x^0)
		Number living at beginning of age interval (l_x)	Number dying during age interval ($_nd_x$)			
0–1 year	0.0076	100,000	757	99,363	7,578,485	75.8
1–5 years	0.0016	99,283	159	396,599	7,479,482	75.4
5–10 years	0.0010	99,084	98	495,153	7,082,883	71.5
10–15 years	0.0013	98,986	125	494,687	6,587,730	66.6
15–20 years	0.0041	98,861	410	493,375	6,093,043	61.6
20–25 years	0.0054	98,451	527	490,964	5,599,668	56.9
25–30 years	0.0060	97,924	583	488,161	5,108,704	52.2
30–35 years	0.0080	97,341	779	484,803	4,620,543	47.5
35–40 years	0.0105	96,562	1,013	480,421	4,135,740	42.8
40–45 years	0.0138	95,549	1,315	474,692	3,655,319	38.3
45–50 years	0.0186	94,234	1,755	467,104	3,180,627	33.8
50–55 years	0.0280	92,479	2,586	456,336	2,713,523	29.3
55–60 years	0.0428	89,893	3,844	440,407	2,257,187	25.1
60–65 years	0.0671	86,049	5,770	416,602	1,816,780	21.1
65–70 yers	0.0983	80,279	7,888	382,527	1,400,178	17.4
70–75 years	0.1461	72,391	10,573	366,442	1,017,651	14.1
75–80 years	0.2126	61,818	13,140	277,041	681,209	11.0
80–85 years	0.3188	48,678	15,520	204,800	404,168	8.3
85 years and over	1.0000	33,158	33,158	199,368	199,368	6.0

SOURCE: National Center for Health Statistics (1997), Table 3.

health care market. Based on the above data, the African-American male population is considerably younger than the remaining three sex–race groupings. Coupled with additional psychographic and behavioral information, specific strategies
for the provision of health services could be formulated for this very different
market segment.

A final use for life tables involves the calculation of survival ratios. These
ratios are a means of determining the proportion of persons surviving from one
age interval to the next. Once calculated, they can be used to determine what
proportion of persons alive now can be expected to be alive at some point in the
future given the assumption that death rates remain relatively constant. Survival
ratios are derived by dividing one L_x figure by another L_x, depending on how far
forward or backward the user wishes to look. For example, the survival ratio of the
age interval 75 to 80 living to the interval 80 to 85 from Table 7.2 is as follows:

$$\text{Survival ratio} = \frac{L_{80-84}}{L_{75-80}} = \frac{204,800}{277,041} = 0.739 \text{ or } 73.9\%$$

That is, about 74% of the persons who are alive at age 75 can be expected to be
alive at age 80. Cause-specific life tables allow the measurement of the effect of
the hypothetical removal of certain causes of death on overall life expectancy.
Clinical researchers and health care administrators alike have a vested interest in
the survival ratios of patients on whom various procedures are performed.

While most life tables are constructed at the national or state levels, methods
have been developed to generate substate life expectancies. Furthermore, simple
life tables can be expanded to include more than one probability of exit. Life table
analysis also can be expanded to include joint probabilities of dying and having a
certain condition, such as a disability. For example, while life expectancy at birth
was 77.6 years for females in 1980, life expectancy without disability was 60.4
years (Crimmins et al., 1989). Box 7.5 focuses on using life tables for estimating
years of life lost. Further research along the same lines has resulted in the creation
of a composite indicator, *healthy life-year* (HeaLY). Life expectancy and morbidity data are combined to produce figures for health life-years lost due to a
variety of conditions (Hyder et al., 1998).

Mortality Trends

The total number of annual deaths in the United States, as indicated in Table
7.3, increased steadily from 1935 to 1998. This increase, to over 900,000 deaths
per year, has been generated in large part by a substantial population increase
(from 127.2 million to 270.3 million), even though death rates have declined. As
the population continues to age, the total number of deaths will continue to rise,
despite decreasing rates of population growth and further increases in longevity.

Box 7.5

Life Tables at a Glance

A life table is based on known mortality rates for specific age groups. Demographers use life table death probabilities for each age and the other functions of the life table subsequently derived. Statisticians can calculate the probability of dying during a particular interval using the following formula:

$$\text{Probability of dying } (nqx) = \frac{{}_nM_x}{1 + .5\,{}_nM_x}$$

where ${}_nM_x$ is the age-specific death rate for the age interval in question and n is the width of the age interval. Thus, for example, using the age-specific death rates calculated earlier, the probability of dying during the interval 80 to 84 years of age in 1984 is as follows:

$$\frac{0.0832(5)}{1 + \frac{1}{2}(0.0832)(5)} = 0.34$$

All life table functions are derived on the basis of one assumption: Age-specific death probabilities remain constant over the period of the life table. That is, if life expectancy at birth, e_0, is 74.7 years, then age-specific death probabilities at all ages must remain constant. A change in any of the probabilities results in a shorter or longer life expectancy, depending on whether the probabilities increased or decreased over time. Therefore, life expectancies derived from any life table must be interpreted with caution and with a view toward prospective changes in medical practice and health technology. While life expectancy at birth today in the United

---

Recently produced population projections show that the number of deaths will exceed 3 million per year early in the twenty-first century. The number of deaths per year during this period would have been approximately twice as high without the reduction in mortality rates that occurred during the twentieth century (White and Preston, 1996).

Given the wide variation in age structure by subnational geographic unit shown in Chapter 5 and area differences in ASDRs, it is not surprising that large differences in death rates exist between regions, divisions, states, counties, and cities. For example, in 1992, the CDR for Anchorage, Alaska, a city with a very young age structure, was 3.3 compared to 15.1 for Sacramento, California, a city with a much older age structure (US Bureau of the Census, 1994: Table c).

States is 74.7 years, age-specific death probabilities are likely to decrease over time and children born now will have a life expectancy somewhat greater than 74.7 years.

The x to $x + n$ column merely refers to the age intervals, such as 5 to 9 years for the population. Single-year intervals could have been chosen along with other age, sex, and race combinations. Other functions are defined as follows:

n^qx The proportion of persons alive at the beginning of the interval who died during the interval. For example, 1.15% of the population born died during the first year of life. In most instances, n^qx is referred to as the probability of dying.

l_x Known as the radix, an arbitrary 100,000 persons are chosen as the starting point. As deaths occur during each interval they are subtracted, and l_x becomes smaller; 100,000 minus 1,155 (n^dx, which is the number of deaths in the interval 0 to 1 years) equals 98,845, or the number of persons alive at age 1.

n^dx This is the number of deaths occurring during the age interval given the number of persons alive at the beginning of the interval, l_x, and the proportion of persons dying during the interval. Deaths in the age interval n^dx are derived by multiplying n^1x by n^qx.

$_nL_x$ The number of person-years lived during the interval. This involves multiplying the number of persons alive at the end of the interval by the width (number of years) of the interval and adding that product to the assumed number of years that those dying during the interval lived.

T_x The reverse sum of $_nL_x$ values. For example T_{80-85} is equal to the sum of T_{85} and over and T_{80-85} or $179,601 + 185,922 = 365,523$.

e_x The life expectancy at any age. For example, life expectancy at age 10 is 65.8 years. This column is derived by dividing T_x by l_x. Life expectancy at birth is calculated by dividing 7,474,573 by 100,000 to yield 74.7 years.

Table 7.4 presents age-specific death rates for the same 60-year period shown in Table 7.2. As can be seen, the time interval has been marked by substantial rate reductions. The largest decreases have been at the youngest ages. The infant mortality rate today is less than one seventh what it was in 1935, and mortality at ages 1 to 4 is only about one eleventh of the 1935 rate. At the older ages, mortality rates at ages 75 to 84 and 85 and over have declined by about one half and one third, respectively.

Figure 7.2 presents the ASDRs for 1935, 1970, and 1995 as three line graphs. The classic J-curve of mortality can be seen, as mortality rates drop to their lowest levels soon after the relatively high rates associated with birth only to rise again in later years. The curve shows a marked upward slope after ages 45 to 54. Compar-

Table 7.3. Total Number of Deaths for the United States, 1935–1998

Year	Deaths[a]	Year	Deaths	Year	Deaths	Year	Deaths
1998	2331	1990	2162	1970	1921	1950	1452
1997	2294	1985	2084	1965	1828	1945	1402
1996	2311	1980	1990	1960	1712	1940	1417
1995	2309	1975	1893	1955	1529	1935	1393

[a]Deaths in thousands.

SOURCES: US Bureau of the Census (1975); US Bureau of the Census (1990), Table 107; National Center for Health Statistics (1986), Table 1; National Center for Health Statistics (1997), Table 1; US Department of Health and Human Services (1997); National Center for Health Statistics (1999).

ing the three time intervals once again illustrate the decline in infant mortality and the increase in older adult mortality.

Infant and maternal mortality rates at 10-year intervals from 1920 are shown in Table 7.5. Since 1920, infant mortality rates have decreased to less than 10% of their former level, although as stated earlier a significant African American–white differential exists. The low relative age of the mother at birth (and therefore the lower birth weight) and the high probability of the mother not being married are important contributors to high African-American infant mortality rates. Maternal mortality rate declines have been even more dramatic. The 1997 rate is about 1% of the 1920 rate, reflecting the significant technological and health care improve-

Table 7.4. Death Rates by Age for the United States, 1935–1995

Age interval	1935	1950	1970	1984	1990	1995
Less than 1	60.9[a]	33.0	21.4	10.9	9.4	7.7
1–4	4.4	1.4	0.8	0.5	0.4	0.4
5–14	1.5	0.6	0.4	0.3	0.2	0.2
15–24	2.7	1.3	1.3	1.0	1.0	1.0
25–34	4.0	1.8	1.6	1.2	1.4	1.4
35–44	6.2	3.6	3.1	2.0	2.2	2.4
45–54	11.6	8.5	7.3	5.2	4.6	4.6
55–64	23.2	19.0	16.6	12.9	11.8	11.1
65–74	43.7	33.3	35.9	28.4	26.7	25.6
75–84	113.1	93.3	80.0	64.0	60.8	58.5
85 and over	224.2	202.0	163.4	152.2	147.8	154.7

[a]Deaths per 1000 population.

SOURCES: US Bureau of the Census (1975); National Center for Health Statistics (1984), Table 2; National Center for Health Statistics (1997), Table 6.

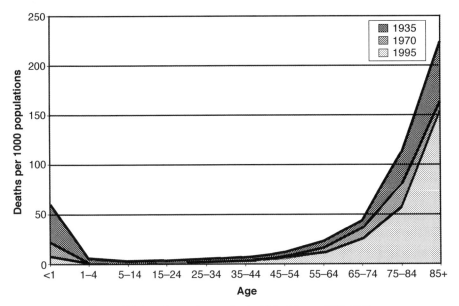

Figure 7.2. Death rates by age for the United States, 1935–1995.

ments that have been made. However, it should be noted that the African-American maternal death rate remains four times higher than the white rate.

Table 7.6 presents death rates for selected causes at approximately 20-year intervals since 1900. These causes were selected based on an examination of the major causes of death in 1900 and 1995. The rates are expressed in deaths per

Table 7.5. Infant and Maternal Mortality Rates in the United States, 1920–1997

Year	Infant mortality[a]	Maternal mortality[b]	Year	Infant mortality	Maternal mortality
1997	7.2	0.8	1960	26.0	3.7
1995	7.7	0.7	1950	29.2	8.3
1990	9.2	0.7	1940	47.0	37.3
1985	10.7	0.8	1930	64.6	67.3
1980	12.6	0.9	1920	85.8	79.9
1970	20.0	2.2			

[a]Deaths per 1,000 live births.
[b]Deaths per 10,000 live births.
SOURCES: US Bureau of the Census (1975); National Center for Health Statistics (1997); Hoyert *et al.* (1990), Tables 27 and 32.

Table 7.6. Selected Causes of Death for the United States, 1900–1995

Year	Major cardiovascular diseases	Influenza and pneumonia	Tuberculosis	Gastritis, duodenitis, enteritis, colitis	Malignant neoplasms
1995	340.8[a]	31.6	<1.0	<1.0	204.9
1990	368.3	32.0	<1.0	<1.0	203.2
1980	436.4	24.1	<1.0	<1.0	183.9
1970	496.0	30.9	2.6	0.6	162.8
1940	485.7	70.3	45.9	10.3	120.3
1920	364.7	207.3	113.1	53.7	83.4
1900	345.2	202.2	194.4	142.7	64.0

[a]Deaths per 100,000 population.
SOURCES: US Bureau of the Census (1975); US Bureau of the Census (1996), Table 129; National Center for Health Statistics (1997), Table 6.

100,000 persons and have not been adjusted for changes in age structure. As can be seen, there have been marked fluctuations in rates, with influenza and pneumonia, tuberculosis, and gastritis, among others, showing significant rate decreases. While these conditions were among the five leading causes of death in 1900, they no longer contribute to overall mortality in any significant fashion. Specifically, in 1900, tuberculosis, pneumonia, and diarrhea and enteritis accounted for nearly 30% of all mortality, while in the mid-1990s they accounted for less than 4%. Cancer (malignant neoplasms) and heart disease accounted for less than 12% of the deaths in the population in 1900. As a result of the growth of cancer as a leading cause of death in the United States, these two disease categories comprise about 55% of all deaths (National Center for Health Statistics, 1997: Table 7).

Deaths by cause also can be classified by race and age and a measure of "excess" deaths subsequently calculated. By examining death rates by cause for whites of both sexes and applying them to standard populations, the number of expected deaths can be derived. Comparing the expected deaths to the number reported results in an "excess" number of deaths (excess because whites have lower death rates). For example, one study has showed that for the category age 45 or younger African-American males had a 73% excess of deaths due to cirrhosis relative to white males in the same age cohort. Excess deaths for African-American males also were found for cardiovascular disorder, 59%; diabetes, 57%; and homicide, 84% (Bonanich, 1989). The excess death concept has also been utilized to assess the impact of influenza epidemics on mortality. A *severity index*, based on calculated excess deaths, has been found to be useful in understanding the effects of various influenza epidemics on mortality (Simonsen et al., 1997).

Table 7.7 presents life expectancy by sex for a number of intervals between 1900 and 1997. Not only has life expectancy increased greatly since 1900 (nearly

Table 7.7. Life Expectancy at Birth by Sex
in the United States, 1900–1997

Year	Males	Females	Year	Males	Females
1997	73.6	79.4	1960	66.6	73.1
1995	72.5	78.9	1950	65.6	71.1
1990	71.8	78.8	1940	60.8	65.2
1985	71.1	78.2	1930	58.1	61.6
1980	70.0	77.5	1920	53.6	54.6
1975	68.8	76.6	1910	48.4	51.8
1970	67.1	74.8	1900	46.3	48.3

SOURCES: US Bureau of the Census (1975); National Center for Health
Statistics (1997), Table 5; Hoyert *et al.* (1999), Table 6.

30 years for females and 25 years for males), but the sex difference in life expectancy has widened. While females outlived males by an average of 2.0 years in 1900, the differential had increased to 7.8 years by 1975. The differential has narrowed since then and was 6.2 years in 1997.

The African American–white life expectancy differential actually has widened in recent years. Life expectancy for African Americans increased by 1.8 years between 1985 and 1997, and during the same period white life expectancy rose by 2.5 years. The explanation given for such a pattern is that the incidence of certain types of morbidity has dropped more slowly in the African-American population. Furthermore, the incidence of diseases such as tuberculosis, which is more concentrated in the African-American population, actually has increased in recent years. Differentials in African American–white rates for cancer, cardiovascular disease, and homicide also contribute to the difference in life expectancy.

Table 7.8 focuses on life expectancies at the older ages for five-year age intervals since 1950. As can be seen, life expectancy at age 65 is substantial and increasing over time. The average person reaching age 65 today can expect to live to nearly age 83. If one lives to age 85, more than 6 additional years of life can be expected. These life expectancy and mortality differences have been tied to socioeconomic status (Duleep, 1989) and occupations (Moore and Hayward, 1990) as well as to health status (Berkman et al., 1989). That is, lower socioeconomic status, higher-risk occupations, and lesser health status are associated with higher mortality rates and therefore lower life expectancy. These issues are addressed more fully in Chapters 10 and 11.

Increases in life expectancy to 80 years or more are expected for the near future. Women will continue to outlive men, though the differential should narrow somewhat. The total number of deaths nevertheless will continue to increase as the population ages, and sometime in the next century deaths will outnumber births.

Table 7.8. Life Expectancy at Age 65 and 85 for the United States, 1950–1997

Year	Age 65	Age 85	Year	Age 65	Age 85	Year	Age 65	Age 85
1997	17.7	6.3	1985	16.8	6.1	1965	14.6	4.7
1995	17.4	6.0	1980	16.4	5.9	1955	14.2	5.1
1990	16.9	6.1	1975	16.0	6.2	1950	14.1	4.9

SOURCES: US Department of Health, Education and Welfare (1954), Table 8.06; US Department of Health, Education and Welfare (1957), Table AZ; US Department of Health, Education and Welfare (1967), Table 5–4; US Bureau of the Census (1977), Table 96; US Bureau of the Census (1984), Table 106; National Center for Health Statistics (1997), Table 4; Hoyert et al. (1999), Table 5.

The cause-of-death structure is likely to remain much the same, although the impact of AIDS and its ultimate contribution to mortality is unknown at this time. While the above trends are surely not exhaustive in regard to all patterns that can be identified, they do reflect both the kinds of information that can be derived through the calculation of rates and life table functions as well as some of the major trends in mortality today.

CONTEMPORARY ISSUES

Current trends in both morbidity and mortality have significant implications for the health care industry. Current sickness and death patterns will drive present and future medical research in terms of treatment modalities and prevention programs. In turn, these medical developments will alter the structure of sickness and death, influencing the research foci of the future.

The demand for medical care, drugs and supplies, health facilities, and health personnel will be shaped by these efforts and the resulting change in patterns of sickness and death. To the extent that certain diseases are eliminated, the market for care related to those diseases (with the possible exception of immunizations) will be eliminated. The introduction of "new" forms of sickness and causes of death, on the other hand, will shape the marketplace. For example, chronic fatigue syndrome, which only recently has been recognized as a set of identifiable symptoms with a somewhat common etiology, was estimated to affect between 2 million and 5 million persons in the United States in the early 1990s (Cowley et al., 1990). An estimated 2.6% of primary care patients age 18 through 45 in England have CFS (Wessely et al., 1997).

The second concern focuses on efforts in sickness and death prevention, which have created an entire market for health services. At the microlevel there are individual prevention programs that are targeted toward people in disease-specific high-risk groups. Efforts targeted at smokers (cancer risk), intravenous

---

Box 7.6

Demographic Modeling and Years of Potential Life Lost

A substantial amount of attention recently has been focused on the relationship between cigarette smoking and health care costs. As states lined up to sue tobacco companies for Medicaid costs purportedly related to cigarette smoking, a mechanism for allocating all Medicaid costs across a range of individual causes was needed. At the same time, models were being developed to estimate the years of potential life lost due to cigarette smoking. These models are used to estimate productive (economic) labor force years lost in lawsuits brought by individuals against tobacco companies when a dollar value is placed on a life that ends prematurely. At an aggregate level, assumptions with regard to productivity, length of employment, and salaries can be attached to estimates of years of potential life lost to arrive at the nonmedical economic effect of a specific cause of death.

Demographers have developed a wide range of complex models to address such issues as this. In order to link tobacco smoking to premature mortality, three related measures have been developed: years of potential life lost (YPLL), lifetime years of potential life lost (LYPLL), and expected (future) years of potential life lost (EYPLL) (Lee, 1997). EYPLL and LYPLL are individual-level measures and are interpreted as the number of years of potential life lost on average due to a specific health factor, in this case to cigarette smoking. YPLL is an aggregate measure of years lost for an entire population, such as a state. Life table modeling is used to produce mortality estimates attributable to smoking across 19 underlying causes of death (Smith, 1992, pp. 99–104).

Smoking is an indirect cause of death in that its effect is realized through a rise in deaths due to certain types of cancer, heart disease, emphysema, and other causes. Therefore, assumptions based on empirical evidence must be made regarding the proportion of deaths from these causes that can be attributed to smoking. Age-specific mortality rates attributable to smoking subsequently can be calculated. Comparisons of the person years lived from two life tables, one for all causes of death and one for smoking-attributable causes, are used to arrive at these measures.

Using life table-based methods, it has been determined that 2,153,700 deaths (or 19.5 percent of all deaths) were attributable to smoking between 1990 and 1994 (Centers for Disease Control, 1997). Smoking-attributable deaths by direct cause over that period were as follows: cardiovascular disease, 906,600; neoplasms, 778,700; non-malignant respiratory diseases, 454,800; diseases among infants, 7,900; and smoking-related fires, 5,500. Between 1990 and 1994, there was an estimated 5,732,900 years of potential life lost due to premature death before age 65 and 28,606,000 years of potential life lost based on average life expectancy attributed to cigarette smoking.

Box 7.7

Hospital Mortality Data Demand Demographic Perspective

In 1986, the Health Care Financing Administration (HCFA) first released information on mortality rates for the Medicare patients of 142 hospitals across the nation. These hospitals were singled out because HCFA considered their rates to be higher than "expected." Since then, HCFA, which has responsibility for administering Medicare funds, has released comparative mortality data for all the nation's hospitals. Based on the records of Medicare patients, the released data identify each hospital and the death rate associated with it.

Although consumer and advocacy groups hailed this as a major step toward accountability and accessibility to comparative data, the hospital industry responded less positively. The first flurry of response came from hospitals that were identified as having higher than "normal" mortality rates among their Medicare patients. Understandably, hospital administrators and their medical staffs at these facilities were called on to justify the institution's apparently poor performance. In turn, HCFA was criticized by these administrators for releasing such data without having received feedback from the affected institutions. More importantly, HCFA's methodology was questioned since it presented raw statistics and failed to distinguish between hospital type and case mix in calculating mortality rates.

The second flurry of response came when hospitals began to try to capitalize on the now-public HCFA mortality data. Many facilities with mortality rates below the average began to advertise their "superior outcomes" and actually identified competitors whose mortality rates were higher according to the HCFA report.

drug addicts (AIDS risk), and prostitutes (AIDS and sexually transmitted disease risk) have the goal of reducing morbidity and mortality.

Reports from the Centers for Disease Control and Prevention indicate that, while nine preventable chronic diseases are responsible for more than one half of the deaths in the United States, only a small portion of all public health dollars spent by the federal and state governments are expended in the screening process required to prevent these conditions. The risk factors for many of these diseases (e.g., cirrhosis of the liver, stroke, and colorectal cancer) are at least partially understood and preventive measures can have a significant impact. For health care providers, prevention programs offer expanding opportunities for addressing a range of health conditions.

At the macrolevel, efforts to link environmental factors to sickness and death have heightened the population's awareness regarding the presence of carcinogens

A more objective response was elicited on the part of health services researchers and policy planners. This more scientific appraisal of the released data criticized the HCFA methodology and the subsequent comparisons. These criticisms were prompted by one major flaw: The demographic dimension had been ignored. All patients are not created equal; therefore, patient mix varies widely from hospital to hospital.

In this case, HCFA had not considered the race, sex, overall morbidity status, or previous health services utilization patterns of the patients in question. Since the data related solely to Medicare patients under study and all patients therefore were considered to be over 65 years of age, little attention was paid to the very important distinction between the "young-old," "middle-old," and "old-old." As a result, hospitals with quite different patient profiles were compared as if they were equal. A hospital at one extreme might admit primarily Medicare patients that are old-old and nonwhite with high levels of comorbidity. A hospital at the other extreme may have a patient mix that is young-old, white, and generally free of other complications.

As a result of such criticisms, HCFA modified its methodology so that, by the time of its 1988 data releases, it had taken sex, age, complicating diseases, and prior hospitalizations into consideration. It further broke patients into 16 diagnostic categories rather than making comparisons on the basis of one global mortality measure. While this methodology was certainly an improvement, this well-intentioned effort created so much controversy that it was eventually abandoned.

The use of such rates by planners and other health professionals is of some use if the appropriate adjustments are made. This calls for an understanding of the significance of such demographic variables as sex, race, age, socioeconomic status, and morbidity level for the outcomes of medical care.

and other environmental health threats. The market here is both directly related to health care (e.g., ongoing research uncovering the connection between pollution and disease) and indirectly related (e.g., the development of a medical waste industry).

Ethical and moral issues emerge when the expenditure of funds in the public and private sectors on disease and death prevention is considered. To a great extent, public pressure affects which health conditions are researched and therefore which segments of the population must wait longer for disease cures. Recent concerns over the spread of the AIDS virus illustrate the wide variety of ethical issues that can emerge in the treatment of disease. One issue concerns the priority level placed on AIDS research and education, a topic hotly debated among various private and governmental agencies. A second issue focuses on how to protect the unaffected public while still guaranteeing individual rights to those who are

Box 7.8

How to Avoid Death: Demographic Clues to Longevity

During the twentieth century, Americans became increasingly obsessed with improving their health and prolonging their lives. Optimism over our ability to eliminate disease and increase life expectancy pervades US society. The health care industry has expanded to address these issues to the point where it now consumes more than 14% of the nation's gross national product.

While US society has become increasingly dependent on the health care system as a means of prolonging life, researchers have become firmly convinced that there are other factors unrelated to health care utilization that are associated with longevity. Many of these factors, as it turns out, are demographic in nature.

The research on life expectancy accumulated over the past three decades suggests the following rules for prolonging life. While there are other factors to consider (e.g., proper diet, exercise, and moderation in lifestyle), the demographic factors are emphasized here. Since the information presented below reflects statistical averages for the US population, readers should not take the data personally.

RULE 1: *Arrange to be born female rather than male.* Females appear to be biologically stronger and more durable than males. The death rate for females is lower for virtually every cause of death and for every age cohort. The crude death rate for the US male population in the 1986 was 9 per 1000 compared to 8 for females. In 1999, life expectancy at birth for females was 79.4 years, compared to 73.1 for males. With the elimination of maternal mortality as a major cause of death, females have become a relatively low-risk group with regard to mortality, resulting in a situation in which males have a 73% higher risk of mortality all things being equal.

RULE 2: *Arrange to be born white rather than nonwhite.* Today whites have a distinct advantage over nonwhites when it comes to mortality. Although white members of US society may not be able to claim inherent biological superiority, the advantages accruing to them by virtue of their standard of living and lifestyles provide a longevity edge. The crude death rate for the black US population is nearly one and one-half that of the white population, with blacks recording a 48% higher risk of death, all things being equal. In the late 1990s, life expectancy for whites was 77.1 years compared to 71.1 for blacks. (Of course, if you could arrange to be born white female, you could expect to live longer than just about anybody.)

RULE 3: *If you must be born into an ethnic group, arrange to be born Asian American.* Although members of most ethnic groups fair less well in terms of mortality risk than the majority white population, some groups actually report better longevity figures. Chief among these are Asian Americans, who record crude death rates about 33% lower than those for the white population. Cultural practices, family support, and other group-specific factors contribute to lower infant mortality and better overall health for Asian Americans in addition to lower overall mortality. Even better, arrange to be born in the nation of origin and then migrate to the US to improve your chances for longevity.

RULE 4: *Arrange to be born rich rather than poor.* An appropriate axiom for contemporary America might be that the rich get richer and the poor get sicker. The relative disadvantage of the poor in US society is reflected in differential mortality rates and life expectancy. The death rate for the lowest socioeconomic status groups is one and one-half times that for the most affluent groups; the rate for the poorest of the poor is twice that for the richest of the rich. The affluent consistently can expect to live several years longer on the average than the nonaffluent. The privileges of class tend to override the effect of the health care delivery system; simply providing the poor more health care has done little to improve their overall health status.

RULE 5: *Get married and stay married.* The contemporary American trend toward later marriages or no marriage at all may bode ill for mortality statistics. Not only are the married healthier overall than the unmarried (whether single, divorced, or widowed), this advantage also shows up in mortality and longevity statistics. Individuals who have never married have a 34% higher risk of mortality, all things being equal. The widowed and divorced face at least a 16% greater risk. (Of course, this means that one must strive to keep one's spouse healthy and happy as well. Becoming divorced or widowed carries a death threat.)

RULE 6: *Have children but not too many.* Having children in the household, to a point at least, appears to prolong life. Married couples with two or three children tend to be better off in terms of longevity than those with one or no children and those with four or more. In fact, the risk of death is 39% greater for married people with four children than those with two children. In contrast, the longevity advantage provided married people by the presence of children turns into a disadvantage for the unmarried. Unmarried individuals with any number of children face a greater risk of death than their married counterparts. An unmarried woman with two children faces an 82% higher risk of death than a married woman with two children.

RULE 7: *Get as much education as possible.* From all indications, the more educated we are, the healthier we are. (This applies primarily to physical health, since it seems the better educated have more mental disorders. Luckily, these are not usually fatal.) This situation is reflected in mortality statistics that indicate a lower death rate for the highly educated than the poorly educated. Those without a high school diploma face a 21% greater risk of death than those who completed high school, all things being equal. Further, those with only a

Continued

Box 7.8. (Continued)

high school education face a 28% greater risk of death than those with a college degree. Similarly, life expectancy increases as education increases. This is partly explained by the higher health consciousness of the better educated, resulting in healthier lifestyles and more appropriate use of the health care delivery system. This situation is also influenced by the fact that income improves with education, as do working conditions. (A college campus *is* a lot safer than a construction site.)

RULE 8: *Get a prestigious job and keep it.* While many jobs are stressful and people think they might be better off without them, employment—at least certain kinds—is good for longevity. Those who are not in the labor force for whatever reason (e.g., retirement, disability) are at over twice the risk of mortality as those who are. Those who are unemployed are better off by virtue of being in the labor force but still at somewhat greater risk than those who are employed. Among the employed, those who occupy lowly occupations have a 59% greater risk of death than those with high status occupations.

RULE 9: *Go West (to the suburbs).* The risk of mortality is related to the section of the country in which one resides. "Go West" is still good advice, since the mortality rate for those living in the West region of the US is 10% lower than the nation as a whole. Further, the type of community in the West or any region is also a factor in mortality risk. The risk of death in core cities of metropolitan areas is nearly 20% greater than it is for those living in the suburbs of these cities. Even rural areas carry a 16% greater risk of death than do the suburbs.

afflicted. A third ethical problem pits the rights of health care providers (for example, doctors, dentists, and nurses) against the rights of AIDS patients to obtain health care services unrelated to their AIDS diagnosis.

The morbidity–mortality–demographic connection has significant marketing implications as well. For example, known diabetes rates in the United States vary markedly by a number of demographic characteristics. The rate for African Americans is about one and one-half times the white rate, and persons with less than 12 years of education have a rate two and one-half times the rate for people with more than a high school education. Persons in families with less than $7000 in yearly income have a rate three times that of persons in families with $25,000 or more in income. The marketing of screening, education, and/or treatment programs must keep these differentials in mind, given the wide range in media habits, health care practices, and purchasing behavior seen in these populations. The providers of private sector health care services in particular must create products with black–white income differentials in mind.

Sickness and death rates impact heavily on population size and age structure, which in turn dictate both the level and type of health care needs. For example, reduced infant and childhood mortality has been a major determinant in increased life expectancy. Increased life expectancy, coupled with an older age structure, means that there is a large proportion of the population at the older ages (with unique health care needs) and many of these persons are relatively healthy; so much so, in fact, that they are likened to populations 15 or 20 years younger in earlier generations. Given an increase in preventive measures such as immunization for influenza, they are likely to maintain their good health for an even longer period of time. Box 7.8 provides some clues on how to avoid death.

REFERENCES

Barhart, H. X., Caldwell, M. B., Thomas, P., Mascola, L., Ortiz, I., Hsu, H. W., Shulte, J., Parrott, R., Maldonado, Y., and Byers, R. (1996). Natural history of human immunodeficiency virus disease in perinatality infected children: An analysis from the pediatric spectrum of disease project. *Pediatrics* 97(5):710–716.

Barber, C., Ozonoff, V. V., Schuster, M., Hume, B., McLaughlin, H., and Janelli, L. (1996). When bullets don't kill. *Public Health Reports* 111:483–493.

Barton, L. J. (1997). A shoulder to lean on: Assisted living in the US. *American Demographics* (July):45–51.

Berkman, L., Singer, B., and Manton, K. (1989). Black/white differences in health status and mortality among the elderly. *Demography* 26:661–678.

Bonanich, E. (1989). Inequality in America: The failure of the American system for people of color. *Sociological Spectrum* 9:77–101.

Brown, S. C. (1989). Chronic conditions in older Americans: What roles do age, sex, and location play? Paper presented at the annual meeting of the Southern Demographic Association, Durham, North Carolina.

Centers for Disease Control. (1997). Smoking attributable-mortality and years of potential life lost. *Morbidity and Mortality Weekly Report* 46(20).

Cowley, G., Hager, M., and Joseph, N. (1990). Chronic fatigue syndrome. *Newsweek* (November 12):62–70.

Crimmins, E. M., Saito, Y., and Ingegneri, D. (1989). Changes in life expectancy and disability-free life expectancy in the United States. *Population and Development Review* 15:235–267.

Department of Health, Education, and Welfare. (1950). *Vital Statistics of the United States, 1964*, Vol. 1. Washington, DC: US Government Printing Office.

Department of Health, Education, and Welfare. (1957). *Vital Statistics of the United States, 1965*, Vol. 1. Washington, DC: US Government Printing Office.

Duleep, H. O. (1989). Measuring socioeconomic mortality differentials over time. *Demography* 26:345–351.

Fleming, S., Rastogi, A., Dmitrienko, A., and Johnson, K. (1999). A comprehensive prognostic index to predict survival based on multiple comorbidities. *Medical Care* 37(6):601–614.

Frisbie, P., Forbes, D., and Pullum, S. (1996). Compromised birth outcomes and infant mortality among racial and ethnic groups. *Demography* 33:469–481.

Hinman, A. R. (1990). 1889 to 1989: A century of health and disease. *Public Health Reports* 105: 374–380.

Hoyert, D., Kochanek, K., and Murphy, S. (1999). Deaths: Final data for 1997. *National Vital Statistics Report* 47(19). Washington, DC: US Government Printing Office.

Hyder, A., Rotllant, G., and Morrow, R. (1998). Measuring the burden of disease: Health life-years. *American Journal of Public Health* 88:196–202.

Jeffrey, R., and French, S. (1998). Epidemic obesity in the United States: Are fast foods and television viewing contributing? *American Journal of Public Health* 88:277–280.

Lee, W.-C. (1997). Quantifying the future impact of disease on society: Life table-based measures of potential life lost. *American Journal of Public Health* 87:1456–1460.

Moore, D. E., and Hayward, M. D. (1990). Occupational careers and mortality of elderly men. *Demography* 27:31–53.

Namboodiri, K., and Suchindran, C. M. (1987). *Life Table Techniques and Their Applications.* New York: Academic Press.

National Center for Health Statistics. (1986). *Advance Report of Final Mortality Statistics, 1984.* Monthly Vital Statistics Report, Vol. 35, No. 6. Washington, DC: US Government Printing Office.

National Center for Health Statistics. (1990). *Vital Statistics of the United States, 1987*, Vol. 11, Mortality, Part A. Washington, DC: US Government Printing Office.

National Center for Health Statistics. (1997). Report of final mortality statistics, 1995. *Monthly Vital Statistics Report*, Vol. 45, No. 11, Supplement 2. Washington, DC: US Government Printing Office.

National Center for Health Statistics. (1999). Births, marriages, divorces, and deaths: Provisional data for 1998. *National Vital Statistics Reports*, Vol. 47, No. 21. Washington, DC: US Government Printing Office.

Orlando Sentinel. (1990). Nine deadliest diseases are preventable. (January 16):A6.

Pressat, R. (1972). *Demographic Analysis.* Chicago: Aldine.

Richarddus, J., Graafmans, W., Verlove-Vanhorick, S. P., and Mackenbach, J. (1988). The perinatal mortality rate as an indicator of quality of care in international comparisons. *Medical Care* 36(1):54–66.

Schoen, R. (1988). *Modeling Multigroup Populations.* New York: Plenum Press.

Shryock, H. S., Siegel, J. S., and Associates. (1973). *The Methods and Materials of Demography.* Washington, DC: US Government Printing Office.

Simonsen, L., Clarke, M., Williamson, G. D., Stroup, D., Arden, N., and Schonberger, L. (1997). The impact of influenza epidemics on mortality: Introducing a seventy index. *American Journal of Public Health* 87:1944–1950.

Smith, D. P. (1992). *Formal Demography.* New York: Plenum Press.

Sowards, K. A. (1997). Premature birth and the changing composition of newborn infectious disease mortality: Reconsidering "exogenous" mortality. *Demography* 34:399–409.

Swanson, D. A. (1989). A state-based regression model for estimating substate life expectancy. *Demography* 26:161–170.

US Bureau of the Census. (1975). *Historical Statistics of the United States, Colonial Times to 1970.* Part I, Series B1-4. Washington, DC: US Government Printing Office.

US Bureau of the Census. (1977). *Statistical Abstract of the United States, 1977.* Washington, DC: US Government Printing Office.

US Bureau of the Census. (1984). *Statistical Abstract of the United States, 1984.* Washington, DC: US Government Printing Office.

US Bureau of the Census. (1990). *Statistical Abstract of the United States, 1990.* Washington, DC: US Government Printing Office.

US Bureau of the Census. (1996). *Statistical Abstract of the United States, 1996.* Washington, DC: US Government Printing Office.

US Bureau of the Census. (1994). *County and City Data Book, 1994.* Washington, DC: US Government Printing Office.

US Bureau of the Census. (1997). *Statistical Abstract of the United States, 1996*. Washington, DC: US Government Printing Office.

US Department of Health and Human Services. (1994). Births, marriages, divorces, and deaths from 1996. *Monthly Vital Statistics Report*, Vol. 45, No. 12. Washington, DC: US Government Printing Office.

Verbrugge, L. (1988). Life and death paradox. *American Demographics* (July):34–37.

Ware, J., and Sherbowrne, C. (1992). The MOS 36-item short-form health survey (SF-36). *Medical Care* 30(6):473–483.

Warnecke, R. (Ed.) (1995). *Health Survey Research Methods* (6th Ed.). Hyattsville, MD: US Department of Health and Human Services.

Wessely, S., Chalder, T., Hirsch, S., Wallace, P., and Wright, D. (1997). The prevalence and morbidity of chronic fatigue and chronic fatigue syndrome: A prospective primary care study. *American Journal of Public Health* 87(9):1449–1455.

White, K. M., and Preston, S. H. (1996). How many Americans are alive because of twentieth century improvements in mortality. *Population and Development Review* 22:415–429.

Winslow, R. (1990). Heart disease linked to habits in early years. *Wall Street Journal*, January 16, p. B1, 4.

SUGGESTED RESOURCES

Carnes, B. A., Olshansky, S. J., and Grahn, D. (1996). Continuing the search for a law of mortality. *Population and Development Review* 22:231–264.

Dawber, T. R. (1980). *The Framingham Study*. Cambridge, MA: Harvard University Press.

Olshansky, S. J., Carnes, B., Rogers, R. G., and Smith, L. (1997). Infectious diseases—New and ancient threats to world health. *Population Bulletin* 52(2). Washington, DC: Population Reference Bureau.

Nathanson, C. A. (1996). Disease prevention as social change: Toward a theory of public health. *Population and Development Review* 22:609–637.

Preston, S. H. (1976). *Mortality Patterns in National Populations*. New York: Academic Press.

Riley, J. C. (1989). *Sickness, Recovery and Death: A History and Forecast of Ill Health*. Iowa City: University of Iowa Press.

Wallace, D. C. (1997). Mitochondrial DNA in aging and disease. *Scientific American* 277:40–47.

Migration

INTRODUCTION

Migration, or geographic mobility, is the third component of population change (along with fertility and mortality). Migration is the most dynamic and complex of these components, as well as the most difficult to measure. While death occurs only once to each individual and the average number of births per woman over a lifetime in the United States is about two, migration is a much more frequent event for most Americans. Recent estimates indicate that the typical American moves 11 times between birth and death (Kulkarni and Pol, 1994). About 17% of the US population changes residence each year, and over a 5-year period more than 45% of the population moves from one location to another.

The difficulty in measurement is largely the product of conceptual ambiguity. Measurement is particularly problematic in the United States because no migration registry is maintained. Migration data typically are derived by comparing addresses at two points in time based on a survey or on some type of systematic record keeping. This approach, however, cannot identify the number of moves or the nature of the moves that may have occurred between the two dates specified. The migration concept therefore is difficult to apply to certain categories of people in transit (e.g., migrant workers and "snowbirds"), for whom the move is not expected to be permanent. Moreover, the growing complexity of living arrangements reflected in nontraditional households and blended families makes the measurement of migration even more difficult. While the distinction between the migration of an individual and the migration of a household always has been important, the households of the 1990s are often marked by the periodic migration of certain household members (e.g., children going to live with the "other" parent for the summer), while other members of the household do not move. These types of "moves" have important implications for health care delivery.

Data on migration within the United States are derived from censuses, surveys, and administrative records. Respondents are typically asked where they lived at an earlier period of time (e.g., 5 years ago) on the decennial census of population and housing and the US Census Bureau's Current Population Survey. The comparison of current address with the location 5 years ago allows for the creation of different types of migrant and nonmigrant categories. On another survey more relevant for the issues addressed in this volume, the National Health Interview Survey, respondents are asked how long they have lived at their current address and how many times they have moved in the last three years (Tucker and Urton, 1987). The other source of migration data, administrative registries such as Social Security and the Internal Revenue Service, use a two-points-in-time comparison of addresses to generate data on the volume and nature of moves. None of these data sources, however, captures the complexity of contemporary migration patterns.

In recent decades, migration has become the most important component of population change in the United States. At the subnational level, the impact of migration is felt much more immediately than the effect of fertility or mortality on a community. As birth rates and death rates have fallen, migration has come to play an even more important role in population change. The effects of migration can be significant in the short run for population size and composition at both the point of origin and the point of destination. Persistent long-term migration flows affect subsequent population change in the areas receiving migrants through the births and deaths of the "new" residents. Areas losing residents through out-migration do not realize the births and deaths of their former residents, and therefore do not benefit from the "lost" births with respect to population growth. This chapter begins by introducing the concepts and measures used in the study of migration. Current trends are then described and the health care implications of migration are discussed.

MIGRATION CONCEPTS AND MEASURES

Concepts

Migration refers to a physical move by an individual involving a permanent change in residence, even though the entity moving is typically a household. A permanent change in residence implies that the person or household in question intends to stay in the new residence for some minimal period of time. The intentions and time dimensions are clearly difficult to ascertain in some instances. Recall from Chapter 4 that a residence is defined as the place where a person usually sleeps and eats. Having any residence at all implies some type of permanency though some categories of individuals (e.g., the homeless) do not have recognized residences. Daily or seasonal movement to and from jobs or for climatic reasons does not qualify as migration, though such short-term changes in location do have implications for the provision of health care. Communities such as Daytona Beach, Florida, encounter short-term population increases due to tourism and a knowledge of the size and composition of the temporary population is crucial in planning for health care needs.

A form of very short-term residence change involves commuting (i.e., the movement of population to and from work and other daily activities), and this type of movement is treated separately by demographers. As discussed in Chapter 4, most cities have radically different daytime and nighttime populations because of commuting flows, and the provision of adequate health care is in part dependent on an understanding of these flows.

Demographers classify migration into two major categories: international and internal. Persons engaged in migration either move between countries or they move within the boundaries of a single country. *International migration* refers to the intended permanent movement between one country and another. Persons migrating to a country are referred to as *immigrants*, while individuals moving out of a country are labeled *emigrants*. Every country has laws and policies that govern international migration, especially immigration. In the United States the flow of immigrants is regulated by immigration laws that establish the conditions for immigration into the country. Currently these laws involve country-specific limits on the number of persons who may legally move to the United States in any given year. Immigration law in the United States has limited effect on emigration from this country; most US citizens are free to leave as long as some country will allow them entry.

Internal migration refers to change of residence within a country. Internal migration is generally less regulated (and measured) than is international migration. Within the United States, internal migration is basically unimpeded, though laws designed to limit the growth of certain communities have a relatively long history (Barnett and Reed, 1985). Demographers refer to internal migrants coming into an area as in-migrants, while those leaving an area are termed out-migrants.

Internal migration is divided into subcategories that distinguish between short-distance and long-distance movement. Moreover, a hierarchy of definitions has been created to reflect the distance of the move. Initially, anyone who permanently changes residence (regardless of distance) is classified as a *mover*. However, in order for a mover to be technically a *migrant*, the mover must change his or her county of residence. The county is chosen for the mover–migrant distinction because it is assumed that movement across such a boundary involves substantial change in social and economic milieu. Thus, a migrant is a mover, but a mover is not necessarily a migrant. Other useful distinctions also reflect the distance and nature of the movement. *Intrastate migration* refers to movement within a state, while *interstate migration* refers to movement between two states.

Migration streams, or the flow of relatively large numbers of persons from one area to another, are a common phenomenon. For example, the flow of African Americans from the South to the Northeast and Midwest regions during the 1930s and 1940s constituted a migration stream. More recently, African-American migration streams from the Midwest and Northeast to the South have been identified (Frey, 1998). Some of these recent migrants are return migrants; that is, they were part of the earlier migration stream to the Midwest or Northeast. These *return migrants* are identified by comparing data on current residence, residence at some earlier time (e.g., 5 years age), and place of birth. Thus, some African Americans were born in the South, resided in the North for some period of time, and returned to the South at a later point in time.

Several current migration streams characterizing the United States are considered as important from a demographic perspective. Rural-to-urban migration, which began in some areas of the nation as early as 1800, has altered the course of industrial development. The east-to-west and city-to-suburb migration flows have forever changed the social, economic, and political structure of the United States. In more recent years the migration of persons from the Snowbelt to the Sunbelt has markedly affected both the place of origin and the place of destination.

Each type of migration flow can have important implications for health care providers. Rural-to-urban, city-to-suburb, and region-to-region flows are seen as major contributors to the changing health care needs in areas that are either net exporters or net importers of people. For example, a migration stream from the Midwest to central Florida may bring about both an increase in population and a change in demographic characteristics. This may also affect preferences for health services and the ability to pay for care. At the same time, the size and composition of the population at the point of origin is affected.

Measures Migration

Demographers have developed a number of migration measures, and many of the same concerns discussed in the chapters on fertility and mortality are relevant to this discussion. With migration, additional measurement difficulties arise and are related to the concepts being measured as well as the data sources available. As noted earlier, persons and households change residence several times over a lifetime on average, but a person is registered as a birth and death only once.

The United States does not maintain any type of registry to record the movements of individuals, so measurement historically has been limited to indirect methods. Measures of migration in the United States are tied to specific sources of data. In the 2000 Census of Population and Housing, for example, persons were asked about their residence 5 years earlier (i.e., April 1, 1995). Based on responses to this inquiry, individuals were classified as movers or migrants, migration streams were identified, and in-migrant and out-migrant flows were specified. In the Current Population Survey, persons are asked where they lived one year earlier. The comparison of the addresses for the two points in time allows persons to be classified as movers or nonmovers. Furthermore, the type of mover among those changing residence can be identified. Administrative records such as IRS or Medicare reports also can be used to compare addresses at two points in time to identify migrant characteristics.

Two summary measures of migration for application to a specific geographic area have been developed. *Net migration* is the absolute difference between in-migration and out-migration for that area over a given time period. For example, if county X in state Y gained 10,000 in-migrants and lost 5,000 out-migrants between 1990 and 1995, the net figure would be 5,000. *Gross migration*, on the other hand, adds both in- and out-migrants, and the gross migration figure in this example would be 15,000. While gross migration is less frequently used than net migration for analysis or descriptive purposes, the former is a much better measure of population turnover. In turn, the amount of turnover has important implications for both the demand for and the delivery of health services.

While the comparison of the absolute numbers of movers, nonmovers, migrants, and net migrants is important in many instances, rates are frequently calculated when there are size differences between the areas being compared. Because flows of persons from one area to another are responsible for the migration totals, rates that measure the inflow, outflow, and net of both flows are needed. Births and deaths are discrete events usually measured at a person's place of residence. Migration, on the other hand, is an event measured at both the points of origin and destination. The duality of migration measurement makes the calculation of rates more problematic. Rates for in-migration, out-migration, net migration, and gross migration can be generated. The numerator for these rates is the total for each migration category (e.g., in-migrants). The denominator, however, is much more difficult to determine.

The identification of an appropriate population at risk, that is, persons with at least some probability of moving over a given timeframe, is complicated because each rate has a different at-risk group. Consider, for example, the *out-migration* rate for a specific city for a one-year period. The numerator of the rate is the number of out-migrants, while the denominator is the population at the beginning or in the middle of a one-year period. However, identifying the population at risk for the in-migration rate is problematic. Anyone who did not live in the city at the beginning of the interval—virtually the entire population of the United States—is at some risk of moving into the city. However, the *in-migration* rate normally is calculated using the same base as the out-migration rate. Therefore, the base for the rate is no longer the population at risk. Instead, the resulting rate should be interpreted as the percentage of population increase that is due to in-migration. Often, the demographic focus is on the amount of change resulting from net migration. The denominator for the migration rate also is the population of the given city at the beginning of the interval. In this case, the concept of population at risk has no meaning because both flows (in-migrants minus out-migrants) generate one figure.

The data required for the calculation of these rates include population counts or estimates, as well as figures for the number of in- and out-migrants. These data are specific to the geographic units of interest and a specific time frame. If the time interval is more than one year, the denominator chosen for the rate usually is the estimated population at the midpoint of the time interval. Box 8.1 presents examples of migration rate calculations.

The rate of migration has a substantial impact on the population size and characteristics of the community. This in turn affects the nature of the health care needs. When migration rates vary for different communities, the impact on those communities is likely to vary also. An examination of migration trends for Florida illustrates this point. The population size and age structure for Florida and the United States for 1980 and 1990, along with growth rates and components of change, are provided for comparison purposes in Table 8.1. As can be seen, the population of Florida grew more rapidly than that of the United States during the decade (32.5% vs. 9.8%). However, this marked difference tells only part of the story. Net migration accounted for over 87% of the population growth for Florida, compared to only about 24% for the United States (second panel of the table). Migration also was selective by age. Though Florida was characterized by higher percentage population increases at all ages, the largest increases were at the youngest ages (under 15), for young adults (25 through 34), for mature adults (45 through 54), and for the oldest old (85 and over). Increases in the absolute numbers of persons for specific age intervals also were impressive for Florida; age groupings showing a population increase of at least 200,000 persons over the 10-year period include the age cohorts under 15, 25 to 34, 35 to 44, 45 to 54, 65 to 74, and 75 to 84.

The trends illustrated in this table have important implications for the demand for health services. Certainly the growth in Florida's population (an estimated 4000 per week during the late 1980s) means that the overall demand for health services is increasing rapidly. More importantly, substantial changes in the level and types of services are expected as a result of the state's rapidly changing population composition. On the one hand, there is rapid growth among the young, working-age population (the 25–34 age cohort). This cohort does not require high levels of health services overall and in fact seldom uses inpatient hospital services. However, it is a population that is characterized by high rates of substance abuse, certain mental disorders, accidents, homicide, and suicide. These problems are significant enough that adequate services are required.

On the other hand, there is tremendous growth in two populations that are high utilizers of health services: the oldest old and the very young. Florida, of course, is a major retirement area, and the senior population constitutes more than 30% of the population in some areas of the state. Clearly, the senior population utilizes a disproportionate share of health services, especially hospital services. In areas such as this, it is difficult for the infrastructure to keep up with the demand

---

Box 8.1

The Calculation of Migration Rates

Focusing on rates for the Midwest region of the United States (1993–1994), the following migration rates can be derived:

$$\text{In-migration rate} = \frac{706,000 \text{ (in-migrants 1993–1994)}}{61,040,000 \text{ (midpoint of interval 1994)}}$$

$$= .0115, \text{ or } 11.5 \text{ per } 1,000 \text{ residents}$$

$$\text{Out-migration rate} = \frac{737,000 \text{ (out-migrants 1993–1994)}}{61,040,000 \text{ (midpoint of interval 1994)}}$$

$$= .0121, \text{ or } 12.1 \text{ per } 1,000 \text{ residents}$$

$$\text{Net migration rate} = \frac{-31,000 \text{ (out-migrants 1993–1994)}}{61,040,000 \text{ (midpoint of interval 1994)}}$$

$$= -.0005, \text{ or } -0.5 \text{ per } 1,000 \text{ residents}$$

$$\text{Gross migration rate} = \frac{1,430,000 \text{ (total in-migration and out-migration)}}{61,040,000 \text{ (midpoint of interval 1994)}}$$

$$= .0234, \text{ or } 23.4 \text{ per } 1,000 \text{ residents}$$

A measure of migration efficiency also can be calculated. Migration efficiency is the ratio of the net gain or loss divided by the total number of moves it took to generate the figure:

$$\text{Migration efficiency} = \frac{\text{net migrants (absolute value)}}{\text{gross migration}}$$

$$= \frac{31,000}{1,430,000} = .022$$

These figures indicate that in the Midwest there are approximately four moves for each net migrant, a relatively inefficient exchange of persons. By comparison, the South, noted for its population growth during the 1970s, experienced the following rates during the 1975–1980 time interval:

In-migration rate: 14.9 per 1,000 population
Out-migration rate: 10.7 per 1,000 population
Net migration rate: +4.2 (a net gain) per 1,000 population
Gross migration rate: 25.7 moves (in or out) per 1,000 population
Migration efficiency: .164

These calculations indicate that the Midwest had a lower in-migration rate than the South, a higher out-migration rate, a comparable net migration rate (though in a negative direction), a lower gross migration rate, and less migration efficiency.

Table 8.1. Population Change, Age Structure, and
Components of Growth for Florida and the United States, 1980–1990

	1980[a]	1990[a]	Florida % change (1980–1990)	US % change (1980–1990)	Ratio of Florida change to US change
Under 5	570	850	49.1	14.7	3.3
5–14	1,307	1,562	19.5	0.4	48.8
15–24	1,623	1,670	2.9	−12.9	—
25–34	1,411	2,116	50.0	16.4	3.0
35–44	1,039	1,811	74.3	46.0	1.6
45–54	989	1,291	30.5	9.9	3.1
55–64	1,120	1,268	13.2	−2.7	—
65–74	1,059	1,369	29.3	15.8	1.8
75–84	511	789	54.4	29.5	1.8
85 and over	117	210	79.5	34.9	2.3
Total	9,746	12,938	32.5	9.8	3.3
Median age	34.7	36.3			

	Florida	United States
Births	1,596	37,508
Deaths	1,188	20,636
Net migrants	2,786	5,300
Migration as a percentage of total growth	87.2%	23.9%

[a]Numbers in thousands.
SOURCES: US Bureau of the Census (1983, 1992); US Bureau of the Census (1996), Table 21; National Center for Health Statistics (1980–1990).

for services. This same situation is true for the high-growth population in the under-5 age cohort. Obstetrical and pediatric problems require high levels of both ambulatory and inpatient services. Childbirth, in fact, accounts for the largest number of admissions to general hospitals. Not only is it difficult for facilities to keep up with the demand, but chronic shortages of geriatricians, obstetricians, and pediatricians can be expected under such conditions. These issues are explored in more detail later in the chapter.

US IMMIGRATION

Legal and Illegal Distinctions

Legal restrictions control the flow of immigrants to the United States. However, illegal immigration adds to the immigrant population in ways that are difficult to enumerate. In the late 1990s, approximately 800,000 legal immigrants entered the country each year. While the extent of illegal immigration can only be estimated, the number of illegal immigrants residing in the United States was estimated at fewer than 5 million persons during the mid-1980s (Passel, 1985; Warren and Passel, 1987), and in 1992 the estimate was placed at 3.2 million (US Immigration and Naturalization Service, 1997).

The volume of legal immigration is controlled by law, using a quota system that dates back to 1921. Recent legislative efforts have focused on quota adjustment, preferences for certain types of immigrants, and immigrant worker reform. The immigration reform bills that were enacted by the US Congress in 1986, 1990, and 1996 brought about some important changes in immigration law. However, the impact of that legislation on immigration (legal and illegal) is not precisely known. The 1990 immigration law, for example, increased the authorized annual level of immigration from 513,000 for 1992 to 700,000 for 1994, with a slight decrease (to 675,000) for 1995 and beyond. The bill also increased the number of visas granted to skilled workers and managers from 54,000 to 140,000 (US Congress, 1990). By 1996, the level of legal immigration, including changes in the status of persons already in the United States, stood at about 761,000 (US Immigration and Naturalization Service, 1997).*

Volume of Immigration

The volume and nature of immigration to the United States have varied greatly over the history of the country. Table 8.2 provides a decade-by-decade analysis of immigrant flows, along with the percentage of total decade population growth accounted for by immigrants.† Comparisons of the data by decade show a low of 528,000 immigrants for the period 1931 to 1940 and a high of 8.8 million from 1901 to 1910. The number of immigrants during the 1990s decade is expected to be the highest in US history. While the largest annual number of immigrants was recorded during the first two decades of this century, the contribution of immigration to population growth declined markedly in the 1930s. It was not until the 1980s that immigration's contribution to growth began to approach pre-1930s levels. Clearly, the recent trend has been toward increased absolute numbers and

*The Illegal Immigration Reform and Immigrant Responsibility Act of 1996 is designed to: (1) improve border control and interior enforcement; (2) enhance enforcement and penalties against alien smuggling and document fraud; (3) improve inspection, apprehension, detention, adjudication, and removal procedures; (4) provide new tools to reduce the employment of unauthorized workers; (5) restrict the benefits provided to aliens; and (6) modify refugee, parole, and asylum procedures (US Immigration and Reform, 1997).

†It should be noted, that while 38 million persons immigrated to the United States between 1901 and 1990, an estimated 10 million emigrated (Warren and Kraly, 1985; Immigration and Naturalization Services, 1997).

Table 8.2. Number of Immigrants and the Proportion of Population
Growth Due to Immigration by Decade for the United States, 1831–1996

Decade	Immigrants (in thousands)	Population growth for decade (in thousands)	Percent of population growth due to immigration
1831–1840	599	4,203	14.3
1841–1850	1,713	6,122	28.0
1851–1860	2,598	8,251	31.5
1861–1870	2,315	8,375	27.6
1871–1880	2,812	10,337	27.2
1881–1890	5,247	12,792	41.0
1891–1900	3,688	13,047	28.3
1901–1910	8,795	15,978	55.0
1911–1920	5,736	13,738	41.8
1921–1930	4,107	17,064	24.1
1931–1940	528	8,894	5.9
1941–1950	1,035	19,028	5.4
1951–1960	2,515	27,767	9.1
1961–1970	3,322	23,979	13.9
1971–1980	4,493	23,244	19.3
1981–1990	7,338	22,143	33.1
1991–1996	6,146	16,566	37.1

SOURCE: US Bureau of the Census (1996), Tables 2 and 8; US Census Bureau and Immigration and Naturalization Service websites: http://www.census.gov and http://www.ins.usdoj/gov.

contribution to growth. Immigrants accounted for 37% of US growth during the 1990s, second only to 55% recorded in the first decade of this century.

Immigrant Origin

The country of origin is an important consideration in the analysis of immigration trends. Table 8.3 presents historical data, with four continent groupings as points of origin. Up until 1920, the vast majority of immigrants were from Europe. Since 1920, most of the share lost by Europe has been gained by Asia, and during the 1980s nearly half of all immigrants originated in Asia. All together, 82% of immigrants have come from Asia or other countries in North and South America during the 1990s. In 1996, the major sources of legal immigrants by country were Mexico (163,572), the Philippines (55,876), India (44,859), Vietnam (42,067), and China (41,728). As a result of this shift in country of origin, the immigrant population is quite different in culture and language from the majority European-origin population in the United States at this time. See Box 8.2 on the "new" immigrants.

Table 8.3. Immigrants to the United States by Continent of Origin, 1831–1996

Decade	Total immigrants[a]	Europe		Asia		Other America		Africa	
1831–1840	599	496	(83)	—	(0)	33	(6)	—	(0)
1841–1850	1,713	1,598	(93)	—	(0)	62	(4)	—	(0)
1851–1860	2,598	2,453	(94)	41	(2)	75	(3)	—	(0)
1861–1870	2,315	2,064	(89)	65	(3)	167	(7)	—	(0)
1871–1880	2,812	2,262	(80)	124	(4)	404	(14)	—	(0)
1881–1890	5,247	4,722	(90)	68	(1)	426	(8)	—	(0)
1891–1900	3,688	3,559	(97)	71	(2)	39	(1)	1	(0)
1901–1910	8,795	8,136	(93)	244	(3)	362	(4)	7	(0)
1911–1920	5,736	4,377	(76)	193	(3)	1,144	(20)	8	(0)
1921–1930	4,107	2,478	(60)	97	(2)	1,517	(37)	6	(0)
1931–1940	528	348	(66)	15	(3)	160	(30)	2	(0)
1941–1950	1,035	622	(60)	59	(3)	355	(34)	7	(0)
1951–1960	2,516	1,492	(53)	157	(6)	841	(33)	17	(1)
1961–1970	3,322	1,239	(37)	445	(13)	1,579	(48)	39	(1)
1971–1980	4,493	801	(18)	1,634	(36)	1,929	(43)	92	(2)
1981–1990	7,338	706	(10)	2,817	(38)	3,581	(48)	192	(3)
1991–1996	6,146	876	(14)	1,942	(32)	3,085	(50)	213	(3)

[a]Numbers in thousands, percentages in parentheses. —, Less than 1000.
SOURCE: US Bureau of the Census (1922), Table 65; US Bureau of the Census (1931), Table 86; US Bureau of the Census (1953), Table 105; US Bureau of the Census (1985), Table 125; US Bureau of the Census (1996), Table 8. Source data came from the US Immigration and Naturalization Service, *Statistical Yearbook*; US Immigration and Naturalization Service website.

Immigrant Characteristics

Information regarding the characteristics of immigrants is important in understanding the impact this population might have on health-related issues. Table 8.4 provides data on sex, age, and occupation for immigrants to the United States in 1996. As can be seen, females account for 54% of the immigrant population. Over one half of all immigrants are under age 30. Only about 5% are 65 and over. (For the United States as a whole the comparable figure for the 65 and over population is over 12%.) The median age of immigrants is 28 years versus 34 years for the total US population. Data on immigrants categorized by occupation are shown in the third panel of the table. The three leading occupational groups are professionals, operators, and services. The occupation was unknown for over 47% of the immigrant population in 1996.

The relatively young age structure of the immigrant population means that the health service demands of these persons are theoretically lower than those normally expected from a population of comparable size. Nevertheless, to the extent that immigrants have been exposed to health conditions and diseases not

---

Box 8.2

The "New" Immigrants and Health Care Delivery

Since the 1970s, the United States has experienced a resurgence of immigration. The annual influx of legal immigrants reached a level not experienced since the 1930s. By the 1980s, there was evidence that a comparable number of illegal immigrants were entering the country. These numbers of legal immigrants were thought to be matched during the 1980s by immigrants entering the United States illegally. For the first time in decades, immigration became a major issue for scholarly research and public policy debate.

The interest in immigration has not been inspired so much by the renewed volume (although that certainly is an issue for some parts of the country) as by the nature of the immigrants. These "new" immigrants have for the most part originated in Southeast Asia, the Caribbean, and Latin America. Unlike the well-educated, often professional immigrants to whom we have grown accustomed, these new waves include large numbers of refugees from the wars of Southeast Asia and Latin America. They often arrive with only the clothes on their backs. Those coming from Asian cultures bring very "foreign" ways with them. Similarly, the estimated 4 to 8 million illegal aliens in the United States from Mexico, Central America, and the Caribbean often come from lower socioeconomic backgrounds.

The influx of such immigrants carries many implications for health status and health care delivery. For those legally admitted immigrants in need of medical care—especially refugees—the problems may be serious. These immigrants often come from countries where health care delivery is poorly developed and/or disrupted by political conflict. These groups also present special problems in that the cultural distance between them and the US system is great and they are typically impoverished. Some groups (e.g., Southeast Asians) have introduced new health problems that call for additional personnel and programs. High birth rates, by US standards, mean that certain communities may face demands on their obstetrical services that cannot be met.

---

found in the United States, their need for care is often different. For example, diseases such as typhoid, shigellosis, tuberculosis, and rubella are much more prevalent in developing countries than in the United States (Olshansky et al., 1997). To the extent that conditions—or at least preconditions—are transported by immigrants to the United States, the health care system will be affected. Of course, cultural preferences that may result in greater or lesser care demand, as well as the use of "nontraditional" health care practices.

The burden imposed by illegal immigrants—to the extent that it can be documented—is several times more severe. In the late 1980s, the US Immigration and Naturalization Service estimated the annual cost of providing care for this population at over $93 million for every 1 million illegal immigrants. These problems are exacerbated due to the concentration of illegal immigrants in certain parts of the country. These areas include parts of Florida, Texas, and California, along with New York City. Since most of the health care provided illegal immigrants is uncompensated, a severe strain is placed on the health care system. Many hospitals lose considerable amounts of money caring for legal immigrants. Although the federal government has provided some financial assistance to health care systems serving certain groups (e.g., Haitians, Nicaraguans, and Cubans), this subsidy does not begin to cover the costs of this care.

Even as some hospitals are overwhelmed by the volume of medically indigent immigrants, fear and distrust keep many immigrants away from the health care system. Immigrants are likely to enter the system after considerable delay, and the use of preventive measures such as prenatal care is rare. Problems associated with communications and cultural differences are multiplied for illegal immigrants who fear that any contact with an "official" can result in deportation. Members of some groups still utilize traditional health care techniques and where possible traditional healers.

Providers of health care have attempted to adapt to this new category of patient, even to the point of catering to those among them that can pay. Individual hospitals have modified their policies and practices in keeping with the concerns of ethnic patients, and at least one marketing firm has emerged to provide guidance to health care organizations desiring to target ethnic patients. Hispanics and ethnic Asian populations are the ones most often targeted so far. Some institutions are finding, contrary to the above, that immigrants often pay out of pocket for services, making them relatively desirable customers. Some hospitals, in fact, have attempted to capitalize on their ethnic connections by encouraging the flow of more affluent foreigners into the United States for purposes of using the particular hospital's services. This has led to an unprecedented interest in "international medicine" among health care providers and planners.

In recent years, the sex composition of immigrants has shifted. Until recently, males tended to predominate among immigrants. During the late 1970s, for example, the sex ratio of immigrants to the United States was 111, or 111 male immigrants for every 100 females. However, during the mid-1980s, the ratio dropped to 100. By 1996, the sex ratio had fallen to 96, in large part due to changed provisions in the immigration laws. After 1990, nearly 90% of all immigrants to the United States were family members of persons already here.

Table 8.4. Immigrants to the United States by Selected
Social and Economic Characteristics, 1996

	Number	Percent		Number	Percent
Sex			Immigrants aged 16–64	669,814	
Male	422,740[a]	46.2[a]	Professional, specialty and	74,220[b]	11.1
Female	493,142	53.8	technical		
Total	915,882	100.0	Executive, administrative and	31,115	4.6
Age			managerial		
<15	183,362	20.3	Sales	14,955	2.2
15–29	304,855	33.3	Administrative support	21,526	3.2
30–44	246,823	26.9	Precision production, craft,	23,421	3.5
45–64	135,980	14.8	and repair		
≥65	41,780	4.6	Operators, fabricators, and	75,551	11.3
Median age	28		laborers		
			Farming, forestry, and fishing	13,195	2.0
			Services	60,722	9.1
			No occupation recorded	317,349	47.4

[a]Based on immigrants aged 16–64.
SOURCE: Immigration and Naturalization Services website (1999), http://www.ins.usdoj.gov.

Immigrant Destination

When immigration trends are analyzed at the subnational level, it is found that the majority of immigrants settle in relatively few states. Data regarding the intended residence of immigrants in 1996 are provided in Table 8.5. The table lists the 10 states and 10 metropolitan areas receiving the largest numbers of immigrants in 1996. California, New York, and Texas are the destinations for nearly 47% of all immigrants, and the top 10 states receive about 77% of all immigrants. The addition of immigrants to the population is the only factor that prevented New York state from losing population between 1980 and 1990. Among metropolitan areas, New York and Miami accounted for over 21% of all immigration in 1996. The top ten metropolitan statistical areas (MSAs) accounted for over 44% of all immigrants. Without question, the heavy flow of immigrants to selected states and MSAs significantly alters the demand for health services. Furthermore, these figures do not take into account refugees who numbered over 825,000 between 1981 and 1990 (US Immigration and Naturalization Service, 1997), nor do they consider illegal immigration. In view of the language and cultural differences characterizing the immigrant population, the provision of health care may be significantly impacted at the point of destination.

Table 8.5. States and Metropolitan Statistical Areas
Receiving Largest Numbers of Immigrants, 1996

	Number	Percentage of total immigrants to the United States
High immigration states		
California	201,529	22.0
New York	154,095	16.8
Texas	83,385	9.1
Florida	79,461	8.7
New Jersey	63,303	6.9
Illinois	42,517	4.6
Massachusetts	23,085	2.5
Virginia	21,375	2.3
Maryland	20,732	2.3
Pennsylvania	18,833	2.1
High immigration metropolitan areas		
New York,NY	133,168	14.5
Los Angeles-Long Beach, CA	64,285	7.0
Miami, FL	41,527	4.5
Chicago, IL	39,989	4.4
Washington, DC-MD-VA	34,327	3.7
Houston, TX	21,387	2.3
Boston, MA	18,726	2.0
San Diego, CA	18,226	2.0
San Francisco, CA	18,171	2.0
Newark, NJ	17,939	2.0

SOURCE: Immigration and Naturalization Serivce website (1999); http://www.ins.usdoj.gov.

INTERNAL MIGRATION

Introduction

The second component of geographic mobility—internal migration—involves population movement within the United States. As with the discussion of international migration, the focus here is on the volume of mover–migrants, the characteristics of these persons, and the origins and destinations of internal migrants.

Volume of Internal Migration

Every year, from 1980 through the late 1990s, between 16 and 20% of the US population changed residence. This translates into about 42 million persons moving between 1996 and 1997 alone. Of this 42 million, 28 million or 66% were classified as movers (within the same county) and nearly 14 million or 37% were classified as migrants (across county lines) (US Bureau of the Census, 1998). Focusing on the nearly 14 million migrants, about 8 million moved to another residence within the same state and 6 million moved to another state.

Migrant Characteristics

Additional insight into internal migration can be gained by examining the respective characteristics of movers and nonmovers. Table 8.6 presents the age structure of the total US population as well as that for both movers and nonmovers. Movers are considerably younger than nonmovers and have a median age that is about 9 years less. The youthfulness of movers is reflected in the relative proportions of persons under age 30 (58.9%) and age 65 and over (4.0%) included within this group. The comparable figures for nonmovers are 40.3% and 13.7%, respectively, and for the total population 43.2% and 11.3%. Therefore, areas receiving migrants gain a younger population in general, while areas losing migrants "age" more rapidly because of the loss of younger persons. A notable exception to this pattern of migration is the movement of older persons to certain retirement areas of the United States. Even so, the overall proportion of persons above the age of 55

Table 8.6. Mover and Nonmover Population by Age, United Staes, 1996–1997

Age interval	Total[a]		Same house		Different house	
	Number	Percent	Number	Percent	Number	Percent
Total	262,976	100	219,585	83.5	42,088	16.5
Under 5	15,965	6.1	12,203	5.6	3,667	8.7
5–9	20,271	7.7	16,400	7.5	3,794	9.0
10–14	19,506	7.4	16,504	7.5	2,930	7.0
15–19	19,164	7.3	15,998	7.3	3,065	7.3
20–24	17,489	6.6	11,667	5.3	5,614	13.3
25–29	19,260	7.3	12,980	5.9	6,065	14.4
30–44	64,956	24.7	53,851	24.5	10,718	25.5
45–64	54,488	20.7	49,622	22.6	4,749	11.3
65–74	18,015	6.8	17,197	7.8	806	1.9
75–84	10,954	4.2	10,441	4.8	501	1.2
85 and over	2,909	1.1	2,723	1.2	179	0.4
Median age	34.7		37.0		26.6	

[a]Numbers expressed in thousands.
SOURCE: Faber (1998), Table b.

Table 8.7. Educational Attainment by Mover–Nonmover Status,
United States, 1993–1994

	Elementary (0–8 years)	High school (1–4 years)	College (1–4 years)	College (over 5 years)
Total (25 years old and over)	7.8[a]	43.8	40.5	7.8
Nonmover	8.0	44.1	39.9	7.9
Mover	6.2	42.5	44.2	7.1
Same county	7.2	44.2	42.2	7.6
Migrant	4.4	38.8	47.9	8.9
Same state	4.5	39.4	49.0	7.1
Different state	4.3	38.0	46.6	11.0

[a]Percentages to be summed across rows.
SOURCE: Faber (1998), Table 4.

that do move is relatively low. Sustained population gain or loss can have a significant impact on both the size and age structure of the populations sending and receiving migrants.

Table 8.7 examines differences in educational attainment between nonmovers and various categories of movers. Overall, nonmovers are less educated than movers. Within the mover category, longer-distance movers are better educated in general. Short-distance movers (within the same county) are less educated than migrants, and among migrants longer-distance movers (between states) are the most highly educated. Nearly 57% of those moving to a different state have at least some college education, while the comparable figure for nonmovers is about 46%.

Regional Migration Flows

Table 8.8 presents data on the 1993–1994 flow of migrants between and among regions, along with the net figure resulting from both in-migration and out-migration. There was substantial movement of persons during this one-year interval, resulting in a net inflow for the South region and a net outflow for the Northeast, Midwest, and West. However, the net flows only tell part of the story. While the West had a net loss of 31,000 persons to the South, 380,000 persons nevertheless moved from the South to the West. The Northeast suffered a 248,000 person net loss to the South; at the same time over 201,000 persons moved from the South to the Northeast. Though the net flows have important implications for health care, gross migration is a better measure of population turnover than net migration. A net gain or loss of 25,000 persons for a region over a 5-year period may seem like a small number, but if those who left the area were demographically very different from those who entered it, the impact could be substantial.

Table 8.8. Region to Region Migration, United States, 1996

| Region of destination | Region of origin[a] | | | | |
	Northeast	Midwest	South	West	Total
Northeast					
In migration	—	118	252	71	441
Out migration	—	127	366	182	675
Net migration	—	−9	−114	−111	−234
Midwest					
In migration	127	—	480	235	842
Out migration	118	—	449	208	775
Net migration	9	—	31	27	67
South					
In migration	366	449	—	469	1,284
Out migration	252	480	—	401	1,113
Net migration	114	−31	—	68	151
West					
In migration	182	208	401	—	791
Out migration	71	235	469	—	775
Net migration	111	−27	−68	—	16

[a]Numbers expressed in thousands.
SOURCE: Hansen (1995), Fig. b.

IMPLICATIONS OF MIGRATION FOR HEALTH AND HEALTH CARE

Migration in its various forms has a number of implications for health status, health behavior, and health services utilization. The most direct consequences of migration include immediate changes in population size and population composition. Over the longer term, fertility and mortality levels are likely to be affected. There are related health care consequences both for the points of origin and destination. Migrants contribute to changing health care needs in areas experiencing net in-migration through the growth and change in composition of health care consumers. At the same time, the size and composition of areas losing migrants are affected as well.

Health Status

Migration involves some level turnover in the population in a particular area. In some cases, the newcomers will resemble the existing residents and, except for the impact of changes in population size, will not affect the area much in terms of health status. In other cases, turnover in population impacts the composition of the population at the points of both origin and destination. Immigrants, for example, can markedly alter compositional aspects related to health status and health care demand. This means that the number and type of health conditions will be modified. Further, changes in the mortality rate, as well as in the dominant causes of death, are likely to result.

Examples of changes in morbidity and mortality due to migration flows are almost endless. A community experiencing a wholesale exodus of its working-age residents and their children will find itself left with the health problems of an older population that may be less educated, poor, and less likely to practice good health habits. The resident health problems will involve the chronic conditions of the elderly such as heart conditions, respiratory disease, arthritis, and diabetes. The mortality rate will increase as those less at risk of death leave the community. Problems of infectious and parasitic conditions, digestive disorders, and accidents associated with the young are likely to decrease. Along these same lines, an urban fringe area undergoing rapid suburbanization may find itself with an "excess" of acute conditions such as pediatric problems, obstetrical problems, neurotic conditions, and even acne. The mortality rate is likely to decline due to the influx of relatively low-risk in-migrants. The communities of origin will find their remaining residents proportionately more likely to die from heart disease, cancer, and stroke. The receiving community will find its residents dying from accidents and suicide rather than any of the causes stated above.

Two other considerations are important with regard to health status, and both relate to the characteristics of the migrants themselves. Some research has indicated that migrants are often characterized by higher levels of both physical and mental disorders than nonmigrants. This is not to suggest that less healthy individuals choose to migrate—the opposite is probably true, in fact—but that migration itself takes a toll on health. The most clear-cut evidence relates to mental illness symptoms, in that the migration process is stressful to the point of inducing psychiatric symptoms. It has been found that even very affluent executives and their families often suffer traumatic effects due to mobility even when it means a substantial career advance. Dislocation, with its loss of family, friends, and schoolmates, involves a substantial health risk.

The other health status factor related to the migrants themselves has to do with the particular disorders that migrants carry with them. This has not been an issue with regard to migration within the United States since the end of the great rural-to-urban migrations in the middle of the twentieth century. Now, however, the influx of international immigrants has led to a concern over the health consequences of these population movements. These "new" immigrants include Southeast Asians, Latin Americans, and Caribbean residents, among others. In some cases the concern is over the introduction of diseases indigenous to their homelands and not found in the United States (e.g., rare tropical diseases). Of greater

Box 8.3

Foreign Doctors in US Health Care

A major controversy that continues to rage in health care relates to the participation of foreign-trained doctors in the US health care system. Referred to as foreign medical graduates (FMGs) or international medical graduates (IMGs), these doctors account for over 20% of the physicians practicing medicine in the United States today. This situation and the controversy that surrounds it has been scantily covered by the popular press and, except for an occasional newspaper article, the average American knows little about this aspect of medical care. However, if one requires the services of an anesthesiologist, a psychiatrist, or certain other specialists, there is a good chance that the care will be provided by someone who went to medical school in a foreign country.

In medical circles the continued influx of FMGs and the implications of their presence in American health care remain highly controversial issues. Organized medicine has always voiced concern over the quality of training that foreign physicians receive, contending that it does not meet American medical school standards. In the 1980s, with physicians facing increased competition for patients and revenue, the threat of additional competition from foreign-trained physicians led to attempts to limit immigration, introduce more difficult qualifying examinations, and preclude foreigners from specialty training and licensure.

Since World War II, FMGs have become an increasingly significant component of the US physician pool. At present, over 120,000 FMGs are in practice in this country. Another 17,000 FMGs annually are enrolled in residency training programs at various hospitals and other health care facilities. An undetermined number of FMGs (possibly in the tens of thousands) are in this country attempting to obtain residency positions or licenses to practice. Most of these are "alien FMGs," who are typically citizens of foreign countries who have received their basic training (i.e., the MD degree) in their homelands and subsequently immigrated to the United States for specialty training and for most the establishment of practices. Some are "US FMGs," American citizens who have received medical school training overseas and subsequently returned to the this country for residency training. Some of these have been educated at long-established medical schools in Europe; most, however, have attended newly created medical schools in the Caribbean or Mexico. The numbers of US FMGs, however, remain small compared to alien FMGs.

The medical education process should be briefly described in order to place this discussion in context. In the United States and in most other countries, individuals enter medical school with an undergraduate degree. The medical school curriculum includes approximately two years of basic science training, followed by two years of clerkship. These third and fourth years are spent essentially as apprentices, with students rotating through various clinical departments in addition to attending classes. At the end of this program, ranging from 3½ to 5 years, medical students are awarded an MD degree. In the United States, at least two years of postgraduate or residency training are required for licensure. While in residency training, physicians provide much of the charity care that is offered and staff hospital emergency rooms. In effect, the actual training in patient care takes place during the residency program.

Although there has been some influx of FMGs into the United States throughout this century, the size of the current pool is primarily the result of national policies formulated during the 1960s. At that time, it was widely held that a severe physician shortage existed. Measures were taken to facilitate the immigration of FMGs to fill the gap until an adequate supply of American-trained physicians could be established. These policies resulted in an influx of large numbers of FMGs, with several thousand entering practice annually from the early 1970s to the present. By the mid-1970s, however, concerns over a shortage were replaced by fears of a physician surplus. The number of domestically trained physicians had increased dramatically, and large numbers of alien physicians had been added to the pool. In response to these developments, immigration policies were made more restrictive, and more difficult qualifying examinations were introduced for FMGs. Both formal and informal measures were introduced to discourage entry of FMGs into training and practice, and legislation was proposed to limit the entry of US FMGs into the market.

During the 1970s and 1980s, the circumstances under which immigration occurred changed significantly. Previously, immigrant physicians entered under temporary visas, and most returned to their homelands. By the 1970s, however, the majority of FMGs were seeking permanent immigration status with the intention of practicing medicine in this country. The earlier immigrants typically entered by means of a formal exchange program, while the later ones were more likely to obtain entry though a nonmedical status, such as tourist, student, family reunification, or even refugee. Even those who entered on a temporary exchange basis often subsequently petitioned for a change of status once here.

The changing basis for admission was accompanied by a change in the national origin of the FMGs. This, perhaps, contributed to the controversy as much as issues of quality and competition. In the years immediately following World War II, the typical physician–immigrant was from Europe. However, by the late 1960s, the influx was dominated by Asian immigrants, particularly those from India and the Philippines. While both of these groups continue to be important, they have been joined by large numbers of physicians from Southeast Asia and Iran. By the 1980s, increasing numbers of immigrants were arriving from Latin America. Many of these newer immigrants entered as refugees, often without complete documentation of their medical background. During the late 1970s, this flow was augmented by thousands of US FMGs.

There are numerous subissues involved here that relate to testing, training

Continued

Box 8.3. *(Continued)*

requirements, licensure requirements, and even the issue of discrimination, which is currently being explored by the legal system. What is important to focus on for this brief discussion is the significance of physician–immigrants for the US health care system. Opponents of FMGs argue that foreign-trained physicians are less qualified to provide care than American-trained physicians. They are increasingly arguing that they are contributing to physician oversupply and causing unnecessary competition. These opponents are primarily representatives of organized medicine—presenting the view of medical schools, specialty associations, and practicing physicians—who have a vested interest in limiting physician supply.

On the other hand, FMGs and their supporters contend that foreign-trained physicians historically have made important contributions to US medical teaching, research, and practice. There is evidence that FMGs enter specialty areas that are considered undesirable by domestic medical school graduates. Further, they are found to practice in areas (such as inner cities and rural communities) in which American-trained physicians are reluctant to practice. Many residency programs contend that FMGs are essential for the provision of care to their indigent patients, particularly in inner-city hospitals that are not attractive to US medical school graduates.

Regardless of the merits of the above arguments, one fact is clear: FMGs will continue to be a major factor in US medical care for the foreseeable future. Each year thousands of FMGs enter practice, despite increasing restrictions. The estimated tens of thousands who are in "limbo," seeking training and practice opportunities, must be dealt with. With the introduction of antidiscrimination legislation in the late 1980s, it appears that the FMG issue will be finally opened to public debate.

---

consequence, however, has been the reintroduction of certain health problems long ago eradicated within this country. Since many of these immigrants originate in less developed countries, they sometimes "import" the health problems characteristic of those countries. These include infectious and parasitic diseases, as well as other long-eliminated conditions such as tuberculosis.

Health Behavior

The impact of migration also is likely to be felt with regard to health behavior. Health behavior involves patterns of service utilization and health practices (e.g., preventive health), as well as preferences for certain types of care, attitudes toward the health care delivery system, and lifestyles that may affect health status. Migrants may differ from nonmigrants in terms of all these factors,

Box 8.4

Migration and Rural Health Services

Much of rural America has experienced significant out-migration for a number of decades. In some instances, this pattern of movement can be traced back to very early in this century. Given the selectivity of migration in terms of age (Table 8.6), areas that lose migrants over a period of years experience premature aging of the populations. They end up with a disproportionately elderly population with a growing need for health services. as can be seen from Figure 5.1 (p. 124, the population pyramid for Garfield County, Nebraska, is characterized by a small base (relatively few young persons) and a relatively large top (many older persons). This type of pyramid has become common for many rural counties.

Many rural areas are similarly characterized by a growing demand for specific types of health services related to an older population and a shrinking base of health resources. Areas losing population through out-migration also experience a decline in the economic base required to support health services provision. Hospitals and clinics may close and new physicians are not drawn to these areas. The existing. physician base may begin to age and is not likely to be replenished by other physicians. In sum, while the size of the population in many rural counties is declining, the overall demand for health services is remaining constant or in some instances increasing. At the same time, economic forces are pushing providers to locate in more populous areas.

While this scenario is certainly a cause for concern, it should be noted that some rural areas have been creative in overcoming some of the problems associated with service shortages. Physician shortages have been addressed in two ways. First, physician networks may be created with family practitioners and some specialists traveling to different communities throughout a larger region. Second, physician assistants and other health professionals may play a larger role in care delivery than they do in urban and suburban areas. The combination of physician networks and expanded responsibilities for nonphysician health professionals brings a much higher level of care to rural areas than the distribution of physicians alone would imply.

The use of medical technology also fosters the delivery of adequate care. Many rural clinics and hospitals are "linked" by satellite or cable to specialists at larger urban hospitals. Images and other patient indicators are "delivered" to specialists for their opinion, thereby enhancing the effectiveness of rural physicians and rural hospitals.

Recent evidence has emerged that indicates that, while rural health care providers do not have all of the "state-of-the-art" equipment and training, patient–physician relationships in those communities foster greater continuity of care. Turnover among physicians and patients in urban and suburban clinics undermines continuity of care, while in rural areas, patients and physicians often have long-term relationships that enhance the quality of the care delivered.

Box 8.5

Geographic Mobility and Mental Health

Research on mental illness in the United States over the past 50 years has accumulated a large body of data that gives us a picture of the distribution of mental disorders within the American population. This research has indicated that mental illness, like physical illness, is not randomly distributed within the population but is disproportionately found among certain segments of the population. Distinct patterns have been found based on age, sex, race, social class, and a variety of other factors. While the distribution pattern is very complex (in keeping with the complexity of mental illness itself), the patterns are distinct enough to allow for relatively high levels of predictability for both the volume and type of mental disorders characterizing a subsegment of the population.

These same research efforts have attempted to link mental illness to geographic mobility, but with somewhat less success. Given the clearly disruptive nature of the migration process, whether across town or across the ocean, hypotheses linking migration to mental disorder inevitably have been posited. To examine this possible relationship, a variety of studies have been conducted over the past several decades, and some evidence has been accumulated that geographic mobility is a factor in the development of mental disorder. However, as seen below, the relationship is quite complex.

Part of the problem in testing this relationship has to do with the operationalization of the variables in question. The migration process has to be defined in such a way that it can be measured and quantified. Given the usually clear pattern of movement from one geographic location to another, this is not particularly difficult. However, operationalizing the other variable in the equation—mental illness—is extremely problematic. Experts in the field cannot agree on what constitutes mental illness, and even if there were consensus, accurate measures of the phenomenon would be difficult to come by. Some of the indicators of mental illness prevalence that have been utilized include admissions to state mental hospitals, referrals to treatment centers by the courts and other agents of social control, reports by social workers, and self-reports by the affected individuals themselves. All the measures have significant flaws, thus making it difficult to test the hypothesis conclusively. Given the fact that we are often dealing with populations whose "normal" behavior might be considered deviant by the receiving community, these measurement problems are multiplied.

Studies that have been conducted utilizing a variety of types of migration, migrant populations, and mental health measures do suggest that there is a correlation between geographic mobility and mental disorder. Many of these studies have focused on immigrants (international migrants), often emphasizing the implications of being "uprooted" as a factor in the onset of mental disorder. Further, conditions of social isolation, cultural conflict, identity crises, and discrimination associated with the move also are seen as etiologic considerations. Despite these obvious negative aspects of migration, the research findings related to the hypothesis have been mixed for international migrants. Much of the research has found rates of mental illness to be higher among immigrants than among native-born Americans. Other studies, however, have found rates to be lower among immigrants. It should be noted that much of the research, at least in the United States, linking international migration to mental disorder was conducted on certain immigrant groups and at a particular time in our social past. It has been argued that the type of immigrant, the circumstances surrounding emigration, and the conditions in the receiving country are more important factors than the physical move itself.

While the evidence relating international migration to mental disorder has become less conclusive as more data have become available, there is strong support for a relationship (at least within the United States) between internal migration and mental illness. Regardless of the time period in question, there appears to be a persistent correlation between psychiatric disorder and internal migration. This effect seems to be stronger for longer-distance moves, with limited evidence found to link short distance moves to mental disorder. For long moves, however, studies have consistently found higher rates of psychiatric disorder for migrants than for non-migrants. When the prevalence of severe disorders is examined—based, for example, on rates of psychiatric hospitalization—rates for interstate migrants have been found to be disproportionately high. These rates have remained high at a time, as noted above, that differentials in psychiatric hospitalization for foreign immigrants and native Americans have almost disappeared.

These findings must be qualified in the same manner as those for international migrants. The preexisting characteristics of the migrant, the conditions surrounding migration, the respective character of the points of origin and destination, and other factors affect the likelihood of onset of mental disorder. The fact that certain groups have consistently high identified rates of mental disorder (e.g., blacks who have migrated from the South to the North) may be a function of the migrant background, conditions in the receiving community, and the impact of the migration process itself.

Despite the inconclusiveness of some of the research, clear implications for the health care system are present. Any community experiencing an influx of migrants, whether international or internal, is likely to see an increase in the demand for mental health services. The extent of the demand and the type of services required will depend on such factors as the nature of the migrants themselves (e.g., nationality, reasons for migration), the social climate of the receiving community, and the existing resources from which the migrants can draw. The health care system will require some "education" as to the cultural backgrounds, value systems, normative systems, and health care behavior patterns of these populations in order to be able to appreciate the nature of mental disorders among them and to provide appropriately conceived mental health services.

with implications for the points of both origin and destination. For some countries, emigrants may be among the best educated and most affluent, and in fact often include large numbers of physicians. The originating country may lose the bulk of its population that is committed to modern medical practice, while those remaining behind are likely to be much more traditional in their health care orientations. In other cases, those with less desirable health characteristics may be "exported" by governments eager to rid themselves of problems. Box 8.3 discusses foreign doctors in US health care.

Since there is wide variation in health care environments and practice patterns across the United States, migrants from one region to another are likely to be characterized by differing patterns of health behavior. A migrant from the West Coast to the rural South would probably be surprised at the lack of emphasis placed on preventive care and health education, the absence of health maintenance organizations, and the generally low level of concern over health issues. Conversely, migrants from rural areas to urban communities are likely to be overwhelmed by the complexity of the health care system and the seeming obsession with health displayed there. International immigrants are likely to originate in societies with quite different orientations toward health care. Those entering the United States as refugees may have developed attitudes of distrust toward government agencies and be apprehensive with regard to public health programs.

Health Services Infrastructure and Utilization Patterns

An important health care implication of migration relates to health services utilization. As noted throughout this chapter, the volume and type of health services consumed depend primarily on the size and composition of the population. As the population increases or decreases in number, the demand for health services typically will follow. Many destination communities have difficulty accommodating increased health care demand because the local infrastructure and the physician pool cannot be enlarged rapidly enough. On the other hand, areas losing population cannot easily scale back the infrastructure in order to adjust services to the needs of a smaller population. Box 8.4 addresses issues facing rural areas.

As population composition changes, not only will overall demand be affected but the type of services needed will change. Changes in age distribution are perhaps the best predictor of changes in utilization, since both volume and type of services are linked directly to age composition. Changes in the educational level or income level also are likely to have a substantial impact on health services. Education plays an important role in the use of a number of services. Income and the ability to pay for health services also are important factors in health services utilization. Occupational characteristics may determine the type of insurance available, and even religious affiliation may influence preferences for the type of care obtained or the hospital chosen.

These same factors play a part in the demand for physician services. The retirement community undergoing a major influx of elderly migrants may face heavy demand for cardiologists, oncologists, urologists, gynecologists, and ophthalmologists. The suburban community undergoing rapid growth will find an increasing need for obstetricians, pediatricians, dermatologists, allergists, and ear, nose, and throat specialists. The relationship between geographic mobility and mental health is the focus of Box 8.5.

REFERENCES

Barnett, L. D., and Reed, E. F. (1985). *Law, Society, and Population: Issues in a New Field*. Houston, TX: Cap and Gown.

Faber, C. S. (1998). Geographic mobility: March 1996 to March 1997 (update). *Current Population Report*, Series P-20, No. 510. Washington, DC: US Government Printing Office.

Hansen, K. (1995). *Geographic Mobility: March 1993 to March 1994*. Current Population Reports, Series P-20, No. 485. Washington, DC: US Government Printing Office.

Kulkarni, M., and Pol, L. (1994). Migration expectancy revisited: Results for the 1970s, 1980s and 1990s. *Population Research and Policy Review* 13:195–202.

National Center for Health Statistics. (1980–1990). *Vital Statistics of the United States* (Natality and Mortality, Part A). Washington, DC: US Government Printing Office.

Olshanksy, S. J., Karnes, B., Rogers, R. G., and Smith, L. (1997). Infectious diseases—New and ancient threats to world health. *Population Bulletin* 52(2). Washington, DC: Population Reference Bureau.

Passel, J. (1985). Undocumented immigrants: How many? In *Proceedings of the Social Statistics Section of the American Statistical Association* (pp. 65–72). Washington, DC: American Statistical Association.

Tucker, C. J., and Urton, W. L. (1987). Frequency of geographic mobility: Findings from the national health interview survey. *Demography* 24(May):265–270.

US Bureau of the Census. (1922, 1931, 1953, 1985, 1996). *Statistical Abstract of the United States, 1996*. Washington, DC: US Government Printing Office.

US Bureau of the Census. (1983, 1992). *Census of Population, General Population Characteristics, Florida*. Washington, DC: US Government Printing Office.

US Bureau of the Census. (1997). Website: http://www.census.gov.

US Bureau of the Census. (1998). Website: http://www.bls.census.gov/cps/pub/1997/mobility.htm

US Congress. (1990). Legal immigration revision. *Congressional Record* (October 27).

US Immigration and Naturalization Service. (1997). Website: http://www.ins.usdoj.gov.

Warren, R., and Kraly, E. (1985). *The Elusive Exodus: Emigration from the United States*. Population Trends and Public Policy Series, No. 8. Washington, DC: Population Reference Bureau.

Warren, R., and Passel, J. (1987). A count of the uncountable: Estimates of undocumented aliens counted in the 1980 census. *Demography* 24(August):375–394.

ADDITIONAL RESOURCES

Borjas, G. J. (1990). *Friends and Strangers: The Impact of Immigrants on the US Economy*. New York: Basic Books.

Edmonston, B., and Passel, J.S. (Eds.) (1994). *Immigration and Ethnicity: The Integration of America's Newest Arrivals*. Washington, DC: The Urban Institute Press.

Farley, R. (Ed.) (1995). *State of the Union: America in the 1990s*, Vol. 2. New York: Russell Sage Foundation.

Heer, D. M. (1996). *Immigration in America's Future: Social Science Findings and Policy Debate*. Boulder, CO: Westview Press.

Isbister, J. (1996). *The Immigration Debate: Remaking America*. West Hartford, CT: Kumarian.

Jensen, L. (1989). *The New Immigration: Implications for Poverty and Public Assistance Utilization*. Westport, CT: Greenwood.

Martin, P., and Midgley, E. (1999). Immigration to the United States. *Population Bulletin* 31(2). Washington, DC: Population Reference Bureau.

Long, L. (1989). *Migration and Residential Mobility in the United States*. New York: Russell Sage.

Loveless, S. C., McCue, C. P., Surette, R. B., and Norris-Tirrel, D. (1996). *Immigration and Its Impact on American Cities*. Westport, CT: Praeger.

Simon, J. L. (1989). *The Economic Consequences of Immigration*. Cambridge, MA: Basil Blackwell.

Smith, J. P., and Edmonston, B. (Eds.) (1997). *The New Americans: Economic, Demographic, and Fiscal Effects of Immigration*. Washington, DC: National Academy Press.

Stevens, R., Goodman, L. W., and Mick, S. S. (1978). *The Alien Doctors: Foreign Medical Graduates in American Hospitals*. New York: Wiley.

Data Sources for Health Demography

INTRODUCTION

The health care industry has always presented something of a paradox. Although historically awash in data, it has been very difficult to convert these data into usable information. Health data often have not been very accessible even to the organizations that generate them. When data sets have been accessible, they typically have been of limited use to health demographers and other analysts, since they were generated for some operational or administrative purpose. Further, even when data have been made accessible, the tools were not available for their efficient management and exploitation.

This situation has existed in the face of increasing demand for health-related data of all types, as health care organizations have striven to adapt to the new health care environment. During the 1990s, organizations and individuals that historically had little interest in or need for health-related data found that efficient data gathering and analysis were necessary to maintain successful operations. Today's health care environment is demanding further improvements in the quality, quantity, and specificity of the data used for marketing, planning, and business development.

In fact, the demand for health-related data has grown far beyond the organizations directly involved in the provision of health care. Health plans, employers, policymakers, health lawyers, and a variety of other interests are increasingly requiring health-related data. Entities both inside and outside of health care are now using health data to address a range of business challenges, as well as for cost containment, quality monitoring, and regulatory purposes. Entire issues of scholarly journals have been devoted to debates regarding the management of health data (e.g., *Health Affairs*, December 1998).

The compilation of health data can be approached at two different levels: the community level and the organizational level. The former involves the analysis of communitywide health data, whether the "community" is the nation, a state, a county, or a planning district. This macrolevel approach historically has characterized public sector activities usually involving government agencies. At the organizational level, data analysis focuses on the characteristics and concerns of specific corporate entities such as hospitals, physician groups, and health plans. The organization-level approach is more typical of the private sector in health care. However, in recent years there has been a blurring of the distinction between public and private planning activities, as a number of joint public–private initiatives have been undertaken, and the two sectors are becoming increasingly interested in the same types of data.

At both levels, these perspectives require the use of data on both the internal environment and the external environment. While it has been natural for health care organizations to turn first to internal information sources, data on the external environment have become increasingly important. Data related to the external environment are sometimes difficult to locate and access but, relative to internal data, are more available to the public. The health care organization's ability to access, manipulate, and interpret external data sets is increasingly the difference between success and failure.

Internally generated data represent a ready source of information at the organizational level. Health care organizations routinely generate a large volume of data as a by-product of their normal operations. These include data related to patient characteristics, utilization patterns, referral streams, financial transactions, personnel, and other types of information that almost always have a demographic dimension. To the extent that these data can be extracted from internal data management systems, they serve as a rich source of information on the organization and its operation. This chapter, however, will focus on sources of external data, since these are the data sets to which the health demographer is most likely to have access.

In addition to the internal–external dimension noted above, a useful distinction is made between primary and secondary data. Primary data collection involves the administration of surveys, focus groups, observational methods, and other studies for the stated purpose of obtaining information on a specific topic. Secondary data refer to data gathered for some other purpose besides planning, marketing, or business development but that are nevertheless of value in the formulation of strategy or policy.

This chapter focuses on secondary sources of data rather than primary research. Primary research requires a much more detailed treatment than can be afforded in this framework and is better addressed in a research methodology context. Further, primary research activities are usually focused narrowly on specific issues facing an organization at a particular time under certain conditions. While the value of primary research has become well established within health care as evidenced by the growing number of patient satisfaction surveys and focus groups being conducted, these activities usually generate proprietary data that are not likely to be disseminated outside the institution. (A useful introduction to primary research methods for health demographers is provided in Berkowitz et al., 1997.)

The primary purpose of this chapter is to describe the broad range of data sets of use to analysts, planners, and decision makers in health care. There is no way, of course, that this discussion could be exhaustive, especially in view of the growing number of sources of health-related data. While many of these information sources have been introduced in specific contexts earlier in the volume, important characteristics of these sources, such as the frequency of publication, geographic specificity, and methodological limitations, are presented in this chapter.

A number of the data sets described here are not what many users would label "health care data." However, health care data is an elusive notion in that much of what affects the health care industry does not result directly from health-related events. During the 1990s, there has been an increase in the demand for data thought in the past to be unrelated to health care, including data on such topics as employment, housing, and crime. Therefore, this discussion has been expanded to include data sets that reflect the more general environment affecting health care-related activities.

Admittedly, a chapter such as this can become tedious reading when some of the data sets described seem to lack specific relevance to issues currently being confronted. The reader, therefore, is encouraged to focus first on the information sources that appear to be most relevant and then to examine the others for ideas, insights, and information perhaps related, albeit indirectly, to the issues being addressed. Familiarity with these data also will prepare the researcher for problems and opportunities that may arise in the future.

DATA COLLECTION METHODS

The methods for data collection discussed in this chapter are divided into four general categories: censuses, registration systems, surveys, and synthetically produced data. Censuses, registries, and surveys are the more traditional methods of generating demographic data, although synthetically produced statistics such as population estimates and projections have become standard tools for most planning, marketing, and business development activities.

Census

A census involves a complete count of individuals (or entities) residing in a specific place at a specific time. The best known census involves a count of the population (including its housing characteristics); a lesser known census involves

Box 9.1

The Year 2000 Census

In 2000, the US Bureau of the Census administered the twenty-second decennial census. Although an attempt will be made to enumerate the entire US population, a complete count is not likely to be accomplished. In 1990, for the first time in 50 years, the census was less complete than its predecessor (1980). The 1990 census failed to count millions of Americans, especially the poor, racial and ethnic minorities, and children. Overall, nearly 2% of the 1990 US population was not counted. Efforts to produce more accurate data resulted in a plan to utilize statistical sampling for a survey of 750,000 households in the 2000 census. These sample data would have been used to "adjust" the 2000 count so that the resulting numbers would better reflect the demographic reality of the nation. However, on January 25, 1999, the US Supreme Court ruled the use of this method to adjust data unconstitutional in regard to reapportionment for the US Congress. The US Bureau of the Census subsequently agreed not to use statistical sampling for this purpose. Still to be resolved at the time of this writing is whether or not adjusted data will be available for other uses, such as the reapportionment of state legislatures.

Like recent censuses, the 2000 count utilized a mail out–mail back approach to enumeration. One week prior to the official enumeration date (April 1, 2000), a questionnaire will be sent to most US households. Included with the questionnaire were instructions for completing the form and an envelope for return mail. Three changes in this procedure for the 2000 census were noteworthy, however. First, before the initial questionnaire is sent, a postcard was mailed to these households notifying residents that the census questionnaire would arrive soon and urging their cooperation. Soon after the questionnaire was mailed another postcard was sent thanking those who had returned their questionnaire and reminding others to do so. The use of both postcards was designed to increase the response of the mail out–mail back effort. Second, people will be able to obtain questionnaires in other locations (e.g., community centers) and respond by telephone and the Internet. Third, an extensive and continuous effort designed to emphasize the importance of the census was made with a much heavier emphasis on advertising and other means of promotion. An estimated 35% of all households did not respond to these efforts, and Census Bureau enumerators were sent out to collect the remainder of the data.

Consistent with its 1990 predecessor, the 2000 census made use of two ques-

a count of businesses. The US Census Bureau (within the Department of Commerce) has conducted population censuses since 1790 and in 1810 added economic (manufacturing only until 1930) census to its responsibilities. The population and housing census is conducted every 10 years (in years that end in zero) and the 2000 census was being conducted as this volume was going to press. Economic cen-

tionnaires, a short form covering eight subjects mailed to five out of every six households and a long form consisting of 53 subjects sent to the remaining households. It should be noted that the short form is the shortest one used in 180 years. Other types of questionnaires are used for single persons with non-household living arrangements such as those individuals living in nursing homes and college dormitories.

The 1990 and 2000 census forms contained comparable questions, although five items from the 1990 census did not appear in 2000. One important change was the questions related to race and ethnicity. In 2000, for the first time in US census history, respondents could select more than one racial category. This revision was made in order to more accurately enumerate persons of mixed racial heritage.

Other differences from the 1990 efforts included:

1. New streamlined forms that are easier to understand, use larger fonts, and offer color contrasts.
2. The first fully computerized census beginning with the optical scanning of all questionnaires and ending with the release of the final results on the Internet.
3. Improved household lists before the initial mailing takes place.
4. The use of improved methods to enumerate difficult-to-count populations.

Significant dates and intervals for the 2000 Census are:

1. Mid-March 2000: postcard sent to households, census questionnaire delivered.
2. April 1, 2000: Census Day.
3. Early-April 2000: follow-up postcard sent to households.
4. April–June 2000: census takers visit housing units that did not return questionnaires.
5. October–November 2000: all field work complete.
6. December 31, 2000: national apportionment counts delivered to the President.
7. April 1, 2001: all states receive redistricting counts.

SOURCE: US Bureau of the Census website (1999). URL: www.census.gov/dmd/www/dropin2.htm.

suses are conducted every five years and involve complete counts of all US business operations. Box 9.1 provides an overview of the 2000 census and discusses some of the controversial issues surrounding its administration.

By definition, a census includes a complete count of the population. However, it is increasingly difficult to strictly apply this term to the decennial census conducted in the United States. While the US census ostensibly counts every resident, it falls short of a true census in two aspects. First, as noted in Chapter 4, every decade a certain segment of the population is missed in the enumeration, resulting in some level of undercount. While the undercount is typically less than 3% and in 1990 was less than 2%, its mere existence creates myriad problems. This undercount tends to be concentrated among certain segments of the population, resulting in a situation in which members of some groups have a greater chance of being enumerated than members of others. This has significant implications, since the results of each census are used as the basis for redistributing Congressional seats and allocating government funds. Because of the undercount, the publication of initial census figures every 10 years produces a spate of lawsuits related to the accuracy of the census itself. For the first time in American history, in fact, the 1990 census was less accurate than its predecessor, the 1980 census. This is one of the factors that has led to the significant changes implemented for the 2000 census.

The second factor diminishing the enumeration's value as a census is the fact that a large portion of the data on population and housing characteristics is obtained from a sample of the nation's households. In 1990, for example, only 7 of the 33 population questions and 12 of the 32 housing questions were asked of all US households. The remainder were asked of approximately one out of every six households. While the use of sampling significantly reduces the cost of conducting the census, it generates figures that some might assume (sometimes incorrectly) to represent complete counts.

Typical census items elicit data on the number of persons residing in each living unit (e.g., house, duplex, apartment, or dormitory) and the characteristics of those individuals. Data are gathered on the age, race, ethnicity, marital status, income, occupation, education, employment status, and industry of employment for each resident. There also are questions about the dwelling unit in which the respondent lives, including information on the type of dwelling unit (e.g., apartment or duplex), ownership status, value of owned house, monthly rent, age of dwelling unit, and a number of other topics. For a more complete discussion of the 1990 census questionnaire and the methodology employed, see Lavin (1996). Census 2000 methodology is provided on the Census Bureau's website at www.census.gov.

For the most part, health-related items are noticeably absent from the census, since very few have been mandated for collection through legislative action. (The only directly health-related question in the 1990 census addressed functional disabilities and the ability to perform daily activities.) In the 2000 census, a question on long-lasting conditions, e.g., blindness, was asked along with one on limits to activities (e.g., concentrating and dressing). As will be shown later, other government agencies have a much more significant role in the collection of health-related data than does the Census Bureau.

Census data are made available by the Census Bureau for virtually every formally designated geographic unit in the United States. Statistics generated by the census are disseminated for states, counties, zip codes, metropolitan areas, and cities. Data also are published for specially designated areas created by the Census Bureau, including census tracts, block groups, block numbering areas, and blocks.

Most census-generated statistics are now available on computer tape, microfiche, CD-ROM, and via the Internet (http://www.census.gov). These databases—referred to as summary tape files (STFs)—do not include the raw data (i.e., individual records) from the census but preselected aggregations of information. Public use microdata samples (PUMS) include raw data and are available for the 1990 census, stripped of any information that would identify individual respondents. PUMS files involve a sample of records from areas containing at least 100,000 persons.

Census data may be obtained from a variety of sources. Many libraries are designated as depositories of US government publications and maintain most or all of the census reports in print, microfiche, or CD format among their holdings. The US Government Printing Office also makes the reports available to the public at a reasonable cost. Computer tapes, microfiche, and CD-ROM data are sold directly through the Census Bureau's Data User Services Office. The bureau's website referenced above has become an increasingly important source of census data. By simply "pointing and clicking" through an alphabetical list of key terms, most census data can be easily found. With each successive census, the number of printed reports is being reduced, with the intent of eventually restricting census output to electronic formats.

After the 1980 census, many private vendors began to repackage census data and sell them to the public. In fact, joint public–private projects were involved in converting census data to the zip code level, a geographic unit with a great deal of utility for the business community. Private sector marketing of census data was even heavier after the 1990 census, with commercial data vendors providing population estimates and projections at the census tract level during the intercensal period. Data vendors are expected to even more intensively exploit the 2000 census.

Economic censuses can be traced back to the early nineteenth century, although it was not until 1929 that continuous data gathering for a broad range of business entities was begun by the Census Bureau. The modern economic census was initiated in 1954 and is conducted every 5 years (currently in years ending in 2 and 7). The census covers businesses engaged in retail trade, wholesale trade, service activities, mineral industries, transportation, construction, manufacturing, and agriculture, as well as government services. The information collected through the economic census includes data on sales, employment, and payroll, along with other, more specialized data. These data are available for a variety of geographic units, including states, metropolitan areas, counties, and places with 2500 or more residents.

While it may appear that these data are unrelated to health issues, it should be kept in mind that information on economic activities from the economic censuses are classified by Standard Industrial Classification (SIC) code, which recently has been revised. The SIC system assigns a code to all businesses, allowing them to be grouped into standard categories for statistical purposes. Thus, aggregated data on businesses within the SIC category that involve health-related activities (e.g., physician practices) are available from this source. (As this volume goes to press, the SIC system is being replaced by the *North American Industry Classification System.*)

Figures from the 1992 census of service industries show, for example, that there were 319 physician offices (SIC 801) in Orlando, Florida, with receipts of over $319 million and an annual payroll of approximately $178 million (US Bureau of the Census, 1994a: Table 5). Furthermore, there were 27 medical and dental laboratories (SIC 807), with over $17 million in receipts and over $5 million in annual payroll. Finally, data from the 1992 census of retail trade industries indicate that there were 22 optical goods stores (SIC 5995), with over $9 million in sales and $2.2 million in annual payroll in Orlando (US Bureau of the Census, 1994b: Table 5).

The formats in which these summary data are distributed include printed reports, CD-ROM, and the Internet. The reports and CDs may be obtained from the same government sources and locations as the population and housing data.

Registration Systems

A second method of data collection that generates information for health demography is represented by registration systems. A registration system involves the systematic registration, recording, and reporting of data on a broad range of events, institutions, and individuals (Shryock et al., 1973, p. 27). The implied characteristics of a registry include the regular and timely recording of the phenomenon in question. Most of the registration systems relevant to this discussion are sponsored by some branch of government, although other types of registration systems will be discussed below as well.

The best-known registration activities in the United States are those related to "vital events," including births, deaths, marriages, and divorces maintained by the National Center for Health Statistics. Other registries can prove valuable when examining changes in the level and types of health services required by a population. These include registration systems sponsored by the Centers for Disease Control and Prevention (CDC), the Social Security Administration, the Health Care Financing Administration, and the Immigration and Naturalization Service, among others.

A variation on registries that is finding increasing use in health demography is "administrative records" (Judson, 1996). Administrative records systems are not necessarily intended to be registries of all enrollees or members of an organization or group but a record of transactions involving these individuals. Thus, the list of all Medicare enrollees would constitute a registry, but the data generated by virtue of Medicare enrollees' encounters with the health care system would be under the heading of administrative records (since not all Medicare enrollees would use services during a given time period). Data sets made available by the federal government on Medicare and Medicaid activity involve administrative records that are useful for a number of purposes.

Administrative records serve a useful function in that they provide access to sources of data not otherwise available. However, unlike other forms of data generation such as censuses and surveys, the raw data are not strictly under the control of those who establish the data file. Administrative records may be submitted by a variety of parties, creating inherent problems in data quality and standardization. A great deal of effort is currently being expended to improve the quality of administrative records for use in health care. For example, Medicare data, including the number of enrollees, are now available for all US counties.

In addition, lists maintained by professional associations such as the American Medical Association (AMA) are placed in this category because such lists have many of the characteristics required of registries. Some of the more important registration systems in place in the United States are described below.

Vital Statistics

As noted above, vital statistics in the United States involves data collection for births, deaths, marriages, and divorces (US Department of Health and Human Services, 1997a). The collection of vital statistics has a long history in the United States, predating the Declaration of Independence by many years. By 1933, all states and the District of Columbia were part of the death registration system. In order to be part of a death registration area (DRA), a state must record at least 90% of the deaths that occur and obtain certain data for the death certificate.

A comparable system has been established for the collection of data on births. Participation in the birth registration area (BRA) requires the same 90% coverage and the use of standard items on the birth certificate. The collection of data on births developed more slowly than that for deaths, but by 1933, all states were in the BRA (National Center for Health Statistics, 1998b: Section 4). Today, virtually all deaths and births in the United States are reported through this process.

The collection of data on vital events is initially the responsibility of the local health authority. Health departments at the county (or county equivalent) level are charged with filing certificates for births and deaths. These data are forwarded to

Box 9.2

The National Center for Health Statistics

The National Center for Health Statistics (NCHS) is considered by many to be the Census Bureau of health care. As a division of the Centers for Disease Control and Prevention, the NCHS performs a number of invaluable functions related to data on health and health care. For over 30 years, the center has carried out the tasks of data collection and analysis, data dissemination, and the development of methodologies for research on health issues. The NCHS also coordinates data collection with the organization responsible for health statistics.

One of the center's responsibilities includes the compilation, analysis, and publication of vital statistics for the United States and each relevant subarea. This is a massive task, but the results provide the basis for the calculation of fertility and mortality rates. These statistics, in turn, provide the basis for various population estimates and projections made by other organizations. The compilation and analysis of data on morbidity is another important function, and the center has been responsible for the development of much of the epidemiological data available, for example, on chronic disease and AIDS.

In addition to the data compiled from various registration sources, the center is the foremost administrator of health care surveys in the nation. Its sample surveys are generally large scale and fall into two categories: community-based surveys and facility-based surveys. Perhaps the center's most important survey is the National Health Interview Survey (NHIS), in which data are collected annually from approximately 49,000 households. The NHIS is the nation's primary source of data on the incidence–prevalence of health conditions, health status, the number of injuries and disabilities characterizing the population, health services utilization, and a variety of other health-related topics. Other surveys that involve a sample from the community include the Medical Expenditure Panel Survey, the National Health and Nutrition

the vital statistics registry within the respective state governments. The appropriate state agency compiles the data for use by the state and the state transmits the files to the National Center for Health Statistics (NCHS). The NCHS has the responsibility of compiling and publishing vital statistics for the nation and its various political subdivisions (Ventura et al., 1997; Anderson et al., 1997). See Box 9.2 for a description of the National Center for Health Statistics.

The standard birth certificate is used to collect data on the time and date of birth, place of occurrence, mother's residence, birth weight, pregnancy complications, mother's pregnancy history, mother and father's age and race (ethnicity in selected states), and mother's education and marital status. Data gathered on the

Examination Survey, and the National Survey of Family Growth. Another survey, the National Maternal and Infant Health Survey, involves a sampling of certificates of birth, fetal death, and infant death.

One of the newer surveys has become the most important source of information on the increasingly important topic of ambulatory care. The National Ambulatory Medical Care Survey samples the patient records of 2500 office-based physicians to obtain data on diagnosis, treatment, and medications prescribed, along with information on the characteristics of both physicians and patients. Other important facility-based surveys include the National Hospital Discharge Survey and the National Nursing Home Survey.

The data collected through the NCHS studies are disseminated in a variety of ways. Much of the information is disseminated as printed material. The center's publications include annual books such as *Health, United States* (the "official" government compendium of statistics on the nation's health), and publications such as *Vital and Health Statistics*. Data from NCHS surveys also are available in tape, diskette, and CD formats. The NCHS sponsors conferences and workshops offering not only the findings from the center's research but training in its research methodologies. NCHS-generated data sets increasingly are being made available via the Internet and can be accessed at www.cdc.gov/nchswww.

From the perspective of a health data user, there are other resources that the center can offer. By contacting the appropriate NCHS division, it is possible to obtain detailed statistics, many unpublished, on all the topics for which the center compiles data. Center staff also are available to help with methodological issues and provide that "one number" that the health data analyst might require. In short, the NCHS is a service-oriented agency that provides a number of invaluable functions for those who require data on health and health care. Much of the information required for the US system to adapt to the changing health care environment, in fact, will be generated by the NCHS.

standard death certificate include age, race (ethnicity in selected states), sex, place of residence, usual occupation, and industry of the decedent, along with the location where the death took place. In addition, data are collected on the immediate and contributing causes of death and on other significant conditions. A separate certificate is used for fetal deaths.

Birth and death statistics are regularly reported in federal government publications and now via the Internet (http://www.fedstats.gov). The compiled statistics are typically presented based on both the place of occurrence of the event (e.g., the location of the hospital) and the place of residence of the affected individual. Considerable detail is provided in the reports for a wide range of geographic units including states, metropolitan statistical areas (MSAs), counties, and urban places. Data for other geographic areas may be available through state and local government agencies. Yearly summary reports are produced and published by the NCHS, though monthly summaries also are available through the monthly vital statistics reports. Data sets including individual-level data ("microdata") are available on computer tape, though these files typically do not include all data, all states, or all variables.

Vital statistics reports also are made available by most state governments and most local health departments. Although basic data always will be reported by these agencies, the format, detail, and coverage varies from state to state and county to county (Kowalski, 1997).

Marriage and divorce registration areas were established using the same criteria as birth and death registration areas, that is, at least 90% coverage, central reporting, and standard items on the marriage and divorce certificates. The marriage registration area does not include eight states—Arizona, Arkansas, Nevada, New Mexico, North Dakota, Oklahoma, Texas, and Washington—and the divorce registration area contains only 31 states.

Standard data collected on the marriage certificate includes age of each spouse, type of ceremony (civil or religious), and previous marital status of spouses, as well as the race and educational status of the bride and groom. Data available from divorce certificates are limited to age of wife and husband at the time of marriage and divorce, previous marital history, number of children under age 18 involved, and the educational status of husband and wife.

Marriage and divorce statistics historically have been disseminated by the NCHS through monthly and yearly published reports for states, MSAs, and counties. However, the compilation of detailed data on marriages and divorces by the NCHS was suspended in January 1996. The latest published data are for 1989–1990 (Clarke, 1995a,b); data for 1991–1995 soon will be available in electronic format (National Center for Health Statistics, 1998a). Publications by state and local government sources may offer more detailed statistics on marriages and divorces and, with the reduction in federal reporting, are likely to become more important sources of such data.

CDC Disease Surveillance

The Centers for Disease Control and Prevention (CDC) have been involved in disease surveillance activities since the establishment of the Communicable Disease Center in 1946. Its initial responsibility involved the study of malaria, murine typhus, smallpox, and other communicable diseases. In 1954, a surveillance section was established within the epidemiology branch of the CDC to plan and conduct continued surveillance of communicable diseases. Surveillance activities now include programs in human reproduction, environmental health, chronic disease, risk reduction, occupational safety and health, and infectious diseases. Recently, controversy has surrounded CDC surveillance efforts with regard to HIV/AIDS. The purpose of the surveillance system is to provide weekly provisional information on the occurrence of diseases defined as notifiable by the Council of State and Territorial Epidemiologists (CSTE).

Notifiable disease reports are received by the CDC from 52 US jurisdictions (Washington, DC, and New York City report separately) and five territories. The number of diseases and conditions reported is quite large. The list of monitored diseases includes, among others, anthrax, botulism, cholera, diphtheria, foodborne disease, leprosy, mumps, and toxic shock. Statistics on notifiable diseases are published weekly by the CDC in *Morbidity and Mortality Weekly Report* (MMWR) and compiled in an annual report published by the agency.

A note of caution must be introduced regarding these data, particularly since the reporting of notifiable diseases is essentially voluntary. As the CDC notes, diseases that cause severe clinical illness and are associated with serious consequences are subject to adequate reporting. Less virulent diseases, on the other hand, are less likely to be reported. Data quality is significantly affected by the availability of diagnostic facilities and the priorities of officials who are responsible for reporting. Furthermore, while state laws and regulations mandate disease reporting, notification of the CDC is voluntary. As a result, underreporting is a problem with regard to some diseases, and further inquiry is recommended if these data are to be used. On the positive side, disease surveillance data as currently collected make analyses at the individual, group (e.g., age cohort), and geographic levels possible (Bennett et al., 1998).

In today's health care environment, existing methods of tracking disease have significant limitations. By definition, the list of reportable diseases is restricted essentially to communicable diseases, thereby omitting chronic conditions for all practical purposes. In the past three decades, however, chronic conditions (along with behavioral and lifestyle-caused diseases) have come to be the main factors in both morbidity and mortality within modern, industrialized countries. Cardiovascular disease, cancer, diabetes, and depression are now leading contributors to mortality.

Although chronic diseases generally are not officially tracked as part of the public health agenda, our knowledge of these conditions has been advanced through surveys such as the National Health Interview Survey and the analysis of data sets like hospital discharge files. Even so, these indirect sources limit our understanding of the epidemiology of chronic conditions, and thus, the system's ability to monitor their prevalence. As a result, the CDC and other agencies are currently exploring possibilities for improving capabilities for identifying and monitoring chronic conditions.

Immigration Data

Data on immigration patterns and the characteristics of immigrants historically have been of interest to health demographers because of the implications of
these phenomena for population change. Today, however, data on immigration are
of increasing interest due to the growing appreciation of the health conditions
associated with immigrants into the United States. The types of information collected by federal agencies and of use to demographers include data on immigrant
numbers and characteristics, legalization applicants, refugees, asylum applicants,
nonimmigrant entries, naturalizations, and immigration law enforcement.

The Immigration and Naturalization Service (INS) within the US Department of Justice has the primary responsibility for collecting data on immigration.
The INS activities involve both the recording of specific occurrences (e.g., immigrant entry) and the ongoing monitoring of the status of immigrants in the United
States. These data are generated from immigrant visa information that in theory is
available on everyone legally entering the United States. After a person is admitted to this country, visa and adjustment forms are forwarded to the INS data
capture facility for processing. Information collected includes port of admission,
country of birth, last residence, nationality, age, sex, occupation, and the zip code
of the immigrant's intended residence (US Department of Justice, 1996).

Data on immigration are made available through yearly published statistical
summaries, more frequent shorter reports, and computer tapes (which are available for 1972 through 1996). Each tape covers a 3-year time period. While the
published reports and now data on the Internet (http://www.ins.usdoj.gov/stats/
annual/fy96/index96.html) contain information for states and MSAs, tabulations
by county and zip code are possible using the tapes.

Health Personnel

Registries constitute the main source of data on many categories of health
personnel. Most health professionals must be registered with the state in which
they practice. In addition, most belong to professional associations whose rosters
become de facto registries. Like other registries, the registration of health care
personnel involves the regular and timely recording of persons entering a given
profession. Registries of health personnel, whether government or association-
sponsored, require constant updating, making them more prone to error than
certain other types of registries.

The federal government is an important source of health personnel registry
data at the national level. As a result of various federal mandates, the Department
of Health and Human Services has been directed to collect and disseminate annual
reports on the status of certain health personnel in the United States. These
requirements have led to the establishment of "registries" for various categories

of health professionals. The department also generates projections of the future personnel pool for each category of professional. Recently, the Health Resources and Services Administration (HRSA) within the US Department of Health and Human Services has begun maintaining a national medical practitioner database in an effort to make additional physician information available (Health Resources and Services Administration, 1998). This database can be accessed by authorized parties via the HRSA website (http://www.hrsa.dhhs.gov).

State governments often represent more direct sources of information on health personnel, since the various states have the primary responsibility for the licensing and monitoring of virtually all health professions. As part of their administrative activities, they necessarily establish registries for specific categories of health personnel. The databases created at the state level for physicians, nurses, physician assistants, and other categories of health personnel are typically up to date. However, the detail provided and the usefulness of the data collected for planning, marketing, and business development purposes vary widely from state to state.

Other sources of data on health professionals include the AMA physician master file; medical, osteopathic, dental, and nursing school enrollments; the American Academy of Physician Assistants master file; the American Dental Association dental practice survey; the Inventory of Pharmacists; and licensure information from the National Council of State Boards of Nursing, among others. Important sources of health-related registry data are described below.

Physician Supply. The records of the AMA represent a comprehensive registry of physicians, and the AMA has maintained a master file of physicians since 1906. This file contains data on virtually every physician in the United States, regardless of AMA membership. The data are collected and updated on an ongoing basis, and the database presently contains about 730,000 records. A file is initiated upon entry into medical school, and foreign medical school graduates entering the United States are added upon certification for residency training. A wide variety of data is collected on physicians, including demographics (e.g., age, sex, race) and practice-related data (e.g., specialty, group structure, activity level).

The master file also is used as a sampling frame for periodic surveys of physicians to collect detailed information on the characteristics of physician practices, earnings, expenses, work patterns, and fees (American Medical Association, 1998, 1999). Aggregated statistics from the master file are available for the entire nation, states, metropolitan areas, and counties in such AMA annual publications as *Physician Characteristics and Distribution in the US* and in compendia such as *Health, United States*, *Statistical Abstract of the United States*, and the *County and City Data Book*. A database of physicians extracted from the master file can be purchased from the AMA in print or electronic format. Other useful data sources described on the AMA website (http://www.ama-assn.org/catalog)

include medical *Group Practice in the US* and *Graduate Medical Education Directory.*

Another major source of data on physicians is the MEDEC database. This database is maintained and updated annually by Medical Economics Data Production Company. The information included is based on data returned by physicians who receive Medical Economics' publication *Physician's Desk Reference.* The coverage of the MEDEC database is not as extensive as that of the AMA master file, but some variables are included that are not available in the AMA database. The MEDEC database is available for purchase and also is available through some proprietary desktop market analysis systems.

These traditional sources of physician data have been joined by other vendors in recent years. One reasonably reliable source of physician data is the database maintained by *info*USA. Originally the American Medical Information database, the *info*USA physician file represents a comprehensive and detailed listing of US physicians regularly updated through telephone interviews. The database includes much of the data found in the AMA and MEDEC databases and is formatted in a manner useful for marketing, planning, and business development activities. A more recently developed physician database has been established by Health Market Science and is referred to by its developers as "a database of databases." HMS has combined data from a variety of sources and cross-checked them against each other to create a more highly refined database. Further, the HMS database is regularly updated and includes certain data (such as hospital affiliation and health plan affiliation) not typically found in other physician databases. One other source to note in passing is the physician database based on the telephone Yellow Pages. Information from the "Physicians" section of the Yellow Pages is extracted and packaged in CD format for resale. Although a Yellow Pages database may be useful for some purposes, it could not possibly include the scope and detail of information found in databases developed specifically to register physicians.

Each physician database has its advantages and disadvantages. All, however, suffer from the shortcomings inherent in having to constantly update a registry in a very dynamic industry. Thus, these databases should be used with caution, with a great deal of verification necessary to assure their usefulness.

State licensure agencies also maintain databases on physicians registered in the respective states. While this information is often available to the public, mere registration in a jurisdiction does not necessarily indicate an active medical practice. Further, these databases are likely to include only the barest of data required to carry out the mandated functions of the licensing agency. Specialty boards and other organizations also maintain registries on their members or certification recipients. While this information is often available in printed directories, the availability of the actual databases varies.

Many local organizations have begun to develop and maintain physician databases for their particular service areas. Since most health care markets are local, national databases are often of limited usefulness. However, it is a considerable challenge to maintain such a database successfully. Those that exist tend to be proprietary in nature.

Nurse Supply. Data on the number and characteristics of nurses are generated through the National Sample Survey of Registered Nurses conducted by the Bureau of Health Professions. Based on questionnaires sent to each licensed nurse in the United States, this database serves as the only federal source of such data. In addition, nurse supply estimates by states, including information on those who currently have licenses to practice as well as those who are working part-time or full-time (and full-time equivalents), are generated from a model that uses data from the National League for Nursing and the National Council of State Boards of Nursing. In addition, state licensure boards maintain data on active (and sometimes inactive) nurses within their jurisdictions. These data vary in accessibility, content, and format from state to state.

Health Care Facilities

The federal government is the major source of nationwide data on health facilities. The National Master Facility Inventory is a comprehensive file of inpatient facilities maintained by the National Center for Health Statistics (National Center for Health Statistics, 1996). The institutions included in the NCHS data collection include nursing homes and related facilities and other custodial or remedial care facilities. The National Master Facility Inventory is kept current by periodically adding the names and addresses of newly established facilities licensed by state boards and other agencies. Annual surveys are used to update information on existing facilities.

The facilities databases established by the NCHS include data on facility size, personnel, admissions, discharges, services offered, type of ownership, and type of certification. These data are available through various published reports and much of this information is provided by the American Hospital Association. These data are also available on computer tape (National Center for Health Statistics, 1998a).

The Health Care Financing Administration (HCFA) is now making available a set of data files on health care facilities and other providers of care. Its "Provider of Services" files include every provider that has filed claims with Medicare. The list covers 22 types of providers, including hospitals, nursing homes, ambulatory surgery centers, community health centers, and home health agencies. Although there are likely to be some providers who have not filed claims with Medicare and therefore are not listed, this number is small. These data files are available on magnetic tape from HCFA.

The nation's most complete hospital registry is maintained by the American

Hospital Association. Data are compiled annually on availability of services, utilization patterns, financial information, hospital management, and personnel (American Hospital Association, 1996). The database is continuously updated through an ongoing survey of the nation's hospitals. These data are available for a variety of geographic units (including regions, divisions, states, counties, and cities). They are available in the form of published reports and on computer diskettes and CD-ROMs. Some of the information is reprinted in secondary sources such as the *County and City Data Book* and *Health, United States.*

Commercial data vendors also have established hospital databases. HCIA, one of the nation's largest health data vendors, produces an annual profile of hospitals drawn from its database. Health Market Science has recently established a hospital database that represents a database of databases. Information is drawn from a wide variety of sources and combined to create what is considered to be a superior commercial database.

Since most health facilities are licensed by the state, information is usually available from the state agency charged with that responsibility. Increasingly, local organizations such as planning and regulatory agencies and business coalitions maintain facilities databases. For facilities other than hospitals, some private data vendors have begun to collect and disseminate data. There are now vendors selling data on health maintenance organizations, urgent care centers, freestanding surgery centers, and a variety of other types of facilities. Some of the commercial databases have developed to the point that they rival the official databases in usefulness.

Mental Health Organizations

An inventory of mental health organizations is maintained by the Center for Mental Health Services (within the US Department of Health and Human Services). The inventory is updated every 2 years. Questionnaires are sent to psychiatric hospitals, nonfederal general hospitals offering psychiatric services, Veterans Administration psychiatric services, residential treatment centers for emotionally disturbed children, freestanding outpatient psychiatric clinics, and other types of partial care organizations. The most recently published government compendium on mental health services, *Mental Health, United States, 1998* (Center for Mental Health Services, 1998), summarizes a wide range of data related to this topic. Information can also be obtained from the center's website (http://www.samhsa. gov/cmhs/htm).

Since many mental health services are administered by state governments, the respective state agencies represent a source of mental health statistics, although the data provided vary in terms of accessibility, content, and format. While rather detailed statistics have become available on ambulatory care services for physical illness, this is not the case for mental illness. Some limited data on mental health outpatient activity may be available through reports filed by comprehensive community mental health centers.

Surveys

Sample surveys are frequently used to supplement data from other sources. A sample survey involves the administration of an interview form to a portion of a target population that has been systematically selected. The sample is designed so that the respondents are representative of the population being examined. This allows conclusions to be drawn concerning the total population based on the data collected from the sample.

The use of sample surveys for data collection has several advantages relative to the census and registry methods. Two of the major advantages are more frequent data collection and more in-depth treatment of health-related issues. The relatively small sample sizes for such surveys have the additional advantages of quicker turnaround time and easier manipulation than large-scale operations such as the census. Clearly, the use of a sample reduces the cost of research.

On the other hand, surveys have their disadvantages. Since they involve a sample, there is potential slippage in accuracy relative to censuses and in comprehensiveness relative to registries. Perhaps the most serious shortcoming related to health care planning, marketing, and business development is the inability to compile adequate data for small geographic units due to small sample sizes. Also, special subject areas addressed by some surveys may not be featured on a regular basis, so that the interval between surveys that address a particular issue can become lengthy.

The federal government is the major source of survey research data related to health care. Primarily through the National Center for Health Statistics, the federal government maintains a number of ongoing surveys that deal with hospital utilization, ambulatory care utilization, nursing home and home health utilization, medical care expenditures, and other relevant topics. The National Institutes of Health and the Centers for Disease Control and Prevention also conduct surveys, although more episodically, that generate data of interest to health demographers. Some of the more useful sample surveys for health demographers are discussed in Box 9.3. The American Community Survey (ACS), a new effort by the Census Bureau to collect census-type data on a continuing basis, is presented in Box 9.4.

There also are a few surveys sponsored by commercial data vendors that contain data useful to health demographers. Inforum, Inc., sponsors a nationwide survey every 2 years of approximately 100,000 households to collect information on health status, health behavior, and health care preferences. A similar survey is conducted annually by National Research Corporation. Other data vendors may extract health-related data from national syndicated surveys and package this information with their demographic data. Some of these data sets are considered

Box 9.3

Federal Sources of Survey Data

The combined agencies of the federal government represent the nation's largest data collection force. Led by the National Center for Health Statistics (NCHS), federal agencies conduct a variety of surveys on health-related issues. The sections below describe a sample of these federal survey activities that have particular relevance for health care planning, marketing, and business development.

The *National Health Interview Survey* (NHIS) is an ongoing national survey of the noninstitutionalized civilian population in the United States. Each year, a multistage probability sample of approximately 49,000 households is drawn and household members interviewed. The data gathered are quite detailed and include demographic information on age, race, sex, marital status, occupation, and income. Information is compiled on physician visits, hospital stays, restricted-activity days, long-term activity limitation, health status, and chronic conditions. Recently, questions regarding AIDS knowledge and attitudes have been added to the survey. Food nutrition knowledge, smoking and other tobacco use, cancer, and polio are also subjects sometimes addressed.

The *Current Population Survey* (CPS) is the Census Bureau's mechanism for gathering detailed demographic data between the decennial censuses. Since 1960, the sample size has ranged from 33,500 to 65,500 households per year. Data are collected on many of the items included in the census of population and housing (e.g., age, race, and education). Questions are included on some health issues and on fertility issues that have implications for health care. Of particular interest to the health care industry are the data on health insurance coverage for the US population. These data were the basis for recent estimates of the size the population that lacks health insurance.

The *National Hospital Discharge Survey* (NHDS) is a continuous nationwide survey of inpatient utilization of short stay hospitals. All hospitals with six or more beds reporting an average length of stay of less than 30 days are included in the sampling frame. A multistage probability sampling frame is used to select hospitals from the National Master Facility Inventory and discharge records from each of the hospitals. The resulting sample has ranged from 192,000 to 235,000 discharge records. Information is collected on the demographic, clinical, and financial characteristics of patients discharged from short-stay hospitals. (See, for example, US Department of Health and Human Services, 1997b.)

The *National Ambulatory Medical Care Survey* (NAMCS) is a nationwide survey designed to provide information about the provision and utilization of ambulatory health services (Woodell, 1997). The sampling frame is the medical records of ambulatory patients to physicians engaged in office practice. A multistage probability sampling approach is used to select physicians from the databases maintained by the American Medical Association and the American Osteopathic Association. A sample of the records of these physicians for a randomly assigned one-week period then are examined. Recent samples contain about 35,000 records. Data regarding the age, race, ethnicity, and sex of the patient are gathered, along with the reason for the visit, expected source(s) of payment, principle diagnosis, diagnostic services provided, and disposition of visit.

The *National Nursing Home Survey* (NNHS) is a periodically conducted national survey of nursing and related care homes, their residents, their discharges, and their staffs. The data are collected using a two-stage probability design. Once facilities are selected, residents and employees of each facility are sampled. Six separate questionnaires were used to gather data in the most recent survey. The first addresses characteristics of the facility and involves an interview with the administrator or a designee. The second focuses on cost data and is completed by the facility's accountant or bookkeeper. Information on current and discharged residents is obtained by interviewing the staff person most familiar with the medical records of the residents. Additional resident data are gathered using telephone surveys of the resident's families. Full-time and part-time employees, including nurses, complete a nursing staff questionnaire. Last administered in 1997, this data set includes approximately 1,400 facilities, 5,100 discharges, 3,000 residents, and 14,000 staff records.

The *National Home and Hospice Care Survey*, last conducted in 1998, involves the collection of data from a sample of 1200 home health agencies and hospices. Patient questionnaires were administered for the various agencies and information was collected on the demographic and health characteristics of the patients served by these agencies.

The *National Survey of Family Growth* (NSFG), last administered in 1995, involved a survey of approximately 10,000 women ages 15–44 years (US Department of Health and Human Services, 1997c). The survey collects data on factors affecting birth and pregnancy rates, adoption, and maternal and infant health. Specific characteristics that are examined include sexual activity, contraception and sterilization practices, infertility, pregnancy loss, low birth-weight, and the use of medical care for family planning and infertility.

The *National Master Facility Survey* (NMFI) involves a comprehensive field survey of inpatient health facilities in the United States. Sponsored by the NCHS, it covers nursing and related care homes and custodial and remedial care facilities. Data are collected on both the facilities and their clients. Updated annually, this represents the most extensive government database of nursing facilities.

The *Medical Expenditure Panel Survey* (MEPS) was initiated in 1996 as a replacement for previous surveys focusing on expenditures for health services. Cosponsored by the Agency for Healthcare Research and Quality (AHRQ) and the NCHS, MEPS is designed to generate data on the types of health services

Continued

Box 9.3. *(Continued)*

Americans use, the frequency with which they use them, how much is paid for these services, and who pays for them. In addition, the MEPS provides information on health insurance coverage.

The *Behavioral Risk Factor Surveillance System* (BRFSS), sponsored by the Centers for Disease Control and Prevention, was initiated in 1995 to collect information on the health behavior and lifestyles of the US population. Over 150,000 persons respond to the survey annually. The survey includes data collection on such timely items as smoking, alcohol and drug use, seat beat use, and obesity, as well as other factors that might contribute to one's health risk profile.

In the area of behavioral health, the Center for Mental Health Services (CMHS) conducts an annual survey of mental health organizations and general hospitals that provide mental health services. These surveys collect data on the characteristics of all providers of behavioral health services and on the characteristics of the patients served. Other related surveys include samples of patients admitted to various treatment programs.

This does not exhaust the list of government sources of data relevant to health demography but only provides a sampler. The publications list of the federal National Technical Information Service (NTIS) provide a good starting point for finding other relevant databases.

---

proprietary and generally are only available to established clients; other data may be available for sale to the public.

Synthetic Data

Demographic Data. Synthetic data are created by merging existing demographic data with assumptions about population change to produce estimates, projections, and forecasts. These data are particularly valuable given that census and survey activities are restricted because of budgeting and time considerations. Consequently, there is a large and growing demand for information between years when data are actually collected. This demand is being met by both government agencies and commercial data vendors (Cheeseman, 1995).

Population estimates for states, MSAs, and counties are prepared each year as a joint effort of the Census Bureau and the state agency designated under the Federal–State Program for Local Population Estimates. The purpose of the program is to standardize data and procedures so that the highest-quality estimates

---

Box 9.4

American Community Survey—
Moving toward Continuous Data Collection

The decennial census is the most rigorous and expensive social and economic data collection endeavor in the world. However, its cost prevents the Census Bureau from gathering data more frequently. Most users of the data understand clearly that the further away in time they get from a year in which a census was taken, the less "accurate" census data become. That is, intercensal population change, which occurs most rapidly in small geographic areas such as census tracts, makes the count that took place in the previous census obsolete in many cases. There is a need for detailed data on a timely basis for large and small units of geography.

While there are several federal, state, and local government efforts to estimate the demographic characteristics of the United States and smaller units of geography (e.g., cities and counties) during intercensal periods, these efforts are limited to very few variables for smaller units of geography. The CPS, for example, provides good data for the United States, and selected MSAs, but its relatively small sample size prevents the production of small-area estimates. While many data vendors advertise that they can estimate the social and economic characteristics of almost any geographic unit no matter the size, in fact, their data have been shown to be lacking in accuracy.

In the mid-1990s, the Census Bureau began to test a system that will ultimately lead to continuous data collection for the intercensal period, with sample sizes large enough to allow for small-area data generation. This endeavor, the American Community Survey (ACS), is scheduled for full implementation in 2003. At that time, the ACS will cover about 3 million persons and gather data for households and persons in every county in the United States. Data for larger geographic areas such as states, cities, counties, metropolitan areas, and population groups of 65,000 or more will be generated annually. For smaller areas (as small as census tracts), data for two to five years will have to be aggregated in order to make the figures reliable. Long-term plans call for the ACS to replace the Census Bureau long-form for the 2010 census. More detail on the ACS can be found at http://www.census.gov/acs.

---

can be generated (Long, 1993). Additional goals of the program include reducing duplication of efforts in the production of population estimates and improving techniques and methodologies (US Bureau of the Census, 1999).

A number of commercial data vendors have emerged in recent years to supplement the population estimates and projections generated by government agencies. Data generated by these vendors have the advantage of being available down to small units of geography (e.g., the census tract) and they often are provided in greater detail (e.g., sex and age breakdowns) than government-produced figures. They also offer the flexibility to generate estimates and projections for "custom" geographies (e.g., a market area) that government statistics do not have the ability to do. The drawback, of course, is that some precision is lost as one develops calculations for lower levels of geography and for population components. However, the ease of accessibility and timeliness of these vendor-generated figures have made them a mainstay of health services planners, marketers, and business developers.

Issues have been raised concerning the quality of the synthetic data produced by vendors. Users stress the need for having the latest information possible, and in an effort to be expedient the question of quality sometimes has become a secondary concern. Any evaluation of synthetic data requires a knowledge of the recency and quality of the historical data being used as a basis for the estimates and projections. Furthermore, attention must be paid to the methods and assumptions utilized to generate the figures. If, for example, one assumes that population growth in an area is gradual and can be described by a simple mathematical function, population estimates and projections will be reasonably accurate as long as the assumptions hold. However, to the extent that an assumption is wrong, the (incorrect) mathematical function will yield inaccurate estimates and projections. While it is not possible to be aware of all the nuances of data quality and method, users are urged to evaluate underlying assumptions critically and to ascertain the accuracy of the synthetic data that are available.

Demand Estimates and Projections. A major category of synthetic data involves estimates and projections of health services demand. Since there are few sources of actual data on the use of health services and projections of future demand are often required, a variety of approaches have been developed for synthetically generating demand estimates and projections. The general approach involves applying known utilization rates to a current or projected population figure. To the extent possible, these figures are adjusted for, at a minimum, the age and sex composition of the target population. Utilization rates generated by the National Center for Health Statistics are the basis for most such calculations, and the demographic data used are likely to be obtained from a variety of sources.

Commercial data vendors have led the way in the development of demand estimates and projections. Some vendors have developed calculations for the full range of inpatient and outpatient services, although these are often available only to established customers. Other vendors may provide selected data on, for example, the demand for a particular service line.

Demand estimates and projections have become essential for virtually any planning, marketing, or business development activity in health care, and there has been growing pressure for the generation of increasingly detailed figures. However, there are at least three major concerns related to the use of such data. First, the estimates and projections are based on historical utilization rates at a time when patterns of utilization are changing dramatically. Second, the results of such calculations are likely to vary widely depending on the source of demographic data (particularly in years distant from the last census). Third, estimates and projections become increasingly tenuous as the size of the geography becomes smaller. While certain utilization rates may be fairly dependable down to even the county level, they tend to become unstable when subcounty units such as zip codes and census tracts are considered. Anyone using synthetically generated demand estimates and projections therefore should use them with caution.

Occupational Projections. The Bureau of Labor Statistics (within the US Department of Labor) maintains data on all occupational categories within the economy, including health care occupations. As part of the Bureau's responsibilities, it produces projections on the size of various occupational categories in the United States for 10 to 15 years into the future (US Bureau of Labor Statistics, 1998). Six projection models are generated, each containing a number of variables reflecting different scenarios related to changes in the total labor force, the aggregate economy, industry demand, and industry employment, among other factors. Three sets of employment projections are created based on differing sets of assumptions. Of interest here are the various categories of clinical occupations (e.g., dentists, physicians, and therapists) and nonclinical occupations (e.g., insurance claims managers, medical records personnel). In recent years, health professions have been prominent among the occupations with the greatest projected growth. Table 9.1 presents projections for the growth of selected health professions.

Data on occupational categories are available from the Department of Labor through regularly published reports. The percentage distribution for the labor force (matrix coefficients) also can be obtained, and these are sometimes used by other organizations to produce subnational occupational projections.

Perhaps more directly related to health care are data from the Bureau of Health Professions (within the Department of Health and Human Services). The Bureau of Health Professions is the federal agency responsible for monitoring the supply of health professionals across the nation. The Bureau provides information on the training, distribution, utilization, and quality of personnel staffing the US health delivery system. The bureau also provides technical assistance to states, educational institutions, professional associations, and other federal agencies concerning health personnel information and analysis. (Additional information on health professions can be obtained by accessing http://www.hrsa.dhhs.gov/bhpr.)

Table 9.1. Fastest Growing Health Care Occupations
(with Overall Rank), 1996–2006

Occupation	Rank	Percent increase
Personal and home care aides	4	85
Physical therapy aides/assistants	5	79
Home health aides	6	76
Medical assistants	7	74
Physical therapists	9	71
Occupational therapy aides/assistants	10	69
Occupational therapists	12	66
Medical records technicians	16	51
Speech pathologists/audiologists	17	51
Dental hygienists	18	48
Physician assistants	20	47
Respiratory therapists	21	46
Emergency medical technicians	24	45
Dental assistants	29	38

Note: Many of the occupations that are not listed here will involve significant employment in the health care field. Examples (and rank) include computer support specialists (1), computer engineers (2), and systems analysts (3).
SOURCE: US Bureau of Labor Statistics (1998).

SOURCES OF DATA FOR HEALTH DEMOGRAPHY

There are numerous sources of data for health demography available today and the number of sources continues to grow. The sections below group these sources into four main categories: government agencies, professional associations, private organizations, and commercial data vendors.

It should be noted that the "products" that might be obtained from these sources fall into two categories: (1) reports that summarize the data, and (2) the actual data sets themselves. Historically, data access was essentially limited to summary tables provided by an organization, agency, or vendor. Today, however, there is a trend toward providing the entire data set for use by the health data user. In reviewing the sources that follow, this distinction in products should be kept in mind.

Although the sources presented in each section refer to the agencies and publications responsible for the specific data set being discussed, numerous compendia exist that users should find quite useful. Box 9.5 describes the more important of these compendia. Table 9.2 outlines sources of specific categories of data.

Box 9.5

Compendia of Health Data

There currently is no clearinghouse for data on health and health care in the United States. This makes identifying and acquiring needed data a challenge for health data users. There are, however, a few compendia of health data that might prove useful for many purposes. While no one of these publications provides all the data a health care analyst is likely to need, they offer a reasonable starting point. Not only do they compile specific data on certain topics but they often can direct the reader to the origin of the data and other useful resources.

The best known of the compendia of health-related data is entitled *Health, United States*. This work is published annually by the National Center for Health Statistics (NCHS) and includes data gathered from the NCHS and many other sources. The publication includes data on health status, health behavior, health services utilization, health care resources, health care expenditures, and insurance coverage. These data are available mostly at the national level, although some state and regional data are available.

A companion publication, *Mental Health, United States*, is published less frequently than *Health, United States*, but represents the primary source of data on behavioral health care. The statistics are based on data collected by the Center for Mental Health Services.

Another more specialized compendium is also published by the Health Care Financing Administration (HCFA). Simply referred to as *Data Compendium* (with the publication year presented as part of the title), this source brings together data on Medicaid and Medicare. The data presented are drawn primarily from HCFA files, although data from sources outside the agency are also included. The information compiled by the HCFA is presented only at the national level, with some data reported at the state level. No data are presented for substate levels of geography.

Continued

Government Agencies

Governments at all levels are involved in the generation, compilation, manipulation, and/or dissemination of health-related data. The federal government, through the decennial census and related activities, is the world's largest processor of demographic data. Other federal agencies are major managers of data in the related areas of fertility, morbidity, mortality, and migration statistics.

The federal government is a major generator of health-related databases. Through the National Center for Health Statistics, the Centers for Disease Control

---

Box 9.5. (Continued)

Health and Healthcare in the United States: County and Metro Area Data, first published by NationsHealth Corporation in 1999, represents another approach to presenting basic health-related data. For each of the nation's counties and metropolitan areas, this compendium provides county-by-county data related to demographics, vital statistics, Medicare, health care businesses, facilities, and personnel. The data set is also available in CD format.

NIHCM Health Care System Data Source (2nd ed.), published in 1999 and available in print and diskette formats, contains state and national data on HMO and PPO penetration, personnel, Medicare and Medicaid expenditures, hospital capacity and hospital utilization among a larger set of variables. For metropolitan areas, there are data on HMO penetration, physicians, hospital capacity, and hospital utilization among a larger set of variables.

Since demographic data are so important to health planners, it is worthwhile to mention some compendia that focus on this type of data. The *County and City Data Book* is published every 2 years by the Census Bureau and includes over 200 separate items for each county and 134 items for each city of 25,000 or more persons. Data of interest to health care analysts include population statistics, vital records, and hospital, physician, and nursing home statistics, as well as certain insurance data.

The *State and Metropolitan Area Data Book* is published by the Census Bureau every 4 years and contains 128 data items for each state, 298 variables for each metropolitan statistical area (MSA), and 87 variables for each MSA's central city. *County Business Patterns*, prepared by the Bureau of the Census, provides a comprehensive count of the various health care businesses operating in each US county.

The *Statistical Abstract of the United States* is published every year by the Census Bureau. The abstract contains detailed data for the nation as a whole for 31 different subject categories (e.g., vital statistics, nutrition), as well as data for states and metropolitan areas. Most states publish a statistical abstract that includes comparable data for that state and its counties and cities. Recently, the abstract was made available on the Census Bureau website.

---

and Prevention, the National Institutes for Health, and other organizations, a large share of the nation's health data is generated. Other federal sources outside of health-related agencies, such as the Bureau of Labor Statistics (e.g., health occupations) and the Department of Agriculture (e.g., nutritional data), create databases of supporting data. State and local governments also generate data that are often aggregated into accessible databases. The number and variety of databases generated by federal agencies is impressive, but the variety of agencies involved means that databases vary in coverage, content, format, cost, frequency, and accessibility.

Table 9.2. Sources of Selected Health-Related Data

Information category	Sources[a]
Population data	
Size	Census, CPS, vendors
Characteristics	Census, CPS, vendors
Estimates and projections	Census, CPS, vendors
Vital statistics	
Births	NCHS
Deaths	NCHS
Marriages	NCHS
Divorces	NCHS
Fertility patterns	NCHS[1], census
Migration data	
Internal	Census, CPS, NCHS[2], IRS
International	INS
Morbidity data	
Disease surveillance	CDC
Acute conditions	NCHS[2]
Health assessment	NCHS[2]
Health personnel	
Physicians	BHP, AMA, MEDEC, InfoUSA, HMS
Nurses	BHP, AHA, BLS, census
Dentists	BHP, BLS, census
Other	BHP, AMA, BLS, census
Health facilities	
Hospitals	NCHS, AHA, HCFA
Nursing homes	NCHS, HCFA
Mental health facilities	NIMH, HCFA, CMHS
Health care utilization	
Physician visits	NCHS[2], vendors
Hospital stays	NCHS[2]
Restricted activity	NCHS[2], vendors
Ambulatory care	NCHS[3], vendors
Nursing homes	NCHS[4]
Expenditures	NCHS[5], BLS

[a]NCHS[1], National Survey of Family Growth; NCHS[2], National Health Interview Survey; NCHS[3], National Ambulatory Medical Care Survey; NCHS[4], National Nursing Home Survey; NCHS[5], Medical Expenditure Panel Survey; AHA, American Hospital Association; AMA, American Medical Association; BHP, Bureau of Health Professions; BLS, Bureau of Labor Statistics; CDC, Centers for Disease Control and Prevention; Census, US Bureau of the Census; CMHS, Center for Mental Health Services; CPS, Current Population Survey; HCFA, Health Care Financing Administration; HMS, Health Market Sciences; INS, Immigration and Naturalization Service; IRS, Internal Revenue Service; MEDEC, Medical Economics Data Products Company; NCHS, National Center for Health Statistics; NIMH, National Institute of Mental Health; Vendors, various commercial data vendors.

State and local governments also are major sources of health-related data. In fact, a survey of health data users indicated that various state agencies were their primary source of data for planning, marketing, and business development (Thomas, 1996). State governments generate a certain amount of demographic data, with each state having a state data center for demographic projections. Vital statistics data often can be obtained in the most timely fashion at the state level, in fact. States vary, however, in the types and quality of data they generate. University data centers also may be involved in the processing of demographic data. Local governments may generate demographic data for use in various planning functions. City or county governments may produce population projections, while county health departments are responsible for the collection and dissemination of vital statistics data.

Professional Associations

Industry associations represent another source of health-related data. Chief among these are the American Medical Association (and related medical specialty organizations) and the American Hospital Association. There also are other organizations of personnel (e.g., American Dental Association) and facilities (e.g., National Association for Home Care) that maintain databases on their members and on activities related to the organization's membership. These databases are typically developed for internal use, but are increasingly being made available to outside parties.

A number of organizations have been formed in recent years that focus specifically on health data, while others have established formal sections that deal with health data within their broader context. The National Association of Health Data Organizations, for example, brings together disparate parties from the public and private sector who have an interest in health data. The National Association of City and County Health Officers has become very active in terms of access to health data for local planning purposes. The Health Information and Management Systems Society is one of the largest organizations that is addressing this issue as a collateral consideration to data management systems issues.

In recent years, many professional associations have made an increasing amount of information on their members available to the research and business communities. Not only do such organizations have an interest in exchanging information with related groups, but they also have recognized the revenue generation potential of such databases. Some of these databases include only basic information, while others offer a wealth of detail.

Private Organizations

Many private organizations (mostly not-for-profit) collect and/or disseminate health-related data. Voluntary health care associations often compile, repackage, and/or disseminate such data. The American Cancer Society, for example, distributes morbidity and mortality data as it relates to its areas of interest. Some organizations, like Planned Parenthood, may commission special studies on fertility or related issues and subsequently publish this information.

Many organizations repackage data collected elsewhere (e.g., from the Census Bureau or the National Center for Health Statistics) and present it within a specialized context. The Population Reference Bureau, a private not-for-profit organization, distributes population statistics in various forms, for example. Some, like the American Association of Retired Persons, not only compile and disseminate secondary data but are actively involved in primary data collection, as well as the sponsorship of numerous studies that include some form of data collection.

Commercial Data Vendors

Commercial data vendors represent a fourth source of health-related databases. These organizations have emerged to fill perceived gaps in the availability of various categories of health data. These include commercial data vendors that establish and maintain their own proprietary databases, as well as those that reprocess and/or repackage existing data. For example, SMG Marketing maintains databases on nursing homes, urgent care centers, and other types of facilities and makes this information available in a variety of forms. The major data vendors (e.g., CACI Marketing, Claritas) who do not necessarily create health-related databases but incorporate health-specific databases into their business database systems are also included in this group.

Because of the demand for health-related data, several commercial data vendors have added health data to their inventories, and a few health-specific data vendors have emerged. These vendors not only repackage existing data into more palatable form, but some also are developing their own proprietary databases. At least three vendors are conducting major nationwide health consumer surveys.

As a result of the increasing demand for health-related data, improvement in the quality, coverage, timeliness, and availability of such data has become a priority with many organizations. The federal government has taken the lead in the public sector through its efforts to make its extensive health-related databases and registries available to the research and business communities. Through its various programs, the federal government is supporting projects that involve the application of contemporary computer technology to the processing, manipulation, and dissemination of health-related data, an area in which health care lags far behind other industries. Commercial data vendors continue to develop proprietary databases and to repackage and distribute databases produced by government and/ or association sources.

The ability to process, manipulate, and disseminate health-related data has improved tremendously owing to the advances that have occurred in computer

technology. New developments in the areas of data warehousing, data standardization, and large-scale database management capabilities continue to improve the
prospects for those requiring health data. Advanced techniques, such as artificial
intelligence, fuzzy logic, and neural networks, are now being applied in the health
care arena.

The Internet is already becoming a force with regard to health data. Although
the focus at the time of this writing has been on consumer-oriented health
information on the worldwide web, data for use by health professionals is not far
behind. Bibliographical and text files are already becoming available, and some
health care organizations are transferring patient data over the Internet. In the
future, there is every reason to believe that data for health services planning,
marketing, and business development will be widely available on the worldwide
web. (See Box 9.6 for a discussion of health data on the Internet.)

HEALTH DATA MANAGEMENT

The expansion in the availability of health data has generated a problem of a
different sort for those involved in health care planning, marketing, and business
development. This involves the challenge of managing and ultimately exploiting
the growing mountain of data on health and health care. Early attempts at managing health data were primitive by any measure and focused almost entirely on such
practical dimensions as patient billing. The mainframe environment characterizing hospitals and other large health care organizations created a slow, inflexible
process. Data management was controlled by information systems technicians
who were essentially isolated from the operation of the organization. If health care
professionals were to harness the power of the growing volume of data and exploit
it for planning, marketing, and business development purposes, a better technical
solution was necessary.

During the early 1980s, it was realized by some that the ability to manage this
growing volume of data was going to be critical. Most other industries had already
addressed this issue and had developed fairly sophisticated means of processing
and analyzing industry data. Because of its peculiar characteristics, the health care
industry lagged well behind other sectors of the economy in terms of information
management.

The introduction of the microcomputer opened the door for more efficient
data management. Bringing the power of the mainframe to the desktop, micro-
computers quickly transformed the data management environment. The transformation involved more than technical capabilities, however, as it allowed the
control of data management to shift back to the administrators and health professionals who ultimately used the data.

In the mid-1980s, as the health data industry expanded, computerized applications for managing this growing wealth of data emerged. Several companies

Box 9.6

Health Care Data and the Internet

As the world has now discovered, the worldwide web is becoming a global informa-tion depository that easily can be accessed via the Internet. At the time of this writing, more data were thought to be available via the Internet on health care than on any other topic. Not only are there more sites dealing with various aspects of health, but some of the most extensive sites have been established by health care organiza-tions.

Despite the spate of health-related data available via the Internet, most of it is of limited usefulness to the health professional. The overwhelming majority of these sites offer data geared to health care consumers. The ready "market" was for consumer data, and there was no shortage of organizations eager to establish a presence on the web that catered to health care consumers. Today, health care consumers can find a doctor, diagnose a condition, and order prescription drugs and nutritional supplements via the Internet.

The information needs of health professionals finally are beginning to be recognized. In response to this need, various organizations have responded by actually distributing *data* via the Internet. This involves making data files available that can be viewed, browsed, and downloaded. More advanced sites may actually allow the user to manipulate the data in some basic ways. Even commercial data vendors are searching for ways to make data more accessible via the Internet.

The federal government has led the charge to make data available on the web. Agencies such as the Bureau of the Census, the Centers for Disease Control and Prevention, the National Center for Health Statistics, and the Health Care Financing Administration have expended significant efforts toward posting their data files on the web. Not only do these data files represent improvements over the cumbersome output formats (e.g., print, magnetic tape) that these agencies historically used, but web-based files can be posted much more expeditiously than the data can be published in print form. In addition, many of the sites offer free data for downloading that in the past would have had to be purchased in some other format.

Some of these data would never be published in print form, and data are now available for levels of geography that would be too cumbersome to provide in a print format in any case. As print versions are cut back by the federal government and other data generators, the importance of Internet distribution will increase.

The initial response of health data users has been enthusiastic. At last it is possible to obtain data on a variety of topics from a "single source." However, as one gets serious about using web-based data files from any of these sources, this enthusiasm can be quickly dampened. The following issues face health professionals who see the worldwide web as a valuable source of data:

Continued

Box 9.6. (Continued)

1. *Ease of access*. While the sites that are posting data files are generally easy to access, the user can quickly run into roadblocks when searching for data. (As is always the case, if one knows exactly where to look, it is less of a problem.) Sites maintained by the Census Bureau or the Centers for Disease Control, for example, are extensive and complex. Further, the provision of data files for use or download may not be the primary function of these organizations and their websites. Thus, the data user may have to wade through a number of screens before the issue of data is even broached. Even then, the data files are likely to be numerous and in the absence of any standard categories the search becomes highly idiosyncratic. One also might speculate that those disseminating the data do not have a total understanding of the ways in which they are likely to be used.

2. *Ease of use*. One of the advantages of electronically formatted data files should be their ease of use. By being posted in what is typically a "spreadsheet" format, the user should be able to easily navigate through these files and manipulate the data in a number of ways. Unfortunately, many of these files simply replicate the print version in electronic format. As such, they are not searchable and their use as spreadsheets is limited. Worse, there are some advantages that print versions actually offer over those in an electronic format.

3. *File size and structure*. In many cases, web-based files represent too much of a good thing. Since the amount of data that can be included in an electronic file is essentially unlimited, there is a tendency to post such large files that it becomes difficult to manage them. There also appears to be a tendency to place "unedited" files out on the web. For example, a federal database may be made available for downloading that contains mostly internal variables that are of no use to the user. Thus, processing an otherwise useless file may require more effort than it is worth in some cases.

4. *Documentation*. Any data file is going to require an extensive amount of documentation in terms of sources of data, calculation methodologies, explanation of variable names, and so forth. The electronic format offers the advantage of unlimited space for the presentation of documentation. However, the rush to post data files on the web has caused many to overlook an important intermediate step: developing standard documentation formats. Even within a single government agency, the data files posted may include a variety of different formats with different approaches to documentation.

5. *Downloading issues*. One of the advantages of web-based data files should be the ability to download them for use in another environment. While this advantage generally exists with regard to these data files, there are issues related to download-ing that represent barriers to efficient use of these resources. Many of the files are in formats that require specialized software for downloading and reading. While these

utilities are readily available and often free via download, they are not necessarily intuitively obvious to the beginner trying to access these data files. Some of these downloading applications do not work on all computers and downloading the utilities themselves requires a certain level of technical expertise. Further, some of the files are huge and appropriate software may be required for decompressing these files.

6. *Quality issues.* As with other Internet sources of data, it is easier and quicker to post health-related data on the Web than it is to verify their accuracy and usefulness. Data files that are posted may include provisional data or otherwise may be incomplete. If they include data collected from different states, for example, the data may vary in methodology or time period. This may not be obvious to the user, although this is an issue with print data files as well.

The ability of the Internet to make data files available and to allow downloading of these files represents a giant step forward in health data distribution. The web truly may come to be a single source for health-related data. Today, however, there are significant issues associated with the data files that are being made available via this environment. There are obvious barriers to efficient use that users will find and others that are not so obvious that could be disastrous since they are not immediately apparent. In many cases, users may still be better off consulting print versions for many data files.

introduced desktop marketing and planning systems designed to run on micro-computers. Many were patterned after those developed in other industries, but most of these could not survive the transition. Others developed health care-specific desktop systems and two major vendors emerged to serve primarily the hospital market. These have been joined by a couple more systems in recent years.

Some early attempts at data management involved the development of management information systems, executive information systems, and decision support systems. Each variation on the same theme involved particular capabilities. However, they were all primarily focused on internal data. They typically did not incorporate "market" data and those that did had limited ability to interface internal and external data sets.

The concept of desktop data management essentially involves installing the necessary market data on-site at the health care organization. The desktop system subsequently interfaces data from a variety of databases and allows the user to manipulate the files in a variety of ways. The ability to work with several files simultaneously was a breakthrough for health services planners and it became possible to interface internal data with the external market data provided by the vendor. Another innovation was the incorporation of mapping capabilities into the data management package. (See below for more on mapping.)

The introduction of desktop market analysis systems made possible the transformation of marketing research from a slow, plodding process of questionable accuracy to a scientific, relatively precise, and expeditious activity. Proprietary desktop analysis systems offer a number of advances over previous approaches to market analysis. They offer access to data sets not otherwise easily accessible or not available at all. They include software applications that perform a wide variety of functions. They have the ability to integrate data sets from disparate sources—both internal and external—and to interface them within the various software applications. They can produce standardized or custom reports, tables, graphics, and maps pertinent to any application. They have the capability to import data sets in a variety of formats and to incorporate them easily into existing applications.

While these desktop systems represented a breakthrough in the 1980s, they are likely to face a challenge from organizations that are now beginning to capitalize on new technology. Even loyal customers of existing vendors are concerned over the cost, limitations in market coverage, and timeliness of the data. While the major vendors are responding by making certain of their resources available electronically, they still cling to the traditional approach of carefully controlling data and only providing it to high-end clients.

The next revolution in health data management will be the distribution of health data via the Internet. Although some technical details have yet to be resolved with regard to web-delivered data, it appears that the distribution of health-related data via the worldwide web is gaining momentum. While the mainframe environment emphasized the centralization of data management, the burgeoning personal computer environment has served to fragment data within an organization.

The Internet represents the opportunity to create the best of both worlds. By serving as a virtual data warehouse, the worldwide web allows the accumulation of data from a variety of sources in the same environment. At the same time, it allows for individual users to maintain control of the data sets that they are contributing to the "warehouse."

Another important consideration with regard to the management and analysis of data for health demography is the growing importance of geographic information systems (GIS). Spatial analysis, in its various forms, has always been an inherent aspect of demographic analysis. At the same time, epidemiological fieldwork includes spatial analysis as a basic component. The interest in GIS has been spurred by the growing importance of spatial relationships for planning, marketing, and business development in health care.

The introduction of high-performance, low-cost GIS applications has contributed greatly to the use of spatial analysis in health-related research. The power of mainframe-based spatial analysis has been brought to the desktop by applications such as MapInfo and ArcView, and even unsophisticated computer users can now generate complex maps. The opportunity for advanced spatial analysis is available to those who require it. Further advances in GIS applications are likely to make these systems even more important for health demographers in the future.

Ultimately, all these developments reflect the changes that are occurring in the manner in which health data are being utilized. The demand for better data management and analysis capabilities is being driven by the new approach to health data engendered by the changing environment. While being able to simply describe a situation in terms of data was a major breakthrough in the past, the new health care environment is calling for a much more proactive approach to the use of data. It is no longer sufficient to be able to describe a market area, for example; the data must be used proactively for decision support and strategic planning. A static picture of health conditions has become less useful as the environment has become increasingly dynamic.

REFERENCES

American Hospital Association. (1996). *Hospital Statistics, 1996–1997 ed*. Chicago: American Hospital Association.
American Medical Association. (1998). *Socioeconomic Characteristics of Medical Practice, 1997*. Chicago: American Medical Association.
American Medical Association. (1999). *Physician Characteristics and Distribution in the US, 1997*. Chicago: American Medical Association.
Anderson, R. N., Kochanek, K. D., and Murphy, S. L. (1997). Report of final mortality statistics, 1995. *Monthly Vital Statistics Report*, 45(11). Hyattsville, MD: National Center for Health Statistics.
Bennett, S., Wharton, M., and Rush, S. (1998). Analysis of surveillance data. Website at URL: http://www.cdc.gov/nip/manual/analysis/analysis.htm.
Berkowitz, E. N., Pol, L. G., and Thomas, R. K. (1997). *Healthcare Market Research*. Chicago: Irwin Professional Publishing.
Center for Mental Health Services. (1998). *Mental Health, United States, 1998*. Manderscheid, R. W., and Henderson, M. J. (Eds.). Washington, DC: US Government Printing Office.
Cheeseman, J. D. (1995). Population projections of the United States by age, sex, race and Hispanic origin: 1995–2050. *Current Population Reports*, Series P-25-1130. Washington, DC: US Government Printing Office.
Clarke, S. (1995a). Advance report of final marriage statistics, 1989 and 1990. *Monthly Vital Statistics Report*, 43(12)(s). Hyattsville, MD: National Center for Health Statistics.
Clarke, S. (1995b). Advance report of final divorce statistics, 1989 and 1990. *Monthly Vital Statistics Report*, 43(9)(s). Hyattsville, MD: National Center for Health Statistics.
Health Resources and Services Administration. (1998). *National Practitioners Data Bank*. Website at URL: http://www.hrsa.dhhs.gov/bhpr.dqa/factshts/fsprac.htm.
Judson, D. H. (1996). Research use of administrative records. Paper presented at the 6th International Congress of Applied and Business Demography held at Bowling Green State University, September 19–21, 1996.

Kowalski, J. (1997). *State Definitions and Reporting Requirements for Live Births, Fetal Deaths, and Induced Termination of Pregnancy* (1997 rev.). Hyattsville, MD: National Center for Health Statistics.

Lavin, M. R. (1996). *Understanding the Census.* Kenmore, NY: Epoch Books.

Long, J. F. (1993). Postcensal population estimates: States, counties and places. *Technical Working Paper, No. 3.* Washington, DC: US Bureau of the Census.

National Center for Health Statistics. (1996). *Organization and Activities.* Hyattsville, MD: Public Health Service.

National Center for Health Statistics. (1998a). Change in the Reporting of Marriage and Divorce Statistics. Website at URL: http://www.cdc.gov/nchswww/releases/96facts/96sheets/mardiv.htm.

National Center for Health Statistics. (1998b). *Health, United States, 1998.* Hyattsville, MD: National Center for Health Statistics.

Shryock, H. S., Siegel, J., and Associates. (1973). *The Methods and Materials of Demography.* Washington, DC: US Government Printing Office.

Thomas, R. K. (1996). *An Assessment of Health Data Users Problems and Needs.* Memphis, TN: Medical Services Research Group.

US Bureau of the Census. (1994a). *1992 Census of Service Industries.* Geographic Area Series: Florida. Washington, DC: US Government Printing Office.

US Bureau of the Census. (1994b). *1992 Census of Retail Trade.* Geographic Area Series: Florida. Washington, DC: US Government Printing Office.

US Bureau of the Census. (1996). *County Business Patterns, 1995 (Florida).* Washington, DC: US Government Printing Office.

US Bureau of the Census. (1999). *United States Census 2000.* Website at URL: http://www.census.gov/dmd/www/(January 15 1998).

US Bureau of Labor Statistics. (1998). Fastest growing occupations. *Occupational Outlook Handbook.* Website at URL: http://stats.bls.gov/news.release/ooh.table1.htm.

US Department of Health and Human Services. (1997a). *US Vital Statistical System.* Hyattsville, MD: Centers for Disease Control and Prevention.

US Department of Health and Human Services. (1997b). National hospital discharge survey: Annual summary, 1994. *Vital and Health Statistics*, Series 13, No. 128. Hyattsville, MD: Centers for Disease Control and Prevention.

US Department of Health and Human Services. (1997c). Fertility, family planning and women's health: New data from the 1995 national survey of family growth. *Vital and Health Statistics*, Series 23, No. 19. Hyattsville, MD: Centers for Disease Control and Prevention.

US Department of Justice. (1996). *1996 Statistical Yearbook of the Immigration and Naturalization Service.* Washington, DC: US Government Printing Office.

Ventura, S., Martin, J. A., Curtin, S., and Matthews, T. J. (1997). Report of final natality statistics, 1995. *Monthly Vital Statistics Report*, 45(11)(s). Hyattsville, MD: National Center for Health Statistics.

Woodell, D. A. (1997). National ambulatory medical care survey: 1996 summary. *Advance Data*, No. 295. Hyattsville, MD: Centers for Disease Control and Prevention.

ADDITIONAL RESOURCES

Hospital Statistics 2000. (1999). Chicago: American Hospital Association.

Anderson, R. N. (1999). *Decennial Life Tables for 1989–1991.* Hyattsville, MD: National Center for Health Statistics. Morbidity and Mortality chapter.

Anderson, M., and Feinberg, S. E. (1999). *Who Counts?* New York: Russell Sage.

Moskowitz, D. B. (Comp.). *2000 Health Care Almanac & Yearbook.* New York: Faulkner and Gray.

CHAPTER 10

The Demographic Correlates of Health Status

INTRODUCTION

In the final analysis, this volume is concerned with the exploration of the demographic determinants and consequences of health status and health behavior. The study of health status focuses on the implications of demographic characteristics for the level and nature of morbidity within a population. The study of health behavior indicates the extent to which one's demographic characteristics influence their actions with regard to health services utilization. This treatise should provide the means whereby an analyst, knowing something about demographic conditions and the prospects for population change, can make assumptions about the health status and health behavior of a particular population. The application of this concept can be applied to a population as large as the nation to one as small as a census tract.

This chapter focuses on the demographic correlates of health status, while Chapter 11 addresses their implications for health behavior. These two chapters taken together represent what might be considered the essence of health demography. In this chapter, each demographic characteristic and process is taken in turn and examined in the light of its relationship with health status.

The exploration of statistical associations between various indicators of health status and population characteristics is the basis of all social epidemiology. The information generated from the study of the relationship between demographic characteristics and health status provides the foundation for health demography. Only in recent years have we begun to generate the baseline information necessary to develop a true appreciation of the epidemiology of health conditions.

The relationships discussed in this chapter represent the distillation of a substantial amount of research on the factors associated with health status. Despite the volume of research that has been completed, the demographic correlates of health status only now are beginning to be understood. Many beliefs attributed to "conventional wisdom" have been challenged as the result of recent studies. Research on lifestyles and their implications for health status have served to further complicate the analysis of these relationships.

Despite the growing body of research, caution should be exercised in reviewing the correlates of health status discussed below. The interplay of the numerous variables that influence health status is obviously complex. Some studies have simply explored the direct effects of a particular demographic variable on health status without controlling for the influence of other factors. Some of the findings reported below are derived from such studies.

Quite often, when controls for additional variables are introduced, the impact of the original variable may be reduced, eliminated, or otherwise modified. For example, a strong relationship has been repeatedly found between race and health status. Virtually every indicator of health status is found to be higher for whites than for African Americans, suggesting a direct correlation between race and health status and perhaps implying causation (National Center for Health Statistics, 1998a: Table 70). However, when other variables like income are taken into consideration, the relationship between race and health status is substantially reduced (Kim et al., 1998; Waidmann and Shoenbaum, 1996).

Additional complexity is added when a time dimension is introduced into these studies. For example, as mortality rates for the elderly declined during the 1970s and 1980s, the self-reported health status of this population grew worse. The initial interpretation of these data led to the "failure of success" hypothesis; that is, as mortality rates declined a more frail, less healthy population was left behind. However, a more recent analysis and interpretation posits that a combination of social factors that affect the perception of health status of the elderly—for example, the upward shifts in the standard for good health status during this time interval—led to a decline in *reported* health status but not necessarily actual health status (Waidmann et al., 1995).

Every effort has been made in the sections that follow to identify any variables that might affect the relationship under study. Since this cannot be done in every case and some relationships have not yet been explored, the research results reported here should be interpreted with caution.

This effort at isolating the factors involved in morbidity and mortality has been aided significantly by the recent work of Rogers, Hummer, and Nam (2000). Their landmark analysis involved the matching of death records with data on respondents drawn from several years of federal health surveys (i.e., the National Health Interview Survey). This approach allowed the researchers to link for the first time actual mortality data with the characteristics of both survivors and decedents. Even given this additional information, however, the research results reported here should be interpreted with caution.

Finally, it should be noted that measures of health status are now incorporated into more global efforts to measure perceived health, medical outcomes, quality of life, and functional status in primary care settings (Essink-Bot et al., 1997). For example, Ware and his colleagues have developed the SF-36 which is a short form based on 36 health status items found in the Medical Outcomes Study (Ware and Sherbourne, 1992). These measures are organized along eight dimensions: mental health, physical functioning, role limitations due to physical health problems, role limitations due to emotional problems, bodily pain, general health perceptions, vitality, and reported health transition (one year). Global indicators are used to assess the success or failure of treatment modalities as well as to grade the overall efforts of health care providers. It is this latter application that is driving a great deal of both research and controversy.

MEASURES OF HEALTH STATUS

One of the major challenges in health care over the past three decades has been the development of acceptable measures of health status. Attempts to develop a single indicator of health status have not been very successful, and specific measures continue to be utilized as indicators. Recent efforts to develop a single indicator incorporating measures of mortality and morbidity that reflect healthy life years have been more successful (Hyder et al., 1998). Several different health status indicators are described below. Box 10.1 addresses the development of health status indices.

Global Indicators

The most direct, and probably the most subjective, approach to measuring health status involves self-assessments by survey respondents. These are referred to as "global indicators" because they address overall health status. With global indicators, survey respondents are typically asked to rate their health status on some type of scale. Although some scales may be relatively complex, the most common response categories are "poor," "fair," "good," "very good," and "excellent." Once such ratings have been obtained from a number of respondents, assessment of the health status of a population or subgroups can be performed and the demographic correlates of health status identified.

While self-reported ratings of health status are attractive in their simplicity, critics contend that they are too subjective. Indeed, the discussion in Chapter 3 of what constitutes health and illness clearly points to the dangers of this approach. One respondent's health may be another's illness, and it is difficult to control for

Box 10.1

The Health Status Index

One of the more elusive measures in health care has been the health status index. Beginning with the social indicators movement of the 1960s, there has been periodic interest expressed in the development of a index that could be used to indicate the health status of a population or community in either absolute or relative terms. While the interest in such an index had waned for a period, there now is renewed interest at a time when community health planning is being revitalized.

A health status index is a single figure that represents the health status of a population or a community. It involves an attempt to quantify health status in objective and measurable terms. A health status index is constructed by combining a number of individual health status indicators into a single index. A health status index can be used to compare the level of need from community to community. It can be used as a basis for setting priorities and evaluating the worthiness of proposed programs. It also can serve as a basis for allocating resources and as a tool for evaluating the effectiveness of existing programs.

A number of conceptual problems surround the development of health status indices. These problems begin with the issue of what indicators to include. To this are added the issues of quantification and measurement. Further, the question of how to weight the various component indicators also is raised. There are no simple means for resolving these issues. Every analysis must address them in the best manner possible. The key need is to carefully document the process that is used in developing the index.

A variety of indicators can be utilized in the creation of a health status index. Many of the indicators that might be included, for example, death rates, are fairly obvious. Others, such as certain demographic indicators, might not be. Nevertheless, it is common to use demographic traits such as the proportion nonwhite, the dependency ratio, and educational attainment as component indicators in a health status index. Some of these are referred to as "proxy" measures of health status, in that they are not direct indicators of health conditions but can be assumed to indirectly indicate the level of health status within a population.

In addition to this type of measure, the major categories of health status indicators utilized include morbidity indicators, outcome indicators, utilization indicators, resource availability indicators, and functional status indicators. Morbidity measures are obvious indicators of health status, since they reflect the prevalence and/or incidence of various conditions, as well as the level of disability within a population. Thus, the extent to which a population is affected by various acute and chronic conditions constitutes an important component in any health status index. (Unfortunately, it is difficult to obtain actual data on morbidity, and although extremely important, this remains a problematic area in health status index construction.)

Outcome measures are so named because they ostensibly reflect the extent to which the health care system is effective. Outcome measures include such indicators as death rates, infant death rates, life expectancy, and potential years of life lost. Of these measures, the infant mortality rate is probably the most useful as a component of a health status index, since it represents far more than just the rate at which infant deaths occur; it speaks volumes about living conditions, nutritional levels, domestic violence, and a number of other dimensions of socioeconomic and health status.

Utilization measures also are used as components of a health status index. This includes indicators such as the hospital admission rate, the rate of emergency room visits, the physician visit rate, and so forth. These measures tend to be among the more controversial, since it could be argued alternately that these are positive or negative indicators.

Resource availability entails another important set of indicators. These include the ratio of hospital beds to the population, the ratio of physicians to the population, and other measures of resources. The rationale for the use of such indicators is that the level of resource availability should be correlated with higher health status. Although this too is controversial, such indicators are frequently employed in index construction.

Measures of functional state constitute an additional category of health status indicators. These include a range of measures such as days of work lost, days of school lost, bed-restricted days, activity-restricted days, and so forth. The use of these measures reflects the notion that individuals who are limited in their functional abilities are a reflection of poor health status (regardless of the source of the limitation).

Health status indices can be calculated for any level of geography for which data are available. However, the smaller the unit of geography, the finer the distinction that can be made. Many health planning agencies conduct analyses down to the census tract level, while others utilize the zip code or county as the unit of analysis.

Once the indicators have been chosen, values must be assigned to each indicator for each unit of geography being analyzed. A number of different methodologies can be used for this process, and the important factor is to come as close to both scientific rigor and face validity as possible. Assuming that all indicators are to be equally weighted, one approach might be to score each indicator on a scale of 1 to 5 for each geographic unit. Negative characteristics would be scored closer to 1 and positive characteristics closer to 5. The scores for each indicator could be summed and then divided by the number of indicators to provide an average score for each geographic unit somewhere between 1 and 5. It should be noted that the absolute number generated through the process means little; its value is derived from the ability to compare it with other figures. This index number could be used, for example, to compare one community to another or track the health status of a particular community over time.

The current methodologies for constructing health status indices are certainly not without their critics. There are numerous conceptual, methodological, and practical issues that must be addressed in the development of a health status index. Nevertheless, the need to better understand the health characteristics of our communities mandates continued efforts toward the development of defensible health status indices.

these variations in perspective. Recent research has found, in fact, that African-American and white respondents use a different framework for their self-evaluation, thereby limiting the value of comparative data (Larsen et al., 1998). Even so, the landmark analysis by Rogers et al. (2000) found a high correlation between self-assessed health status and mortality rates. Table 10.1 presents a breakdown of self-assessed health status by demographic characteristics.

A reasonable correlation has been found between self-reported ratings of health status and more objectively derived indicators of health status. When self-assessments are correlated with responses to a symptom checklist, for example, a relatively strong association is evidenced (Proctor et al., 1998). That is, respondents with a large number of symptoms (either self-reported or observed) tend to rate their health status lower than those with few identified symptoms. Self-reported health status has even been shown to be a strong prognostic indicator of subsequent mortality (McGee et al., 1999).

Table 10.1. Self-Assessment of Health Status
by Selected Characteristics, United States, 1995

Characteristic	Self-assessment (percent)				
	Poor	Fair	Good	Very good	Excellent
Total	2.9	7.3	23.2	29.2	37.4
Age					
Under 5 years	0.4	2.4	16.4	27.8	53.0
15–17 years	0.3	2.2	17.4	28.1	52.0
18–24 years	0.7	3.9	21.1	32.8	41.6
25–44 years	1.7	5.6	22.5	32.2	38.1
45–64 years	5.7	11.0	27.4	28.3	27.6
65 years and over	8.8	19.6	33.6	22.9	15.1
Sex					
Male	2.7	6.4	21.8	29.1	40.0
Female	3.0	8.1	24.5	29.4	35.0
Race					
White	2.7	6.9	22.4	29.7	38.3
African American	3.9	10.1	27.8	26.6	31.6
Family income					
Less than $10,000	7.7	15.1	28.3	25.8	23.0
$10,000–19,999	5.1	12.1	28.7	26.7	27.3
$20,000–34,999	2.6	7.3	25.2	29.9	35.0
$35,000 or more	0.9	3.3	17.8	30.6	47.4

SOURCE: Based on the National Health Inteview Survey and published in National Center for Health Statistics (1998a), Table 70.

Outcome Measures

The most frequently utilized measures of health status are called outcome measures. They are so called because they purportedly measure the end result of the operation of the health care delivery system. The two primary outcome measures are morbidity and mortality, with the latter being the most frequently used historically. Such measures are appealing to clinicians and increasingly to health care administrators and health policy analysts, since they are thought to be indicators of the quality of care provided by the health care system. More recently, outcomes measures have been expanded and extended to include indicators of patient well-being and ability to function as well as variables that reflect the health services delivery process.

As noted in Chapter 7, morbidity refers to the level of sickness and/or disability within a population. Measures of morbidity are certainly important, especially in a society where chronic conditions predominate, but they are particularly difficult to operationalize. Little success has been achieved in establishing an overall indicator of morbidity for individuals or populations, so a variety of more specific morbidity measures are utilized. Some of the indicators that are currently utilized are incidence statistics for specific conditions, symptom checklists, and various measures of disability.

Disability as an indicator of morbidity is particularly difficult to operationalize, and, as noted in Chapter 7, it is often necessary to use proxy measures for the level of disability within the population. These most often take the form of "restriction" indicators. Thus, the number of work-loss days, bed-restricted days, and level of activity limitation are often used rather than the proportion of individuals in the population with some type of handicap.

The outcome measure of longest standing is mortality. This is considered the ultimate outcome measure in that it could be interpreted as a failure of the health care system. Its pervasive use, however, is probably more a function of its ready availability and its ease of interpretation than of its current relevance as a health status indicator. Unlike morbidity measures, mortality measures are not meaningful measures for individuals but only for populations. At the same time, it is perhaps the least refined of the various measures of health status, unless it is adjusted to account for interpopulation variations in demographic, socioeconomic, and health care utilization characteristics. The fact that it uses the total population as its denominator masks a great many subgroup differences.

There are two major drawbacks to the use of mortality measures today. First, in modern industrial societies so few people die that the calculation of mortality rates is not very meaningful. Second, with chronic disease predominating, the cause of death does not provide a true reflection of the conditions that affect individuals within the population. Few people die from chronic diseases, so the official cause of death is likely to reflect some complication or consequence of one or more chronic conditions. Thus, the role of chronic diseases is likely to be minimized if mortality data are relied on. Most often, a group of comorbidities interact to determine the survival of an individual diagnosed earlier with a particular disease.

A subsidiary issue here involves cause-specific mortality rates. As discussed in Chapter 7, some refinement can be introduced into mortality rates by calculating rates based on the specific cause of death. An overall mortality rate of 10 deaths per 1000 residents really is an aggregate figure that combines the death rates for a wide variety of causes. Thus, the rate of 10 may be the end result of three persons per 1000 dying from heart disease, two from cancer, and two from stroke. The remainder of the 10/1000 rate reflects the aggregate mortality induced by hundreds of other causes of death. The use of cause-specific data makes comparisons between populations more meaningful.

Another frequently utilized mortality indicator is the infant mortality rate. Although this measure applies only to a limited segment of the population (i.e., those under 1 year of age), it is considered by many as more useful than the overall mortality rate. The premise is that the infant mortality rate is much more than an outcome measure for the health care system. Rather, the level of infant mortality is a function of environmental safety, diet, prenatal care, the educational and economic status of the parents, the age of the mother, the incidence of neglect and abuse, and a number of other factors. Thus, infant mortality is seen as a proxy for a variety of indicators of health and well-being. As with the overall mortality rate, however, infant deaths occur rarely enough that measures of infant mortality have less salience as indicators of a population's health status than they did historically. (See Chapter 7 for a more detailed discussion of mortality indicators.)

DEMOGRAPHIC CORRELATES OF HEALTH STATUS

Introduction

Demographic characteristics offer a useful basis for examining the correlates of health status. Compositional variables such as age, sex, and racial classification allow health demographers to infer a great deal about a population's health characteristics. This chapter builds on the growing knowledge of the ways in which population composition can contribute to an understanding of the need for health services. It extends the presentations in Chapters 6 and 7, where compositional factors were introduced to describe and explain differentials in fertility, mortality, and morbidity. After a discussion of overall health status, the sections that follow focus on the relationship between both biosocial factors and socioeconomic factors and a population's health status.

Overall Health Status

Various community surveys have used global indicators as a means of measuring health status based on self-reports. The major government study to take this approach is the National Health Interview Survey (NHIS) conducted by the National Center for Health Statistics. The center's 1995 study found that, on a five-point scale, most respondents (66.6%) rated their health as "very good" or "excellent." Only 10.2% rated it as "poor" or "fair" (National Center for Health Statistics, 1998b: Table 70). Overall, most respondents (89.8%) rated their health as at least good and 37.4% as "excellent." Table 10.1 presents assessment data expressed as a scale from poor to excellent cross-classified by age, sex, race, and income.

As can be seen in the table, health status assessment based on self-reports declines as people age. While less than 3% of those aged 15 to 44 describe their health as only poor or fair, 28.4% of those 65 and over assessed their health this unfavorably. Interestingly, over one third of all persons 65 and over assess their health as excellent or very good, and this proportion actually increased between 1987 and 1995 (National Center for Health Statistics, 1998b: Table 70).

The difference in the self-assessment of health status between males and females is narrow, with males more positive in their self-assessments overall. Forty percent of males, for example, considered themselves to be in excellent health, compared to 35.0% for females (National Center for Health Statistics, 1998b: Table 70).

The discrepancy in self-assessed health status by race is substantial, with African Americans being much less positive in their self-assessment. While 68.0% of whites assessed their health as excellent or very good in 1995, only 58.2% of African Americans report such a positive evaluation. A higher proportion of African Americans than whites (14.0% vs. 9.6%) described themselves as being in poor or fair health. Given that African Americans have a younger age structure, the "true" differential in health status is probably even greater (National Center for Health Statistics, 1998a: Table 70).

When self-reported health status is examined by family income, a clear pattern is produced. The proportion reporting excellent health increased steadily with income, while the proportion reporting poor health declined steadily with income.

Indicators of health status are sometimes combined into a health status index in an attempt to generate a single objective indicator of health status. Box 10.1 presents a discussion of health status indices, their construction, and their applications.

Biosocial Characteristics

Age.   There has been long-standing acceptance of the notion that health status is linked closely with age. Conventional wisdom suggests that as the person ages, the more numerous and more serious his health problems become. While there is some truth to this assertion, research conducted in recent years indicates that the situation is much more complex than had been previously thought. Patterns of morbidity, disability, and even mortality display complicated relationships with the age structure of the population.

The most well established relationship has been the association between age and mortality. Overall, there is a direct and positive relationship between age and mortality in contemporary US society. The 1993–1995 average mortality rate of 23/100,000 for those aged 5 to 14, the cohort with the lowest death rate, increases gradually up through age 50. After 50, the increase in the mortality rate is dramatic. The rate of 23 increases to 461/100,000 for the 45–54 age group and 5,887/100,000 for the 75–84 age group. This same age-related pattern holds for all race–sex categories (National Center for Health Statistics, 1997: Table 37). It is noteworthy that all of these rates have declined since 1990.

The increase in overall life expectancy for the US population has been well documented. One of the findings derived from the analysis of life tables is the fact that longevity appears to feed on itself. (In other words, the longer one lives, the longer one lives.) In 1995, projected life expectancy at birth was 75.8 years. However, for individuals who live to age 65, life expectancy increases to 82.4 years. Similarly, individuals who survive until age 75 experience an increase in life expectancy to 85.4 years.

Not only does each age cohort carry its particular risk of death, but the causes of death vary widely among the age cohorts. For example, the leading causes of death for infants (under 1 year) are birth defects, respiratory conditions, and infectious diseases. The leading causes for young adults are accidents and suicide; for young adult African-Americans homicide is added to the list. The elderly are more likely to fall victim to the major killers: heart disease, cancer, and stroke. Each age cohort thus has its own peculiar cause-of-death configuration.

In terms of morbidity, a certain amount of disagreement exists when age is being considered. Historically, conventional wisdom has held that the number of health problems increases as the population ages. This has turned out to be only partially true. The prevalence of chronic conditions does in fact increase with age, and there appears to be a clear cumulative effect. However, the incidence of acute conditions actually declines with age. Thus, while the younger age cohorts are characterized by high rates of respiratory conditions, injuries, and other acute conditions, the elderly are less affected by these types of conditions. Instead, they are faced with a growing number of chronic conditions such as hypertension, arthritis, and heart problems. It has been suggested that the actual average number of conditions does not differ much from the youngest age cohorts to the oldest. The differential is primarily in the types of conditions that are common.

Another perspective is provided by examining acute and chronic conditions cross-classified by two compositional factors: age and sex. Table 10.2 contains

Table 10.2. Incidence of Selected Acute Conditions
by Selected Characteristics, United States, 1995[a]

Characteristic	Infectious and parasitic	Influenza	Digestive disorders	Injuries
Total	20.1	41.2	6.0	24.7
Age				
Under 5 years	52.0	53.6	11.7	27.0
15–17 years	39.6	59.4	7.3	30.2
18–24 years	18.3	43.1	6.3	25.1
25–44 years	13.5	45.2	5.0	23.4
45–64 years	8.7	28.0	4.5	23.3
65 years and over	5.9	14.0	5.4	19.7
Sex				
Male	21.5	43.4	6.4	22.3
Female	18.6	39.0	5.7	27.2
Race				
White	17.6	26.5	9.6	18.1
African American	21.2	44.0	5.7	26.1
Family income				
Less than $10,000	21.6	47.7	11.2	29.1
$10,000–19,999	21.6	39.7	6.4	24.3
$20,000–34,999	18.2	41.6	5.1	26.0
$35,000 or more	22.2	44.8	5.4	24.3

[a]Figures are expressed per 1000 population and are age adjusted.
SOURCE: Based on the National Health Inteview Survey and published in National Center for Health Statistics (1998a), Tables 1–4.

selected data on the incidence of acute conditions, while Table 10.3 presents data on five chronic conditions that reflect differing composition–condition relationships. While there is the expected significant increase in prevalence for heart disease, hypertension, and arthritis found as age increases, bronchitis and diabetes show much less marked increases, and rates for these conditions actually decrease at the oldest ages.

At the same time, there is a clear correlation between age and the level of disability characterizing a population. The proportion of the population experiencing some level of activity limitation increases steadily with age, and the oldest age cohorts are characterized by limited-activity days several times as numerous as those for the younger age cohorts. For example, 9.8% of the 15–44 age cohort in 1995 reported some limitation of activity. The comparable figure for the 65–74 age group was 33.2% (National Center for Health Statistics, 1998b: Table 60).

There is a well-documented relationship between the prevalence of mental illness and age, although the nature of the relationship has undergone substantial

Table 10.3. Prevalence of Selected Chronic Conditions
by Selected Characteristics, United States, 1995[a]

Characteristic	Heart disease	Chronic hypertension	Chronic bronchitis	Arthritis	Diabetes
Total	80.6	114.4	55.5	124.7	33.2
Age					
Under 18 years	18.6	0.6	53.6	2.1	2.6
18–44 years	35.8	52.8	50.2	46.9	11.4
45–64 years	120.8	222.7	63.9	232.9	63.8
65–74 years	268.1	391.9	66.0	447.9	133.0
75 years and over	363.9	419.7	61.4	548.5	117.1
Sex					
Male					
Under 45 years	24.0	34.0	44.2	22.4	6.2
45–64 years	143.1	223.2	37.4	176.7	62.1
65–74 years	316.3	352.0	58.1	385.5	131.4
75 years and over	439.4	344.5	45.6	437.0	110.6
Female					
Under 45 years	34.0	30.3	58.9	36.0	9.7
45–64 years	100.0	212.9	88.7	285.4	65.4
65–74 years	229.3	423.8	72.4	498.2	134.3
75 years and over	318.0	465.3	70.9	616.1	121.1
Race					
White					
Under 45 years	31.0	30.1	55.0	29.2	7.1
45–64 years	126.9	207.8	65.0	234.2	55.8
65–74 years	282.2	381.5	66.0	443.0	121.7
75 years and over	361.0	412.8	62.3	548.0	114.2
African American					
Under 45 years	24.4	46.1	38.5	32.0	8.8
45–64 years	93.2	344.7	59.6	250.2	121.4
65–74 years	197.1	561.8	46.9	536.6	239.9
75 years and over	387.9	477.8	71.3	641.4	117.6

[a]Figures are express per 1000 persons and are age adjusted.
SOURCE: Based on National Health Interview Survey and published in National Center Health Statistics
(1998a), Table 60.

modification in recent years. Until the 1970s, it was believed that aging had a
cumulative effect on mental health just as it was thought to have on physical health
(Warheit et al., 1975), with the prevalence of mental illness thought to increase
with advancing age. However, many observers argued that this pattern reflected
selectivity in terms of the mental disorders measured, use of statistics on institutionalized patients, and the tendency to attribute many symptoms of old age to
mental illness.

A more contemporary graphic depiction suggests a nonmonotonic and much more irregular relationship. This change in perceived relationship between age and mental illness is a function not so much of actual changes in distribution of mental illness within the population as of a revision in terms of the conditions classified as mental disorders. The inclusion of alcoholism, drug abuse, and suicide under the heading of mental illness has created a "bulge" in the 15–25 age cohort. At the same time, attributing many symptoms of aging to Alzheimer's disease has reduced the perceived prevalence of mental illness among the elderly. Further, the advent of adolescent treatment centers has meant that many more adolescents are being defined as mentally disturbed than in the past (Ilfeld, 1978).

Because of the aging of the US population, increasing attention must be paid to the relationship between age and health status. The growing number of elderly residents will result in an increasing number of cases of life-threatening conditions. The aging pattern portends an increase in the proportion of hospital patients who are very sick. At the same time, an aging population brings with it a growing number of persons with chronic conditions that must be "managed" in order to enhance the quality of life for those persons. These trends obviously have significant implications for health resource utilization, and this will be discussed in Chapter 11. Box 10.2 describes the implications of the "new" elderly for health status.

Sex. One of the most perplexing yet important correlations discussed in this context is that between sex and health status. There is perhaps no other demographic variable for which differentials in health status are so clear-cut. Yet, at the same time, there is probably none for which more questions are raised concerning the validity of the findings and the possible explanations for the apparent relationship.

Any discussion of the relationship between sex and health status must begin with what has become a maxim: Women are characterized by higher levels of morbidity than men, but men have a much higher mortality rate. Although this is a somewhat simplistic summary of a complex situation, there is a great deal of evidence to suggest that, by any measure of morbidity one would care to use, women are "sicker." On the other hand, there is no doubt that mortality rates are higher and life expectancy is considerably lower for males. In fact, the mortality rate for males is higher than that for females for every age cohort and for virtually every cause of death. This assertion has recently been verified by Rogers et al. (2000). They found 73% higher odds of mortality for men without controls for other factors. When demographic, social, and economic factors were controlled, the odds ratio for males actually increased to 2.0.

When global measures are utilized, females tend to characterize themselves as being in slightly poorer health than males (National Center for Health Statistics, 1998b: Table 70). On symptom checklists for both physical and mental symptoms,

Box 10.2

The "New" Elderly

No demographic trend has received more attention over the past decade than the aging of the US population. Along with increases in life expectancy has come tremendous growth in the size of the older American population. By the late 1990s, the median age had crept up close to 35 years, and in mid-1998 there were approximately 57 million Americans 55 years or older, representing 21% of the total population. By 2025, there will be 62 million citizens 65 or older, accounting for nearly 20% of the population. While all older age groups will increase significantly in numbers for the foreseeable future, the 85 and over age group will grow faster than any other cohort.

The numbers by themselves are noteworthy, since the current cohort of seniors constitutes a population 1.5 times the total population of Canada. As this age group has grown in size, it also has increased its economic, political, and market clout. "Mature" Americans are living longer and enjoying greater health, while having more money to spend than any previous generation. As with many demographic trends, however, the size of the phenomenon may not be as important as the characteristics of the population under consideration.

The attributes of this new generation of seniors are noteworthy along two dimensions. First, these new seniors have distinct characteristics that set them apart from previous cohorts of seniors. While today's oldest seniors share many characteristics with the elders of previous generations, even they are also likely to be distinct from their forebears in a number of ways. While today's 80-year-olds grew up during the Depression and are likely to carry scars from that period, today's 65-year-old, on the other hand, was 10 years old when World War II ended and grew up in a much different world. In fact, this cohort as a group is unlike any previous generation, and it appears that its behavior, including the use of health services, will be strikingly different from that of its forebears throughout the aging process. (Indeed, they are so different that the term "elderly" has been essentially taken out of use.)

The mature consumer of the 1990s represents the first cohort in history to benefit from the extraordinary advances in medicine and technology of this century. The additional 10–20 years of life expectancy gained in recent decades appears to have been added to the middle rather than to the end of the life span. This means today's 65-year-old is roughly equivalent to yesterday's 50-year-old, with all that implies for senior lifestyles. In fact, the oldest old have gained more in terms of health status than any other cohort. Their tastes, interests, and concerns are quite different from those of their parents. These seniors are interested in autonomy, self-sufficiency, personal growth, and revitalization.

Second, there is significant differentiation *within* the nation's older population.

For almost two decades it has been realized that the senior population was not simply one homogeneous cohort of individuals. Now, as more data have become available, researchers know (and marketers are beginning to find out) that American seniors are a highly differentiated population with wide variations in needs, preferences, and behaviors. In fact, it has been suggested that we are becoming less alike, rather than more, as we age. For demographic purposes, this generation of seniors has been categorized as the "young-old," the "middle-old," and the "old-old." Other more descriptive terms ("working mature," "young retirees," and even the traditional "elderly") also may be applied. However differentiated, each subgroup has specific implications for health status and health services utilization.

Key indicators of health, social, and economic characteristics among older Americans vary considerably by race and ethnicity, for example, often mirroring disparities in wider racial and ethnic populations. In addition to living longer, Americans are becoming more racially and ethnically diverse. While the number of older whites will increase 97% between 1995 and 2050, elderly African Americans will increase by 265%, Native Americans by 294%, Hispanic Americans by 530%, and Asian Americans by 643%.

Of course, the nature of future seniors will be driven to a great extent by the characteristics of the baby boomers. Nearly 78 million Americans were born between 1946 and 1964, and the oldest among them were in their 50s as the century ended. Boomers are determined to reinvent retirement, a process that appears already to be underway. Retirement is no longer seen as a type of "default" condition but as a context for a new and different lifestyle. Boomers, in fact, have already influenced the health care delivery system in significant ways. They were primarily responsible for the establishment of health maintenance organizations, birthing centers, urgent care centers, and outpatient surgery centers as components of the health care landscape. Now they are driving the demand for a wide range of new services such as laser eye surgery, skin rejuvenation, and menopause management.

The new generation of seniors is not likely to be nearly as docile as previous ones. Baby boomers are used to having things their way and already are much more demanding as "middle-agers" than previous cohorts. Their expectations are much higher, they are better informed, and they are used to being in charge. The stereotype of the docile grandmother happily accepting whatever Medicare metes out will not persist very long under the onslaught of demanding men and women baby boomers.

The health status of the senior population will be a critical issue for the United States during the twenty-first century. Today's seniors are living longer, and they tend to suffer fewer limitations than previous generations of elderly. In fact, self-assessed health status improved significantly for seniors between 1987 and 1995, according to the National Center for Health Statistics. Recent research has found an actual generation-to-generation improvement in functional ability among those 65 and older.

Continued

Box 10.2. (Continued)

Today's seniors are staying active longer as a result of being in better health than previous generations. Although there is an understandable drop in the proportion involved in outdoor recreation and more strenuous activities, the numbers of seniors involved in other types of exercise programs have increased dramatically. Seniors, in fact, are demanding exercise programs tailored to their needs in an effort to stay healthy. A new generation of health professionals is also encouraging lifelong physical activity, and sports products companies are modifying their equipment to meet the needs of seniors.

Nevertheless, an increase in chronic conditions and activity limitations is inevitable among seniors. Physical and mental deterioration can be delayed but not eliminated. This means that we can expect a growing proportion of the US population to be characterized by one or more chronic conditions and one or more activity limitations in the future. Even with improved health status, the numbers alone will assure that health care costs for this population will increase significantly.

Despite the evidence of improving health status among the seniors, older Americans still account for the majority of federal health care expenditures. Over half the federal health care dollar is spent on Medicare beneficiaries. While seniors account for only 12% of Medicaid enrollment, they account for over one third of Medicaid expenditures (primarily for nursing home care). Americans over 50 account for 60% of health care spending and 80% of prescription drug spending, while representing 35% of the total population.

The good news, for seniors at least, is that over 99% of the elderly have health care coverage. Virtually all elderly are covered under Medicare, and more than two thirds of those 65 and over have supplementary coverage. The role of the federal government in subsidizing care for American seniors will continue to be an issue to be faced as the "new elderly" begin to dominate the health care system.

---

females tend to score much higher (i.e., they report more symptoms). For reported conditions and diagnoses, females are characterized by higher incidence rates. (The one acute "condition" more common among males is injuries.) While females report an even higher level of chronic conditions than acute conditions, these tend to be conditions that are not particularly life-threatening. Comparable proportions of males and females are characterized by some level of activity limitation. Females, however, accumulate on the average more work-loss days, more school-loss days, and more bed-restricted days than males (National Center for Health Statistics, 1998b: Table 67).

Males, while scoring "better" on the indicators of morbidity discussed above, are at greater risk of mortality. In effect, the overall mortality rate for males is nearly twice that of females, with males reporting a mortality rate of 621 per 100,000 in 1996 compared to 381 per 100,000 for females (National Center for Health Statistics, 1998b: Table 31). For each of the 15 leading causes of death in 1995, males recorded a higher mortality rate, and for some causes the male–female ratio exceeds 3:1.

The mortality rate for males is higher, in fact, at every age. At the ages 15–24 and 35–44, it is almost three times as high. Even the fetal death rate for males is higher than that for females, indicating that the greater mortality risk characterizing males predates birth. These figures, of course, are reflected in differentials in life expectancy. In 1996, life expectancy from birth for males was 73.9 years compared to 79.7 years for females (National Center for Health Statistics, 1998b: Table 29).

On one hand, it can be argued that males die from different causes than do females. However, for every condition except diabetes and sex-related disorders, the mortality rate is higher for males. Interestingly, the excess male mortality for each age cohort is attributable to a different cause in each case. For example, a major killer of infants is chronic respiratory disease, and this is more common among male infants. Accidents are the major cause of death for children aged 1 to 14, and males have approximately twice the risk of accidents. One other anomaly beclouding these relationships is the fact that, although males are sick less often, when they are sick it is more likely to be serious or even fatal. All things being equal, the disease acuity level for males who do become ill is higher than for females with comparable conditions.

It is beyond the scope of this volume to evaluate the various explanations that are offered to account for these phenomena. Briefly, these explanations include reporting anomalies, differential exposure to environmental conditions and social stress, cultural expectations, and outright biological differences. There is evidence that women are more sensitive to the existence of symptoms of both physical and mental illness, and that they more readily take action in response to perceived symptoms, thereby showing up more often in the data compilations. On the other hand, recent research has found that men and women do not differ in their reporting of initial conditions (McIntyre et al., 1999). It is argued that men historically have been exposed to more dangerous environmental and occupational conditions, thereby accounting for the excess mortality. But it follows that these same conditions should contribute to morbidity, which they apparently do not.

The relationship between sex and mental health status is fairly well documented, although the conclusions are not without controversy. As noted above with regard to physical health, females appear to be characterized by a higher level of psychiatric morbidity. Based on reported symptoms, clinical evaluations by community researchers, and frequency of presenting themselves for mental health

Box 10.3

Social Support, Demographics, and Health Status

As early as the 1960s and 1970s, researchers were discovering an imperfect relationship between the incidence of various health problems and such standard causative factors as the presence of disease agents, environmental threats, and exposure to various types of risks. Researchers were perplexed by situations in which, on the one hand, individuals with limited exposure to risk suffered more pathology than those with greater exposure, and on the other hand, individuals who were exposed to substantial risk seemed to be immune to the potential health threat. This mismatch between exposure and disease activation was noted for such diverse conditions as myocardial infarction, birth complications, injuries resulting from accidents, pregnancy outcomes, tuberculosis, and various forms of psychosomatic conditions and mental disorders.

Recent research in a number of fields has yielded evidence that helps to explain these anomalies. This research links health status to the availability of "social support." Although no widely accepted definition of social support has yet been formulated, all the definitions in use involve some notion of resources available to the individual that arise out of interpersonal relationships. Thus, social support represents resources available from within the individual's social setting that can be called on in times of excessive stress, but also are available on an ongoing, perhaps indiscernible, basis. Social support has been distinguished from such related concepts as "social integration" and "social networks," although these concepts certainly have significant commonalities.

Research has found social support to have implications for several stages of the health–illness continuum. The availability of social support is now thought to serve to promote health, to prevent the onset of illness, to limit the progression of illness

care, females appear to be characterized by a higher level of mental disorder (Cockerham, 1996). Even this must be qualified. While women exhibit higher scores on indices [Minnesota Multiphasic Personality Inventory-2 (MMPI-2)] of depression, hysteria, and paranoia, men have higher scores for antisocial, authority problems, and type A behavior (Gumbiner and Flowers, 1997).

Many observers suggest that females are not, in fact, "crazier," but that differences in identified prevalence rates are a function of other factors. These factors include a tendency for females to perceive symptoms as emotional rather than physical, a greater tendency for females to admit to symptoms of either physical or mental character, and the willingness of society to interpret females' characteristics as emotional rather than physical. Differential access to social

episodes that do occur, and to speed recovery and return to a healthy state following an illness episode. Social support appears to have an impact throughout the illness process and has relevance for both physical and mental illness. Emerging social support theory argues that individuals who do not have meaningful relationships, who do not participate in social networks, who do not have linkages to various social organizations, and who, in short, are poorly integrated into society do not benefit from the buffering and curative aspects of social support. It is these individuals who are at a risk of illness disproportionate to their exposure to disease agents.

Ultimately, the demographic characteristics of the population have significant implications for the availability of social support. An examination of the types of individuals who lack social support and subsequently suffer disproportionate pathology reveals some important demographic correlates. As it turns out, individuals at high risk can be grouped into certain demographic categories. The high-risk groups include the poor, African Americans, widowers, people who are highly mobile, relocated elderly people, and others who differ from the rest of the community in important ways. Other research has found the unmarried, individuals living alone, and members of certain alienated ethnic groups also to be at greater risk of illness and death. The factor members of these groups often have in common is a deficit of social support.

In order therefore to predict the extent and nature of morbidity within a population, knowledge of the availability of social support is important. It turns out that an important means of determining the availability of social support is through an understanding of the demographic composition of the population and the nature of the demographic processes that characterize it. The demographic traits of a population thus provide (indirectly at least) a clue to the likely amount and seriousness of physical and mental illness within the population. To the extent that the size of the demographic categories characterized by low levels of social support increases, a concomitant increase in the level of morbidity can be anticipated.

---

support is considered a factor here, as it is in the distribution of other conditions. Box 10.3 addresses the issue of social support and health status.

Males and females tend to be characterized by quite different psychiatric disorders. Females tend to be characterized by milder, more common anxiety disorders. Males, on the other hand, tend to predominate with regard to the less common but more serious psychoses such as schizophrenia and personality disorders. A major exception is found in the case of depression, for which women report a rate twice as high as men (Cockerham, 1996). As with physical illness, it appears that females are characterized by a greater occurrence of symptoms, while males are afflicted with more extreme conditions.

Regardless of the ultimate explanation for these sex differentials, the implications for the provision of health services are clear. Women will continue to account for the majority of those with chronic symptoms that will require long-term management, while males will continue to be characterized by a higher level of life-threatening diseases. Sex will continue to be a powerful predictor of levels of morbidity and mortality and of the types of conditions that characterize males and females, respectively. The fact that women will constitute an even greater majority of the patient population in coming years has significant implications for the future demand for health services.

Race–Ethnicity.   Racial groups are defined based on one or more distinguishable physical attributes considered important in the particular society. In US society and many others, skin color is the most important factor in racial categorization. Race is a clearly biosocial attribute, because it combines physical attributes with social connotations.

Ethnic group distinctions are based on differences in cultural heritage. Members of distinct ethnic groups have a common cultural tradition, including values and norms and perhaps even a language, that sets them apart from the larger society. While ethnic distinctions are not primarily biological, prolonged "inbreeding" often leads to the development of distinctive physical characteristics. For this reason the discussion of ethnicity and health status is included in this section. The major ethnic groups in US society include Hispanics, Jews, and certain large national groups that, in some parts of the country at least, have been able to maintain their ethnic identity.

When the various racial groups in the United States are examined in terms of health status, significant differences are found (Shoebaum and Waidman, 1997). The major distinction is between whites and African Americans, with Asian Americans and Native Americans manifesting less distinct health status characteristics. Whites historically have rated themselves high in terms of health status relative to African Americans, with other racial–ethnic categories falling somewhere in between. Differences in global health assessment and functional limitations in daily activities by race and ethnicity persist even when income and education are controlled (Ren and Amick, 1996). Differences in self-assessment should be interpreted with caution, however, since there are indications that members of different racial groups may use different criteria for assessing their own health status (Larsen et al., 1998).

Clear-cut differences in morbidity are found primarily between whites and nonwhites. The number of symptoms, the number of episodes, and the severity of the conditions all place African Americans at a health status disadvantage. Although relatively more prone to acute health conditions, African Americans actually suffer higher rates of both acute and chronic conditions than whites. African Americans represent 12% of the population, for example, but account for 28% of the diagnosed hypertension (Hidreth and Saunders, 1992). Further, all things being equal, African Americans contracting life-threatening conditions are more at risk of death from them than are whites with the same conditions.

The explanations offered for racial and ethnic differences in health measures are complex. In the case of substance abuse, for example, differences in socioeconomic status account for variations between races. On the other hand, strong racial dissimilarities in rates of infant mortality and hypertension persist even after differences in socioeconomic status are accounted for (Lillie-Blanton et al., 1996).

Differences in cause-specific morbidity exist between various racial and ethnic groups, with the epidemiology of cancer being a good example. Whites in the United States are more likely to suffer from colon/rectal cancer, breast cancer, and bladder cancer, to name a few, than are African Americans. However, the incidence rate for several other types of cancer are higher for African Americans. These include lung, prostate, stomach, and esophageal cancer.

Specific ethnic groups are likely to display unique morbidity and mortality profiles. Polish-Americans suffer from relatively high levels of lung and esophageal cancer, for example, while among Italian-Americans bladder, intestinal, and pharyngeal cancer are more common. Japanese-Americans suffer from stomach cancer at rates many times higher than Japanese nationals, while cervical cancer is almost unknown among Jewish women. Hispanics report by far the highest incidence of AIDS among the various racial and ethnic groups (National Center for Health Statistics, 1998b).

When racial differences in the level of disability are examined, it is found that the proportion of African Americans reporting some level of activity limitation is nearly half again as high as that for the white population. The figure with activity limitation is 18% for African Americans compared to 14% for whites.

Mortality rates for the African-American population are considerably higher than those for the white population. When the 1994–1996 average mortality rate is examined, the overall age-adjusted mortality rate is 501 per 100,000 population. The mortality rate for the white population as a whole was 475 deaths per 100,000 population, compared to a rate of 759 per 100,000 population for African Americans (National Center for Health Statistics, 1998b: Table 30). African Americans are characterized by higher mortality risks at nearly all ages and for nearly all causes (Rogers et al., 2000). The gap in mortality rates for whites and African Americans has actually increased since 1990.

This mortality differential is reflected in life expectancy for the two racial categories. In 1996, life expectancy for whites was 76.8 years compared to 70.2 years for African Americans. The greatest differential in life expectancy is between white females (79.2 years) and African-American males (66.1 years). Overall, Hispanic mortality rates compare favorably to those for both whites and African Americans. This advantage is particularly apparent for the major killers like heart disease and certain forms of cancer (National Center for Health Statistics, 1998b: Table 29). Interestingly, life expectancy for African-American males has been found to actually improve relative to that of other age-sex groups once they reach the older age groups. Although it has been suggested that this is an artifact of age misreporting, there is evidence that African-American males do in fact have an advantage in this regard (Corti et al., 1999).

The mortality rates for Asian populations in the United States generally fall between the rates for African Americans and whites. However, Asian Americans represent a rather diverse population, and certain Asiatic nationality groups record a rate lower than that for the white population. The Asian-American population reported an overall mortality rate of only 299 per 100,000 in 1995, and even the overall Hispanic rate of 386 is more favorable than that for the non-Hispanic white population. Recently, much of the mortality advantage characterizing Asian Americans and Hispanics has been attributed to the foreign born among these populations. Subsequent generations of Asian Americans and Hispanics, it seems, do not fare as well in comparative mortality analyses (Rogers et al., 2000).

Interestingly, Native Americans have made the greatest gains of any group in reducing mortality in recent years, with a 1993–1995 average mortality rate of 468 per 100,000. Native Americans record the lowest mortality rate for cancer for any group but by far the highest mortality rates for diabetes, suicide, and accidents. (Note that all of these rates are age adjusted, thereby eliminating any distortion caused by differential age distributions.)

Further, important differences exist between African Americans and whites in terms of the common causes of death. To a great extent these differentials reflect the differences in morbidity characteristics discussed above. Whites in the United States are more likely to be characterized by chronic conditions, especially those associated with aging. African Americans and certain ethnic groups are more likely to be characterized by acute conditions. Further, nonwhites are more likely to be affected by environmentally caused health problems and life-threatening problems associated with lifestyles (such as homicide and accidents). Consequently, the dominant causes of death among the white population are heart disease, cancer, and stroke. While these are important among various other racial and ethnic groups, African Americans in particular are more likely to die as a result of infectious conditions, respiratory and digestive systems conditions, and the lifestyle-associated problems noted above. Table 10.4 presents data on death rates by age and sex.

Another relatively important cause of death for African Americans is infant mortality. Although infant mortality has been dramatically reduced in the United States in this century, it continues to be a serious health threat for many groups of nonwhites (Hummer, 1996). The infant mortality rate for African Americans in 1996 was more than twice that for whites (14.7 per 1000 live births vs. 6.8). The rates for both groups had declined since the late 1980s, with the gap between the two actually narrowing in recent years (National Center for Health Statistics, 1998b: Table 24).

Table 10.4. Death Rates for Selected Causes by Sex and Race, 1996[a]

Causes	White males	White females	Black males	Black females
All causes	918.1	896.2	939.9	753.5
Diseases of heart	293.3	294.2	234.8	229.0
Cerebrovascular diseases	49.1	76.3	50.1	59.7
Malignant neoplasms	225.8	201.8	207.3	157.9
Chronic obstructive pulmonary disease	46.1	43.0	24.9	17.0
Pneumonia and influenza	30.5	36.9	26.2	21.6
Diabetes mellitus	21.1	23.9	26.0	37.9
Accidents and adverse effects	47.3	25.4	54.3	22.8
Motor vehicle accidents	22.4	11.0	24.3	9.5

[a]Figures expressed as rates per 100,000 population.
SOURCE: Peters et al. (1998), Table 8.

One of the major factors in infant mortality is low birth weight, and this is a condition that is much more common among African-American newborns. For all births in 1996, 7.4% were classified as low birth weight. However, the figure for African-American newborns (13.0%) was more than twice that for white newborns (6.3%). Most other major racial and ethnic groups were closer to the white rate for low birth weight than the African-American rate. Asian Americans recorded a figure of 6.9%; Native Americans, 6.6%; and Hispanics, 6.9%. Particularly low rates were recorded by Chinese Americans (5.0%) and Mexican Americans (5.9%) (National Center for Health Statistics).

Other racial and ethnic groups recorded quite disparate rates of infant death. Certain Asian groups, for example, report much lower than average infant mortality, while Hispanics as a group record infant mortality rates between those of whites and African Americans. Native Americans and native Alaskans historically have recorded very high infant mortality rates; however, since the 1950s, their rates have come to resemble the US average. Rates for selected groups in 1995 include 7.0 deaths per 1000 live births for whites, 16.6 for African Americans, 7.1 for Hispanics, 4.6 for Chinese Americans, and 4.2 for Japanese Americans (National Center for Health Statistics, 1998b: Table 20).

Indicators of disability also are found to be higher among African Americans. Data from the 1995 National Health Interview Survey indicated that 14.8% of the white population had some limitation due to disability, compared to 15.9% of the African-American population (National Center for Health Statistics, 1998b). In addition, African Americans are characterized by higher levels of disability than whites, whether measured by the actual presence of handicaps or by such proxy measures as work-loss days and bed-restricted days. While 22.0% of whites aged

45 to 64 had activity limitations in 1995, the corresponding percentage for African Americans was 30.0% (National Center for Health Statistics, 1998b: Table 60).

The distribution of mental illness with regard to race and ethnicity has been of great interest to researchers and health professionals. This interest has been sparked in part by the controversial nature of the relationship, especially as it relates to racial comparisons. Since the development of modern concepts of mental illness in the nineteenth century, attempts have been made to profile the mental health status of various racial and ethnic groups. In its most malevolent form, this effort has been subverted in an attempt to portray certain groups as mentally inferior.

Historically, it was believed that African Americans and certain other racial and ethnic groups in US society had worse mental health status than whites. Even after the scientific study of mental illness became established, evidence was developed that suggested higher rates of mental disorder among these groups. Most often singled out were African Americans, who often were depicted as a group as being characterized by relatively high levels of psychotic behavior.

After several decades of research, it is now believed by many that the impression of higher rates of mental disorder among African Americans and certain other racial and/or ethnic groups is a function of at least three factors. These include: (1) collection of data historically from public mental institutions; (2) a middle-class bias in the diagnosis of mental disorders; and (3) a failure to consider important intervening variables such as social class. Recent studies in fact have found little support for significant differences between African Americans and whites in terms of the prevalence of mental disorders. However, Hispanics have been found in these same studies to have higher than average rates, while Asian Americans record lower than average prevalence rates. Differences in education and occupational status, for example, may account for some of the variation. More importantly, social class is often pointed to as the major contributing factor to prevalence differentials. Thus, many researchers consider differences in mental health status between African Americans and whites to be a function of social class. This would explain apparent differences in both prevalence and types of disorders. (See the discussion below on the relationship between social status and health status.)

The relationship between mental disorder and ethnicity is even cloudier, given the wide variation in the types of ethnic groups in US society. Some groups, such as Mexican Americans, appear to be characterized by higher than average rates of disorder (Robertson, 1981). Others, such as Japanese and Chinese Americans, appear to be relatively "disease-free" (Kuo, 1984).

Once again, the observed differences may reflect differentials in types of disorders rather than prevalence. These differentials in turn may be a function of social class or other socioeconomic differences, or even migration status. In any case, it is extremely difficult to compare subgroups of the population in terms of either prevalence or types of disorder due to numerous possible intervening variables.

Sociocultural Characteristics

Sociocultural characteristics refer to those traits that characterize individuals related to their position or status in society. While biosocial traits are ascribed essentially at birth, sociocultural traits are typically acquired through the actions of the individual. Sociocultural traits are important not only because they indicate one's place in society, but also because of their correlation with health status.

Marital Status. Although one of the earliest sociological studies (Durkheim, 1951) found marital status to be a factor in differential suicide rates, it is only recently that the association between marital status and both physical and mental illness has been fully appreciated. Today, many consider marital status to be one of the best predictors of both health status and health behavior, although (as will be shown) the relationship is actually a very complex one.

The categories of marital status for the discussion below include: never married, married, divorced, and widowed. (The term "single" generally has been eliminated from research terminology, since it can be interpreted to mean never married, widowed, or divorced.) By the mid-1980s, most researchers counted couples living together as married for analytical purposes. Separated individuals are not treated in a consistent manner in the literature but are most often listed under their official status, which is married. Some studies list these couples as divorced if they are legally separated. This group is small enough that its variable definition does not distort the relationships that are identified.

In general, it is held that health status, both mental and physical, is higher for the married in US society than for those of any other marital status. Married individuals are found to have lower levels of morbidity and mortality, to have lower levels of disability and restriction of activity, and to perceive themselves as being in much better health. Similarly, the married are found to have lower levels of mental disorder. Married persons have a higher level of physical and psychological well-being than their unmarried counterparts (Mookherjee, 1997). It has also been found that married individuals, when affected with a health problem, suffer less serious problems, face a more favorable prognosis, and report a more favorable outcome.

With regard to disability, only 15% of married men and 14% of married women were found to be restricted in the performance of their normal activities in the 1995 National Health Interview Survey (NHIS), compared to 20% or more of both men and women in other marital status categories. This same pattern is found with regard to other indicators of disability. The NHIS found that married men are restricted in their work, home, or school activities an average of 10 days per year;

the figure is 12 days for married women. Only never-married males, with 9 days of restrictions, fared better; all other categories were substantially worse off. The same was true for bed-restriction days. Married and never-married men and women were similar in the number of days they were restricted to bed annually, but divorcees and widows were clearly worse off.

These patterns hold, incidentally, for every age cohort. In fact, the advantage for the married increases with age for some conditions. While the prevalence of chronic conditions for the married and never-married is approximately the same for the 18–24 age cohort, the NHIS found that in 1995 one third of the never married in the 45–64 age group suffer from chronic disabilities, compared to one fifth of the ever married.

The exception to these patterns relates to the incidence of acute conditions. Married men and women report slightly more acute conditions than never-married men and women. However, the married are still better off than the divorced and widowed on this indicator of morbidity. It has been suggested, as in the case with sex differentials, that the never-married may suffer fewer episodes of acute conditions but are affected by more serious and prolonged conditions. The incidence of injuries also represents something of an exception; while married people are less prone to injuries than never-married and divorced individuals, they are more at risk for injuries than are the widowed. The fact that married persons may be more likely to have their acute conditions diagnosed is a consideration in interpreting these data.

Although never-married, divorced, and widowed individuals have poorer health status overall than the married, there is no clear-cut ranking among these three groups. The relative health status of members of these three groups actually depends on the measure that is being utilized. Although the never-married are better off on some measures of morbidity, they are more likely to commit suicide or die as a result of homicide or an accident. The never-married also are at greater risk of developing mental illness.

It is sometimes argued that there are other factors that actually explain these differences in morbidity and mortality, and some of these factors are discussed below. However, evidence for the importance of marital status as a predictor of health status can be drawn from data on changes in health status that accompany changes in marital status. When individuals shift from one status to another, changes in health status are frequently seen. The change is probably the most extreme when the shift is from married status to the divorced or widowed category. Increases in both morbidity and mortality have been documented for individuals undergoing such a transition (Waldron et al., 1997). In addition, poor health status has been shown to increase the probability that divorce will occur (Joung etal., 1998).

Such a general overview tends to mask a number of inconsistencies in the overall patterns noted. If figures for the various categories are decomposed on the basis of other variables and if specific health problems are considered, substantial variation is indicated by the data. One of the best differentiating factors is sex. When comparisons are made between various marital status–sex categories (e.g., married females, unmarried males, divorced females), the patterns of relationship become more complex. For example, while married individuals are healthier overall and married females are in relatively good physical health, married females have been found to account for a large amount of the depression reported among the mentally ill. Similarly, married males are better off than the unmarried in general, but are likely to have higher mortality rates than never-married females. In fact, married males are the ones found to suffer the most deterioration (both physically and mentally) in making the transition from married to unmarried statuses.

Limited research has been conducted on the mortality implications of marital status and household characteristics. However, recent work by Rogers et al. (2000) has found that married individuals living with their spouses and children are at the lowest risk of morality of any marital status/living arrangement combination. Situations that are characterized by high mortality levels include unmarried individuals who live with their parents, members of particularly large families, and single parents with three or more children living in the household.

The preponderance of research now indicates that the different marital statuses—never-married, married, divorced (with separation sometimes considered), and widowed—are at varying risks of mental illness. The consensus is that the married are much better off overall in terms of mental health than are those in any of the other marital categories. There is less consensus concerning the category at greatest risk; different studies have variously identified the never-married, the divorced, and the widowed. Changes in marital status also are contributors to higher levels of morbidity, with divorce being a contributor to the onset of major depression for both men and women. The impact of such changes, however, is clearly greater for women (Bruce and Kim, 1992).

As for many of the demographic variables discussed, the relationship may not be as direct as it appears. There are those that argue for marital status-specific disorders and others that contend that reliance on marital categories overlooks important differences between sexes. Another school of thought suggests that it is not marital status per se that correlates with risk of mental disorder but living arrangements. That is, those living alone (regardless of marital status) have been found to be at greater risk of mental disorder (Hughes and Gove, 1981). Until the complexities of these relationships can be unraveled, it appears that marital status will be retained as a reasonable predictor of the prevalence of mental disorder at the group level at least.

Socioeconomic Status. During the 1960s and 1970s, when poverty in the United States was being rediscovered, one of the by-products of this research was the emergence of a relationship between socioeconomic status and health status. This relationship had not been fully explored heretofore, despite episodic reporting of surprisingly poor health status within pockets of disadvantaged populations such as Native Americans and Appalachian residents. Only in the 1970s was the extent of the health–social class relationship recognized.

Social scientists generally see US society as being divided into three to six social classes. The three major divisions are the upper, middle, and lower classes. When more divisions are utilized, the categories are typically subdivisions of the three major groupings. A common variation involves the carving out of a "working class" category out of the lower-middle and upper-lower classes.

Social scientists often emphasize objective measures of class status such as income, education, and occupation. While these are the demographic dimensions that will be utilized in the discussion below, it should be noted that the subjective component cannot be ignored. This "lifestyle" component of social class involves not only notions of normative behavior and values, but attitudes, perceptions, and opinions. While the objective measures are the easiest to operationalize and thereby to use as a basis for dividing the population into measurable groups, these groups' lifestyles have important implications for health status and health behavior.

Income. Since income is the measure of social class most easily quantified, it has been the socioeconomic variable most frequently linked to health status. It has been found that no matter what indicator of health status is utilized, there generally is an inverse relationship between income and health status. This is true whether the indicators are outcome measures, prevalence indicators, disability measures, or (as will be seen in the next chapter) utilization measures. There is a strong inverse relationship between income level and morbidity for both physical and mental disorders. As income increases, the prevalence of both acute and chronic conditions decreases. When symptom checklists are utilized, the lower the income, the larger the number of symptoms identified. Not surprisingly, members of lower-income groups assess themselves as being in poorer health than do the more affluent. While 20% of those with annual household incomes less than $15,000 considered themselves in poor or fair health, only 3.7% of those with household incomes over $50,000 reported poor or fair health (National Center for Health Statistics, 1998b: Table 70).

Not only are there more episodes of both acute and chronic conditions recorded as income decreases, but the severity of the conditions is likely to be greater when income is lower. When afflicted by acute conditions, the poor tend to have more prolonged episodes characterized by greater severity. Interestingly, in a society that has become characterized by chronic health conditions, acute disorders remain surprisingly common among the lower-income groups. In fact, the disease profiles of many low-income communities more closely resemble those of developing countries than they do the United States.

There also is an inverse relationship between income and indicators of disability. There is a direct and monotonic relationship between income level and activity limitation. Among the population with annual household incomes in 1995 less than $10,000, 28.2% reported some limitation of activity due to chronic conditions. This figure drops dramatically to 14.9% for the $20,000–34,999 income group. The rate continues to drop to a level of only 9.2% for those with household incomes of $35,000 or more.

The lower the income, the greater the number of bed-disability days, work-loss days, school-loss days, and restricted-activity days. For example, while persons in households with incomes under $10,000 experienced on average 13.2 bed-disability days in 1995, the corresponding percentage for persons living in households with $35,000 or more income was 3.7 days (National Center for Health Statistics, 1998b).

The relationship between income and health status persists when mortality is examined. The mortality rate for the lowest income levels may be twice that of the most affluent in some communities, even after adjusting for age. This assertion has been recently reaffirmed by the landmark study by Rogers et al. (2000). The poor also are characterized by relatively high levels of infant mortality and even maternal mortality. Virtually all infant mortality in the United States today is accounted for by the lowest income groups, and maternal mortality (which has been virtually eliminated societywide) is disturbingly common among the poor.

Early on in the study of the social epidemiology of mental disorder, it was asserted that the lower classes were more prone to psychiatric pathology than the affluent (Hollingshead and Redlich, 1958). However, more recent studies have failed to consistently demonstrate a clear relationship. What has been demonstrated is the fact that the relative prevalence of mental illness by social class depends heavily on the type of disorder examined (Cockerham, 1997). Even so, for some disorders apparent correlations that exist with many variables (e.g., race and age) are essentially eliminated when socioeconomic status is controlled (Warheit et al., 1973).

Of course, there are numerous considerations in examining this relationship. Social class is extremely difficult to operationalize. Income (and sometimes education or occupational status) is often used as a proxy measure since no generally agreed-upon indicator exists. Unfortunately, this approach relies on objective measures of social class and ignores the subjective component that would be assumed to be important in the examination of mental illness. At the same time, possible intervening variables also need to be considered.

Much useful information on the distribution of mental disorders within US society has been generated by the federally funded Epidemiological Catchment Area Study initiated in the early 1980s. Data were collected from a sample of residents in five-sites across the nation using the Diagnostic Interview Schedule. This community survey has made it possible to reexamine earlier conclusions drawn with regard to the relationship between the prevalence of psychiatric disorders and socioeconomic status. Conclusions drawn from this survey indicate an inverse relationship between socioeconomic status and three major disorders—schizophrenia, alcohol abuse, and major depression (Dohrenwend, 1990). Socioeconomic status here was measured by a combination of income, education, and occupational characteristics. Other surveys have found a similar relationship between symptoms of major depression and both education and income (Eaton and Ritter, 1988).

Although the possibility of diagnostic bias is always present, the preponderance of evidence indicates that different disorders characterize those at different socioeconomic levels. Further, those at the lower levels are likely to be characterized by more severe disorders. This explains why early studies concluded that mental disorders were concentrated within lower-income groups; the available statistics were for schizophrenia and from public mental hospitals. It is still felt that schizophrenia, certain forms of depression, and sociopathy are more common among lower-income groups. Manic–depression and anxiety disorders, on the other hand, appear to be more common among upper-income groups. The rate of suicide, it should be noted, is much higher for the affluent than for the nonaffluent. This, however, is generally attributed to differing styles of coping characterizing various socioeconomic groups.

Education. While other socioeconomic indicators are useful for predicting a population's health status, education appears to be the single most important indicator in this regard (Cockerham, 1997). Those at higher educational levels are likely to rate themselves as being in better health than those with less education (National Center for Health Statistics, 1998b: Table 70). Typically, the higher the educational level, the lower the morbidity level. This is true for both acute and chronic physical conditions, with a clear inverse relationship demonstrated between educational levels and major health threats such as cardiovascular disease (Wamala et al., 1999). These relationships also hold for indicators of disability. For example, an analysis of data from the 1996 National Health Interview Survey found an inverse relationship between educational levels and chronic conditions, limitation of activities, and number of bed days for disability.

The pattern with regard to mortality resembles that for income. The death rate for the poorly educated is much higher than for those with higher educational achievement (National Center for Health Statistics, 1998b: Table 36). The age-adjusted death rate for those with less than 12 years of education is three times that for those with thirteen or more years of schooling. Infant mortality, in fact, has been virtually eliminated from the groups with the highest educational levels. The poorly educated, however, account for the bulk of infant deaths. Like the poor, the causes of death for the poorly educated are more likely to be the acute problems typically associated with less developed countries than the chronic conditions characterizing much of American society. Also like the poor, the less educated are likely to be characterized by lifestyle-related deaths such as homicides and accidents. Education, it fact, has been recently shown to demonstrate a stronger influence on mortality than income (Rogers et al., 2000).

The correlation between educational level and infant mortality rates is reflected in differences in low birth weight babies. Nine percent of mothers with less than a high school education deliver low birth weight babies. Mothers with a year or more of college record a figure of 5.5% (National Center for Health Statistics, 1998b: Table 21).

The relationship between educational level and mental illness, like that for physical illness, appears fairly clear-cut. In fact, some researchers have suggested that the social class differentials noted above are a function of differing levels of education. As the level of education increases, there appears to be an increase in the prevalence but a decrease in the severity of disorders. The better educated appear to be more characterized by anxiety disorders, while the less educated appear to be more frequently psychotic. Gallo et al. (1993) found a clear relationship between educational level and the likelihood of depression onset in older adults. Ironically, the rate of suicide is much higher among the better educated, but this is generally attributed to the differing means of coping characterizing various educational levels.

As with income, the relationship does not necessarily reflect the level of income per se but the differential consequences of varying income levels. Those with less education also are likely to have more financial problems, poor housing conditions, and unsafe environments, all contributing to an unhealthy situation (Schrijvers et al., 1999).

Occupation and Employment Status. The relationship between occupation and health status is somewhat more complex than that for the measures of socioeconomic status discussed above. Occupation can be examined in terms of occupational status (e.g., blue-collar, white-collar, professional) or in terms of specific occupations. In the first case, there is a relatively direct and positive relationship between the relative importance of the occupation one holds and health status. In general, the higher the occupational prestige, the better the health status. Those at lower occupational levels tend to be characterized by higher rates of morbidity and disability. Like the poor and the uneducated, they tend to be characterized both by more conditions and by more serious conditions. Levels of disability (as measured by restricted-activity days and lost days from work and school) are higher for lower occupational levels (Marmot et al., 1991).

At the same time, mortality rates and longevity vary directly with occupational status. Past research has consistently found a clear link between mortality and occupational status. A study in Great Britain found a clear link between mortality and occupational status, with age-standardized death rates for the lowest occupational group (unskilled laborers) being approximately twice that of the highest (professionals). The recent research by Rogers et al. (2000) has reaffirmed this finding. The causes of death for those lower in terms of occupational status are similar to those for the poor and uneducated.

Although attempts have been made to link mental disorder with occupational status, the results have been less than satisfactory. Occupational status is a difficult concept to operationalize and is further complicated by American society's complex stratification system. It has been argued that an association exists between occupational status and mental health status in that the lower the former, the higher the latter. Such a monotonic relationship has not been adequately demonstrated, however.

Researchers on this issue have been successful at establishing that both prevalence and types of disorders may be to a certain extent occupation specific (Roman and Trice, 1972). Based on data from treatment records, self-reports, and even suicide records, it has been determined that occupations carry varying risks of mental disorder. Unfortunately, the most concrete examples of this phenomenon relate to conditions that have been omitted from the scope of this discussion (e.g., suicide and alcoholism). Nevertheless, continuing research is likely to uncover other linkages, especially with the increased interest in research on lifestyles and health status.

A second approach to examining the relationship between the conditions of employment and health status involves an analysis of health status in terms of specific industries and occupations. Although this is a highly complex process, it is found that certain industries tend to be characterized by inordinately high levels of both morbidity and mortality. Among the standard industry categories utilized by the Department of Labor, the industry with the highest rate of injuries involving work loss is the transportation–communications–utilities industry. This industry reports 5 injuries per 100 full-time equivalent employees for 1995, compared to a rate of less than 1 per 100 for the finance–real estate–insurance industry.

A similar pattern is displayed with regard to work-related deaths. In 1993, the mining industry reported 25 deaths for every 100,000 workers. This was followed by agriculture–forestry–fishing with 18 deaths per 100,000. This contrasts vividly with the "safest" industry (services), which reported a death rate of around 1 per 100,000.

High-morbidity occupations often include those whose workers are exposed to environmental risks. Similar patterns have been identified for mortality, although the occupations most affected may be different. The single most dangerous occupation is fishing, with 117 deaths per 100,000 workers (1994–1995 average). This occupation is followed by lumberjacks (115/100,000) and airplane pilots (111/100,000). The overall rate for all occupations is only 5 deaths per 100,000 workers (National Center for Health Statistics, 1997). Some professions, such as psychiatry and dentistry, are noteworthy for their high suicide rates.

One other consideration when examining occupational categories is the issue of employment status. This issue may in fact be more significant than occupational differentials. When the employed are compared to the unemployed, clear-cut differences surface in terms of physical and mental illness. The unemployed appear to be sicker in terms of most health status indicators; they have higher levels of morbidity and higher levels of disability than the employed. While it could be argued that poor health leads to unemployment, it has been found that otherwise healthy individuals who have undergone loss of employment often develop symptoms of health problems. In fact, even perceived threats to job security have been found to be associated with an increase in morbidity (Ferrie et al., 1998). It has also been suggested that, among those who cannot find employment, developing an illness serves as something of a rationale for a failure to find work.

Apart from evidence linking unemployment to high suicide rates, little research has been conducted on the relationship between the lack of employment and mortality. However, the recent research by Rogers et al. (2000) has demonstrated that the employed tend to have a lower risk of mortality than the unemployed. Interestingly, the analysis also found that individuals who were not in the labor force (i.e., neither employed nor looking for employment) were at the greatest risk of mortality of all employment statuses.

The same pattern holds for employment status and mental illness. The unemployed tend to be characterized by higher levels of mental illness symptoms than the employed. In fact, for both physical and mental disorders, it has been suggested that the lack of social integration resulting from unemployment serves as a "trigger" for various health problems.

Religion. Perhaps the least well-documented relationship between a demographic variable and health status is the link between religion and health conditions. Religion is relatively poorly studied in US society, and information linking religious affiliation or religiosity with health status is fragmented. However, a growing body of empirical evidence suggests that religious involvement has beneficial effects on health status and mortality rates (Oman and Reed, 1998).

Ecological studies have found a correlation between overall health status and religious affiliation (Fuchs, 1974). In addition, specific conditions have been linked to degree of religious commitment (Jarvis and Northcott, 1987). A recent study (Dwyer et al., 1990) found that religious "concentrations" are associated with lower rates of digestive cancer, respiratory cancer, and overall morbidity. Even more recently, Hummer et al. (1999) found a clear relationship between church attendance and mortality rates. People who never attend church services exhibit a risk of death 1.87 times that for those who attend services 2 or more times per week. This calculates out to a 7-year difference in life expectancy (at age 20) between nonattenders and frequent attenders. These studies also have associated higher frequency of church attendance with lower blood pressure, mortality from cardiovascular disease, and physical disability (Oman and Reed, 1998). The lifestyles of strict religious groups such as Mormons and Seventh Day Adventists have been found to contribute to their higher health status.

Some religion-specific differentials in morbidity that have been found typically are not in terms of overall prevalence but in regard to group-specific conditions. For example, the Jewish population in the United States is characterized by higher levels of some conditions and lower levels of others. However, it is usually argued that these differences reflect cultural variations rather than religious differences.

The findings on mental illness and religion are not particularly clear-cut. For one measure of mental disorder at least—feelings of nervous breakdown—it has been found that the highest rates were among members of fundamentalist denominations, followed by Baptists and Jews (Gurin et al., 1960), although others have uncovered conflicting evidence. In terms of religiosity, it has been found that the more religious are characterized by lower levels of psychiatric morbidity (Stark, 1971).

Research is now underway to determine the impact on the perceived relationship between religious involvement and health status of such factors as lifestyle, diet, psychological well-being, and the availability of social support.

REFERENCES

Bruce, M. L., and Kim, K. M. (1992). Differences in the effects of divorce on major depression in men and women. *American Journal of Psychiatry* 149(7):914–917.

Cockerham, W. C. (1997). *The Sociology of Mental Disorder.* Englewood Cliffs, NJ: Prentice-Hall.

Corti, M.-C., Guralnik, J. M., Ferrucci, L., et al. (1999). Evidence for a black–white crossover in all-cause and coronary heart disease mortality in an older population: The North Carolina EPESE. *American Journal of Public Health* 89:308–314.

Dohrenwend, B. P. (1990). Socioeconomic status (SES) and psychiatric disorders: Are the issues still compelling. *Social Psychiatry and Psychiatric Epidemiology* 25:41–47.

Durkheim, E. (1951). *Suicide.* New York: Free Press.

Dwyer, J. W., Clarke, L. L., and Miller, M. K. (1990). The effect of religious concentration and affiliation on county cancer mortality rates. *Journal of Health and Social Behavior* 31(June): 185–202.

Eaton, W. W., and Ritter, C. (1988). Distinguishing anxiety and depression from field survey data. *Psychological Medicine* 18:155–166.

Essink-Bot, M.-L., Krabbe, P. F., Bonsel, G. J., and Aarsonson, N. K. (1997). An empirical comparison of four generic health status measures. *Medical Care* 32(5):522–537.

Ferrie, J. E., Shipley, M. J., Marmot, M. G., Stansfeld, S. A., and Smith, G. D. (1998). An uncertain future: The health effects of threats to employment security in white-collar men and women. *American Journal of Public Health* 88(7):1030–1036.

Fuchs, V. R. (1974). *Who Shall Live: Health, Economics and Social Choice.* New York: Basic Books.

Gallo, J. J., Royall, D. R., and Anthony, J. C. (1993). Risk factors for the onset of depression in middle age and later life. *Social Psychiatry and Psychiatric Epidemiology* 28(3):101–108.

Gumbiner, J., and Flowers, J. (1997). Sex differences on the MMPI-1 and MMPI-2. *Psychological Reports* 81:479–482.

Gurin, G., Veroff, J., and Feld, S. (1960). *Americans View Their Mental Health.* New York: Basic Books.

Hollingshead, A., and Redlich, F. C. (1958). *Social Class and Mental Illness.* New York: Wiley.

Hughes, M. D., and Gove, W. R. (1981). Living alone, social integration, and mental health. *American Journal of Sociology* 87:48–74.

Hummer, R. A. (1996). Black–white differences in health and mortality: A review and conceptual model. *Sociological Quarterly* 37(1):105–125.

Hummer, R. A., Rogers, R. G., Nam, C. B., and Ellison, C. G. (1999). Religious involvement and US adult mortality. *Demography* 36(May):273–285.

Hyder, A. A., Rotllant, G., and Morrow, R. H. (1998). Measuring the burden of disease: Healthy life-years. *American Journal of Public Health* 88(February):196–202.

Ilfeld, F. W. (1978). Psychological status of community residents along major demographic dimensions. *Archives of General Psychiatry* 35:716–724.

Jarvis, G. K., and Northcott, H. C. (1987). Religion and differences in morbidity and mortality. *Social Science and Medicine* 25:123–140.

Joung, I. M., Van de Mheen, H. D., Stronks, K., Van Poppel, F., and Mackenbach, J. P. (1998). A longitudinal study of health selection in marital transition. *Social Science and Medicine* 46(February):425–435.

Kim, J. S., Bramlett, M. H., Wright, L. K., and Poon, L. W. (1998). Racial differences in health status and health behaviors of older adults. *Nursing Research* 47(July–August):243–250.

Kuo, W. H. (1984). Prevalence of depression among Asian-Americans. *Journal of Nervous and Mental Disease* 161:449–457.

Larsen, C. O., Colangelo, M., and Goods, K. (1998). African-American–white differences in health perceptions among the indigent. *Journal of Ambulatory Care Management* 21(2):35–43.

Lillie-Blanton, M., Parsons, P. E., Gayle, H., and Dievler, A. (1996). Racial differences in health: Not just black and white, but shades of gray. *Annual Review of Public Health* 17:411–448.

Macintyre, S., Ford, G., and Hunt, K. (1997). Do women "over-report" morbidity? Men's and women's responses to structured prompting on a standard question on long standing illness. *Social Science and Medicine* 48(January):89–98.

Marmot, M. G., Davey Smith, G., Stansfield, S., Patel, C., North, F., Head, J., et al. (1991). Health inequities among British civil servants: The Whitehall II study. *Lancet* 337:1387–1393.

McGee, D. L., Liao, Y., and Cooper, R. S. (1999). Self-reported health status and mortality in a multi-ethnic cohort. *American Journal of Epidemiology* 149(January):41–46.

Miller, C. A. (1985). Infant mortality in the US. *Scientific American* 253(1):31–37.

Mookherjee, H. N. (1997). Marital status, gender and perception of well-being. *Journal of Social Psychology* 137(February):95–105.

Moustafa, A. T., and Weiss, M. (1968). *Health Status and Practices of Mexican-Americans. Advanced Report II, Mexican-American Study Project.* Los Angeles: University of California.

National Center for Health Statistics. (1991). Annual summary of births, marriages, divorces, and deaths: United States, 1990. *Monthly Vital Statistics Report* 39(10). Washington, DC: US Government Printing Office.

National Center for Health Statistics. (1997). *Health, United States, 1997.* Washington D.C.: US Government Printing Office.

National Center for Health Statistics. (1998a). Current estimates for the national health interview survey. *Vital and Health Statistics*, Series 10, No. 199. Washington, DC: US Government Printing Office.

National Center for Health Statistics. (1998b). *Health, United States, 1998.* Washington D.C.: US Government Printing Office.

Oman, D., and Reed, D. (1998). Religion and mortality among the community-dwelling elderly. *American Journal of Public Health* 88:1469–1475.

Peters, K., Kuchanek, K., and Murphy, S. (1998). Deaths: Final data for 1996. *National Vital Statistics Reports*, Vol. 47, No. 9. Washington, DC: Centers for Disease Control.

Proctor, S. P., Heeren, T., White, R. F., Wolfe, J., Borgos, M. S., David, J. D., Pepper, L., Clapp, R., Sutker, P. B., Vasaterling, J. J., and Ozonoff, D. (1998). Health status of persian Gulf War veterans: Self-reported symptoms, environmental exposure and the effect of stress. *International Journal of Epidemiology* 27(December):1000–1010.

Ren, X. S., and Amick, B. C. (1996). Racial and ethnic disparities in self-assessed health status: Evidence from the national survey of families and households. *Ethnic Health* 1(September): 293–303.

Roberts, R. E. (1981). Prevalence of depressive symptoms among Mexican-Americans. *Journal of Nervous and Mental Disease* 169:213–219.

Rogers, R. G., Hummer, R. A., and Nam, C. B. (2000). *Living and Dying in the USA: Behavioral, Health and Social Differentials of Adult Mortality.* New York: Academic Press.

Roman, P. M., and Trice, H. M. (1972). Psychiatric impairment among "middle Americans": Surveys of work organizations. *Social Psychiatry* 7:157–166.

Schrijvers, C. T. M., Stronks, K., van de Mheen, D., and Mackenbach, J. P. (1999). Explaining educational differences in mortality: The role of behavioral and material factors. *American Journal of Public Health* 89:535–540.

Shoenbaum, M., and Waidmann, T. (1997). Race, socioeconomic status and health: Accounting for race differences in health. *Journal of Gerontology B: Psychological and Social Sciences* 52(May): 61–73.

Stark, R. (1971). Psychopathology and religious commitment. *Review of Religious Research* 12: 165–176.

Verbrugge, L. M. (1976). Females and illness: Recent trends in sex differences in the United States. *Journal of Health and Social Behavior* 17:387–403.

Verbrugge, L. M. (1989). The twain meet: Empirical explanations of sex differences in health and mortality. *Journal of Health and Social Behavior* 30(September):282–304.

Waidmann, T., Bound, J., and Schoenbaum, M. (1995). The illusion of failure: Trends in the self-reported health of the US elderly. *The Milbank Quarterly* 73(2):253–287.

Wamala, S. P., Mittleman, M. A., Schenck-Gustafsson, K., and Orth-Gomer, K. (1999). Potential explanations for the educational gradient in coronary heart disease: A population-based case-control study of Swedish women. *American Journal of Public Health* 89:315–321.

Ware, J. E., and Shelbourne, C. D. (1992). The MOS 36-item short form health survey (SF-36). 1. Conceptual framework and item selection. *Medical Care* 30:473–483.

Warheit, G., Holzer, C. E., III, and Schwab, J. J. (1975). An analysis of social and racial differences in depressive symptomatology. *Journal of Health and Social Behavior* 14:291–299.

ADDITIONAL RESOURCES

Center for Mental Health Services, US Department of Health and Human Services (1999). *Mental Health, United States, 1998.* Washington, DC: US Department of Health and Human Services.

Centers for Disease Control and Prevention (Weekly). *Morbidity and Mortality Weekly Review.* Atlanta, GA: Centers for Disease Control and Prevention.

Johnson, N. J., Sorlie, P. D., and Backlund, E. (1999). The impact of specific occupation on mortality in the US national longitudinal mortality study. *Demography* 36(3):355–367.

Morgan, K. O., and Morgan, S. (Eds.) (1999). *Health Care State Rankings, 1999*. Lawrence, KS: Morgan Quitno Press.

National Center for Health Statistics World Wide Website: www.cdc.gov/nchswww

Wellner, A. (1998). *Best of Health: Demographics of Health Care Consumers*. Ithaca, NY: New Strategist.

US Department of Labor. (1998). *Occupational Injuries and Illnesses: Counts, Rates, and Characteristics, 1995*. Washington, DC: US Department of Labor.

CHAPTER 11

The Demographic Correlates of Health Behavior and Health Services Utilization

INTRODUCTION

This chapter focuses on the relationship between various demographic characteristics and the response of individuals and groups to health-related conditions. Chapter 10 examined the demographic correlates of health status, and this chapter represents a natural extension of that discussion. *Health behavior* might be broadly defined to include the utilization of formal health services as well as the informal health behavior characterizing a population. Some of these actions are taken by individuals who have been formally diagnosed as ill. However, much health behavior is initiated by relatively healthy individuals who are attempting to maintain or enhance their existing health status or to prevent a decline in health status.

The introductory sections of this chapter summarize the demographic variables that are to be used and provide definitions of various indicators of health behavior and health services utilization. The next section constitutes the core of the chapter and identifies the demographic correlates of health behavior. A final section addresses the meaning of these relationships for health services planning.

HEALTH BEHAVIOR

The concept of health behavior is a relatively new one in both social science and medical circles. The earliest discussions singling out a pattern of behavior in response to health threats are found in the literature in the 1950s. Many consider the early work by Parsons (1951) to be the first scientific treatment of health behavior. Since then, a considerable amount of research has been accumulated on the responses of individuals and groups to ill health. The significance of the concept of health behavior cannot be overemphasized in a society as highly "medicalized" as the United States as the twenty-first century begins.

The concept of health behavior can be interpreted broadly to include virtually any action aimed at restoring, preserving, and/or enhancing an individual's health status. From a medical perspective, the focus is on the formal utilization of health services. Physician visits, hospital admissions, outpatient procedures, and drug prescriptions are typically used as indicators of the volume and types of health behavior. Although this type of indicator is the major focus of this chapter, health behavior also includes such activities as preventive health practices, fitness and wellness activities, self-medication and treatment, and diet-related activities. This discussion, then, necessarily must include the gamut of health behavior from toothbrushing to heart transplantation.

It has become increasingly clear that variations in health behavior reflect variations in demographic characteristics, with the implications of demographics for health behavior even greater than they are for health status. There are enough biological underpinnings to morbidity and mortality to keep them from being totally "social" constructs. The variations in health behavior, however, are infinite and very much influenced by demographic characteristics. Despite a correlation between health status and use of some services, most health behavior is ultimately elective.

Individuals sometimes choose to use health services because these services are ordered; however, if all dimensions of health behavior are considered, it is obvious that a great deal of volition is involved in the use of such services. This is clearly demonstrated by the fact that there are three health status–health services utilization combinations found in US society: those with "real" illnesses who utilize health services; those with real illnesses who do not utilize health services; and those without real illnesses who utilize health services.

The discussion below focuses primarily on the demographic correlates of formal measures of health services utilization. This approach reflects both conventional usage and the fact that data on formal participation in the health care system are more readily available than are data on informal forms of health behavior. However, in those cases where information is available on such activities as dieting, exercise, self-medication, and preventive care activities, their demographic correlates are discussed.

UTILIZATION INDICATORS

Health Services Utilization

This section begins with a description of commonly used indicators of health services utilization. In Chapter 10, outcome measures were discussed in relation to health status, while utilization indicators discussed here frequently are thought of as process measures. The impact of the health care delivery system is measured, in this case, not in terms of the amount of sickness or death found in society, but in terms of the number of surgical procedures performed, drugs prescribed, or hospital admissions recorded. Each of the key utilization indicators will be discussed in turn.

Hospital Admissions

One of the most frequently used process indicators historically has been hospital admissions. By the middle of the 20th century, the hospital had become the center of the US health care system. It is only appropriate that the operation of the system be monitored on the basis of hospital utilization. The terms "admissions" and "discharges" are used to refer to episodes of inpatient hospital utilization. Although they are often used interchangeably to refer to an episode of hospitalization, they technically refer to different processes, one being the act of entering a hospital and the other being the act of leaving a hospital.

Although the numbers are generally comparable, a noteworthy exception is found with regard to maternity cases. One person (a pregnant woman) is admitted to the hospital, but two persons (the mother and newborn infant) are discharged. Given the fact that childbirth is a leading reason for hospitalization in the United States, this distinction becomes important in the tracking of hospital utilization. Other factors that may sometimes result in discrepancies between the numbers of admissions and discharges for a particular institution include the categorization of patients who have expired or have been internally transferred. Most hospitals today follow conventionally accepted guidelines for such definitions. It is important, however, when working with hospital data sets to clarify the criteria used in allocating patients to the admission and discharge categories.

The hospital discharge rate is generally stated in terms of a number per 1000 population. Some other denominator occasionally may be used, or the rate might be converted into a proportion of the population that has been hospitalized. For example, the hospital discharge rate for the United States in 1995 of 86.2 discharges per 1000 population might be expressed in terms of nearly 9 out of every 100 residents (or 8.6%) being discharged from a hospital during that year (National Center for Health Statistics, 1998: Table 87). Although the latter presentation may be more intuitively understandable to the general public, it masks the possibility of multiple discharges on the part of those who were hospitalized more than once in 1995.

Despite a shift from inpatient care to outpatient care, the hospital discharge rate remains an important indicator of the volume of utilization of health services. It serves as a proxy for a variety of other indicators, since hospital discharges are correlated with tests performed, surgeries performed, and other related activities. Since hospital care is so labor- and capital intensive, one discharge carries a great deal of weight in terms of its significance in overall health care expenditures. It is certainly important to health planners because of the investment required for hospital care and the amount of resources that a hospital episode entails.

Under certain circumstances, discharge and admission rates will be provided specific to a particular category of patient. For example, an age-specific hospital admission rate, or one based on area of residence and/or category of diagnosis might be used. Thus, for planning and policy purposes, the admission rate for those under 65 years of age might be compared to that for those over age 65, the rate for Medicare patients compared to that for commercially insured patients or the rate of admission for respiratory problems compared to that for circulatory problems. While such comparisons have utility in their own right, they are particularly useful when comparing admission patterns for different hospitals or different geographic areas. With this information available, the various standardization techniques discussed in Chapter 4 can be applied.

One other consideration is the reporting of hospital admissions by type of hospital. Since there are several different types of hospitals that could be considered, a global indicator such as hospitalization rate per 1000 population masks important distinctions within the numerator. Most of these institutions would be classified somewhat interchangeably as "general," "community," "acute care," or "medical–surgical" facilities. However, there are large numbers of hospitals that do not fall into one of these categories. Included among these are hospitals specializing in a particular problem (e.g., mental illness or tuberculosis), in a particular population (e.g., children or veterans), or in a nonacute type of problem (e.g., chronic care or rehabilitation). Rates of admission to mental hospitals are discussed in some detail later in this chapter.

Patient Days

An indicator of utilization related to hospital admissions is hospital patient days. This indicator is calculated, like hospital admission rates, with respect to the number of patient days generated per 1000 population. In some ways, this indicator is a better reflection of the utilization of resources than is hospital admissions. Measuring patient days serves to adjust for variations in length of stay for various conditions. Two hospitals with comparable admission levels may generate quite different numbers of patient days because of differences in their patient mix. For example, Hospital X and Hospital Y may both report 5000 annual admissions but record patient-day totals of 15,000 and 30,000, respectively. This would happen, for example, if the former were a woman's hospital specializing in obstetrical care and the latter were a general hospital with a more typical patient mix.

Like admission rates, patient days may be calculated in terms of diagnosis, type of hospital, patient origin, and payer category. Changes in reimbursement procedures, in fact, have made the patient day more of a standard unit for resource utilization than the admission episode.

Length of Stay

One other commonly used indicator related to hospitalization is the average length of hospital stay. This is typically reported in terms of the average number of days a patient remains in the facility. For example, the average length of stay (ALOS) at a general hospital in the mid 1990s was around 5.5 days. On the other hand, the ALOS for a maternity hospital might be around 2 days and for a psychiatric facility around 45 days. This indicator has been important historically, since it has been a good measure of resource utilization and because many insurance and governmental health care programs have reimbursed hospitals on a per diem rate. Changes in reimbursement procedures in the mid-1980s, however, have given a different meaning to the average length of stay in that such entities are increasingly limiting the number of days for which they will provide reimbursement. For this reason, hospitals have become more sensitive to ALOS as a predictor of reimbursement levels and as an indicator of the efficiency of their operations.

Nursing Home Admissions

The other major institutional indicator of health care utilization is nursing home admissions, although the increase in availability of home care services and the rise in the popularity of assisted living facilities is changing the distribution of living arrangements for the elderly population. (Interestingly, the term "discharge" is not generally associated with nursing home use.) The nursing home admission rate is usually calculated in the same manner as the hospital admission rate and expressed in terms of nursing home admissions per 1000 population or as a percentage of the population admitted to nursing homes. This represents something of an incidence rate, but quite often a prevalence rate might be found more useful. That is, the level of nursing home use might be expressed in terms of the number of patients resident in nursing homes at a particular point in time, rather than the number of admissions during some time period. In this case, the number of annual admissions is less meaningful owing to the long tenure of most nursing home residents.

The rate of nursing home utilization is often expressed in terms of the population aged 65 years or older. This allows for a more precise depiction of nursing home utilization, as well as comparison between populations with differing characteristics. In addition, a variety of nursing home types are emerging that will require more precise indicators of utilization. Until recently, the two types of nursing homes were those providing actual nursing care and those providing custodial care with medical backup. The introduction of such variations as "step-down" facilities (between a hospital and a nursing home), hospital-based skilled nursing facilities, chronic care facilities, life-care facilities, and geriatric day hospitals has complicated the calculation of this indicator. The extent of these changes reflects the growing significance of nursing care in US society.

Other Facilities Indicators

There are several other facility indicators that also might be mentioned. While not all have the significance of hospital admissions, each is important in its own way. All, in fact, have a particular linkage with some aspect of demographic composition. These additional facilities for which utilization rates may be calculated include hospital emergency rooms, hospital outpatient departments, freestanding emergency centers, freestanding minor medical centers, freestanding surgery centers (surgicenters), and freestanding diagnostic centers. Some of these facilities have come to compete with traditional sources of care, especially hospitals. As the emphasis has shifted toward more outpatient care, these indicators have become increasingly important.

Utilization rates for these facilities may be calculated in the same manner as hospital and nursing home admission rates. In actual practice, however, there seems to be more interest in determining the proportion of the population that uses a particular type of facility during a certain time period. As will be seen, there are demographically based differences in the rates of utilization of these facilities.

Physician Utilization

Perhaps one of the most useful indicators of health services use is the level of physician utilization. The physician, of course, is the pivotal practitioner in the health care system and the "gatekeeper" for most other types of service utilization. This is a more direct measure of utilization levels than hospital admissions in that virtually everyone uses a physician's services at some time. Hospitalization, in fact, is a relatively rare occurrence for most of the population.

Typically, calculations of physician utilization are based on physician office visits. In some cases, however, the level of physician contact might be calculated with the inclusion of telephone contact and physician visits of hospitalized patients. Physician utilization might be calculated in terms of annual visits per 1000 population. For example, a community of 10,000 might be expected to generate 30,000 physician visits per year. More commonly, however, utilization is calculated in terms of the number of annual visits per person or as the proportion of the population that has visited a physician. In 1995, Americans averaged 3.3 physician office visits per year; 80% of the population had visited a physician at least once during the last year (National Center for Health Statistics, 1998: Tables 74 and 77). As will be demonstrated, clear-cut patterns exist with regard to the level of physician use that can be linked to demographic characteristics.

Physician utilization varies by specialty, so in many cases rates for physician visits are figured separately for the various specialties. Primary care physicians are likely to be visited more often than specialists. In fact, planners might gauge the efficiency of an area's health care system by making a comparison of the visit rates for various specialists. Interestingly, specialty utilization varies on the basis of demographic characteristics. Members of groups with certain attributes (e.g., age, income levels, educational levels, ethnic background) display different patterns of physician utilization.

Utilization of Other Health Care Personnel

There are other types of personnel for whom utilization rates might also be calculated. Most of these, like physicians, are independent practitioners who practice without supervision of other medical personnel. Examples of these are dentists, optometrists, podiatrists, chiropractors, nurse practitioners, and physician assistants, as well as various mental health counselors and therapists. Other health care personnel who generally cannot operate independently but for whom utilization rates might be calculated include home health nurses, physical therapists, and speech therapists. The various methods discussed above for calculating utilization levels may be applied to these personnel as well. A visit or utilization rate per 1000, the average number of visits per person annually, or the proportion of the population using the particular type of therapist might be calculated.

These nonphysician practitioners and paraprofessionals have been growing in number at a much faster rate than physicians and are playing a growing part in the provision of care. The roles of many of these practitioners have been expanding, often to the point of competing with physicians for certain types of patients. Their role in the US health care system also is worth noting in that various demographic traits are correlated with utilization of some of these practitioners. For example, individuals who utilize podiatrists generally can be differentiated demographically from those who use orthopedic surgeons for similar problems. The same is true for those who use chiropractors rather than physicians for back problems.

Treatment Rates

Some of the most direct indicators of health services utilization are those calculated for various diagnostic tests and therapeutic procedures. While hospital admissions and physician visits give a general picture of health services use, rates for specific procedures provide a much more detailed description of the functioning of the health care delivery system. Diagnostic procedures include the various clinical tests that are performed to determine the nature and causes of a health problem. A large proportion of them, in fact, are performed on "well" individuals who are simply obtaining routine preventive examinations.

Therapeutic procedures involve the treatments directed toward curing or managing a particular health problem; these are usually categorized as surgical or medical. The former type of procedure is usually "invasive" in that it involves an incision in the patient. Medical procedures are typically those that involve the administration of drugs, topical applications, or some ameliorative treatment such as physical therapy. The trend, however, has been toward performing an increasing proportion of both diagnostic and treatment procedures on an outpatient basis. For example, between 1980 and 1996, the proportion of all surgeries performed on an outpatient basis increased from 16.3 to 59.5% (National Center for Health Statistics, 1998: Table 94). Utilization rates for diagnostic and therapeutic procedures are generally calculated like the rates described above.

Fairly detailed information now is available on procedures that are performed on an inpatient basis. Data from the National Hospital Discharge Survey, the Medicare program, and other sources allow a relatively accurate calculation of use rates. Data on the performance of diagnostic and therapeutic procedures done on an outpatient basis are not as complete. Information on procedures performed in physician offices is fragmented, with the most accurate information being collected through a sampling of cases from physician offices through the National Ambulatory Medical Care Survey. Many other types of outpatient facilities (e.g., freestanding diagnostic centers) are so recent in development that meaningful data are not always available. Nevertheless, enough information is available to develop reasonable estimates for the level for utilization of most outpatient procedures. The surveys referred to in this section are described in Chapter 9.

Given the hundreds of different diagnostic and therapeutic procedures that are performed, utilization patterns are understandably complex. However, when the demographic correlates of utilization are explored, the picture is somewhat simplified. Wide variations exist in use rates for various procedures, and many of these can be linked to demographic factors. Certainly educational and income levels influence the number and type of procedures performed, and many other examples can be cited. Granted, part of the difference in utilization patterns (e.g., from region to region) can be attributed to variations in physician practice patterns. Even these variations can be indirectly linked to the demographic characteristics of the practice's patients. As will be seen, variations in use rates for diagnostic and therapeutic procedures are very much a function of demographic characteristics.

Insurance Coverage Indicators

An indirect indicator of the level of health services utilization is the type and extent of health insurance coverage for individuals and families. Historically, this would have simply involved the calculation of the proportion of the population covered under standard health plans. However, the 1970s and 1980s witnessed a proliferation in the variety of financial arrangements available to cover health services. Traditional insurance coverage, whether through an individual policy or a group policy sponsored by an employer or some other organization, is referred to as indemnity insurance. Since the coverage is usually offered through a for-profit insurer, it is often referred to as commercial insurance. This insurance is strictly reactive and only comes into effect in response to an illness episode. Most indemnity policies, in fact, historically did not go in effect unless the insured was hospitalized. This arrangement, on a not-for-profit basis, has developed into a nationwide network of "Blues" (e.g., Blue Cross).

The Medicare and Medicaid programs were established in the mid-1960s, the former to provide medical insurance for the elderly and the latter to insure the poor. Medicare is available to all citizens aged 65 years and older, to some individuals under 65 if certain conditions are met, and to the disabled. Medicaid, although federally sponsored, is administered through the various states, who provide matching funds. The degree of participation is left up to the individual state, so that a wide range of benefits are available among the states. Individuals must qualify in terms of income to participate in the Medicaid program. There are a few other health care insurance programs that are federally funded, the most important of which is the Civilian Health and Medical Program of the Uniformed Services (CHAMPUS) for military retirees and dependents.

The 1970s witnessed the emergence of several alternative financing mechanisms for the coverage of health care costs, and by the 1980s the concept of "managed care" had become well established. Health maintenance organizations (HMOs), preferred-provider organizations (PPOs), and other alternative forms of financing that attempt to control costs by managing the utilization of physicians and hospitals have become common.

The extent of insurance coverage is important at the societal level, since it is a gauge of the ability of US citizens to pay for the health services they receive. The type of reimbursement available from patients becomes a crucial determinant of revenue for hospitals and other providers. Each type of insurance involves different patterns of coverage, rates of reimbursement, and payment arrangements.

Insurance coverage is typically calculated in terms of the proportion of the population covered by all types of insurance or covered under a particular insurance program. The level and type of coverage may be calculated using either individuals or households as the denominator. A typical breakdown (or "payer mix") may include the percentage of the population covered by commercial insurance, Blue Cross, Medicare, and Medicaid. HMOs and other forms of managed care are now often listed as separate categories. There are a few other miscellaneous categories of coverage (such as state-sponsored worker's compensation programs), and there is also a category for those without coverage, usually identified as either "self-pay" or "no insurance." Although this last group is often referred to as the "medically indigent," the uninsured actually represent a surprisingly diverse population.

The relevance of the discussion here is reflected in the fact that various demographic categories of the population are characterized by different mixes of insurance. The relationship is so strong that if one knows certain demographic characteristics for a particular population, the payer mix can be rather accurately estimated. Conversely, if one has information on the payer mix of a population, it is possible to estimate some of its demographic characteristics. (See Chapter 2 for a more detailed discussion of health care financing.)

Drug Utilization

The level of drug utilization is another indicator that is sometimes used. This typically focuses on the consumption of prescription drugs, since these (rather than over-the-counter medicines) are thought to reflect actual utilization of the formal health care system more closely. While the level of drug prescription can be determined from physician and pharmacist records, rates of consumption of nonprescription drugs must be determined more indirectly.

Rates of drug utilization typically are calculated in terms of the number of prescriptions written, for example, within a given year per 1000 population. Alternatively, the average number of prescriptions written annually per person may be calculated. Moreover, this may be adjusted to include only those persons with any prescriptions written. Occasionally, the level of drug consumption might be estimated based on the quantities of pharmaceuticals prescribed. All these approaches are flawed to a certain extent, due to the fact that a drug prescribed is not necessarily a drug consumed. Rates that are calculated should be seen more as an indicator of activity level of the health care system rather than actual behavior on the part of patients.

In any case, there are important demographic differences in the level and types of drugs prescribed and nonprescription drugs purchased. Part of these differences can be attributed to variations in lifestyles characterizing different groups in society. Interestingly, another part can be attributed to the prescription patterns of physicians in relation to patients with varying demographic traits.

DEMOGRAPHIC CORRELATES OF UTILIZATION

Biosocial Characteristics

Age. Age is considered by many to be the best single predictor of the utilization of health services. Age is related not only to levels of service utilization but to the type of services used and the circumstances under which they are received. This is true whether the indicator is for inpatient care, outpatient care, tests and procedures performed, insurance coverage, or virtually any other measure of utilization. It also is true for measures of informal health behavior.

There are several reasons for the close association between age and health behavior in its various forms. Different conditions are associated with each age cohort, resulting in demands for differing types of services. In addition, age is likely to be related to living conditions and marital status, and these in turn influence both health services utilization and informal health behavior. Another factor is the relationship between age and lifestyle. The attitudes and perceptions accompanying various lifestyles, as well as associated values, have historically changed as individuals age. Attitudes toward one's health and toward the health care delivery system are likely to vary with age. Younger people generally are more accepting of innovations and alternative care arrangements. Older people tend to be more traditional in their use of services and practitioners.

Although it has become conventional wisdom in US society that the consumption of health services increases with age, this primarily reflects the heavy weight accorded to hospital care. The rate of hospitalization for individuals under 45 is very low, with the lowest rate 24.2 per 1000 being recorded by the 5 to 14 age cohort. The only exception to low rates at the younger ages, of course, is for women during their childbearing years. After 45, however, admission rates begin increasing dramatically, with the rate more than doubling from the 15 to 44 age cohort to the 45 to 64 cohort. Those 65 and over recorded and admission rate of 266.9 per 1000 in 1995, a rate ten times that for the least hospitalized cohort. The average length of stay increases significantly from the 5 to 14 age group to the 65 and over cohort, from 5.0 days to 7.1 days (although this difference is substantially reduced over previous years). Historically, the greatest jump in admissions has been at the 60 to 65 age break; however, with the improved health status of the elderly in US society, by the late 1980s age 70 or older had become the breakpoint at which hospital utilization soars (National Center for Health Statistics, 1998: Table 87). Table 11.1 presents data on average length of stay by age and sex.

Within this framework of overall high rates for the elderly and generally low rates for the nonelderly, there are some important variations. To the extent that health problems are age specific, there are conditions that have a very different configuration from that above. Childbirth already has been mentioned as one example; those admitted for tonsillectomies or myringotomies (ear tubes) virtually all are children, while those admitted for alcoholism and drug abuse treatment are more likely to be in the 20 to 35 age range. The most frequent reasons for hospitalization for those under 15 are acute conditions associated with respiratory and digestive systems. For those aged 15 to 44, there are major differences related to sex. Childbirth and related conditions account for nearly half of the female hospitalizations, while injuries and mental disorders are the most common among males. For the 45 to 64 and 65 and over cohorts, heart disease and cancer predominate (National Center for Health Statistics, 1998: Table 90). In terms of emergency room utilization (for true emergencies), teens and those in their early twenties (particularly males) account for a disproportionate share due to injuries and accidents.

Table 11.1. Average
Hospital Stay in Days
by Age and Sex, 1994

Age	Male	Female
Under 1	5.6	6.0
1–4	3.4	3.5
5–14	5.5	4.7
15–24	5.4	3.1
25–34	5.8	3.3
35–44	6.1	4.5
45–64	5.8	5.9
65–74	6.7	7.0
75 and over	7.6	7.8

SOURCE: US Bureau of the Census
(1997), Table 190.

The discrepancy between the elderly and the nonelderly in terms of admissions is magnified with respect to patient days. The seriousness of conditions for which the elderly are hospitalized means that long lengths of stay are common. For example, a general hospital with an average length of stay of 6 days may record an ALOS of 10 days for elderly patients. Alternatively, a hospital that reports that 35% of its admitted patients are 65 or older may find that 50% of its patient days are accounted for by the elderly.

The relationship between nursing home utilization and age is predictable. Few nursing home residents are under 65. However, within the nursing home population itself, there are significant differences in age distribution. Overall, fewer than 5% of those aged 65 and older resided in nursing homes in 1995, a figure that has changed little in the last two decades. However, of those aged 85 and over around 20% were institutionalized. Looked at another way, the age distribution of nursing home residents is around 13% aged 65 to 74, nearly 36% aged 75 to 84, and over 50% aged 85 or older. Thus, as the American population has aged, the average age of nursing home residents has actually increased. Similarly, those 65 and over account for 72% of home health patients, with clients for home health services concentrated in the 75–84 age group. A similar pattern exists with regard to the use of hospice services (National Center for Health Statistics, 1998: Table 86).

Age differences also are found in the use of other types of facilities. Among the older population, there is a preference for inpatient rather than outpatient care. The ingrained notion of better care and a more secure environment among older age cohorts tends to favor hospitalization. On the other hand, tendencies toward utilization of outpatient facilities among the younger age cohorts have developed.

(This preference appears to be increasingly mitigated by the impact of changing reimbursement patterns and the influence of the aging baby boomers.) The primary users of freestanding urgent care clinics, for example, are in the 25 to 40 age group. The under-45 population also is more likely to utilize other outpatient settings, such as freestanding diagnostic centers or surgicenters. These differences are partly a reflection of age-generated differences in perceptions. But they also reflect the fact that younger age cohorts are more likely to be enrolled in some alternative delivery system that mandates outpatient care and to have physicians with more "contemporary" practice patterns than those of the older age groups.

Age differences do exist in the utilization of physician services, although they are not as dramatic as those for hospital and nursing home services. With the exception of the youngest age cohorts, there is a direct relationship between age and number of physician office visits (National Center for Health Statistics, 1998: Table 74). The elderly overall visit physicians 1.5 times as often as the nonelderly taken as a group. Thus, in 1995, those aged 75 and over reported an average of 6.3 office visits compared to 2.0 for the 15 to 44 age group, which recorded the lowest visit rate. This difference reflects the fact that a large proportion of visits for the elderly are for regular checkups and monitoring of chronic conditions and not for acute problems. Table 11.2 presents information on the number of visits by age and sex category.

A significant difference exists in the utilization of specialists by the age of the patient. With increases in age, the utilization rate for primary care physicians decreases and that for specialists increases. The increase in chronic problems with age means that more specialized services are necessary. While populations aged 45 and under are more likely to use general or family practitioners, OB-GYNs, and pediatricians (for their children), the older age cohorts are relatively more likely to patronize medical and surgical specialists such as cardiologists, oncolo-

Table 11.2. Annual Physician Office
Visits by Age and Sex, 1996

Age group	Both sexes	Males	Females
0–14	2.4[a]	2.4	3.2
15–44	2.0	1.4	2.7
45–54	3.0	2.4	3.5
55–64	3.5	3.2	3.8
65–74	5.1	5.0	5.3
75 and over	6.3	6.8	6.0
Total	2.7	2.3	3.1

[a]Average office visits per year.
SOURCE: US Department Health and Human Services
(1998), Table 81.

gists, and urologists. Thus, the age structure of the population becomes a key factor in the types of physicians needed by a particular community.

Age is probably the best predictor of the types of services that will be utilized. Although some diagnostic tests and therapeutic procedures may be performed throughout the age spectrum, most clinical procedures carry a particular age configuration. For example, some tests and procedures are typically performed only on children. Women of childbearing age tend to be virtually the only users of certain other tests and procedures. In general, diagnostic procedures are less frequently performed on those under age 45 than they are on those over 45. Box 11.1 addresses an important issue in the aging of the population.

Insurance coverage in terms of both its presence and type varies with age. With the insurance coverage patterns in the 1990s, the elderly were the one group with essentially universal coverage because of Medicare. On the other hand, householders aged 25 and under were the least well insured of any age cohort. Differences in type of coverage also can be identified. Older age cohorts (e.g., 45 and older) are more likely to have traditional indemnity insurance, including Blue Cross, than are those under 45. The under-45 group is more likely than the older group to be enrolled in a health maintenance organization or some other form of managed care. As the number of uninsured has grown over the past few years, the number of children without health insurance has increased disproportionately. In 1997, 10.7 million children age 18 or younger did not have health insurance (US Bureau of the Census, 1999).

Although there are some exceptions, utilization of prescription drugs tends to increase with age. This reflects the use of drugs for the management of chronic health problems, which tend to accumulate with age. Those aged 65 and older constitute the age cohort with by far the highest rate of prescription drug use. In fact, frequent assertions of overuse of drugs by the elderly population are made. The current debate over drug coverage by Medicare reflects the significance of this issue.

The population aged 65 and over is markedly different from younger age cohorts in terms of most of its health behavior. In addition, there are several linear relationships, such as breakfast eating (percentage going without declines with age), perceived stress (declines with age), and heavy drinking (declines with age). Other factors show less clear patterns, though differentials do still exist. The percentage having never smoked is highest at the youngest and oldest ages. The percentage considering themselves somewhat or very overweight is highest among old persons. Table 11.3 presents a breakdown of health behavior by age and sex.

As can be seen in the table, there are some large differences in health-related behaviors across age groups and between sexes. For example, the percentage of both males and females who eat breakfast almost every day increases from about 44% to 85% between the age intervals 18–29 and 65 and over. In addition, men are

Box 11.1

The Elderly Are Not as Old as They Used to Be

The aging of the American population is a more complex process than meets the eye. Gross measures such as the increasing percentage of the total population that is 65, 75, or 85 years old and over or the rise in median age tells only part of the story. Even focusing on the population aged 50, 60, or 65 and above and examining the age structure of those populations leaves important information aside. The older population is younger than it used to be.

A confusing claim? Not really. At the turn of the century, and even only 50 years ago, a man or woman who was age 65 or over was "old." Many had lived "hard lives," working in dangerous and physically demanding occupations, and few imagined living to, much less beyond, "retirement" age. Many men never retired. They just worked until they died. Women outlived their husbands but not by many years.

While the latter part of the twentieth century has been filled with concerns over environmental pollution, a rise in exposure to toxic products, and calls for healthier lifestyles, the average elderly person today is healthier than her or his parents in an absolute sense (increased life expectancy at age 60, 65, 70, and beyond and lower morbidity rates) and from subjective evaluation. That is, health status based on self-assessment is rising for the elderly population. Overall, persons reaching age 50 or 60 can expect more person years without serious illness and disability than in previous generations, and they feel better about their health.

The resulting "younger" older population has been the target of a number of health services providers and many more organizations that try to affiliate their products or services with healthy lives. Whether it be an advertisement for Centrium and "it is a great time to be silver," or a pitch to look 20 years younger by having a facelift, marketers of health care "products" push to have their offerings associated with being a fit and attractive senior. Healthy "behavior," whether it be exercising or taking the right kind of dietary supplements, is believed to result in better health. Undoubtedly, some of those efforts to look and feel better not only result in elderly who report that they feel better (and report an increase in self-assessed health status), but in fact cause them to be physically better off because they are exercising more or eating healthier foods.

Because there is a self-fulfilling dimension to the process of being a healthier senior, thinking one is a healthier senior, and exhibiting behavior that is consistent with both the physical and physociological dimensions of health, there is every reason to believe that the elderly, in general, will continue to be healthier. This fact should not be lost on any organization that offers health products or services targeted to the older population.

Table 11.3. Health Behavior by Age and Sex, 1990

| Health behavior | Sex | Age[a] | | | |
		18–29	30–44	45–64	65 and over
Eat breakfast almost every day	M	45	45	59	86
	F	43	50	63	85
20% or more over desirable body weight	M	20	32	38	26
	F	16	25	34	28
Had a Pap smear in the last year (females only)	F	64	55	44	30
Experienced a moderate or a lot of stress in last 2 weeks	M	57	64	52	28
	F	64	69	61	37
Currently smoke cigarettes	M	29	34	29	15
	F	25	26	25	11
Had two or more drinks a day in the last 2 weeks (on average)	M	10	10	10	8
	F	2	2	2	2
Wore seatbelts all or most of the time	M	56	64	64	67
	F	67	74	72	72

[a]Figures expressed as a percentage.
SOURCE: US Department of Health and Human Service (1993).

more likely than women to smoke and are more likely to average two or more alcoholic drinks a day over the last 2 weeks.

As was the case with physical illness, the quantity and type of mental health services utilized vary dramatically with age. The very young use few such services, while the utilization rate for other cohorts varies widely. In terms of inpatient care for the mentally ill, the elderly historically have been overrepresented, although this may be a reflection of selective data. By the 1970s, young adults had become overrepresented among psychiatric inpatients. This shift reflects changes in institutionalization policies and the redefinition of certain behaviors as mental illness. In 1996, the highest inpatient admission rates to all facilities were for the 25 to 44 cohort. By far the lowest rates were for the 18 and under cohort and the 65 and older cohort (National Center for Health Statistics, 1998: Table 97).

The inclusion of alcoholism, drug abuse, and suicide under the heading of mental illness has created a "bulge" in the 15 to 25 age cohort. Attributing many symptoms of aging to Alzheimer's disease has reduced the perceived prevalence of mental illness among the elderly. Further, the advent of adolescent treatment centers has meant that many more teenagers are being defined as mentally disturbed than in the past. Trends such as these have served to cloud the association between age and mental illness treatment.

All these factors tend to muddy the waters with regard to the relationship between mental illness and aging. In fact, it may be impossible to clearly discern a positive or negative relationship between the variables. It therefore may be appropriate to focus not on overall prevalence but on the distribution of mental illness among age cohorts by type of disorder. Even here, quality data on outpatient treatment are lacking.

For outpatient care overall, the 15 to 35 age cohort appears to dominate. However, this pattern is probably more a function of help-seeking by females in these age cohorts than of mental problems in this age group overall. The picture is further complicated when source of treatment is considered. Those using community mental health center services, which have become the most common settings for care, tend to have demographic characteristics different from those using psychiatrists or psychoanalysts. Further, those using medical doctors or clergymen for mental health counseling are also characterized by differing demographic characteristics.

Sex.   In US society, females are more active than men in terms of health behavior and are much heavier users of the health care system. Women are heavier consumers of health services, in fact, regardless of the indicator used. They tend to visit physicians more often, take more prescription drugs, and use other facilities and personnel in general more often. Further, women in US society are more active with regard to informal health behavior. They tend to be more conscious of proper diet and other keys to wellness and are more active when it comes to preventive health care.

Part of the heavier use attributed to females in US society in the 1990s can be explained by the higher reported levels of morbidity. As noted in Chapter 10, women report more symptoms and more illness episodes than men. The relative complexity of their reproductive systems also necessitates more use of health care. It also should be noted that women are more conscious of the health services that are available and are more willing to use them. It appears that sex role differentiation in US society has encouraged use of health services by females and discouraged their use by males.

Utilization of services also can be measured in terms of how long, on average, people stay in a hospital. While hospital stay comparisons can be misleading, especially if shortened-stay trends overall are not considered, there are compositional differences worthy of note. The hospital admission rate was comparable for males and females in 1995, with reported rates of 88.5 and 84.8 per 1000, respectively. The pattern for length of stay is similar, although males tended to remained hospitalized 1⅓ times as long as females on the average. As noted earlier, Table 11.1 presents data on average length of stay cross-classified by age and sex. As might be expected, the average length of stay increases substantially for both sexes as people age. While the average stay for females aged 25 to 34 is

4.2 days, at the ages 75 and over the average stay is 9.4 days. At the younger ages (but beyond age 4), males have longer stays. However, at the older ages, beyond age 65, females have longer stays, and at age 75 that difference is more than one-half day on average.

The average number of annual physician encounters (for all physicians) for females in 1995 was 6.1, compared to 4.9 for males (National Center for Health Statistics, 1998: Table 74). The average number of office visits in 1995 for females was 3.7 compared to 2.7 for males. Obviously, the rate of utilization for the range of specialties varies by sex. OB-GYNs are utilized almost exclusively by females, while men are overrepresented among the patients of urologists. Similar rate differentials are found for other health care practitioners. For example, females use dentists at a rate 1.25 times that of males.

Women also tend to be hospitalized at a slightly lower rate overall than are males. The hospital admission rate for males in 1995 was 88.5 per 1000 males and 84.8 per 1000 females in the population. Much of the female hospitalization can be accounted for by childbirth, which remains one of the leading causes of hospitalization. When tertiary care is examined, males tend to be particularly predominant. Although males become sick less often than females, they are more likely to contract serious conditions, perhaps as a result of later diagnosis. For example, in 1995 the male admission rate for heart disease was considerably higher than that for females. Females averaged 5.3 days per hospital stay in 1995, compared to 6.0 days for males. The shorter length of stay associated with many "female" conditions tends to reduce the patient days generated by females (National Center for Health Statistics, 1998). Males, particularly adolescents and young adults, are more likely to utilize hospital emergency rooms for true emergencies, primarily owing to the large number of injuries and accidents occurring among this sub-population.

Despite comparable admission rates females tend to be subjected to twice as many procedures on the average once admitted. This differential primarily reflects the heavy use of service by obstetrical patients, and when the older age cohorts are examined, it is found that among those 65 and older males are subjected to a much greater number of procedures.

Females comprise the majority of nursing home admissions. The nation's nursing home population is nearly 75% female. For the 85 and over cohort, the female proportion is over 80% (National Center for Health Statistics, 1998: Table 95). This reflects the fact, discussed in Chapter 5, that there is a preponderance of females at the older age levels. The higher mortality rate for males, coupled with the lower survival rate for males who do become ill means that there are more female candidates for nursing home admission. Further, males surviving into the older age cohorts are likely to have a wife to care for them. This is not true for females surviving to advanced ages; they typically outlive their spouses.

The distribution of insurance coverage historically has not been related to sex, although most recent data show that 14.8% of females lack health insurance compared to 17.6% of males (US Bureau of the Census, 1999). Insurance policies typically involve family coverage, so calculations are made in terms of the head (presumably male) of the household. With the changes that have occurred in household and family structure during the last third of the twentieth century, this stance requires modification. The dramatic increase in the numbers of female-headed households is a particularly important factor. Many households that are without insurance or are covered only under the Medicaid program fall into this category. In addition, because of mortality, and therefore life expectancy differentials, the majority of Medicare participants are female. The nature of the female component of the population thus must be taken into consideration in planning for health services.

Females are much heavier users of prescription drugs in the United States than are males. This partly reflects the greater participation of females in the health care system and their more assertive behavior in seeking out cures. However, if calculations are made eliminating those who have received no prescriptions, females still retain an edge. One explanation offered for this has been the historical practice patterns of physicians. A tendency for physicians (typically male) to prescribe more drugs for females than for males, all other things being equal, has been documented.

Females tend to be much heavier users of mental health services than are males. Females are more likely to see symptoms in psychiatric terms and more likely to present themselves for treatment. This predominance, however, primarily reflects use of outpatient services; when inpatient mental health care is examined, males appear to be heavier users of these services. Females exhibit higher levels of utilization regardless of the type of therapist. For psychiatrists, clinical psychologists, social workers, and even general practitioners and clergymen, females constitute the majority of the patients–clients.

In terms of psychiatric hospital admissions, females do not hold the same edge as for outpatient services. As shown in Table 11.4, females have slightly higher admission rates to private psychiatric hospitals and general hospitals but significantly lower admission rates to public mental institutions. This is explained to a certain extent by contemporary patterns of mental hospitalization. The conditions most likely to warrant institutionalization are the extreme psychotic conditions such as schizophrenia and manic–depression. Males tend to have higher rates of the former and females of the latter. However, depressed patients are much more likely to be admitted to general hospital psychiatric wards than they are to mental hospitals. Women therefore turn up less often in the mental hospitalization statistics.

In addition, by the late 1980s, substance abuse had become a leading cause for mental hospital admission. The various types of substance abuse tend to be much more common among males than females. The apparent discrepancy between outpatient and inpatient treatment rates for women reflects the greater likelihood of their being admitted to a private mental facility. Males are proportionately more likely to be admitted into public facilities. For both inpatient and outpatient mental health treatment, females are overrepresented among those voluntarily seeking care and males among those involuntarily seeking care.

Race and Ethnicity.   A correlation has been found between racial and ethnic characteristics and the utilization of certain types of health services. The most clear-cut differences have been identified between the health behaviors of African Americans and whites. Certain Asian populations and ethnic groups also display somewhat distinctive utilization patterns. To a limited extent, differences in utilization may be traced to differences in the types of health problems experienced. However, many of the differences reflect variations in lifestyle patterns and cultural preferences. For some racial and ethnic groups, in fact, differences in health care utilization patterns may have little relationship to differences in health status.

The hospital admission rate for whites tends to be around 20% lower than that for African Americans, despite the older age structure of the white population. In 1995, the hospital admission rate for whites in the United States was 84.2 per 1000 population. This compares to a rate of 108.0 per 1000 African Americans (National Center for Health Statistics, 1998: Table 87). Other racial and ethnic groups tend to display rather idiosyncratic patterns for admission rates.

Although whites generate a greater number of patient days per 1000 population than African Americans, their average number of patient days per hospital episode is not that different from the figure for African Americans. In fact, when African Americans are hospitalized, they tend to record longer lengths of stay, presumably because they have more serious conditions on the average at the time of hospitalization. As with admissions, there is no consistent pattern with regard to patient days and length of stay for other racial and ethnic groups.

Whites are overrepresented among the nursing home population. While whites account for approximately 83% of the US population, in 1995 they accounted for over 91% of the nursing home population. African Americans and other racial and ethnic groups tend to be underrepresented, although Hispanics increasingly report a pattern similar to that of non-Hispanic whites (National Center for Health Statistics, 1998). The underrepresentation among African Americans is particularly telling in view of the heavy burden of chronic disease and disability affecting this population. These differences are partially explained in terms of the ability to pay for care, since nursing home care is not satisfactorily financed in this country. In fact, nursing home care is typically paid for out-of-pocket or through the Medicaid program. That means that nursing home residents are either relatively affluent or relatively poor. The absence of African Americans, Asian Americans, and various other ethnic group members from nursing homes, however, is probably more a reflection of cultural preferences and the relatively strong family and social support systems that characterize some ethnic groups than it is of economic factors. It also may reflect the higher mortality rates characterizing certain nonwhite populations prior to the elderly years.

In general, whites tend to utilize physicians at a rate higher than the rest of the population. In 1995, whites in the United States averaged 3.4 physician office visits; this compares to 2.6 for African Americans. Thus, while African Americans constitute 12.6% of the US population, they only account for 10.5% of the physician office visits despite higher rates of both acute and chronic conditions (National Center for Health Statistics, 1998). Whites are particularly overrepresented among the patients of specialists. African Americans are overrepresented among the patients of obstetricians, but underrepresented among the clients of ophthalmologists and orthopedic surgeons. African Americans are nearly twice as likely to utilize emergency room services as are whites. These differences in utilization patterns reflect differences in lifestyle, income, education, access to care, and cultural preferences. Some ethnic group members (Hispanics, for example) utilize alternative types of care in the form of "traditional" healers. Thus, their physician utilization rate does not provide a full picture of their health care utilization. In fact, recent information on the use of alternative therapies by Americans suggests that the conventional wisdom concerning the utilization of clinic services requires review (Eisenberg and Kessler, 1993).

Differences are found in the types of tests and procedures performed on members of various racial and ethnic groups. Some of these differences may reflect the perceptions and practice patterns of providers in their management of members of various groups. It has been found, for example, that African Americans are likely to be subjected to more invasive forms of treatment than whites, all things being equal. At the same time, African Americans are less likely to receive major diagnostic and treatment procedures compared to whites with the same problem. This pattern has been found for both physical and mental disorders. It is believed, however, that this is more a reflection of the socioeconomic status of the patients and the conditions under which care is received than a function of racial differences (Harris et al., 1997). While the proportion of the older female population receiving mammograms had equalized between whites and African Americans by 1995, Hispanic woman remained much less likely to receive this type of diagnostic test (National Center for Health Statistics, 1998: Table 80). Whites are also 1.5 times more likely to obtain regular dental services than are African Americans or Hispanics.

There are large differences in insurance coverage in terms of racial and ethnic characteristics, although these too are thought in large part to reflect economic differences. In 1997, 12.0% of non-Hispanic whites, 21.5% of African Americans, 20.7% of Asian Americans, and 34.2% of Hispanics did not have health insurance (US Bureau of the Census, 1999). Whites tend to have higher levels of commercial and Blue Cross insurance than African Americans and members of certain other groups. To a great extent this reflects differences in employment levels, since most private insurance is provided through employment. The proportion of Medicaid coverage is higher for African Americans than for other racial and ethnic groups. Hispanics represent an interesting situation, in that they often have low levels of insurance but are willing to pay high out-of-pocket costs to obtain care.

Whites are also heavier consumers of prescription drugs. This partly reflects their heavier use of physician services that might lead to the prescribing of drugs. It also reflects the fact that whites constitute a higher proportion of the elderly than they do of the general population. Selective mortality within younger age cohorts leaves fewer African Americans to suffer the chronic conditions of old age. Members of most other racial and ethnic groups tend to use prescription drugs at a much lower rate than whites. This pattern essentially holds for over-the-counter drugs as well.

The rate of institutionalization for psychiatric treatment is much lower for whites than for nonwhites. This is true whether the site of institutionalization is the government mental institution, a private psychiatric facility, or the psychiatric ward of a general hospital (National Center for Health Statistics, 1998: Table 97). This is true for the second largest racial–ethnic group—Hispanics—as well. It should be noted that African Americans face a greater likelihood of involuntary commitment to psychiatric facilities, and this accounts for some of the difference in hospital utilization.

Other ethnic groups display disparate patterns of utilization for mental health care. Jews, for example, tend to be heavy users of many types of mental health services. Chinese and Japanese Americans, on the other hand, are underrepresented in all mental health treatment settings.

Sociocultural Characteristics

Marital Status. Marital status is a relatively effective predictor of health behavior and the utilization of health services, just as it is of health status. Marital status is related not only to levels of service utilization but to the type of services utilized and the circumstances under which they are received. This is true whether the indicator is for inpatient care, outpatient care, tests and procedures performed, insurance coverage, or virtually any other measure of utilization. It also is true for measures of informal health behavior. The categories of marital status included in the discussion below will be never married, married, divorced, and widowed.

There are several reasons for the close association between marital status and health behavior in its various forms. As indicated in Chapter 10, the level of health status within the population is closely related to marital status. Different levels of morbidity are associated with each marital status category, resulting in demands for differing levels and types of services. Further, lifestyle characteristics vary with marital status, and this includes not only the behavioral aspects of lifestyle but the attitudes–perceptions–preferences component as well. These factors, along with the values associated with various marital statuses, probably have more of an impact on health behavior than do actual differentials in morbidity.

Utilization of health services probably correlates better with health status differences in the case of marital status than for any other demographic variable. However, there are some exceptions to this that reflect the living arrangements and access to social support of those in various statuses. In general, the married require fewer services because they are healthier. Yet, they consume more of certain types of services because they are more aware of the need for preventive care, are more likely to have insurance, and it is argued have some significant other to encourage them to use the health care system.

The social support provided by marriage works in two ways. First, it serves to forestall the need for intensive care by providing an environment that retards the progression of disorders. Second, social support serves to encourage individuals in the use of preventive care. The latter is particularly important in the case of informal health behavior. The married are more likely to be characterized by healthy lifestyles, and to a certain extent this reflects the presence of social support agents that encourage this behavior. The never-married, divorced, and widowed, on the other hand, are more likely to be characterized by negative health behaviors (Umberson, 1987).

The age-adjusted rate of hospitalization for married individuals is relatively low. Admission rates for the never married also tend to be relatively low, while those for the widowed and divorced are high by comparison. If rates of admission for various conditions are considered, the variation among marital statuses is even more pronounced. The pattern identified for the various marital statuses in terms of patient days is similar to that for admissions. Observed differences in length of stay, however, probably reflect factors other than marital status. Box 11.2 focuses on the health implication of the large number of single person households in the United States.

The relationship between nursing home utilization and marital status is one of the most clear-cut to be discussed in this section. Few nursing home residents are married. The bulk of nursing home residents are widowed, although there are small numbers who are divorced or never married. Married individuals requiring nursing care are often maintained in the home and cared for by a spouse.

Some differences also are found in the use of other types of facilities on the basis of marital status. The never-married are more likely to use innovative service offerings, while the married are somewhat more traditional in their orientation. However, income and educational levels no doubt play a role here.

Some differences related to marital status do exist in the utilization of physician services, although they are not as dramatic as those for hospital and nursing home services. Based on 1988–1990 data, the widowed report by far the

---

Box 11.2

No One Else at Home? The Delivery of Health Care at Home

Historically, the delivery of many health services has relied on a caregiver at home to assist in the process. Whether it be a mother who sees that her child gets "plenty of rest" and "drinks enough liquids" when that child has a cold or a spouse who provides transportation to her husband who has just had hip replacement surgery, having a person at home to help during these times is essential to successful convalescence. Moreover, family members and live-in friends also provide the psychic support so often needed when someone has been ill.

At the end of the twentieth century, there were about 26 million persons in the United States who lived alone, up from about 11 million in 1970. Given that there are approximately 105 million households nationwide, this means that more than one in five households was made up of a single person. Is this the product of late twentieth-century demographic trends? Yes. Were there health care implications for single person households? Absolutely.

When health care consumption and related health care behavior are considered, the site of consumption is a vital concern. Nearly 60% of all surgeries today occur on an outpatient basis. And while outpatient procedures tend to be less invasive than their inpatient counterparts of a decade or two ago, extended convalescence and care is often required. In addition, the increase in the number of chronic conditions that need to be managed due to aging of the population means that there also has been an increase in the number of persons who "need help" in managing their conditions. Without a person at home, or someone close by, the process of healing or managing a condition is made much more difficult.

Health care providers and health policymakers must consider the single-person household when instructions are given for the safe administration of drugs, or in addressing larger issues such as national or state level support for home health care provision. There is a long history of research that shows that older people want to live at home and do not wish to be institutionalized in nursing homes. Modern medicine, improvements in other health-related services, and lifestyle changes foster the opportunity to live at home longer. However, living alone serves as a barrier to meeting this desire and limits the ability of such individuals to benefit from home care.

---

greatest number of physician contacts; the never-married report the least (Collins and LeClare, 1996). The rate of contact for divorced and separated women is slightly higher than that for the never married. This may be one of the few cases in this chapter in which utilization corresponds to health status. The rate of physician contact for males is lower than that for females in every marital status category, although little difference exists from one marital status to another for men. Some differences exist in the utilization of specialists by the marital status of the patient, but these are not great.

The patterns of utilization of dentists and other health professionals are similar for the various marital statuses. While the married have fewer dental problems, they are more regular users of dentists than are the other marital status categories. The unmarried are overrepresented among those using mental health professionals (Gove, 1979). Otherwise, no clear-cut marital status differences are found for the use of podiatrists, chiropractors, and physical therapists.

Insurance coverage, in terms of both its presence and type, varies with marital status. The married have by far the best insurance coverage, typically with a commercial or Blue Cross plan. Increasingly, married individuals are opting for enrollment in a health maintenance organization or some other form of managed care plan offered through their place of employment. Never-married individuals are the least likely to have insurance of any type, with the divorced and widowed intermediate. Medicare coverage is somewhat higher among the divorced and widowed because they are older on the average than the married and never-married. Unmarried heads of household have the highest rate of Medicaid coverage.

Although there are some exceptions, utilization of prescription drugs tends to be higher for the married. This partially reflects the higher use of physician services on the part of the married. Those in the unmarried categories are found to have higher rates of utilization of nonprescription drugs.

Income.   Income is probably one of the better predictors of health behavior and the utilization of health services. Income is related not only to levels of service utilization but to the types of services used and the circumstances under which they are received. This is true whether the indicator is for inpatient care, outpatient care, tests and procedures performed, insurance coverage, or virtually any other measure of utilization. It is also true for measures of informal health behavior.

Social class, as measured by income, demonstrates a close association with health behavior in its various forms. As indicated in Chapter 10, the distribution of health problems within the population is highly income specific. There is a direct and negative relationship between income level and outcome measures such as morbidity and mortality. This results in a demand for health services that varies in level and type of service on the basis of income. In addition, income is likely to be related to living conditions and lifestyle, and these in turn influence both health services utilization and informal health behavior. Attitudes and perceptions, as well as health care values, have been found to vary by income.

Hospitalization rates tend to decrease directly with income and in fact greater discrepancies exist among the various income groups than for any of the other demographic variables examined. The rate of hospitalization for the groups with the lowest income in the United States is the highest of any income group, reflecting the higher incidence of health problems. The hospitalization rate is 140.7 per 1000 for those in households averaging less than $15,000 annual income in 1995 compared to 61.6 per 1000 for the highest income group (National Center for Health Statistics, 1998: Table 87). Further, after admission, the length of hospital stay also is longer on the average for members of the lowest income group.

The differences noted for admissions and length of stay reflect the types of conditions for which different income groups are admitted. These differences further appear to reflect disparities in lifestyle. The higher fertility levels of the lower income groups result in a higher rate of admissions for childbirth and related problems. The relatively unhealthy and unsafe environments in which the lower income groups are likely to live result in a higher rate of emergency admissions, especially for children. Admission rates for psychotic conditions and substance abuse problems tend to be higher for the least affluent. The pattern of longer stays for the less affluent is complicated somewhat by unexpected cases of shorter lengths of stay for lower income patients because of their limited ability to pay for services.

The relationship between nursing home utilization and income is not very clear-cut. In fact, the more affluent and the least affluent are likely to be more highly represented among the nursing home population than those in between. This is partially explained in terms of the patient's ability to pay. Nursing home care is typically paid for either out-of-pocket or through the Medicaid program. This would suggest that nursing home residents are either relatively affluent or relatively poor.

Income differences also are found in the use of other types of facilities. Lower-income groups are heavier users of hospital emergency room care, especially for nonemergency conditions. This phenomenon is explained by the lack of family physicians among lower-income patients, the lack of accessible services other than emergency rooms in inner-city areas, the hospital emergency room's obligation to provide treatment, and the now well-established cultural preference for emergency room care. On the other hand, lower-income populations are less likely to utilize freestanding emergency clinics or urgent care clinics. This is presumably due to a lack of knowledge of their availability (they are often located in suburban areas) and the fact that payment is typically demanded when care is rendered.

The primary users of freestanding urgent care clinics, interestingly enough, are middle- and upper-middle-income households. Patients on either end of the spectrum are infrequent urgent care center users. The moderately affluent also are more likely to use other outpatient settings, such as freestanding diagnostic centers or surgicenters. Members of these groups are likely to be highly mobile, to not have an established physician relationship, and to be supportive of innovative and/ or cost-effective forms of care.

In the past, significant differences have existed in the utilization of physicians in relation to income. Historically, the number of annual physician visits per capita increased with income, although the highest income groups always represent something of a anomaly. The lowest income groups tended to be infrequent users of physician services. This reflected a lack of family physicians and the use of alternative sources of care such as public health clinics. This situation has changed due to the availability of government-sponsored insurance programs and efforts at offering physician services in underserved communities. By the 1980s, the rate of physician utilization by income had essentially equalized, and by the mid-1990s the low-income groups reported utilization rates comparable to or greater than those for the high-income groups (National Center for Health Statistics, 1998). However, the lower-income groups continue to be underrepresented among the patients of private practice physicians and overrepresented among emergency department users.

A significant difference exists in the utilization of specialists by the income of the patient. As income increases, the utilization rate of primary care physicians decreases and that of specialists increases. This is something of a reflection of the fact that the affluent are likely to be somewhat older than the nonaffluent and thereby have more chronic conditions. It also reflects the prestige accorded to medical specialists. Their presumed greater expertise and their higher fees make them appealing to the well established. Of course, the advent of managed care has limited the influence of individual volition in the selection of physicians.

The patterns of utilization of dentists and other health professionals are similar to those for physicians. There is direct and inverse relationships between income and dental care. The more affluent see dental care as a preventive service, while the least affluent see it as an expensive service only to be used in emergencies. No clear-cut income differences are found in the use of podiatrists, physical therapists, and mental health counselors. Chiropractors tend to be patronized primarily by those from working-class backgrounds.

Income also has usefulness as a predictor of the types of clinical services that will be used. Although diagnostic tests and therapeutic procedures are typically performed as necessary in the eyes of the physician, many clinical procedures have a particular income configuration. For example, the nonpoor report a mammography rate 1.5 times that of the poor (National Center for Health Statistics, 1998: Table 80). This disparity is further evidenced by the high proportion of elective surgery performed on the affluent. Cosmetic surgery and such elective procedures performed to improve the appearance of the affluent are almost never performed on the poor.

The relationship between insurance coverage and income is fairly clear-cut. The more affluent the person, the better the coverage typically is. The lowest-income groups are the least well insured in terms of commercial insurance. They do, however, often qualify for Medicaid coverage, which covers some of their health care needs. By the late 1980s, the group with the least tenable position insurance-wise was the "near poor." This is the working-class population that may not have employer-sponsored insurance owing to the nature of their employment while not being poor enough to qualify for Medicaid. Middle-income groups are more likely to be enrolled in a health maintenance organization or some other form of managed care owing to the nature of their employment status. A newly emerging group of underinsured involves the postemployment–pre-Medicare population. This includes those individuals in the 55 to 65 age range who have left the labor force (and employer-sponsored insurance) but are not yet eligible for Medicare benefits (Pol et al., 2000).

Although there are some exceptions, use of prescription drugs tends to increase with income. This reflects the fact that the affluent visit private physicians more frequently than the nonaffluent. Since drugs are the treatment of choice, few affluent individuals leave the physician's office without a prescription.

Education. The relationship between education and health behavior resembles that of income, although some of the relationships are stronger. In fact, some have suggested that utilization differentials linked to income actually reflect educational differences. Educational level is probably one of the better predictors of health behavior and the utilization of health services. Education is related not only to levels of service utilization but to the types of services used and the circumstances under which they are received. Educational attainment demonstrates a particularly close association with health behavior in its various forms.

As indicated in Chapter 10, the distribution of health problems within the population is to a certain extent associated with educational levels. There is a direct and negative relationship between educational level and outcome measures such as morbidity and mortality. The relationship between education and health care utilization is even stronger in many ways. In addition, education is likely to be related to living conditions and lifestyle, and these in turn influence service use and informal health behavior. In fact, educational level may have more of an influence on lifestyle differentiation than does income. Attitudes and perceptions, as well as values, have been shown to vary with educational level.

The rate of hospitalization for the least educated segments of the US population is very low, despite the fact that the incidence of health problems is greater for the poorly educated than for any other group. The better educated, although less affected by health problems, have much higher rates of hospitalization. This is thought to be a function of a greater appreciation of the benefits of health care and more insurance coverage on the part of the better educated.

The relationship between nursing home utilization and education is not very clear-cut. Educational differences are found, however, in the use of other types of facilities. Less-educated groups are heavier users of hospital emergency room care, especially for nonemergency conditions. On the other hand, better-educated populations are more likely to use freestanding emergency clinics or urgent care clinics. The better educated also are more likely to use other outpatient settings, such as freestanding diagnostic centers or surgicenters. Those with higher educational levels are likely to be highly mobile and to be supportive of innovative and/or cost-effective forms of care.

Significant differences exist in the utilization of physicians in relation to education. Physician use is considerably higher for the best educated than for the least. In general, the number of annual physician visits per capita increases with education. The lowest educational groups record the lowest rates of physician visits.

A significant difference exists in the utilization of specialists by education of the patient. As education increases, the utilization rate for primary care physicians decreases and that of specialists increases. This partly reflects the prestige accorded to medical specialists and the knowledge required to select a specialist. The presumed greater expertise of specialists makes them appealing to the well educated.

The patterns of utilization of dentists and other health professionals are similar to those for physicians. There are direct and inverse relationships between education and dental care. The better educated see dental care as a preventive service, while the least educated are less likely to appreciate its benefits. No clear-cut educational differences are found in the use of optometrists, podiatrists, and physical therapists. The use of various types of mental health counselors tends to increase with education. Chiropractors tend to be patronized primarily by those with lower educational backgrounds.

Education is something of a predictor of the types of clinical services that will be utilized. Although diagnostic tests and therapeutic procedures are typically performed as necessary in the eyes of the physician, certain clinical procedures that have a correlation with income also are differentiated on the basis of education. This is reflected in the high proportion of elective surgery performed on the better educated.

Insurance coverage in terms of both its presence and type varies with education. The better educated the individual, the better the coverage typically is. The lowest educational groups are the least well insured in terms of commercial insurance. They often do qualify for Medicaid benefits, however, which cover some of their health care needs. The better educated are more likely to be enrolled in a health maintenance organization or some other form of managed care, due to the nature of their employment.

Although there are some exceptions, utilization of prescription drugs tends to increase with education. This reflects the fact that the better educated visit the physician more frequently than the poorly educated. Box 11.3 addresses several issues concerning lifestyles and other behavioral correlates of health. Box 11.4 examines selected health behaviors of America's youth.

Box 11.3

Behavioral Risk Factors: The Decline of Smoking in the United States

There are a host of behaviors that have been linked to increased morbidity, lower levels of satisfaction with one's health and ultimately to shorter life expectancy. While the rule of moderation holds for most behaviors, in some instances any risk at all linked to some behaviors is seen as undesirable. At the end of the day, we all know that too much drinking, being overweight, driving without a seatbelt, working with or near carcinogens, and eating ill-prepared foods, among other things, can be deleterious to one's health. And, we also know that some behaviors are worse than others; for example, not brushing one's teeth twice a day is not as risky as having unprotected sex with multiple partners.

Issues related to behavioral risk are confounded by the fact that there is not always agreement with behavioral guidelines within the medical community, and medical research oftentimes suggests that behavioral recommendations be altered. With regard to the former, there is considerable debate over how often a woman should have a mammogram once she reaches age 40. The American Medical Association, following the recommendations of the American Cancer Society, has established guidelines of annual mammograms for women age 40 and over. However, many physicians and a number of researchers disagree that an annual mammogram beginning at age 40 is the standard to follow. With regard to behavioral recommendations, recent research has shown that a moderate level of alcohol consumption (e.g., two beers an evening, several evenings per week) is linked to a lower incidence of heart disease. The researchers do not recommend that all nondrinkers begin drinking, but clearly this research indicates that a higher level of alcohol intake than was previously thought is not only acceptable but has some health advantage.

There are several behaviors that are known to be related to more frequent sickness and quicker death, and moderation is not recommended. Cigarette smoking is one of those behaviors and the one that has received the greatest amount of

---

Occupation and Employment Status. Occupation can be examined in terms of occupational status (e.g., blue collar, white collar, professional) or in terms of specific occupations. In the first case, there is a relatively direct and positive relationship between the status of the occupation one holds and health status. In general, the higher the occupational prestige, the better the health status. Occupational status is related, in turn, to levels of service utilization, the types of services used, and the circumstances under which they are received. This is true whether the indicator is for inpatient care, outpatient care, tests and procedures

attention in the popular media in recent years. The recent tobacco settlements, including the amount of money going to each state as well as limitations in how the money can be spent, have been both praised and criticized. Praise is given because the settlements are seen as tobacco's acknowledgment that proper use of their products results in sickness and death. Critics note, however, that the amount of money agreed upon was not enough and the restrictions placed on how the money can be spent are too limiting. For example, the most successful antismoking campaign targeted toward and created by teenagers in Florida cannot, by agreement, be duplicated in other states.

The table below indicates the percentage of persons smoking by age and sex for three time periods: 1965, 1985, and 1995. Younger teens, whose percentages have increased in recent years, are not included in the table. As the table shows, smoking percentages are higher for males than females in all three time periods, although a great deal of convergence is seen in the 1995 data. More important, percentages have dropped sharply since 1965. Levels of smoking for males 18 to 24 years of age declined by nearly half, for example. While the rates are clearly lower in 1995, it is still the case that about 25% of the adult population smokes cigarettes. Cigarette smoking continues to be one of the most serious health concerns for individuals as well as for public health in the United States.

	Males			Females		
	1965	1985	1995	1965	1985	1995
18–24 years	54.1[a]	28.0	27.8	38.1	30.4	21.8
25–34 years	60.7	38.2	29.5	43.7	32.0	26.4
35–44 years	58.2	37.6	31.5	43.7	31.5	27.1
45–64 years	51.9	33.4	27.1	32.0	29.9	24.0
65 years and over	28.5	19.6	14.9	9.6	13.5	11.5

[a]Percent of persons in this sex/age group who are current smokers.
SOURCE: US Department of Health and Human Services (1998), Table 62.

performed, insurance coverage, or virtually any other measure of utilization. It also is true for measures of informal health behavior.

There are several reasons for the close association between occupation and health behavior in its various forms. Different levels of morbidity are associated with each occupational status category, resulting in demands for differing levels and types of services. An important factor related to occupational status is its implications for lifestyle. Because of the importance of the economic system in US society, occupation becomes a key factor in the shaping of the individual's

Box 11.4

The Health Risk Behavior of America's Youth

Risky behavior has been the trademark of America's youth for at least several generations. There are some elements of our culture that dismiss certain behaviors as acts of the "young" and in some instances encourage other behaviors that are known to be unsafe. The concept of the "immortal teen," the young person who dismisses the possibility that she or he can get sick, injured, or killed in an automobile accident, or be permanently affected as a result of some behavior is well-understood in American society. Nevertheless, parents, researchers, and policymakers are very interested in these behaviors because they are aware of the negative consequences that may follow.

One of the difficulties in connecting risky behavior to negative outcomes lies in the timeframe in which medical problems arise. While the negative effects of driving a car while intoxicated may be realized immediately, the sickness that may result from cigarette smoking may take several decades to materialize. In a society where most youth are short-term oriented, the warning of problems that might occur 20 or 30 years later may well fall on deaf ears. Even risky behavior that is linked to immediate consequences is accepted because the negative consequences are not a certainty. Not everyone who drives without a seatbelt and has a traffic accident is injured or killed.

Of persons 12 through 21 years of age, over one quarter have had two or more drinks in a row and nearly 30% have driven an automobile after drinking in the last month. About one third wear seatbelts, although females (38.6%) are more likely than males (29.1%) to wear them. Over 30% have used an illegal drug once in their lifetime, 27.5% marijuana, and 5.9% cocaine. Nearly one half have smoked at least one cigarette in their lifetime. Concerning health behavior perceptions, over 43% of young females and 24% of young males consider themselves to be overweight.

While it is clearly understood that some persons over 21 years of age engage in risky behavior, in general the prevalence of risky behavior is higher in the youth population. These behaviors are a concern not only to the persons who engage in this behavior and their parents, but to the society in general that live with the aggregate outcomes (e.g. higher rates of lung cancer in the future) of these behaviors.

SOURCE: US Department of Health and Human Services (1995).

worldview. The attitudes and perceptions associated with various lifestyles, as well as values, vary with occupational status.

To a limited extent, the use of health services by members of the various occupational status categories corresponds with the differentials in health status identified. Other demographic attributes concomitant to occupational status, such as income and education, also tend to influence health behavior and the use of health services. In general, those in higher occupational categories require less services because they are healthier. Yet, they use more of certain types of services because they are more aware of the need for preventive care and tend to have better insurance coverage. Occupational status seems to be particularly important in terms of informal health behavior (e.g., diet and exercise) owing to the influence of coworkers.

The rates of hospitalization for various occupational categories demonstrate patterns similar to those for the income categories discussed above. That is, the higher occupational groups have somewhat higher admission rates. Note that this also might reflect the fact that age increases with occupational status. If rates of admission for various conditions are considered, the variation among occupational statuses becomes more pronounced.

The pattern identified for the various occupational statuses for patient days is comparable to that for admissions. However, the lower-status occupational categories make up for any differences in admissions by recording more patient days. Differences in length of stay for the various occupational categories reflect differences in the reasons for admission.

The relationship between nursing home utilization and occupational status probably reflects income differences more than any other variable. The section on income above should be consulted. Some differences are found in the use of other types of facilities on the basis of occupational status. Income and educational levels no doubt play a role here, and the type of insurance coverage available (which is primarily a function of employment status) is important in the type of health service.

Some differences related to occupational status do exist in the utilization of physician services. Despite the higher incidence of health problems among the lower occupational statuses, these individuals tend to use physicians, dentists, and other health professionals less often than higher occupational groups. Here, as above, income, education, and insurance coverage play an important role in the use of physician services. Some selectivity does occur with regard to certain health professionals. Those in lower occupational statuses are more likely to use chiropractors than those in higher ones. While those in lower-status occupations use fewer outpatient mental health services than those at higher statuses, despite greater identified need, the counselor of choice is seldom a psychiatrist. Less formal sources, such as social workers or clergymen, are likely to be accessed.

Insurance coverage in terms of both its presence and type varies considerably with occupational status. This, in fact, is one of the keys to differentials in service utilization. The extent of insurance coverage generally increases with occupational status. There are important exceptions, however, in unionized occupations where those in relatively low status positions have extensive coverage. Enrollment in a health maintenance organization or some other form of managed care plan offered through the place of employment has been more characteristic of the higher occupational levels in the past, but such options had become common except at the lowest occupational levels by the late 1980s. Those in the lowest occupational levels are likely to be the least insured of any of the employed. Small-scale employers and many service occupations do not offer insurance for their employees. Individuals in these situations find that Medicaid is not available to them either, since they are not indigent enough to qualify. The fact that over 40 million Americans had little or no insurance in the late 1990s reflects low levels of insurance coverage at this occupational level.

Although there are some exceptions, utilization of prescription drugs tends to be higher for those at higher occupational levels. This partially reflects the more frequent use of physician services on the part of these groups. Those in the lower occupational categories are found to have higher rates of utilization of non-prescription drugs.

Differences in health behavior based on employment status are probably greater than those among the various occupational categories. When the employed and unemployed are compared, the employed have significantly higher admission rates, despite the greater level of morbidity identified for the unemployed. The unemployed, in fact, use less of all types of health services. The only exception might be higher use of hospital emergency rooms and public health facilities.

The primary explanation for this differential, of course, is the lack of insurance on the part of the unemployed. Commercial insurance is usually employer-sponsored, and the purchase of policies on the part of individuals is financially prohibitive. The inability to pay for services becomes an important determinant of utilization. This situation is complemented by lower educational levels and a lack of appreciation on the part of coworkers concerning the need for various health services.

The unemployed also are likely to be characterized by informal health behavior that contributes to the poor health status. They are less likely than the employed to eat and sleep properly, to exercise, and to abstain from risk-increasing behavior such as smoking and drinking.

Religion and Religiosity. Associations between religious affiliation and/or degree of religiosity with health behavior are probably the most idiosyncratic of those discussed in this chapter. These relationships have been subjected to limited research so that clear patterns are difficult to discern. Further, in US society in the late twentieth century, religious affiliation and participation tend to

Box 11.5

Market Responses to Health Services Demand

There are a host of health products that have received a significant boost because of changes in the composition of the US population. While most of these are related to shifts in the age structure, other compositional changes also are important. Life insurance, health insurance, and other insurance-related products are frequently modified in response to existing and predicted compositional changes and related behavioral components.

Industry concerns are being raised regarding the patchwork and highly tiered insurance services structure likely to confront baby boomers early in this century. The overall system will require modification of private sector insurance packages supplemented by public sector supports for both routine care and catastrophic backup. Insurance companies are beginning to provide a constellation of services that reflect these needs, though some have been slow to react. Among the considerations for companies providing health care coverage are all the issues surrounding healthier and longer-living retirees. The age structure of retirees is getting older, and therefore more expensive to insure; other factors such as the trend toward earlier retirement, changes in the Medicare program, and increases in average health care costs have added considerable complications. In particular, the aging population is boosting the demand for long-term health care policies.

The aging of the population has also been linked to growth in residential development for retirees. One emphasis in this industry has been the incorporation of health services as an inherent component of the retirement center. Concomitant developments include the introduction of long-term care insurance for individuals and insurance to cover assisted living and nursing home costs in excess of those covered under government programs. On the institutional side, the retirement center business is highly specialized and markedly different from that of the acute care hospital.

Other products are the natural outgrowth of the interaction between the changing tastes and research advances in medicine. To the extent that the public desires healthier lives, services such as wellness centers and exercise clinics have become increasingly popular. Research advances include an increased understanding of the relationships among behavior, environment, and morbidity and mortality. As these relationships become better understood and the public expects better health, products will be offered to facilitate behavior that contributes to lower levels of morbidity and increased life expectancy.

be associated with so many other variables that it is difficult to tease out the influence of these variables per se.

There appears to be little difference in the rate of hospitalization for the major religious groups in the United States. Rates of admission for Catholics, Jews, and Protestants overall have not been found to vary much. There are some patterns specific to particular religions. Jews, for example, are found to have higher rates of psychiatric treatment, particularly outpatient, than other religious groups. (This incidently is in contrast to the finding that Jews have the lowest rate of psychiatric impairment of the three groups.) In another study, Catholics and Baptists were found to have higher rates of admission to public mental hospitals than other denominations. Differences in utilization rates of physicians by religious affiliation are probably related to other factors than religion. Jews report higher use of psychiatrists and other medical specialists, and this is thought to be attributable to both cultural preferences and higher socioeconomic status.

Limited research has been conducted on the relationship between religiosity and health behavior. There is too little information available to make concrete distinctions between patterns of health care utilization and informal health behaviors of those with various degrees of religious commitment. There have been some studies that link religiosity with choice of hospital when there are different religion-affiliated facilities available. The most that can be concluded, however, is that for some religiously committed individuals hospitals supported by their denomination are preferred over other hospitals. The strength of this relationship is probably not such that one would want to predicate health planning decisions on it. Box 11.5 addresses several issues concerning market responses to shifting demand for health services.

REFERENCES

Collins, J. G., and LeClere, F. B. (1996). Health and selected socioeconomic characteristics of the family: United States, 1988–90. *Vital and Health Statistics*, Series 10, No. 195. Washington, DC: US Government Printing Office.

Connolly, J. (1988). Long-tern care market called conservation. *National Underwriter* 92(July 4):7, 40.

Eisenberg, D., and Kessler, R. C. (1993). Unconventional medicine in the United States. *New England Journal of Medicine* 328:246–252.

Gove, W. R. (1979). Sex, marital status, and psychiatric treatment: A research note. *Social Forces* 58:89–93.

Harris, R., Andrews, R., and Elixhauser, A. (1997). Racial and gender differences in the use of procedures for black and white hospitalized adults. *Ethnicity and Disease* 7:91–105.

National Center for Health Statistics. (1998). *Health, United States, 1998*. Washington, DC: US Government Printing Office.

Parson, T. (1951). *The Social System*. New York: Free Press.

Umberson, D. (1987). Family status and health behaviors: Social control as a dimension of social integration. *Journal of Health and Social Behavior* 28(September):306–319.

US Bureau of the Census. (1997). *Statistical Abstract of the United States, 1997*. Washington, DC: US Government Printing Office.

US Bureau of the Census. (1999). Website, URL: http://www.census.gov/hhes/hlthins/hlthin97/hi97t2.html.

US Department of Health and Human Services. (1993). Health promotion and disease prevention: United States, 1990. *Vital and Health Statistics*, Series 10, No. 185. Washington, DC: US Government Printing Office.

US Department of Health and Human Services. (1995). Health risk behaviors among our nation's youth: United States, 1992. *Vital and Health Statistics*, Series 10, No. 192. Washington, DC: US Government Printing Office.

ADDITIONAL RESOURCES

Barton, L. J. (1997). A shoulder to lean on: Assisted living in the United States. *American Demographics* (July):45–71.

Center for Mental Health Services. (1998). *Mental Health, United States, 1998*. Washington, DC: US Department of Health and Human Services.

Dortch, S. (1997). America weighs in. *American Demographics* (June):39–45.

Gochman, D. S. (1997). *Handbook of Health Behavior Research*, Vols. I–IV. New York: Plenum Press.

Health Care Financing Administration. (1998). *1998 Data Compendium*. Washington, DC: US Department of Health and Human Services.

Moskowitz, D. B. (Compiler) (1999). *1999 Heath Care Almanac & Yearbook*. New York: Faulkner and Gray.

Rockett, I. R. H. (1994). Population and health: An introduction to epidemiology. *Population Bulletin* 43(4). Washington, DC: Population Reference Bureau.

Walker, T. C., and Miller, R. K. (1999). *1999 Health Care Market Research and Strategic Planning Handbook*. Norcross, GA: Richard K. Miller & Associates.

Wellner, A. (1998). *Best of Health*. Ithaca, NY: New Strategist.

CHAPTER 12

The Future of Health Demography

INTRODUCTION

As we enter the twenty-first century, health demography is a rapidly evolving discipline. Changes in the discipline are being driven by the actions of policy-makers, health care providers, business entrepreneurs, and patients themselves. The perspectives offered by these diverse parties are changing the ways we think about health care, as well as the ways in which health care is delivered. Physicians may still make the decisions that account for over 60% of the care that is provided, but they are increasingly being forced to share power, risk, and decision-making responsibilities with a variety of other individuals and organizations.

Health care has never before experienced the degree of change that the past decade has wrought. In fact, it is likely that no industry has undergone as much change as rapidly as health care has realized in recent years. These changes have included, among others, the emergence of major for-profit chains, rapid consolidation of providers into a few megasystems, the corporatization of physician practices, the emergence of major employers as significant players, the redirection of the system from inpatient care to outpatient care, and the emergence of managed care as a dominant financial arrangement. The hospital and physician have been removed from the central core, and many decision-making responsibilities have been taken on by nonclinical entities. Insurers, who once bore all the risk for the cost of care, are now sharing that risk with providers and consumers.

Perhaps the major development of the past decade, and the one with the most long-term demographic implications, has been the shift from an emphasis on "medical care" to an emphasis on "health care." This shift has affected the manner in which illness, patients, and treatment are perceived. It has influenced our notions of disease causation and the manner in which health conditions should be managed. More than anything, however, it has served to broaden our notion of the boundaries of health and health care. If health professionals have not yet become convinced of the importance of the demographic dimension of health care, this paradigm shift surely will reinforce the importance of population characteristics for an understanding of both health status and health behavior.

While most public policymakers and members of the general public believe that access to high-quality health care is a right of all Americans, the introduction of business principles and practices into the management of care over the past 15 years has changed the health care system in ways that sometimes run counter to this belief. Physicians and other health care providers today find themselves at the center of powerful and contradictory forces. In fact, the industry continues to be characterized by internal contradictions that make understanding—much less broad reform—almost impossible.

Perhaps the most significant of these is the dilemma posed by the contrast between clinical notions of "quality" and the demands of financial exigency. On the one hand, providers are trained and socialized to diagnose, cure, and manage diseases using the best methods and latest technology available. On the other hand, managed care organizations and others who pay for patient care are demanding that the cost of care be reduced. Although clear excesses on the care side have been documented, there is a growing criticism of efforts to continually cut costs. It is worth noting that the most efficacious approaches to addressing the tension involved in providing high-quality but cost-effective care requires an in-depth understanding of health demography.

HEALTH-RELATED DEVELOPMENTS

As we begin the twenty-first century, at least four noteworthy factors will continue to influence the direction of health demography. First, the relationship between business practices and the clinically oriented delivery of care will continue to evolve. While managed care organizations and other health insurers will seek greater efficiencies, health care providers and patients will emphasize the importance of the non-economic aspects of health care. Greater patient and provider protections are likely to emerge in part through national and state legislative action (e.g., the proposed consumer "bill of rights").

Second, new medical technology and the introduction of new therapeutic procedures will continue to alter how and where disease diagnosis, management, and cure are carried out. On the one hand, these advances will act to drive down the cost of care, for example, by reducing the length of hospital stay for certain procedures. The dramatic shift from inpatient to outpatient settings for care for a wide range of procedures is, in part, the result of improved technology. On the other hand, advancements in medical technology drive up the cost of care as "tests where there were no tests before" emerge and "procedures where there were no procedures before" become accepted. As new technologies become more widespread, the "bar" that identifies acceptable practice is continually raised.

Third, while there always has been a great deal of data on health and health care available to researchers and policymakers, the more recent deluge of information makes it possible to study, document, and describe many dimensions of health care in ways that were impossible in the past. Yet, while health demographers and health professionals have access to much more data than ever before, there are still important gaps in the information available, and the challenge of managing and exploiting the existing information remains. The evolution of the business–medicine relationship, as well as the measurement of the effect of technological advances on the cost of care, will require a broadening of the types of data collected and greater sophistication of data analysis. Much of the data needed is demographic or demographically related in nature.

Finally, the reemergence of health planning at both the community and organizational levels must be considered. Clearly, since the early 1990s, there has been revived interest in communitywide health planning. This is evidenced by the increase in the number of citations in the literature, including Internet listings. It is evidenced by appearance in the content of professional meetings and by the level of public discussion that is now occurring. Most important, it is evidenced by activities on the part of both public and private entities who, while perhaps not using the term, are acting as if they were "planning."

The reasons for this renewed interest are complex and reflect the changing nature of the health care system itself. Among the factors encouraging interest in health planning are (1) an emphasis on local, community-based approaches to health issues; (2) the obvious failures of the laissez-faire approach applied to health care; (3) identified deficiencies in public health; (4) the abuses and excesses that have occurred in the private sector; (5) the costs of providing health services under current conditions; and (6) the perceived ineffectiveness of the health care system overall. The attention (and the threat of legislation) brought to the topic by the Clinton Administration's ill-fated health care reform initiative has no doubt been a contributor to this renewed interest.

At the community level, public health agencies are being asked to become much more proactive in dealing with their areas of responsibility, especially in the light of certain perceived failures of the public health system. They are being pressured to become more strategically oriented in order to intervene more effectively with regard to public health issues. Finally, they are being held to higher standards of accountability while facing greater demands for data. All these factors call for much more of a planning orientation, which in turn calls for greater reliance on demographic concepts, methods, and data.

Private sector health care organizations face an even greater level of urgency in this regard, although for quite different reasons. The competition that has become so heated in health care already has served to weed out some of the "unfit-test." This dog-eat-dog environment is clearly not going to dissipate. Add to this the necessity of adapting to a managed care environment and in its most extreme manifestation to a capitated payment system, the need for sophisticated planning capabilities becomes apparent. As with the public sector, health services planning begins with a sound foundation in demographic concepts, methods, and data.

Virtually all the changes occurring in the health care environment have implications for health demography. These changes are fostering new require-ments for health data and a mandate to examine the demand for and the delivery of health services from a variety of perspectives. Health care providers are being held accountable for their actions in ways never before seen. Accrediting bodies, standards agencies, and managed care providers demand that protocols be fol-lowed and documented and that all costs be justified. The compilation and analysis of information on health behavior, subjective health status, and patient satisfac-tion, for example, are becoming "standard" for most providers, as insurance companies and other interested parties attempt to "grade" providers for a host of reasons (Atlantic Information Systems, 1998).

The relatively recent emphasis on measuring health outcomes also requires a different approach to existing data and the collection of new data. While outcomes research is designed to help decision makers improve the delivery of care, the research is also driven by managed care entities and others who seek greater efficiencies and reduced costs. Although it is possible to increase efficiency and improve the level of care at the same time, many current efforts to reduce cost are thought by some to threaten the quality of care provided (Kimberly, 2000).

The introduction of business practices into the provision of health care has greatly increased the level of competition seen in the industry. Hospitals try to "out-nice" competitors by creating flowery images of their staff and rooms via television advertising. Hospitals often vie with one another by offering the same services as competitors, even when the size of the market does not justify a duplication of services. Not surprisingly, this competition often focuses on demo-graphically delineated groups. The media has provided extensive coverage of attempts to tap the women's market, the geriatric market, the ethnic market, and the baby boomers. If the market is not directly demographic, as in the case of a payer category (e.g., commercial insurance), there are likely to be indirect demo-graphic aspects that need to be taken into consideration. After all, the commer-cially insured are demographically different from the Medicare and self-pay populations. Even if no link is obvious between demographic traits and health services utilization, successful competition rests on the ability to determine the message and the medium that is most appropriate for a target audience, and this is likely to be a function of the demographic traits of that population.

As part of this change in the competitive environment, new partnerships are being formed and reformed on a frequent basis. Real and virtual networks of providers are becoming the norm. These networks often are created to generate referrals to a hospital for services ranging from blood tests to the transplantation of organs. The ebb and flow of activities in these networks is rapid, and physician and staff membership in many of these clinics is often short-lived. In many US metropolitan areas, two or more competing networks have emerged to "stake out" a presence in rapidly growing geographic areas. These networks often experience a great deal of physician, staff, and patient turnover as the geographic areas grow and evolve and their patient bases undergo transition. Changes on the part of employers with regard to managed care providers (employees rarely have any input into this decision) further add to the churning processes as patients find that their current physician is not listed as a provider on their newest health plan.

A major shift has occurred in regard to the end-users of health services involving the transformation of the "patient" into the "consumer." Patients are obviously those who are already using the health care system. Consumers may or may not be using the system and in fact may be only potential patients. Consumers have different attributes than patients and the differences are likely to be demographically derived. An impoverished, frail 85-year-old *patient* represents a different category of senior than the affluent, active 65-year-old *consumer*. This distinction holds throughout the demographic spectrum.

This transformation has been given another twist by the creation of the category of health plan enrollee. The significance of thinking in terms of enrollees rather than patients has to do with the fact that the "relationship" between patient and provider exists *prior* to any episode of illness. Most in the health plan at any point in time are not sick but they nevertheless need to be considered with regard to service provision and financial efficacy. Under this scenario, the "best" enrollees for a health plan are going to be determined demographically.

Another development along these lines has been the introduction under managed care of capitated payment arrangements. Under capitation, a health care provider is responsible for a specified set of services for a specified population for a specified level of reimbursement. Such an approach requires that all parties—providers, managed care plans, employers—have a reasonable understanding of the health status and health behavior patterns of this specified population. Of course, the best predictor of these attributes is the demographic profile of the affected population.

Today, there is a growing emphasis on markets as the notion of service area has given way to "market area." The market area could range from a very small geographic unit served by a pharmacy, for example, to a national or even international market served by a pharmaceutical company or a hospital chain. The market that is profiled should be in keeping with the scope of the organization being planned for.

There may be situations in which the market area is not clear cut and a certain amount of research may be required to define the market that is to be cultivated.

In most cases, the market will be delineated by geography. Certainly local health care providers will be restricted to a relatively circumscribed geographic area. On the other hand, the market may actually involve broad population segments and, except for national boundaries, may not be related to geography at all. Thus, a retail pharmacy mail-order business may have a national market defined in terms of population characteristics that exist independent of geography.

In situations in which the market is not closely linked to geography, the emphasis is often on demographically defined markets. As national health care chains have become increasingly active, their basic approach to expanding their customer base has been through the identification of specific demographic groupings. For example, the market may be made up of active, younger seniors or of women of childbearing age. In either case, the characteristics of the market will be determined initially independent of geography (except for the limitation of national boundaries). Thus, the characteristics of younger seniors or women of childbearing age will be identified in terms of the above dimensions and *then* linked to geography for the spatial dimension.

The new emphasis on markets increases the importance of the market segmentation process. Ultimately, most marketing initiatives are going to involve target marketing in which subsegments of the population are singled out for cultivation. Market segmentation on the basis of demographics is the best known of the approaches to identifying target markets. The links between demographic characteristics and health status, health-related attitudes, and health behavior have been well established. For this reason, demographic segmentation is always an early task in any market analysis. Even when market segmentation is based on geography, psychographics, payer mix, or usage levels, the demographic dimension is not far away.

A form of market segmentation unique to health care involves targeting population groups on the basis of their payer categories. The existence of insurance coverage and the type of coverage is a major consideration in the marketing of most health services. Health plans cover some services and not others, and this becomes an important consideration in marketing. For elective services that are paid for out of pocket, for example, a highly targeted marketing approach is required. The payer mix of the market area population has now come to be one of the first considerations for many marketing planning activities. Realistically, examining the market in terms of payer mix means thinking, indirectly at least, in terms of demographic characteristics. Is there any question that the demographic characteristics of those in managed care plans are different from those covered under Medicare or Medicaid?

Today, the extent to which the demographic perspective has taken root in the industry can be seen in the actions of entities at polar opposites within the health care spectrum. Public health agencies are now thinking in terms of markets for their services. This represents a dramatic shift in the approach characterizing public health agencies and mandates increasingly improved access to a growing range of data. As public health agencies have become more active in the provision of primary care—and many are providers under the Medicaid program—they have had to adopt the demographic analysis techniques long common in other industries.

Conversely, the direct-to-consumer approach adopted by pharmaceutical companies, illustrates how health service and product providers have changed their thinking about "customers and markets." The data needs of market-oriented organizations are different from organizations driven by other forces, as markets are defined demographically, geographically, psychographically, and behaviorally.

Another important dimension of the evolving health care environment is the urgency attached to certain public policy issues related to health care. Proposals for raising the age of eligibility for Medicare from 65 to 67, allowing persons under age 65 to "buy in" early to Medicare, broadening Medicaid benefits, extending health insurance benefits to children who have no health insurance, and offering or restricting state health benefits to certain populations significantly alter the "use" of health services. The changing age structure of the population of the United States is making it nearly impossible for political officeholders to continue to put off needed change in programs like Social Security and Medicare. Any politician who appears in the eyes of the potential voters to be reluctant to "save" Social Security or Medicare considerably increases the probability of an early exit from office. In regard to these two programs, the question of "if" has evolved to the questions of "when" and "how."

DEMOGRAPHIC TRENDS

The demographic shifts noted at many junctures in this volume must be added to the mix. The changing demographic characteristics of the population determine the level of demand for services to a large degree. The politician who signs on to help save Medicare also must deal with the rise in Medicare costs that will make the program account for about 25% of the federal budget by 2030 (Wilensky and Newhouse, 1999). Changes specific to demographic segments of the population must be considered. Aging rural populations, ethnically diverse urban populations, and the poor populations of inner-city areas bring with them unique health care needs. Recent research and policy-oriented statements have focused on the dissimilarities in treatment modalities and health outcomes for Anglos, African Americans, Asian Americans, and Hispanics (Association for Healthcare Research and Quality, 2000). The long term regional and national implications of disparate patterns of care across racial and ethnic groups become clearer when one accounts for the fact that all these ethnic populations are growing at a faster rate than the Anglo population.

Shifts in health behavior and health status that are specific to demographically defined segments of the population further complicate the situation. The incidence of smoking seen in teenagers, for example, can help predict the prevalence of chronic bronchitis and subsequent health complications in the future. The aging baby boom population continues to overeat and get too little exercise. At the same time, this cohort lines up in record numbers for face lifts, liposuction, "tummy-tucks," and other elective procedures designed in part to counteract the physical toll exacted by unhealthy behavior. As baby boomers continue to age, the connection between demography and health behavior in all likelihood will result in more use of existing elective procedures while driving the development of procedures not yet available.

The growth of the elderly population need not be belabored at this point. The elderly represent the fastest growing segment of the US population and the oldest-old are the fastest growing subcohort. The demands of this population are already placing pressure on the Medicare system, and the baby boomers—looming as the largest cohort of seniors ever—are not far behind.

Public and private sector entities not only must plan for the health care needs of today, but they must anticipate the changes in needs and demands for services that appear to be inevitable. The discussion about "saving Medicare" turns largely on projected changes in the age structure of the population linked to the size of the Medicare-eligible segment and their demands for health services. If the US population had a younger age structure, such as the one that existed three or four decades ago, in all likelihood there would not be an ongoing discussion and proposed legislation concerning Medicare.

As the traditional sources of patients and health care revenues have stabilized, the competition for the existing "pie" has become increasingly keen. Every attempt is being made to limit utilization, particularly in capitated reimbursement plans. Providers who perform unlimited tests and procedures are increasingly likely to have reimbursement denied. This has led to growing interest in the provision of elective procedures. Elective procedures generally are not covered by insurance but are paid for out of pocket by the consumers. Most cosmetic surgery procedures fall into this category, as do infertility treatment, discretionary orthopedic surgery (e.g., "tennis elbow"), and laser eye surgery. Despite not being covered by insurance, those desiring these procedures represent a large and growing market. Even more so than general medical procedures, the likely market for elective procedures is demographically defined. Depending on the procedure, the best predictors may be age, income, educational level, ethnicity, or some other demographic attribute. In fact, one of the major challenges facing health care providers over the next few years will be determining the most effective means of targeting these self-selected populations.

THE GROWING NEED FOR HEALTH DATA

As we enter the twenty-first century, health data needs fall into three basic categories: data related to the demand for health services, data related to the delivery of those services, and data for measuring outcomes. On the service demand side, the "usual suspects"—age, income, race–ethnicity, and the like—are prominent determinants of differential demand for health services. Combined with population size data and nondemographic considerations, these factors allow analysts to estimate current and projected health services needs. These linkages are not expected to change in the future. However, researchers and decision makers have learned that health services demand is driven by a complex interaction of factors, and more information is required in order to understand these relationships.

With regard to data on the delivery of health services, substantial effort is going into the compilation of data on the use of all manner of health services. Certainly, the utilization of inpatient facilities is an important dimension of health care, especially given the share of expenditures claimed by this setting. Yet, as the industry has moved toward an outpatient orientation, the demand for data on the use of ambulatory services is perhaps surpassing that for inpatient data. In recent years, the industry has witnessed the rise of interest in alternative therapies and now a great deal of emphasis is being placed on the collection of data on that dimension of the health care system. Ultimately, no process can be controlled unless there is a clear understanding of the process, and that is the point at which health care planners find themselves today.

Outcomes measurement became one of the main themes in health care in the 1990s. Outcomes research attempts to measure the success and efficiency of care modalities by accounting for factors that may contribute to different outcomes. The growing emphasis on across-the-board accountability has meant that virtually all participants in the health care arena are being asked to demonstrate the efficacy of their programs. Managed care plans are demanding that providers in their networks meet performance benchmarks. Report cards are being drawn up on hospitals and health plans. Even public health agencies are being expected to demonstrate the value of their activities.

Needless to say, outcomes measurement, regardless of the form it takes, requires a degree of sophistication in the management of health care data that has not existed in the past. And much of the data content is demographic in nature. The likelihood of individuals developing certain conditions, the course of these conditions, the likely disposition, and ultimately the cost involved in managing these conditions are going to be a function of the demographic characteristics of the affected individuals. If managed care plans and providers are to be judged based on their outcomes, they must develop a much better understanding of the nonclinical factors—more often than not demographic—that contribute to the ultimate outcome of treatment.

Researchers and practitioners are fortunate, however, in that much of the expanded information needs can be addressed through data that already are being collected. As researchers and practitioners learn even more about these complexities, the perceived value of demographic data and demographic analysis is likely to be enhanced.

On the health services delivery side, service usage often is described along demographic dimensions. When researchers specify that a geographic area is characterized by underutilization or overutilization of services, it is because they have calculated the "expected" level of service usage based on average demand data differentiated by demographic and other factors. Like demand, usage is now recognized as being determined by a complex interaction of a number of factors, and the value of demographic input into these studies is becoming increasingly recognized.

Demand management is a rapidly growing area of health care management that attempts to control the utilization of services on the front end. This is done by proactively addressing *potential* health problems through aggressive education, early screening, and incentives for healthy behavior. Demand management also involves the use of call centers and nurse triage systems that provide access to the system prior to actual utilization of services. By routing plan enrollees, for example, through the call center, many trips to physicians, hospitals, and emergency rooms can be eliminated as unnecessary.

Successful demand management calls for a much better understanding of health behavior than has been available in the past. Health demographers are contributing to this educational process, as managed care plans, providers, and others with a stake in controlling demand attempt to identify the segments of the population with various health service needs and develop appropriate methods for targeting the numerous subgroups for education and prevention.

THE FUTURE ROLE OF DEMOGRAPHIC DATA AND ANALYSIS

Such diverse members of the medical community as epidemiologists, actuaries, fertility experts, and clinical researchers have long recognized the value of demographic contributions to their research. However, the analytical focus and the issues addressed by these scientists are likely to shift rapidly in the future. Changes will be brought about by the growing body of knowledge in these fields resulting in the emergence of new theories, hypotheses, and models to be tested. Demographic considerations will continue to be important, but the action and interaction of demographic factors on the research questions deemed important are likely to change due to: (1) the increasing ease with which demographic data can be accessed; (2) a broadening of the list of "demographic" variables that are available; and (3) the shortened time intervals between data collection activities which will result in more timely provision of data. In addition, improvements in analysis software, (including geographic information systems capabilities) are altering both the ways in which analyses take place in the short run and theories are generated in the long run.

The types of demographics-related data needed fall into three categories as well. First, there is "straight" demographic data such as population size, composition, and distribution. These data are used to describe markets or service areas and to establish a priori differential levels of demand between and among areas.

Second, demographic data are frequently used in the calculation of the rates and ratios essential for developing health-related indicators of health status and health behavior. These include rates of utilization, incidence, and prevalence as well as other rates. This is particularly important for interarea or interpopulation segment comparisons.

The third type of demographic data arises in the context of other types of health-related data such as clinical and financial data. The ability to interface demographic data with financial and clinical data is becoming increasingly important. Only by developing a well-rounded picture of the clinical, financial, and patient characteristics will it be possible to proactively address issues as disparate as clinical outcomes, cost containment, and patient satisfaction.

In applied settings such as those involving business planning, resource allocation, and human resource recruitment, the implications of demographic factors have been established more recently. In the private sector, decision makers have brought together findings and models from the sciences with business principles and practices and a demographic perspective to solve problems and take advantage of opportunities. (Public sector applications that involve demographic input have a much longer history.) Because demographic data have proven valuable in these efforts, they have been embraced, and many researchers have focused on ways to extend demographic analysis. As demographic data have become more plentiful and easier to access, their use has been expanded. For example, many of the demographically based demand models produced for larger geographic areas have been revised for smaller geographic areas as demographic data for small areas have become more readily available.

As we enter the twenty-first century, the convergence of the trends described above presents an unprecedented opportunity for both health demography and health demographers. Health care professionals, particularly the more financially astute, are coming to increasingly appreciate the relevance of demographic concepts, methods, and data for health care. Whether the issue is the demand for a service, the nature of particular market, the consumer decision-making process, or levels of patient satisfaction, the demographic traits of the population are of growing significance. Whether the player is a health system, a provider, a health plan, an employer, a business coalition, or any other entity involved in health care today, an understanding of the demographics of the situation is imperative.

This interest in health demography *should* boost the interest in health demographers. The opportunity for health demography—and health demographers—to contribute to what is arguably the most significant social challenge our society has faced is at hand, and it would be to the detriment of all parties if health demography were to fail to take up the call.

REFERENCES

Association for Healthcare Research and Quality. (2000). *Addressing Racial and Ethnic Disparities in Health Care*. Website: www.ahrg.gov.

Atlantic Information Systems. (1998). *Health Care Report Cards: 1998–99*. Pembroke, MA: Atlantic Information Systems.

Kimberly, J. R. (2000). *The Quality Imperative: Measurement and Management of Quality in Healthcare*. London: Imperial College Press.

Wilensky, G. R., and Newhouse, J. P. (1999). Medicine: What's right, what's wrong, what's next. *Health Affairs* 18:92–106.

Index